2018

LEARNING

TO REALIZE EDUCATION'S PROMISE

D1288145

A World Bank Group Flagship Report

LEARNING

TO REALIZE EDUCATION'S PROMISE

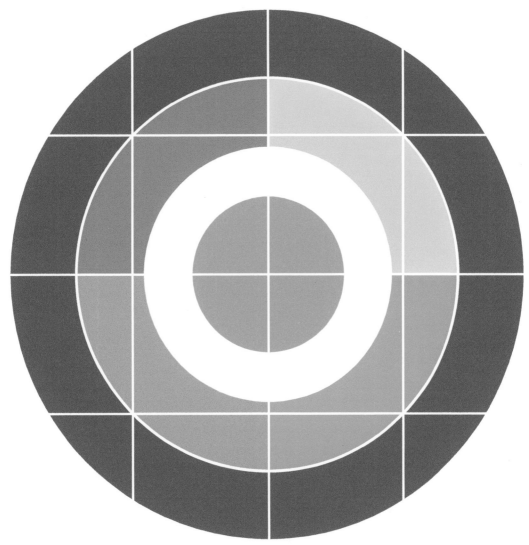

WORLD BANK GROUP

ISSN, ISBN, e-ISBN, and DOI:

Softcover
ISSN: 0163-5085
ISBN: 978-1-4648-1096-1
e-ISBN: 978-1-4648-1098-5
DOI: 10.1596/978-1-4648-1096-1

Hardcover
ISSN: 0163-5085
ISBN: 978-1-4648-1097-8
DOI: 10.1596/978-1-4648-1097-8

Cover design: Kurt Niedermeier, Niedermeier Design, Seattle, Washington.

Interior design: George Kokkinidis, Design Language, Brooklyn, New York, and Kurt Niedermeier, Niedermeier Design, Seattle, Washington.

Contents

Boxes

Figures

Map

Tables

Foreword

Education and learning raise aspirations, set values, and ultimately enrich lives. The country where I was born, the Republic of Korea, is a good example of how education can play these important roles. After the Korean War, the population was largely illiterate and deeply impoverished. The World Bank said that, without constant foreign aid, Korea would find it difficult to provide its people with more than the bare necessities of life. The World Bank considered even the lowest interest rate loans to the country too risky.

Korea understood that education was the best way to pull itself out of economic misery, so it focused on overhauling schools and committed itself to educating every child—and educating them well. Coupled with smart, innovative government policies and a vibrant private sector, the focus on education paid off. Today, not only has Korea achieved universal literacy, but its students also perform at the highest levels in international learning assessments. It's a high-income country and a model of successful economic development.

Korea is a particularly striking example, but we can see the salutary effects of education in many countries. Delivered well, education—and the human capital it creates—has many benefits for economies, and for societies as a whole. For individuals, education promotes employment, earnings, and health. It raises pride and opens new horizons. For societies, it drives long-term economic growth, reduces poverty, spurs innovation, strengthens institutions, and fosters social cohesion.

In short, education powerfully advances the World Bank Group's twin strategic goals: ending extreme poverty and boosting shared prosperity. Given that today's students will be tomorrow's citizens, leaders, workers, and parents, a good education is an investment with enduring benefits.

But providing education is not enough. What is important, and what generates a real return on investment, is learning and acquiring skills. This is what truly builds human capital. As this year's *World Development Report* documents, in many countries and communities learning isn't happening. Schooling without learning is a terrible waste of precious resources and of human potential.

Worse, it is an injustice. Without learning, students will be locked into lives of poverty and exclusion, and the children whom societies fail the most are those most in need of a good education to succeed in life. Learning conditions are almost always much worse for the disadvantaged, and so are learning outcomes. Moreover, far too many children still aren't even attending school. This is a moral and economic crisis that must be addressed immediately.

This year's Report provides a path to address this economic and moral failure. The detailed analysis in this Report shows that these problems are driven not only by service delivery failings in schools but also by deeper systemic problems. The human capital lost because of these shortcomings threatens development and jeopardizes the future of people and their societies. At the same time, rapid technological change raises the stakes: to compete in the economy of the future, workers need strong basic skills and foundations for adaptability, creativity, and lifelong learning.

To realize education's promise, we need to prioritize learning, not just schooling. This Report argues that achieving learning for all will require three complementary strategies:

- *First*, assess learning to make it a serious goal. Information itself creates incentives for reform, but many countries lack the right metrics to measure learning.

- *Second*, act on evidence to make schools work for learning. Great schools build strong teacher-learner relationships in classrooms. As brain science has advanced and educators have innovated, the knowledge of how students learn most effectively has greatly expanded. But the way many countries, communities, and schools approach education often differs greatly from the most promising, evidence-based approaches.

- *Third*, align actors to make the entire system work for learning. Innovation in classrooms won't have much impact if technical and political barriers at the system level prevent a focus on learning at the school level. This is the case in many countries stuck in low-learning traps; extricating them requires focused attention on the deeper causes.

The World Bank Group is already incorporating the key findings of this Report into our operations. We will continue to seek new ways to scale up our commitment to education and apply our knowledge to serve those children whose untapped potential is wasted. For example, we are developing more useful measures of learning and its determinants. We are ensuring that evidence guides operational practice to improve learning in areas such as early-years interventions, teacher training, and educational technology. We are making sure that our project analysis and strategic country diagnoses take into account the full range of system-level opportunities and limitations—including political constraints. And we will continue to emphasize operational approaches that allow greater innovation and agility.

Underlying these efforts is the World Bank Group's commitment to ensuring that all of the world's students have the opportunity to learn. Realizing education's promise means giving them the chance not only to compete in tomorrow's economy, but also to improve their communities, build stronger countries, and move closer to a world that is finally free of poverty.

Jim Yong Kim
President
The World Bank Group

Acknowledgments

This year's *World Development Report* (WDR) was prepared by a team led by Deon Filmer and Halsey Rogers. The core team was composed of Samer Al-Samarrai, Magdalena Bendini, Tara Béteille, David Evans, Märt Kivine, Shwetlena Sabarwal, and Alexandria Valerio, together with research analysts Malek Abu-Jawdeh, Bradley Larson, Unika Shrestha, and Fei Yuan. Rafael de Hoyos and Sophie Naudeau were members of the extended team. Stephen Commins provided consultations support. Mary Breeding, Ji Liu, Christian Ponce de León, Carla Cristina Solis Uehara, Alies Van Geldermalsen, and Paula Villaseñor served as consultants. The production and logistics team for the Report consisted of Brónagh Murphy and Jason Victor.

The Report is sponsored by the Development Economics Vice Presidency. Overall guidance for preparation of the Report was provided by Paul Romer, Senior Vice President and Chief Economist, and Ana Revenga, Deputy Chief Economist. In the early months of the Report's preparation, guidance was provided by Kaushik Basu, former Senior Vice President and Chief Economist, and Indermit Gill, former Director for Development Policy. The team is also grateful for comments and guidance from Shantayanan Devarajan, Senior Director for Development Economics. The Education Global Practice and the Human Development Global Practice Group provided consistent support to the Report team. The team is especially grateful for support and guidance provided by Jaime Saavedra, Senior Director, and Luis Benveniste, Director, of the Education Global Practice.

The team received guidance from an advisory panel composed of Gordon Brown (who, together with the Chief Economist, cochaired the panel), Michelle Bachelet, Rukmini Banerji, Julia Gillard, Eric Hanushek, Olli-Pekka Heinonen, Ju-Ho Lee, and Serigne Mbaye Thiam. Although the team valued their advice and found it very useful, the views expressed in the Report do not necessarily reflect those of the panel members.

The team also benefited at an early stage from consultations on emerging themes with the Chief Economist's Council of Eminent Persons. Council members providing comments were Montek Singh Ahluwalia, François Bourguignon, Heba Handoussa, Justin Yifu Lin, Ory Okolloh, Pepi Patrón, Amartya Sen, Joseph Stiglitz, Finn Tarp, and Maria Hermínia Tavares de Almeida.

Paul Holtz was the principal editor of the Report. Bruce Ross-Larson provided editorial guidance, and Sabra Ledent and Gwenda Larsen copyedited and proofread the Report. Kurt Niedermeier was the principal graphic designer. Alejandra Bustamante and Surekha Mohan provided resource management support for the team. Phillip Hay, Mikael Reventar, Anushka Thewarapperuma, and Roula Yazigi, together with Patricia da Camara and Kavita Watsa, provided guidance and support on communication and dissemination. Special thanks are extended to Mary Fisk, Patricia Katayama, Stephen Pazdan, and the World Bank's Formal Publishing Program. The team would also like to thank Maria Alyanak, Laverne Cook, Maria del Camino Hurtado, Chorching Goh, Vivian Hon, Elena Chi-Lin Lee, Nancy Tee Lim, David Rosenblatt, and Bintao Wang for their coordinating roles.

The team is grateful for generous support for preparation of the Report provided by the Knowledge for Change Program (KCP, a multidonor Trust Fund) and especially from the governments and development agencies of the following KCP donor countries: Finland, France, and Norway. Background and related research, along with dissemination, are being generously supported by the Bill & Melinda Gates Foundation, Early Learning Partnership Trust Fund, LEGO Foundation, and Nordic Trust Fund.

Consultation events attended by government officials, researchers, and civil society organizations were held in Bolivia, Brazil, Canada, China, Côte d'Ivoire, Finland, France, Germany, India, Indonesia, Japan, Kenya, Malaysia, Mexico, Senegal, South Africa, Tanzania, Thailand, Turkey, the United Kingdom, and the United States, with participants drawn from many more countries. The team thanks those who took part in these events for their helpful comments and suggestions. Further information on these events is available at http://www.worldbank.org/wdr2018.

Interagency consultations were held with the Association for the Development of Education in Africa (ADEA), Global Development Network (GDN), Global Partnership for Education (GPE), International Commission on Financing Global Education Opportunity (Education Commission), International Monetary Fund (IMF), Organisation for Economic Co-operation and Development (OECD), United Nations Children's Fund (UNICEF), and United Nations Educational, Scientific, and Cultural Organization (UNESCO). Consultations with bilateral development partners included representatives of the governments of Canada, Finland, Japan, the Republic of Korea, Norway, and Sweden, and of Australia's Department of Foreign Affairs and Trade (DFAT), the French Development Agency (AFD), German Agency for International Cooperation (GIZ GmbH), German Federal Ministry for Economic Cooperation and Development (BMZ), Japan International Cooperation Agency (JICA), U.K. Department for International Development (DFID), and U.S. Agency for International Development (USAID). The team also held consultations with the advisory board of KCP. The team is grateful to all those who took part in these events.

Civil society organizations (CSOs) represented at consultations included, among others, ActionAid, Bill & Melinda Gates Foundation, Education International, Global Campaign for Education, LEGO Foundation, MasterCard Foundation, ONE Campaign, Oxfam, Save the Children, Teach for All, and World Vision. In addition, a diverse group of CSOs participated in a CSO Forum session held during the 2017 World Bank/IMF Spring Meetings and in an e-forum held in March 2017. The team is grateful to these CSOs for their input and useful engagement.

Researchers and academics provided helpful feedback at WDR-oriented sessions at the 2016 Research on Improving Systems of Education (RISE) Conference at Oxford University, 2017 meetings of the Allied Social Sciences Associations (ASSA), 2017 meetings of the Society for Research on Education Effectiveness (SREE), 2017 Mexico Conference on Political Economy of Education, and 2017 meeting of the Systems Approach for Better Education Results (SABER) Advisory Panel. In addition, events dedicated to the WDR were organized by the Aga Khan Foundation and Global Affairs Canada in Ottawa; Brookings Center for Universal Education in Washington, DC; Columbia School of International and Public Affairs and Cornell University in New York; Development Policy Forum of GIZ GmbH, on behalf of BMZ, in Berlin; JICA in Tokyo; Université Félix Houphouët-Boigny in Abidjan; and USAID in Washington, DC.

This Report draws on background papers prepared by Violeta Arancibia, Felipe Barrera-Osorio, Tessa Bold, Pierre de Galbert, Louise Fox, Dileni Gunewardena, James Habyarimana, Michael Handel, Anuradha Joshi, Kanishka Kacker, Michelle Kaffenberger, Upaasna Kaul, Elizabeth M. King, Gayle Martin, Eema Masood, Ezequiel Molina, Sebastián Monroy-Taborda, Kate Moriarty, Anna Popova, Lant Pritchett, Christophe Rockmore, Andrew Rosser, María Laura Sánchez Puerta, Priyam Saraf, M. Najeeb Shafiq, Brian Stacy, Jakob Svensson, Namrata Tognatta, Robert Toutkoushian, Michael Trucano, Waly Wane, Tim Williams, and Attiya Zaidi.

The team drew on the analysis, research, and literature reviews of researchers and specialists from across the world. In addition, the team would like to thank the following for their feedback and suggestions: Christine Adick, Ben Ansell, Manos Antoninis, Caridad Araujo, David Archer, Belinda Archibong, Monazza Aslam, Girindre Beeharry, Penelope Bender, Peter Bergman, Raquel Bernal, Robert Birch, Tarsald Brautaset, Barbara Bruns, Annika Calov, Michael Clemens, Luis Crouch, Rohen d'Aiglepierre, Rossieli Soares da Silva, Momar Dieng, Rob Doble, Amy Jo Dowd, Margaret Dubeck, Sandra Dworack, Alex Eble, Marcel Fafchamps, John Floreta, Eli Friedman, Akihiro Fushimi, Paul Gertler, Rachel Glennerster, Paul Glewwe, Amber Gove, Oliver Haas, James Habyarimana, Jeffrey Hammer, Michael Handel, Christoph Hansert, Blanca Heredia, Sam Hickey, Veronika Hilber, Arja-Sisko Holappa, Naomi Hossain, Huang Xiaoting, Ali Inam, Dhir Jhingran, Emmanuel Jimenez, Maciej Jubowski, Ravi Kanbur, Cheikh Kane, Jouni Kangasniemi, Devesh Kapur, Vishnu Karki, Nina Kataja, Venita Kaul, Kim Kerr, Elizabeth M. King, Kenneth King, Geeta Kingdon, Eiji Kozuka, Michael Kremer, K. P. Krishnan, Kazuo Kuroda, Elina Lehtomäki, Henry Levin, Brian Levy, Krystelle Lochard, Karen Macours, Lu Mai, Akshay Mangla, M. A. Mannan, Santhosh Mathew, Imran Matin, Jordan Matsudaira, Karthik Muralidharan, Essa Chanie Mussa, Charles Nelson III, Aromie Noe, Munaz Ahmed Noor, Mario Novelli, Mead Over, Jan Pakulski, Benjamin Piper, Lant Pritchett, Ritva Reinikka, Risto Rinne, Jo Ritzen, Francisco Rivera Batiz, John Rogers, Caine Rolleston, Andrew Rosser, David Sahn, Justin Sandefur, Yasuyuki Sawada, Andreas Schleicher, Ben Ross Schneider, Dorothea Schonfeld, Olaf Seim, Abhijeet Singh, David Skinner, William Smith, Prachi Srivastava, Liesbet Steer, R. Subrahmanyam, Sudarno Sumarto, Jan Svejnar, Jakob Svensson, Soubhy Tawil, Valerie Tessio, Auli Toom, Miguel Urqiola, Jouni Välijärvi, Olli Vesterinen, Joseph Wales, Libing Wang, Michael Ward, Kevin Watkins, Mark Wenz, Yang Po, Khair Mohamad Yusof, and Andrew Zeitlin. Team members also drew heavily on their own experiences and interactions with the many dedicated educators, administrators, and policy makers who work in often difficult conditions to provide students with the best educational opportunities possible.

A number of World Bank colleagues provided insightful comments, feedback, and collaboration: Junaid Ahmad, Omar Arias, Nina Arnhold, Ana Belver, Hana Brixi, James Brumby, Pedro Cerdan Infantes, Marie-Hélène Cloutier, Aline Coudouel, Amit Dar, Jishnu Das, Amanda Epstein Devercelli, Gregory Elacqua, Emanuela Galasso, Diana Hincapie, Alaka Holla, Peter Holland, Sachiko Kataoka, Stuti Khemani, Igor Kheyfets, Kenneth King, Eva Kloeve, Steve Knack, Xiaoyan Liang, Toby Linden, Oni Lusk-Stover, Francisco Marmolejo, Yasuhiko Matsuda, Julie McLaughlin, Muna Meky, Ezequiel Molina, Caitlin Moss, Matiullah Noori, Anna Olefir, Owen Ozier, Andrew Ragatz, Vijayendra Rao, Dan Rogger, Audrey Sacks, María Laura Sánchez Puerta, Indhira Santos, William Seitz, Shabnam Sinha, Lars Sondergaard, Dewi Susanti, Christopher Thomas, Michael Trucano, Adam Wagstaff, and Melanie Walker.

The team would also like to thank the World Bank colleagues who helped organize and facilitate consultations and advised on translations: Gabriela Geraldes Bastos, Paolo Belli, Moussa Blimpo, Andreas Blom, Leandro Costa, Oumou Coulibaly, Meaza Zerihun Demissie, Safaa El-Kogali, Tazeen Fasih, Ning Fu, Elena Glinskaya, Marek Hanusch, Pimon Iamsripong, Susiana Iskandar, Nalin Jena, Hamoud Abdel Wedoud Kamil, Adriane Landwehr, Dilaka Lathapipat, Khady Fall Lo, Norman Loayza, André Loureiro, Hope Nanshemeza, Mademba Ndiaye, Koichi Omori, Azedine Ouerghi, Tigran Shmis, Taleb Ould Sid'ahmed, Lars Sondergaard, Dewi Susanti, Yasusuke Tsukagoshi, and Michael Woolcock.

In addition, the team is grateful to the many World Bank colleagues who provided written comments during the formal Bankwide review process: Cristian Aedo, Inga Afanasieva, Ahmad Ahsan, Edouard Al Dahdah, Umbreen Arif, Nina Arnhold, Anna Autio, Arup Banerji, Elena Bardasi, Sajitha Bashir, Ana Belver, Raja Bentaouet Kattan, Luis Benveniste, Moussa Blimpo, Erik Bloom, Vica Bogaerts, Susan Caceres, César Calderón, Ted Haoquan Chu, Punam Chuhan-Pole, Fernando Ramirez Cortes, Michael Crawford, Laisa Daza, Bénédicte de la Brière, Gabriel Demombynes, Shanta Devarajan, Sangeeta Dey, Ousmane Diagana,

Ousmane Dione, Safaa El Tayeb El-Kogali, Marianne Fay, María Marta Ferreyra, Carina Fonseca, Marie Gaarder, Roberta Gatti, Ejaz Syed Ghani, Elena Glinskaya, Markus Goldstein, Melinda Good, David Gould, Sangeeta Goyal, Caren Grown, Keith Hansen, Amer Hasan, Caroline Heider, Katia Herrera, Niels Holm-Nielsen, Dingyong Hou, Elena Ianchovichina, Keiko Inoue, Sandeep Jain, Omer Karasapan, Michel Kerf, Asmeen Khan, Igor Kheyfets, Youssouf Kiendrebeogo, Daniel John Kirkwood, Eva Kloeve, Markus Kostner, Daniel Lederman, Hans Lofgren, Gladys López-Acevedo, Javier Luque, Michael Mahrt, Francisco Marmolejo, Kris McDonall, Mahmoud Mohieldin, Lili Mottaghi, Mary Mulusa, Yoko Nakashima, Shiro Nakata, Muthoni Ngatia, Shinsaku Nomura, Dorota Agata Nowak, Michael O'Sullivan, Arunma Oteh, Aris Panou, Georgi Panterov, Suhas Parandekar, Harry Patrinos, Dhushyanth Raju, Martín Rama, Sheila Redzepi, Lea Marie Rouanet, Jaime Saavedra, Hafida Sahraoui, Sajjad Shah, Sudhir Shetty, Mari Shojo, Lars Sondergaard, Nikola Spatafora, Venkatesh Sundararaman, Janssen Teixeira, Jeff Thindwe, Hans Timmer, Yvonne Tsikata, Laura Tuck, Anuja Utz, Julia Valliant, Axel van Trotsenburg, Carlos Vegh, Binh Thanh Vu, Jan Walliser, Jason Weaver, Michel Welmond, Deborah Wetzel, Christina Wood, and Hanspeter Wyss.

The team apologizes to any individuals or organizations inadvertently omitted from this list and expresses its gratitude to all who contributed to this Report, including those whose names may not appear here.

The team members would also like to thank their families for their support throughout the preparation of this Report. And finally, the team members thank the many children and youth who have inspired them through interactions in classrooms around the world over the years—as well as the many others whose great potential has motivated this Report. The *World Development Report 2018* is dedicated to them.

Abbreviations

A4L	Assessment for Learning
ASER	Annual Status of Education Report
BRN	Big Results Now in Education (Tanzania)
CAMPE	Campaign for Popular Education (Bangladesh)
CCT	conditional cash transfer
CSEF	Civil Society Education Fund
DISE	District Information System for Education (India)
EGRA	Early Grade Reading Assessment
GDP	gross domestic product
GNECC	Ghana National Education Campaign Coalition
I-BEST	Integrated Basic Education and Skills Training
ICT	information and communication technology
IDEB	Índice de Desenvolvimento da Educação Básica (Index of Basic Education Development, Brazil)
LLECE	Latin American Laboratory for Assessment of the Quality of Education
MDG	Millennium Development Goal
MENA	Middle East and North Africa
NAFTA	North American Free Trade Agreement
NGO	nongovernmental organization
OECD	Organisation for Economic Co-operation and Development
PASEC	Programme d'Analyse des Systèmes Éducatifs de la Confemen (Programme for the Analysis of Education Systems)
PIAAC	Programme for the International Assessment of Adult Competencies
PIRLS	Progress in International Reading Literacy Study
PISA	Programme for International Student Assessment
PPP	purchasing power parity
SACMEQ	Southern and Eastern Africa Consortium for Monitoring Educational Quality
SAR	special administrative region
SAT	Scholastic Aptitude Test
SDG	Sustainable Development Goal
SIMCE	Sistema de Medición de la Calidad de la Educación (Education Quality Measurement System, Chile)
SNED	Sistema Nacional de Evaluación de Desempeño (National Performance Evaluation System, Chile)
SNTE	Sindicato Nacional de Trabajadores de la Educación (National Union of Educational Workers, Mexico)
TERCE	Third Regional Comparative and Explanatory Study
TIMSS	Trends in International Mathematics and Science Study
TVET	technical and vocational education and training
UNESCO	United Nations Educational, Scientific, and Cultural Organization
UNRWA	United Nations Relief and Works Agency
USAID	U.S. Agency for International Development
WHO	World Health Organization
WIDE	World Inequality Database on Education

OVERVIEW

Learning to realize education's promise

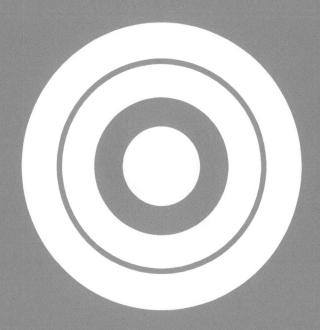

Learning to realize education's promise

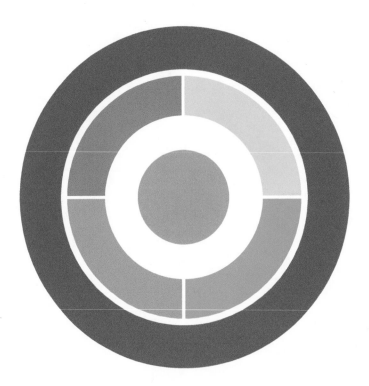

Assess learning

to make it a serious goal

Act on evidence

to make schools
work for all learners

Align actors

to make the whole
system work for learning

OVERVIEW

Learning to realize education's promise

"Education is the most powerful weapon we can use to change the world."

NELSON MANDELA (2003)

"If your plan is for one year, plant rice. If your plan is for ten years, plant trees. If your plan is for one hundred years, educate children."

KUAN CHUNG (7TH CENTURY BC)

Schooling is not the same as learning. In Kenya, Tanzania, and Uganda, when grade 3 students were asked recently to read a sentence such as "The name of the dog is Puppy," three-quarters did not understand what it said.[1] In rural India, just under three-quarters of students in grade 3 could not solve a two-digit subtraction such as 46 – 17, and by grade 5 half could still not do so.[2] Although the skills of Brazilian 15-year-olds have improved, at their current rate of improvement they won't reach the rich-country average score in math for 75 years. In reading, it will take more than 260 years.[3] Within countries, learning outcomes are almost always much worse for the disadvantaged. In Uruguay, poor children in grade 6 are assessed as "not competent" in math at five times the rate of wealthy children.[4] Moreover, such data are for children and youth lucky enough to be in school. Some 260 million aren't even enrolled in primary or secondary school.[5]

These countries are not unique in the challenges they face. (In fact, they deserve credit for measuring student learning and making the results public.) Worldwide, hundreds of millions of children reach young adulthood without even the most basic life skills. Even if they attend school, many leave without the skills for calculating the correct change from a

transaction, reading a doctor's instructions, or interpreting a campaign promise—let alone building a fulfilling career or educating their children.

This learning crisis is a moral crisis. When delivered well, education cures a host of societal ills. For individuals, it promotes employment, earnings, health, and poverty reduction. For societies, it spurs innovation, strengthens institutions, and fosters social cohesion. But these benefits depend largely on learning. Schooling without learning is a wasted opportunity. More than that, it is a great injustice: the children whom society is failing most are the ones who most need a good education to succeed in life.

Any country can do better if it acts as though learning really matters. That may sound obvious—after all, what else is education for? Yet even as learning goals are receiving greater rhetorical support, in practice many features of education systems conspire against learning. This Report argues that countries can improve by advancing on three fronts:

- *Assess learning—to make it a serious goal.* This means using well-designed student assessments to gauge the health of education systems (not primarily as tools for administering rewards and punishments). It also means using the resulting

learning measures to spotlight hidden exclusions, make choices, and evaluate progress.
- *Act on evidence—to make schools work for all learners.* Evidence on how people learn has exploded in recent decades, along with an increase in educational innovation. Countries can make much better use of this evidence to set priorities for their own practice and innovations.
- *Align actors—to make the whole system work for learning.* Countries must recognize that all the classroom innovation in the world is unlikely to have much impact if, because of technical and political barriers, the system as a whole does not support learning. By taking into account these real-world barriers and mobilizing everyone who has a stake in learning, countries can support innovative educators on the front lines.

When improving learning becomes a priority, great progress is possible. In the early 1950s, the Republic of Korea was a war-torn society held back by very low literacy levels. By 1995 it had achieved universal enrollment in high-quality education through secondary school. Today, its young people perform at the highest levels on international learning assessments. Vietnam surprised the world when the 2012 results of the Programme for International Student Assessment (PISA) showed that its 15-year-olds were performing at the same level as those in Germany—even though Vietnam was a lower-middle-income country. Between 2009 and 2015, Peru achieved some of the fastest growth in overall learning outcomes—an improvement attributable to concerted policy action. In Liberia, Papua New Guinea, and Tonga, early grade reading improved substantially within a very short time thanks to focused efforts based on evidence. And recently, Malaysia and Tanzania launched promising societywide collaborative approaches to systematically improving learning.

Progress like this requires a clear-eyed diagnosis, followed by concerted action. Before showing what can be done to fulfill education's promise, this overview first shines a light on the learning crisis: how and why many countries are not yet achieving "learning for all." This may make for disheartening reading, but it should not be interpreted as saying that all is lost—only that too many young people are not getting the education they need. The rest of the overview shows how change is possible if systems commit to "all for learning," drawing on examples of families, educators, communities, and systems that have made real progress.

The three dimensions of the learning crisis

Education should equip students with the skills they need to lead healthy, productive, meaningful lives. Different countries define skills differently, but all share some core aspirations, embodied in their curriculums. Students everywhere must learn how to interpret many types of written passages—from medication labels to job offers, from bank statements to great literature. They have to understand how numbers work so that they can buy and sell in markets, set family budgets, interpret loan agreements, or write engineering software. They require the higher-order reasoning and creativity that builds on these foundational skills. And they need the socioemotional skills—such as perseverance and the ability to work on teams—that help them acquire and apply the foundational and other skills.

Many countries are not yet achieving these goals. First, the learning that one would expect to happen in schools—whether expectations are based on formal curriculums, the needs of employers, or just common sense—is often not occurring. Of even greater concern, many countries are failing to provide learning for all. Individuals already disadvantaged in society—whether because of poverty, location, ethnicity, gender, or disability—learn the least. Thus education systems can widen social gaps instead of narrowing them. What drives the learning shortfalls is becoming clearer thanks to new analyses spotlighting both the immediate cause—poor service delivery that amplifies the effects of poverty—and the deeper system-level problems, both technical and political, that allow poor-quality schooling to persist.

Learning outcomes are poor: Low levels, high inequality, slow progress

The recent expansion in education is impressive by historical standards. In many developing countries over the last few decades, net enrollment in education has greatly outpaced the historic performance of today's industrial countries. For example, it took the United States 40 years—from 1870 to 1910—to increase girls' enrollments from 57

Problem dimension 1: **Outcomes**

percent to 88 percent. By contrast, Morocco achieved a similar increase in just 11 years.[6] The number of years of schooling completed by the average adult in the developing world more than tripled from 1950 to

Figure O.1 Shortfalls in learning start early

Percentage of grade 2 students who could not perform simple reading or math tasks, selected countries

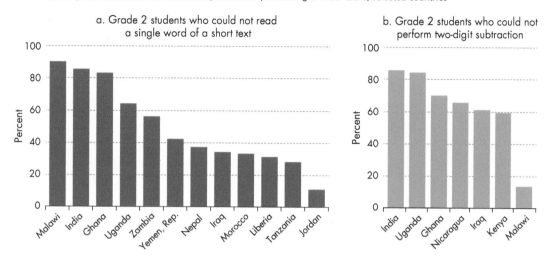

a. Grade 2 students who could not read a single word of a short text

b. Grade 2 students who could not perform two-digit subtraction

Sources: WDR 2018 team, using reading and mathematics data for Kenya and Uganda from Uwezo, Annual Assessment Reports, 2015 (http://www.uwezo .net/); reading and mathematics data for rural India from ASER Centre (2017); reading data for all other countries from U.S. Agency for International Development (USAID), Early Grade Reading Barometer, 2017, accessed May 30, 2017 (http://www.earlygradereadingbarometer.org/); and mathematics data for all other countries from USAID/RTI Early Grade Mathematics Assessment intervention reports, 2012–15 (https://shared.rti.org/sub-topic/early -grade-math-assessment-egma). Data at http://bit.do/WDR2018-Fig_O-1.

Note: These data typically pertain to selected regions in the countries and are not necessarily nationally representative. Data for India pertain to rural areas.

2010, from 2.0 to 7.2 years.[7] By 2010 the average worker in Bangladesh had completed more years of schooling than the typical worker in France in 1975.[8] This progress means that most enrollment gaps in basic education are closing between high- and low-income countries. By 2008 the average low-income country was enrolling students in primary school at nearly the same rate as the average high-income country.

But schooling is not the same as learning.[9] Children learn very little in many education systems around the world: even after several years in school, millions of students lack basic literacy and numeracy skills. In recent assessments in Ghana and Malawi, more than four-fifths of students at the end of grade 2 were unable to read a single familiar word such as *the* or *cat* (figure O.1).[10] Even in Peru, a middle-income country, that share was half before the recent reforms.[11] When grade 3 students in Nicaragua were tested in 2011, only half could correctly solve 5 + 6.[12] In urban Pakistan in 2015, only three-fifths of grade 3 students could correctly perform a subtraction such as 54 − 25, and in rural areas only just over two-fifths could.[13]

This slow start to learning means that even students who make it to the end of primary school do not master basic competencies. In 2007, the most recent year for which data are available, less than 50 percent of grade 6 students in Southern and East Africa were able to go beyond the level of simply deciphering words, and less than 40 percent got beyond basic numeracy.[14] Among grade 6 students in West and Central Africa in 2014, less than 45 percent reached the "sufficient" competency level for continuing studies in reading or mathematics—for example, the rest could not answer a math problem that required them to divide 130 by 26.[15] In rural India in 2016, only half of grade 5 students could fluently read text at the level of the grade 2 curriculum, which included sentences (in the local language) such as "It was the month of rains" and "There were black clouds in the sky."[16] These severe shortfalls constitute a learning crisis.

Although not all developing countries suffer from such extreme shortfalls, many are far short of the levels they aspire to. According to leading international assessments of literacy and numeracy—Progress in International Reading Literacy Study (PIRLS) and Trends in International Mathematics and Science Study (TIMSS)—the average student in low-income countries performs worse than 95 percent of the students in high-income countries, meaning that student would be singled out for remedial attention in a class in high-income countries.[17] Many high-performing students in middle-income countries—young men and women who have risen to the top quarter of

Figure O.2 In several countries, the 75th percentile of PISA test takers performs below the 25th percentile of the OECD average

Performance of 25th, 50th, and 75th percentiles in 2015 PISA mathematics assessment, selected countries

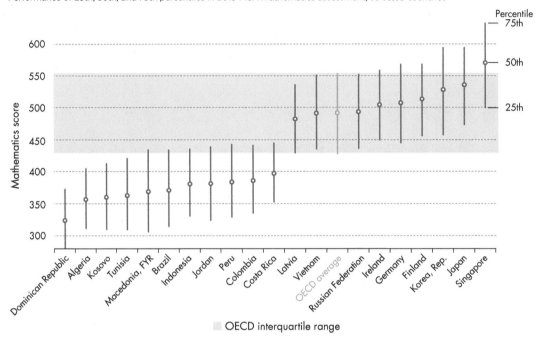

Source: WDR 2018 team, using data from Programme for International Student Assessment (PISA) 2015 (OECD 2016). Data at http://bit.do/WDR2018-Fig_O-2.

their cohorts—would rank in the bottom quarter in a wealthier country. In Algeria, the Dominican Republic, and Kosovo, the test scores of students at the cutoff for the top quarter of students (the 75th percentile of the distribution of PISA test takers) are well below the cutoff for the bottom quarter of students (25th percentile) of Organisation for Economic Co-operation and Development (OECD) countries (figure O.2). Even in Costa Rica, a relatively strong performer in education, performance at the cutoff for the top quarter of students is equal to performance at the cutoff for the bottom quarter in Germany.

The learning crisis amplifies inequality: it severely hobbles the disadvantaged youth who most need the boost that a good education can offer. For students in many African countries, the differences by income level are stark (figure O.3). In a recent assessment (Programme d'Analyse des Systèmes Éducatifs de la Confemen, PASEC, 2014) administered at the end of the primary cycle, only 5 percent of girls in Cameroon from the poorest quintile of households had learned enough to continue school, compared with 76 percent of girls from the richest quintile.[18] Learning gaps in several other countries—Benin, the Republic of Congo, and Senegal—were nearly as wide. Large gaps among learners afflict many high- and middle-

income countries as well, with disadvantaged students greatly overrepresented among the low scorers. Costa Rica and Qatar have the same average score on one internationally benchmarked assessment (TIMSS 2015)—but the gap between the top and bottom quarters of students is 138 points in Qatar, compared with 92 points in Costa Rica. The gap between the top and bottom quarters in the United States is larger than the gap in the median scores between Algeria and the United States.

Students often learn little from year to year, but early learning deficits are magnified over time. Students who stay in school should be rewarded with steady progress in learning, whatever disadvantages they have in the beginning. And yet in Andhra Pradesh, India, in 2010, low-performing students in grade 5 were no more likely to answer a grade 1 question correctly than those in grade 2. Even the average student in grade 5 had about a 50 percent chance of answering a grade 1 question correctly—compared with about 40 percent in grade 2.[19] In South Africa in the late 2000s, the vast majority of students in grade 4 had mastered only the mathematics curriculum from grade 1; most of those in grade 9 had mastered only the mathematics items from grade 5.[20] In New Delhi, India, in 2015, the average grade 6 student performed at a grade 3

Figure O.3 Children from poor households in Africa typically learn much less

Percentage of grade 6 PASEC test takers in 2014 who scored above (blue) and below (orange) the sufficiency level on reading achievement: poorest and richest quintiles by gender, selected countries

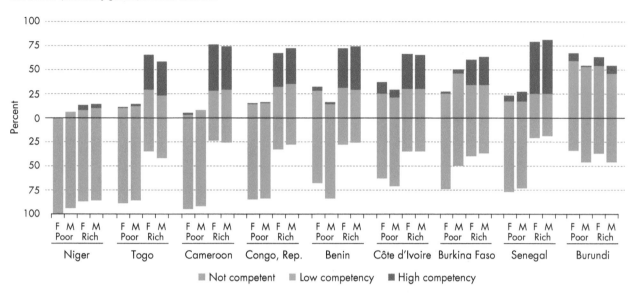

Source: WDR 2018 team, using data from World Bank (2016b). Data at http://bit.do/WDR2018-Fig_0-3.

Note: Socioeconomic quintiles are defined nationally. "Not competent" refers to levels 0–2 in the original coding and is considered below the sufficiency level for school continuation; "low competency" refers to level 3; and "high competency" refers to level 4. F = female; M = male; PASEC = Programme d'Analyse des Systèmes Éducatifs de la Confemen.

level in math. Even by grade 9, the average student had reached less than a grade 5 level, and the gap between the better and worse performers grew over time (figure O.4). In Peru and Vietnam—one of the lowest and one of the highest performers, respectively, on the PISA assessment of 15-year-old students—5-year-olds start out with similar math skills, but students in Vietnam learn much more for each year of schooling at the primary and lower secondary levels.[21]

Although some countries are making progress on learning, their progress is typically slow. Even the middle-income countries that are catching up to the top performers are doing so very slowly. Indonesia has registered significant gains on PISA over the last 10–15 years. And yet, even assuming it can sustain its 2003–15 rate of improvement, Indonesia won't reach the OECD average score in mathematics for another 48 years; in reading, for 73. For other countries, the wait could be even longer: based on current trends, it would take Tunisia over 180 years to reach the OECD average for math and Brazil over 260 years to reach the OECD average for reading. Moreover, these calculations are for countries where learning has improved. Across all countries participating in multiple rounds of PISA since 2003, the median gain in the national average score from one round to the next was zero.

Figure O.4 Students often learn little from year to year, and early learning deficits are magnified over time

Assessed grade-level performance of students relative to enrolled grade, New Delhi, India (2015)

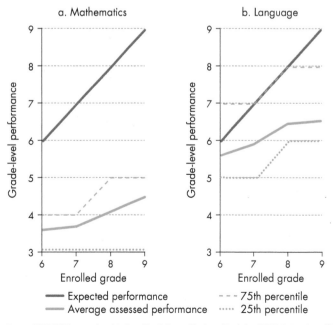

Source: WDR 2018 team, using data from Muralidharan, Singh, and Ganimian (2016). Data at http://bit.do /WDR2018-Fig_0-4.

Figure O.5 The percentage of primary school students who pass a minimum proficiency threshold is often low

Median percentage of students in late primary school who score above a minimum proficiency level on a learning assessment, by income group and region

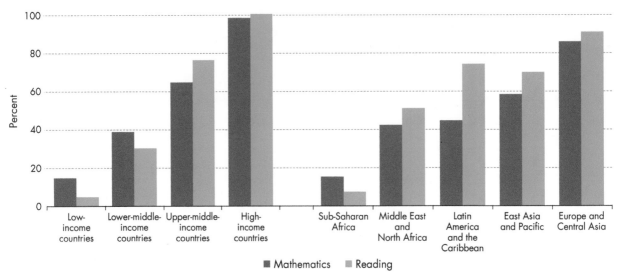

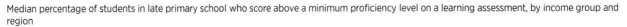

Source: WDR 2018 team, using "A Global Data Set on Education Quality" (2017), made available to the team by Nadir Altinok, Noam Angrist, and Harry Anthony Patrinos. Data at http://bit.do /WDR2018-Fig_O-5.

Note: Bars show the unweighted cross-country median within country grouping. Regional averages exclude high-income countries. India and China are among the countries excluded for lack of data. Minimum proficiency in mathematics is benchmarked to the Trends in International Mathematics and Science Study (TIMSS) assessment and in reading to the Progress in International Reading Literacy Study (PIRLS) assessment. Minimum proficiency in mathematics means that students have some basic mathematical knowledge such as adding or subtracting whole numbers, recognizing familiar geometric shapes, and reading simple graphs and tables (Mullis and others 2016). Minimum proficiency in reading means that students can locate and retrieve explicitly stated detail when reading literary texts and can locate and reproduce explicitly stated information from the beginning of informational texts (Mullis and others 2012).

Because of this slow progress, more than 60 percent of primary school children in developing countries still fail to achieve minimum proficiency in learning, according to one benchmark. No single learning assessment has been administered in all countries, but combining data from learning assessments in 95 countries makes it possible to establish a globally comparable "minimum proficiency" threshold in math.[22] Below this threshold, students have not mastered even basic mathematical skills, whether making simple computations with whole numbers, using fractions or measurements, or interpreting simple bar graphs. In high-income countries, nearly all students—99 percent in Japan, 98 percent in Norway, 91 percent in Australia—achieve this level in primary school.[23] But in other parts of the world the share is much lower: just 7 percent in Mali, 30 percent in Nicaragua, 34 percent in the Philippines, and 76 percent in Mexico. In low-income countries, 14 percent of students reach this level near the end of primary school, and in lower-middle-income countries 37 percent do (figure O.5). Even in upper-middle-income countries only 61 percent reach this minimum proficiency.

The ultimate barrier to learning is no schooling at all—yet hundreds of millions of youth remain out of school. In 2016, 61 million children of primary school age—10 percent of all children in low- and lower-middle-income countries—were not in school, along with 202 million children of secondary school age.[24] Children in fragile and conflict-affected countries accounted for just over a third of these, a disproportionate share. In the Syrian Arab Republic, which achieved universal primary enrollment in 2000, the civil war had driven 1.8 million children out of school by 2013.[25] Almost all developing countries still have pockets of children from excluded social groups who do not attend school. Poverty most consistently predicts failing to complete schooling, but other characteristics such as gender, disability, caste, and ethnicity also frequently contribute to school participation shortfalls (figure O.6).

But it's not just poverty and conflict that keep children out of school; the learning crisis does, too. When poor parents perceive education to be of low quality, they are less willing to sacrifice to keep their children in school—a rational response, given the constraints they face.[26] Although parental perceptions of school quality depend on various factors, from the physical condition of schools to teacher punctuality, parents consistently cite student learning outcomes

Figure O.6 School completion is higher for richer and urban families, but gender gaps are more context-dependent

Gaps in grade 6 completion rates (percent) for 15- to 19-year-olds, by wealth, location, and gender

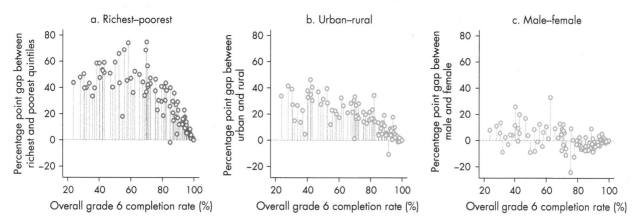

Source: WDR 2018 team, using data from Filmer (2016). Data at http://bit.do/WDR2018-Fig_O-6.

Note: The data presented are the latest available by country, 2005–14. Each vertical line indicates the size and direction of the gap for a country.

as a critical component.[27] These outcomes can affect behavior: holding student ability constant, students in the Arab Republic of Egypt who attended poorer-performing schools were more likely to drop out.[28]

Learning shortfalls during the school years eventually show up as weak skills in the workforce. Thus the job skills debate reflects the learning crisis. Work skill shortages are often discussed in a way that is disconnected from the debate on learning, but the two are parts of the same problem. Because education systems have not prepared workers adequately, many enter the labor force with inadequate skills. Measuring adult skills in the workplace is hard, but recent initiatives have assessed a range of skills in the adult populations of numerous countries. They found that even foundational skills such as literacy and numeracy are often low, let alone the more advanced skills. The problem isn't just a lack of trained workers; it is a lack of readily trainable workers. Accordingly, many workers end up in jobs that require minimal amounts of reading or math.[29] Lack of skills reduces job quality, earnings, and labor mobility.

The skills needed in labor markets are multidimensional, so systems need to equip students with far more than just reading, writing, and math—but students cannot leapfrog these foundational skills. Whether as workers or members of society, people also need higher-order cognitive skills such as problem-solving. In addition, they need socioemotional skills—sometimes called soft or noncognitive skills—such as conscientiousness. Finally, they need technical skills to perform a specific job. That said,

the foundational cognitive skills are essential, and systems cannot bypass the challenges of developing them as they target higher-order skills.

Tackling the learning crisis and skills gaps requires diagnosing their causes—both their immediate causes at the school level and their deeper systemic drivers. Given all the investments countries have made in education, shortfalls in learning are discouraging. But one reason for them is that learning has not always received the attention it should have. As a result, stakeholders lack actionable information about what is going wrong in their schools and in the broader society, and so they cannot craft context-appropriate responses to improve learning. Acting effectively requires first understanding how schools are failing learners and how systems are failing schools.

Schools are failing learners

Struggling education systems lack one or more of four key school-level ingredients for learning: prepared learners, effective teaching, learning-focused inputs, and the skilled management and governance that pulls them all together (figure O.7). The next section looks at why these links break down; here the focus is on *how* they break down.

First, children often arrive in school unprepared to learn—if they arrive at all. Malnutrition, illness, low parental investments, and the harsh environments associated

Problem dimension 2: **Immediate causes**

Figure O.7 Why learning doesn't happen: Four immediate factors that break down

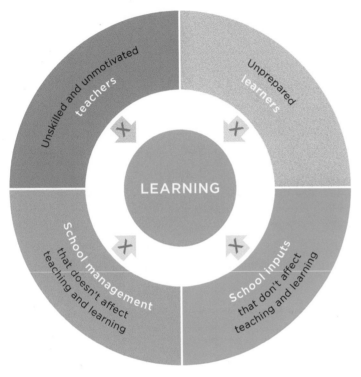

Source: WDR 2018 team.

Second, teachers often lack the skills or motivation to be effective. Teachers are the most important factor affecting learning in schools. In the United States, students with great teachers advance 1.5 grade levels or more over a single school year, compared with just 0.5 grade levels for those with an ineffective teacher.[34] In developing countries, teacher quality can matter even more than in wealthier countries.[35] But most education systems do not attract applicants with strong backgrounds. For example, 15-year-old students who aspire to be teachers score below the national average on PISA in nearly all countries.[36] Beyond that, weak teacher education results in teachers lacking subject knowledge and pedagogical skills. In 14 Sub-Saharan countries, the average grade 6 teacher performs no better on reading tests than do the highest-performing students from that grade.[37] In Indonesia, 60 percent of the time in a typical mathematics class is spent on lecturing, with limited time remaining for practical work or problem-solving.[38] Meanwhile, in many developing countries substantial amounts of learning time are lost because classroom time is spent on other activities or because teachers are absent. Only a third of total instructional time was used in Ethiopia, Ghana, and Guatemala.[39] Across seven African countries, one in five teachers was absent from school on the day of an unannounced visit by survey teams, with another fifth absent from the classroom even though they were at school (figure O.9).[40] The problems are even more severe in remote communities, amplifying the disadvantages already facing rural students. Such diagnostics are not intended to blame teachers. Rather, they call attention to how systems undermine learning by failing to support them.

Third, inputs often fail to reach classrooms or to affect learning when they do. Public discourse often equates problems of education quality with input gaps. Devoting enough resources to education is crucial, and in some countries resources have not kept pace with the rapid jumps in enrollment. For several reasons, however, input shortages explain only a small part of the learning crisis. First, looking across systems and schools, similar levels of resources are often associated with vast differences in learning outcomes.[41] Second, increasing inputs in a given setting often has small effects on learning outcomes.[42] Part of the reason is that inputs often fail to make it to the front lines. A decade ago in Sierra Leone, for example, textbooks were distributed to schools, but follow-up inspections found most of them locked away in cupboards, unused.[43] Similarly, many technological interventions

with poverty undermine early childhood learning.[30] Severe deprivations—whether in terms of nutrition, unhealthy environments, or lack of nurture by caregivers—have long-lasting effects because they impair infants' brain development.[31] Thirty percent of children under 5 in developing countries are physically stunted, meaning they have low height for their age, typically due to chronic malnutrition.[32] The poor developmental foundations and lower levels of preschool skills resulting from deprivation mean many children arrive at school unprepared to benefit fully from it (figure O.8).[33] So even in a good school, deprived children learn less. Moreover, breaking out of lower learning trajectories becomes harder as these children age because the brain becomes less malleable. Thus education systems tend to amplify initial differences. Moreover, many disadvantaged youth are not in school. Fees and opportunity costs are still major financial barriers to schooling, and social dimensions of exclusion—for example, those associated with gender or disability—exacerbate the problem. These inequalities in school participation further widen gaps in learning outcomes.

Figure O.8 Socioeconomic gaps in cognitive achievement grow with age—even in preschool years

Percentage of children ages 3–5 who can recognize 10 letters of the alphabet, by wealth quintile, selected countries

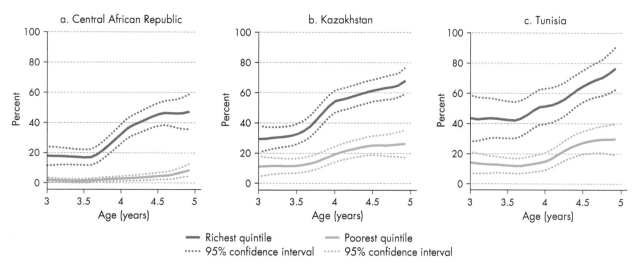

Source: WDR 2018 team, using data from Multiple Indicator Cluster Surveys (http://mics.unicef.org/). Data are for 2010 for the Central African Republic, 2010–11 for Kazakhstan, and 2012 for Tunisia. Data at http://bit.do/WDR2018-Fig_O-8.

fail before they reach classrooms, and even when they do make it to classrooms, they often do not enhance teaching or learning. In Brazil, a One Laptop Per Child initiative in several states faced years of delays. Then, even a year after the laptops finally made it to classrooms, more than 40 percent of teachers reported never or rarely using them in classroom activities.[44]

Fourth, poor management and governance often undermine schooling quality. Although effective school leadership does not raise student learning directly, it does so indirectly by improving teaching quality and ensuring effective use of resources.[45] Across eight countries that have been studied, a 1.00 standard deviation increase in an index of management capacity—based on the adoption of 20 management practices—is associated with a 0.23–0.43 standard deviation increase in student outcomes. But school management capacity tends to be lowest in those countries with the lowest income levels, and management capacity is substantially lower in schools than in manufacturing (figure O.10).[46] Ineffective school leadership means school principals are not actively involved in helping teachers solve problems, do not provide instructional advice, and do not set goals that prioritize learning. School governance—particularly the decision-making autonomy of schools, along with the oversight provided by parents and communities—serves as the framework for seeking local solutions and being accountable for them. In many settings, schools lack any meaningful

Figure O.9 In Africa, teachers are often absent from school or from classrooms while at school

Percentage of teachers absent from school and from class on the day of an unannounced visit, participating countries

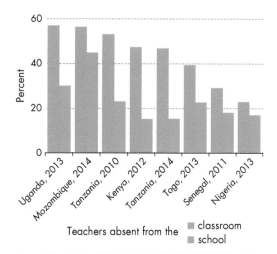

Source: Bold and others (2017). Data at http://bit.do/WDR2018-Fig_O-9.

Note: "Absent from the classroom" combines absences from school with absences from class among teachers who are at school. Data are from the World Bank's Service Delivery Indicators (SDI) surveys (http://www.worldbank.org/sdi).

autonomy, and community engagement fails to affect what happens in classrooms.[47]

Because these quality problems are concentrated among disadvantaged children, they amplify social

Figure O.10 Management capacity is low in schools in low- and middle-income countries

Distribution of management scores by sector, participating countries

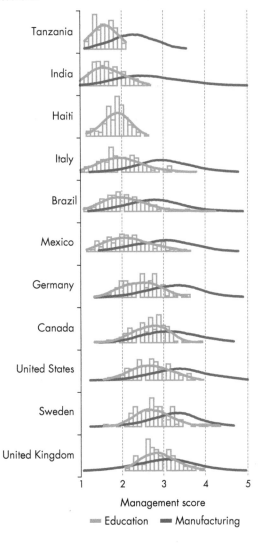

Management score
━━━ Education   ━━━ Manufacturing

Sources: Bloom and others (2014, 2015); Lemos and Scur (2016), with updates. Data at http://bit.do/WDR2018-Fig_O-10.

Note: The underlying distributions for the education data are shown as bars; for both sectors, the smoothed distributions are shown as curves. The indexes are constructed from the nine items that are comparable across sectors. Data on manufacturing are not available for Haiti.

inequalities. In low-income countries, on average, stunting rates among children under 5 are almost three times higher in the poorest quintile than in the richest.[48] In schools, problems with teacher absenteeism, lack of inputs, and weak management are typically severest in communities that serve the poorest students. It's not just that spending patterns

typically disadvantage marginalized communities, but also that resources are used less effectively there, exacerbating the problem. Public policy thus has the effect of widening social gaps rather than offering all children an opportunity to learn.

Systems are failing schools

Viewed from a systems perspective, the low level of learning and skills should come as no surprise. Technical complexities and political forces constantly pull education systems out of alignment with learning (figure O.11).

Problem dimension 3:
Deeper causes

Technical challenges: Reorienting toward learning is hard

Complex systems and limited management capacity are obstacles to orienting all parts of an education system toward learning. First, the various parts of the system need to be aligned toward learning. But actors in the system have other goals—some stated, some not. Promoting learning is only one of these, and not necessarily the most important one. At times, these other goals can be harmful, such as when construction firms and bureaucrats collude to provide substandard school buildings for their financial gain. At other times, these goals may be laudable, such as nurturing shared national values. But if system elements are aligned toward these other goals, they will sometimes be at cross-purposes with learning.

Even when countries want to prioritize learning, they often lack the metrics to do so. Every system assesses student learning in some way, but many systems lack the reliable, timely assessments needed to provide feedback on innovations. For example, is a new teacher training program actually making teachers more effective? If the system lacks reliable information on the quality of teaching and the learning of primary students—comparable across time or classrooms—there is no way to answer that question.

To be truly aligned, parts of the education system also have to be coherent with one another. Imagine that a country has set student learning as a top priority and that it has in place reasonable learning metrics. It still needs to leap a major technical hurdle, however: ensuring that system elements work together. If a country adopts a new curriculum that increases emphasis on active learning and creative thinking, that alone will not change much. Teachers need to be trained so that they can use more active learning methods, and they need to care enough to make the change because teaching the new curriculum may be much more demanding than the old rote learning methods. Even if teachers are on board with curriculum reform, students could weaken its effects if an unreformed examination system creates misaligned incentives. In Korea, the high-stakes exam system for university entrance has weakened efforts to reorient secondary school learning. The curriculum has changed to build students' creativity and socio-emotional skills, but many parents still send their children to private "cram schools" for test preparation.[49]

The need for coherence makes it risky to borrow system elements from other countries. Education policy makers and other experts often scrutinize systems that have better learning outcomes to identify what they could borrow. Indeed, in the 2000s the search for the secret behind Finland's admirable record of learning with equity led to a swarm of visiting delegations in what the Finns dubbed "PISA tourism." Finland's system gives considerable autonomy to its well-educated teachers, who can tailor their teaching to the needs of their students. But lower-performing systems that import Finland's teacher autonomy into their own contexts are likely to be disappointed: if teachers are poorly educated, unmotivated, and loosely managed, giving them even more autonomy will likely make matters worse. South Africa discovered this in the 1990s and 2000s when it adopted a curriculum approach that set goals but left implementation up to teachers.[50] The approach failed because it proved to be a poor fit for the capacity of teachers and the resources at their disposal.[51] Home-grown, context-specific solutions are important.

Successful systems combine both alignment and coherence. Alignment means that learning is the goal of the various components of the system. Coherence means that the components reinforce each other in achieving whatever goals the system has set for them. When systems achieve both, they are much more likely to promote student learning. Too much misalignment or incoherence leads to failure to achieve learning, though the system might achieve other goals (table O.1).

Political challenges: Key players don't always want to prioritize student learning

Political challenges compound technical ones. Many education actors have different interests, again beyond learning. Politicians act to preserve their positions in power, which may lead them to target particular groups (geographic, ethnic, or economic) for benefits. Bureaucrats may focus more on keeping

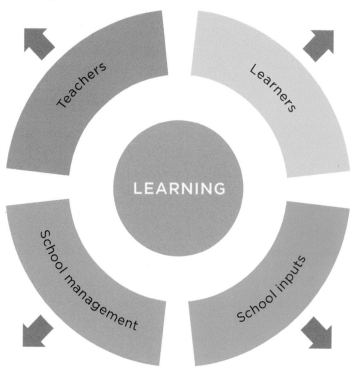

Figure O.11 Technical and political factors divert schools, teachers, and families from a focus on learning

LEARNING

Teachers

Learners

School management

School inputs

Source: WDR 2018 team.

politicians and teachers happy than on promoting student learning, or they may simply try to protect their own positions. Some private suppliers of education services—whether textbooks, construction, or schooling—may, in the pursuit of profit, advocate policy choices not in the interest of students. Teachers and other education professionals, even when motivated by a sense of mission, also may fight to maintain secure employment and to protect their incomes. None of this is to say that education actors don't care about learning. Rather, especially in poorly managed systems, competing interests may loom larger than the learning-aligned interests (table O.2).

Misalignments aren't random. Because of these competing interests, the choice of a particular policy is rarely determined by whether it improves learning. More often, the choice is made by the more powerful actors in the policy arena. Agents are accountable to one another for different reasons, not just learning. Given these interests, it should come as no surprise that little learning often results.

One problem is that activities to promote learning are difficult to manage. Teaching and learning in the

Table O.1 Alignment and coherence both matter

Are system elements . . .		Coherent?	
		Yes	No
Aligned toward learning?	Yes	*High performance:* Systems well organized to promote learning *Examples:* High performers at each level (Shanghai [China], Finland, Vietnam)	*Incoherent strivers:* Systems incoherently oriented toward learning *Examples:* Countries that borrow learning-oriented "best practice" elements but do not ensure that the various elements are coherent with each other
	No	*Coherent nonlearners:* Systems well organized to promote a different goal *Examples:* Totalitarian or authoritarian systems focused on promoting loyalty to the state or nation building (Stalin-era USSR, Suharto-era Indonesia); systems that focus on school attainment rather than learning (many systems)	*Failed systems:* Systems that are not trying to achieve learning or anything else in a coherent way *Examples:* Systems in failed states

Source: WDR 2018 team.

Table O.2 Multiple interests govern the actions of education stakeholders

Stakeholders	Examples of . . .	
	Learning-aligned interests	Competing interests
Teachers	Student learning, professional ethic	Employment, job security, salary, private tuitions
Principals	Student learning, teacher performance	Employment, salary, good relations with staff, favoritism
Bureaucrats	Well-functioning schools	Employment, salary, rent-seeking
Politicians	Well-functioning schools	Electoral gains, rent-seeking, patronage
Parents and students	Student learning, employment of graduates	Family employment, family income, outdoing others
Judiciary	Meaningful right to education	Favoritism, rent-seeking
Employers	Skilled graduates	Low taxes, narrowly defined self-interests
Nongovernment schools (religious, nongovernmental, for-profit)	Innovative, responsive schooling	Profit, religious mission, funding
Suppliers of educational inputs (e.g., textbooks, information technology, buildings)	High-quality, relevant inputs	Profit, influence
International donors	Student learning	Domestic strategic interests, taxpayer support, employment

Source: WDR 2018 team.

classroom involve significant discretion by teachers, as well as regular and repeated interactions between students and teachers.[52] These characteristics, coupled with a dearth of reliable information on learning, make managing learning more difficult than pursuing other goals.[53] For example, improvements in access to education can be monitored by looking at simple, easily collected enrollment data. Similarly, school construction, cash transfer programs, teacher hiring, and school grant programs intended to expand access are all highly visible, easily monitored investments.

The potential beneficiaries of better foundational learning—such as students, parents, and employers—

often lack the organization, information, or short-term incentive to press for change. Parents are usually not organized to participate in debates at the system level, and they may lack knowledge of the potential gains from different policies to improve learning.[54] They also may worry about the potential ramifications for their children or themselves of opposing interests such as teachers, bureaucrats, or politicians. Students have even less power—except sometimes in higher education, where they can threaten demonstrations—and, like parents, they may be unaware of how little they are learning until they start looking for work. Finally, the business community, even if it suffers from a shortage of skilled graduates to hire, often fails to advocate for quality education, instead lobbying for lower taxes and spending. By contrast to these potential beneficiaries of reform, the potential losers tend to be more aware of what is at stake for them and, in many cases, better organized to act collectively.

As a result, many systems are stuck in low-learning traps, characterized by low accountability and high inequality. These traps bind together key stakeholders through informal contracts that prioritize other goals such as civil service employment, corporate profits, or reelection, perpetuating the low-accountability equilibrium. In better-run systems, actors such as bureaucrats and teachers can devote much of their energy to improving outcomes for students. But in low-learning traps those same actors lack either the incentives or the support needed to focus on learning. Instead, they are constantly pressured to deliver other services for more powerful players. As actors juggle multiple objectives, relying on each other in an environment of uncertainty, low social trust, and risk aversion, it is often in the interest of each to maintain the status quo—even if society, and many of these actors, would be better off if they could shift to a higher-quality equilibrium.

This diagnosis has concentrated on the shortfalls in foundational learning, as will the priorities for action discussed in the next section. However, this focus should not be interpreted as a statement that other areas are unimportant. Education systems and their enabling environment are broader and more complex than this Report can cover, so our priority here is to highlight what can be done most immediately to strengthen the foundations of learning on which all successful systems are built. But both the diagnosis and the priorities for action are relevant for other parts of the system, such as higher education or lifelong learning. In these areas, too, many countries suffer from a lack of attention to outcomes, wide gaps in opportunity, and systemic barriers to resolving these problems.

Still, there are reasons for hope

Even in countries that seem stuck in low-learning traps, some teachers and schools manage to strengthen learning. These examples may not be sustainable—and they are not likely to spread systemwide without efforts to reorient the system toward learning—but systems willing to learn from these outliers can benefit. On a larger scale, some regions within countries are more successful in promoting learning, as are some countries at each income level.

These examples reveal that higher-level system equilibriums exist. But is it possible for a whole system to escape the low-learning trap, moving to a better one? There are at least two reasons for optimism. First, as countries innovate to improve learning, they can draw on more systematic knowledge than ever available before about what can work at the micro level—the level of learners, classrooms, and schools. A number of interventions, innovations, and approaches have resulted in substantial gains in learning. These promising approaches come in many flavors—new pedagogical methods, ways to ensure that students and teachers are motivated, approaches to school management, technologies to enhance teaching learning—and they may not pay off in all contexts, but the fact that it is possible to improve learning outcomes should give hope. These interventions can provide substantial improvements in learning: almost one or two grade-equivalents for some students.[55] Even though successful interventions cannot be imported wholesale into new contexts, countries can use them as starting points for their own innovations.

Second, some countries have implemented reforms that have led to sustained systemwide improvements in learning. Finland's major education reform in the 1970s famously improved the equity of outcomes while also increasing quality, so that by the time of the first PISA in 2000, Finland topped the assessment. More recently, Chile, Peru, Poland, and the United Kingdom have made serious, sustained commitments to reforming the quality of their education systems. In all these countries, learning has improved over time—not always steadily, but enough to show that system-level reforms can pay off.

The education systems in Shanghai (China) and Vietnam today—and Korea decades ago—show that it is possible to perform far better than income levels would predict, thanks to a sustained focus on learning with equity. Brazil and Indonesia have made considerable progress, despite the challenges of reforming large, decentralized systems.

How to realize education's promise: Three policy responses

Learning outcomes won't change unless education systems take learning seriously and use learning as a guide and metric. This idea can be summarized as "all for learning."[56] As this section explains, a commitment to all for learning—and thus to learning for all—implies three complementary strategies:

- *Assess learning—to make it a serious goal.* Measure and track learning better; use the results to guide action.
- *Act on evidence—to make schools work for all learners.* Use evidence to guide innovation and practice.
- *Align actors—to make the whole system work for learning.* Tackle the technical and political barriers to learning at scale.

These three strategies depend on one another. Adopting a learning metric without any credible way to achieve learning goals will simply lead to frustration. School-level innovations without a learning metric could take schools off course, and without the system-level support they could prove ephemeral. And system-level commitment to learning without school-level innovation, and without learning measures to guide the reforms, is unlikely to amount to more than aspirational rhetoric. But together, the three strategies can create change for the better.

The potential payoff is huge. When children have a growth mindset, meaning they understand their own great learning potential, they learn much more than when they believe they are constrained by a fixed intelligence.[57] Societies have the same opportunity. By adopting a social growth mindset—recognizing the barriers to learning, but also the very real opportunities to break them down—they can make progress on learning. One overarching priority should be to end the hidden exclusion of low learning. This is not just the right thing to do; it is also the surest way to improve average learning levels and reap education's full rewards for society as a whole.

Assess learning—to make it a serious goal

"What gets measured gets managed." "Just weighing the pig doesn't make it fatter." There is some truth to both of these sayings. Lack of measurement makes it hard to know where things are, where they are going, and what actions are making any difference. Knowing these things can provide focus and stimulate action. But measurement that is too removed from action can lead nowhere. The challenge is striking a balance—finding the right measures for the right purposes and implementing them within an appropriate accountability framework.

Policy response 1: Assess learning

Use measurement to shine a light on learning

The first step to improving systemwide learning is to put in place good metrics for monitoring whether programs and policies are delivering learning. Credible, reliable information can shape the incentives facing politicians. Most notably, information on student learning and school performance—if presented in a way that makes it salient and acceptable—fosters healthier political engagement and better service delivery. Information also helps policy makers manage a complex system.

Measuring learning can improve equity by revealing hidden exclusions. As emphasized at the outset of this overview, the learning crisis is not just a problem for the society and economy overall; it is also a fundamental source of inequities and widening gaps in opportunity. But because reliable information on learning is so spotty in many education systems, especially in primary and lower secondary schools, the way the system is failing disadvantaged children is a hidden exclusion.[58] Unlike exclusion from school, lack of learning is often invisible, making it impossible for families and communities to exercise their right to quality education.

These measures of learning will never be the only guide for educational progress, nor should they be. Education systems should have ways of tracking progress toward any goal they set for themselves and their students—not just learning. Systems should also track the critical factors that drive learning—such as learner preparation, teacher skills, quality of school management, and the level and equity of financing. But learning metrics are an essential starting point for improving lagging systems.

Figure O.12 Many countries lack information on learning outcomes

Percentage of countries with data to monitor progress toward the Sustainable Development Goals for learning by the end of primary or lower secondary school

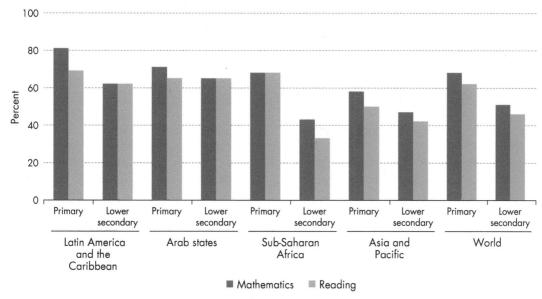

Source: UIS (2016). Data at http://bit.do/WDR2018-Fig_O-12.

Note: Regional groupings follow UNESCO definitions.

There is too little measurement of learning, not too much

A recommendation to start tackling the learning crisis with more and better measurement of learning may seem jarring. Many education debates highlight the risks of overtesting or an overemphasis on tests. In the United States, two decades of high-stakes testing have led to patterns of behavior consistent with these concerns.[59] Some teachers have been found to concentrate on test-specific skills instead of untested subjects, and some schools have engaged in strategic behavior to ensure that only the better-performing students are tested, such as assigning students to special education that excuses them from testing.[60] In the extreme, problems have expanded to convictions for systemic cheating at the school district level.[61] At the same time, media coverage of education in many low- and middle-income countries (and some high-income ones) often focuses on high-stakes national examinations that screen candidates for tertiary education—raising concerns about an overemphasis on testing.

But in many systems the problem is too little focus on learning—not too much. Many countries lack information on even basic reading and math competencies. An assessment of capacity to monitor progress toward the United Nations' Sustainable Development Goals found that of the 121 countries studied, a third lack the data required to report on the levels of reading and mathematics proficiency of children at the end of primary school.[62] Even more lack data for the end of lower secondary school (figure O.12). Even when countries have these data, they are often from one-off assessments that do not allow systematic tracking over time. A lack of good measurement means that education systems are often flying blind—and without even agreement on the destination.

Use a range of metrics with one ultimate goal

Different learning metrics have different purposes, but each contributes to learning for all. Teachers assess students in classrooms every day—formally or informally—even in poorly resourced, poorly managed school systems. But using metrics properly to improve learning systemwide requires a spectrum of types of assessment that, together, allow educators and policy makers to use the right combination of teaching approaches, programs, and policies.

Formative assessment by teachers helps guide instruction and tailor teaching to the needs of students. Well-prepared, motivated teachers do not need to operate in the dark: they know how to assess the learning of students regularly, formally and informally. As the next section discusses, this type of regular check-in is important because many students lag so far behind that they effectively stop learning. Knowing where students are allows teachers to adjust their teaching accordingly and to give students learning opportunities they can handle. Singapore has successfully used this approach—identifying lagging students in grade 1 using screening tests and then giving them intensive support to bring them up to grade level.[63]

National and subnational learning assessments provide system-level insights that classroom assessments by teachers cannot. To guide an education system, policy makers need to understand whether students are mastering the national curriculum, in which areas students are stronger or weaker, whether certain population groups are lagging behind and by how much, and which factors are associated with better student achievement. There is no effective way to aggregate the results of classroom-level formative assessment by teachers into this type of reliable system-level information. This is why systems need assessments of representative samples of students across wider jurisdictions, such as countries or provinces. Such assessments can be an especially important part of tracking systemwide progress because they are anchored in a system's own expectations for itself. And national assessments can provide a check on the quality of subnational assessments by flagging cases in which trends or levels of student achievement diverge across the two. In the United States, the National Assessment of Educational Progress has played this role.[64]

International assessments also provide information that helps improve systems. Globally benchmarked student assessments such as PISA, TIMSS, and PIRLS, as well as regionally benchmarked ones such as PASEC in West and Central Africa and the Latin American Laboratory for Assessment of the Quality of Education (LLECE), provide an additional perspective on how well students are learning. They allow assessment of country performance in a way that is comparable across countries, and they provide a check on the information that emerges from national assessments. And international assessments can be powerful tools politically: because country leaders are concerned with national productivity and competitiveness, international benchmarking can raise awareness of how a country is falling short of its peers in building human capital.

Two other types of learning metrics measured in nonschool settings can be used to strengthen the quality and equity focus of assessment systems. Grassroots accountability movements—led by civil society organizations such as the ASER Centre in India and Uwezo in East Africa—have deployed citizen-led assessments that recruit volunteers to measure the foundational learning of young children in their communities. These organizations then use their learning data to advocate for education reform. Some multipurpose household surveys also collect learning data, enabling researchers to analyze how learning outcomes correlate with income and community variables. Both types of assessments are administered in people's homes, not schools. As a result, they don't suffer from a key weakness of school-based assessments: when marginal students drop out, their absence can improve the average scores on school assessments, thereby creating a perverse incentive for school leaders. But household-based assessments yield learning metrics that reward systems for improving both access and quality. This is crucial to ensuring that no child is written off. Even for students who are in school, household-based assessments provide an alternative source of learning data, which can be important in settings where official assessments are of questionable quality.

Measurement can be hard

Why isn't there more and better measurement of learning? As with system barriers to learning, barriers to better measurement are both technical and political. From a technical perspective, conducting good assessments is not easy. At the classroom level, teachers lack the training to assess learning effectively, especially when assessments try to capture higher-order skills—say, through project-based assessment—rather than rote learning. And at the system level, education ministries lack the capacity to design valid assessments and implement them in a sample of schools. Political factors intrude as well. To paraphrase an old saying, policy makers may decide it is better to avoid testing and be assumed ineffective than to test students and remove all doubt. And even when they do participate in assessments, governments sometimes decline to release the learning results to the public, as happened with the 1995 TIMSS in Mexico.[65] Finally, if assessments are poorly designed or inappropriately made into high-stakes tests, administrators or educators may have an incentive to cheat on them, rendering the assessment results worthless as a guide to policy.

Measurement doesn't need to detract from broader education objectives—it can even support them

A stronger emphasis on measurable learning doesn't mean that other education outcomes don't matter. Formal education and other opportunities for learning have many goals, only some of which are captured by the usual assessments of literacy, numeracy, and reasoning. Educators also aspire to help learners develop higher-order cognitive skills, including some (like creativity) that are hard to capture through assessments. Success in life also depends on socioemotional and noncognitive skills—such as persistence, resilience, and teamwork—that a good education helps individuals develop. Education systems often have other goals as well: they want to endow students with citizenship skills, encourage civic-minded values, and promote social cohesion. These are widely shared goals of education, and it is understandable that people will ask whether, especially in education systems that are already overburdened, increasing the emphasis on measurable learning will crowd out these other goals.

In fact, a focus on learning—and on the educational quality that drives it—is more likely to "crowd in" these other desirable outcomes. Conditions that allow children to spend two or three years in school without learning to read a single word, or to reach the end of primary school without learning to do two-digit subtraction, are not conducive to reaching the higher goals of education. Schools that cannot equip youth with relevant job skills usually will not prepare them to launch new companies or analyze great works of literature either. If students cannot focus because of deprivation, if teachers lack the pedagogical skills and motivation to engage students, if materials meant for the classroom never reach it because of poor management, and if the system as a whole is unmoored from the needs of society—well, is it really plausible to believe that students are developing higher-order thinking skills like problem-solving and creativity? It is more likely that these conditions undermine the quest for higher goals—and that, conversely, improving the learning focus would accelerate progress toward those goals as well.

Paradoxically, lower-performing countries probably do not face the same sharp trade-offs encountered

Figure O.13 Low-performing countries don't face sharp trade-offs between learning and other education outputs

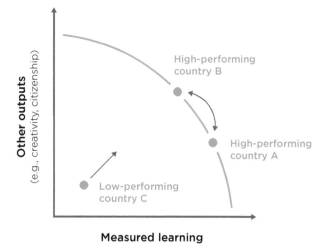

Source: WDR 2018 team.

by high-performing countries on the education frontier. Economists use the concept of the production possibilities frontier to understand how producers—or in this case countries—make trade-offs between the production of different goods. This idea encapsulates the debates on education policy in OECD countries on the learning frontier (figure O.13). For example, in recent years many stakeholders in Korea have argued that their high-performing education system places too much emphasis on test scores (called "measured learning" in figure O.13) and not enough on creativity and certain socioemotional skills such as teamwork ("other outputs"). Implicitly, this Korean debate is about whether to try to move up and to the left on the frontier—that is, from A toward B. But in the low-learning trap, represented by "low-performing country C" in the figure, there is so much slack and such a weak focus on outcomes that this OECD-driven debate is not relevant. Country C has an opportunity to improve on both measured learning and other education outputs at the same time. An experiment in Andhra Pradesh, India, that rewarded teachers for gains in measured learning in math and language led to more learning not just in those subjects, but also in science and social studies—even though there were no rewards for the latter.[66] This outcome makes sense—after all, literacy and numeracy are gateways to education more generally.

Act on evidence—to make schools work for all learners

Policy response 2: Act on evidence

Measurement of learning shortfalls doesn't provide clear guidance on how to remedy them. Fortunately, there is now a lot of experience on ways to improve learning outcomes at the student, classroom, and school levels. Cognitive neuroscience has evolved dramatically in the last two decades, providing insights on how children learn.[67] This work has revealed how important the first several years of life are to a child's brain development.[68] At the same time, schools and systems around the world have innovated in many ways: by deploying novel approaches to pedagogy, using new technologies to enhance teaching and learning in classrooms, or increasing the accountability, and sometimes autonomy, of various actors in the system. The number of systematic evaluations of whether these interventions have improved learning has increased more than 10-fold, from just 19 in 2000 to 299 in 2016.[69]

Many interventions have succeeded in improving learning outcomes. The learning gains from effective interventions translate into additional years of schooling, higher earnings, and lower poverty. For a group of stunted Jamaican children 9–24 months old, a program to improve cognitive and socioemotional development led to much better outcomes 20 years later—lower crime rates, better mental health, and earnings that were 25 percent higher than those of nonparticipants.[70] Programs to improve pedagogy have had an impact greater than the equivalent of an extra half a year of business-as-usual schooling and an 8 percent increase in the present discounted value of lifetime earnings.[71] So while tackling the learning crisis is hard, the fact that there are interventions that improve learning suggests ways forward.

This evidence base does not allow us to identify what works in all contexts because there are no global solutions in education. Improving learning in a particular setting will never be as simple as taking a successful program from one country or region and implementing it elsewhere. Randomized controlled trials and other approaches to evaluate impact place a premium on carefully isolating the causal impact of an intervention. But such approaches may ignore important interactions with underlying factors that affect whether an intervention makes a difference—factors that may not be at play when replicating the intervention in a new context. For example, increasing class size by 10 students reduced test scores by four times as much in Israel as it did in Kenya—and it has had no impact in some contexts.[72] In the words of two commentators on this literature: "Knowing 'what works' in the sense of the treatment effect on the trial population is of limited value without understanding the political and institutional environment in which it is set."[73]

The next section tackles the question of that broader environment, but in the meantime we first address how to use this evidence most effectively. There are four main considerations.

First, more important than the individual results from individual studies are the principles of how and why programs work. In economic terms, "principles" correspond to models of behavior that can then help guide broader sets of approaches to addressing problems. Three types of models can prove especially insightful: straightforward models in which actors maximize their welfare subject to the constraints they face; principal-agent models that incorporate multiple actors with different goals and perhaps different information; and behavioral models that factor in mental models and social norms.

Second, a gap between what the evidence suggests may be effective and what is done in practice points to a potential entry point for action. Understanding why gaps open up helps guide how to address them. For example, when different actors face different information, or some actors lack information, this suggests drawing from approaches that show how information can be disseminated and used better. Gaps point to which types of principles should drive context-specific innovation.

Third, evidence tends to accumulate where it is easiest to generate, not necessarily where action would make the most difference, so policies focused only on that evidence might be misguided.[74] Though the scope of the accumulated evidence in education is broad, just because an approach hasn't been evaluated doesn't mean it lacks potential. Context-specific innovation may mean trying things that have not been tried elsewhere.

Fourth, a focus on underlying principles highlights that the problem can't be solved by one decision maker simply prescribing an increase in the quantity, or even the quality, of one or more inputs. Many of the inputs in learning are the result of choices made by the various actors—choices made in reaction to the actual and anticipated choices of other actors. For example, teachers respond to incentives to attend school and to improve student outcomes, even though the nature of the response varies across contexts.[75] Likewise, students and parents make choices

Figure O.14 It's more complicated than it looks: People act in reaction to the choices of others throughout the system

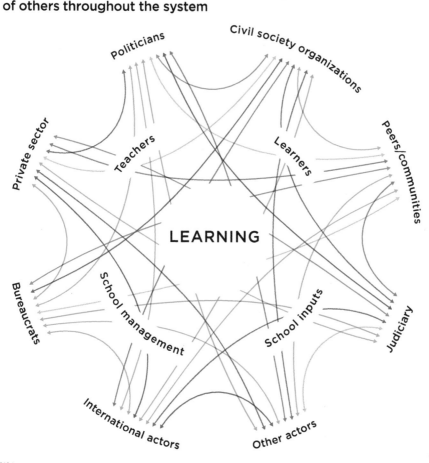

Source: WDR 2018 team.

responding to other decisions. In India and Zambia, government grants to schools led parents to reduce their own investments in their children's schooling.[76] All things considered, a more complete characterization of the learning framework might be closer to the one illustrated in figure O.14: learning how to improve outcomes by intervening at the student, classroom, and school levels involves illuminating the various arrows.

Putting all this together sheds light on three sets of promising entry points: prepared learners, effective teaching, and school-level interventions that actually affect the teaching and learning process. Each of these priority areas is founded on evidence from multiple contexts showing that it can make a real difference for learning.

Prepare children and youth for learning

Getting learners to school ready and motivated to learn is a first step to better learning. Without it, other policies and programs will have a minimal effect.

There are three key entry points to addressing learner preparation:

- *Set children on high-development trajectories through early childhood nutrition, stimulation, and care.* Three approaches stand out from successful experiences. First, target mothers and their babies with health and nutrition interventions during the first 1,000 days to reduce malnutrition and foster physiological development. Second, increase the frequency and quality of stimulation and opportunities for learning at home (starting from birth) to improve language and motor development, as well as to cultivate early cognitive and socioemotional skills. Third, promote day-care centers for very young children and preschool programs for children 3–6 years old—along with caregiver programs that enhance the nurturing and protection of children— to improve cognitive and socioemotional skills in the short run, as well as education and labor market outcomes later in life.[77] Program quality matters a lot: center-based programs with poor process quality (even with relatively good infrastructure, caregiver training, and caregiver-children ratios) can actually worsen developmental outcomes.[78]

- *Lower the cost of schooling to get children into school, but then use other tools to boost motivation and effort because cost-reducing interventions don't usually lead to learning on their own.*[79] To improve learning, demand-side programs need to increase a student's effort or capacity to learn. School-provided meals, for example, have had positive effects on access—and also on learning in places where children have limited access to food at home.[80] Targeted cash transfers have led to more learning when they have incentivized performance itself[81] or were marketed in a way that induces more effort, such as in Cambodia.[82] Some information interventions have motivated efforts as well.[83]
- *To make up for the fact that so many youth lack skills when leaving basic education, provide remediation before further education and training.*[84] Remediation in school is a first best approach. After school, the more successful programs share two main features. First, they provide bridging courses in real-life settings, which allows learners with very low foundational skills to build these in the workplace.[85] Second, accelerated, flexible pathways—not sequential courses over multiple semesters—are associated with greater student retention and ultimate certification.[86]

Make teaching more effective

Effective teaching depends on teachers' skills and motivation, and yet many systems do not take them seriously. Teacher salaries are the largest single budget item in education systems, consuming three-quarters of the budget at the primary level in developing countries. Yet many systems struggle to attract strong candidates into teaching and to provide a solid foundation of subject or pedagogical knowledge before they start teaching. As a result, new teachers often find themselves in classrooms with little mastery of the content they are to teach.[87] Once teachers are in place, the professional development they receive is often inconsistent and overly theoretical. In some countries, the cost of this training is enormous, reaching $2.5 billion a year in the United States.[88] Moreover, education systems often have few effective mechanisms in place to mentor, support, and motivate teachers—even though teachers' skills do nothing for learning unless teachers choose to apply them in the classroom.[89] Fortunately, teachers' skills and motivation can be strengthened, leading to greater effort and more learning, with three main promising principles emerging:

- *For effective teacher training, design it to be individually targeted and repeated, with follow-up coaching—often around a specific pedagogical technique.* This approach contrasts starkly with much of today's professional development for teachers across a range of countries. In the United States, a team of teacher training experts characterized professional development there as "episodic, myopic, and often meaningless."[90] In Sub-Saharan Africa, teacher training is often too short to be effective and too low in quality to make a difference.[91] By contrast, programs in Africa and South Asia that provided long-term coaching led to sizable learning gains.[92]
- *To keep learners from falling behind to the point where they cannot catch up, target teaching to the level of the student.* Over the course of several grades, often only a fraction of learners progress at grade level, with most falling behind and some learning almost nothing. This is partly because teachers teach to the most advanced students in the class, as documented from Australia to Sweden to the United States,[93] or because the curriculum is too ambitious but teachers are required to teach it.[94] Effective strategies to target teaching to the level of the student include using community teachers to provide remedial lessons to the lowest performers, reorganizing classes by ability, or using technology to adapt lessons to individual student needs.[95]
- *Use pecuniary and nonpecuniary incentives to improve the motivation of teachers, ensuring that the incentivized actions are within teachers' capacity.* Education systems typically neither reward teachers for performing well nor penalize them for performing poorly. Incentives are most likely to be effective at improving outcomes when there are straightforward actions that teachers can take to improve learning—such as increasing attendance when absenteeism is the constraint. But incentives do not need to be high stakes (or financial) to affect behavior. In Mexico and Punjab, Pakistan, simply providing diagnostic information to parents and schools about the schools' relative performance improved learning outcomes.[96]

Focus everything else on teaching and learning

School inputs, management, and governance must benefit the learner-teacher relationship if they are to improve learning—but many do not. Debates on improving education outcomes frequently revolve around increasing inputs, such as textbooks, technology, or school infrastructure. But too often the question of why these inputs might actually improve learning is overlooked. The evidence on successful use of inputs and management suggests three main principles:

- *Provide additional inputs, including new technologies, in ways that complement rather than substitute for teachers.*[97] A computer-assisted learning program in Gujarat, India, improved learning when it added to teaching and learning time, especially for the poorest-performing students.[98] A Kenyan program that provided public school teachers with tablets to support instruction increased the reading performance of their students.[99] But simply providing desktop computers to classrooms in Colombia—where they were not well integrated with the curriculum—had no impact on learning.[100] Even more traditional inputs—such as books—often fail to affect teaching and learning when they aren't actually deployed in classrooms, or if the content is too advanced for the students.[101]
- *Ensure that new information and communication technology is really implementable in the current systems.* Interventions that incorporate information and communication technology have some of the biggest impacts on learning.[102] But for every highly effective program—such as a dynamic computer-assisted learning program for secondary school students in Delhi that increased math and language scores more than the vast majority of other learning interventions tested in India or elsewhere[103]—there are programs such as the One Laptop Per Child programs in Peru and Uruguay, which evaluations suggested had no impact on student reading or math ability.[104] Technologies ill-adapted to their settings often fail to reach the classroom or to be used if they reach it.[105]
- *Focus school management and governance reforms on improving teacher-learner interaction.* Training principals in how to improve that interaction—by providing feedback to teachers on lesson plans, action plans to improve student performance, and classroom behavior—has led to a large impact on student learning.[106] In countries ranging from Brazil and India to Sweden, the United Kingdom, and the United States, the management capacity of school principals significantly and robustly relates to student performance—even after controlling for a variety of student and school characteristics.[107] Involving communities, parents, and school actors in ways that promote local oversight and accountability for service delivery can improve outcomes.[108] But community monitoring tends to have more impact when it covers things that parents can easily observe (such as teacher absenteeism when

it is high), and when a range of stakeholders (not just parents) are brought together in ways that lead to action. In Indonesia, school grants improved learning when links between the school and the village council—a center of local authority—were strengthened.[109]

The most effective systems—in terms of learning—are those that have narrowed gaps between evidence and practice. On learner preparation, for example, East Asian countries such as Korea and Singapore have achieved high levels of children ready to learn. Stunting rates among preschool-age children are low, and children are motivated and supported by their families. To promote effective teaching, Finland and Singapore attract some of the most highly skilled graduates from tertiary education into teaching and provide them with effective professional development opportunities and sustained support.

Align actors—to make the whole system work for learning

Working at scale is not just "scaling up." The concept of scaling up in education implies taking interventions that have been shown to be effective on a pilot or experimental scale and replicating them across hundreds or thousands of schools. However, this approach often fails because the key actors are human beings, operating with human aspirations and limitations in a

Policy response 3: **Align actors**

politically charged arena. Real-world complications can undermine well-designed programs, especially when new, systemwide forces come into play. When the Cambodian government tried to scale up early child development centers and preschools—programs that had worked in some parts of the country when implemented by nongovernmental organizations (NGOs)—low demand from parents and low-quality services led to no impacts on child development, and even slowed it for some.[110] When the Kenyan government tried to lower student-teacher ratios by hiring contract teachers—an intervention that had improved student outcomes when implemented by an NGO—the results were negligible because of both implementation constraints and political economy factors.[111] And when the Indonesian government tried to increase teacher capacity by nearly doubling the salaries of certified teachers, political pressures watered down the certification process and left only the pay increase in place. The result was much larger budget outlays on salaries, but no increase in teachers' skills or student learning.[112]

The lesson, then, is that better interventions at the school and student levels will sustainably improve learning only if countries tackle the stubborn system-level technical and political barriers to change. Technical barriers include the complexity of the system, the large number of actors, the interdependence of reforms, and the slow pace of change in education systems. Political barriers include the competing interests of different players and the difficulty of moving out of a low-quality equilibrium, especially in low-trust environments where risks predominate. All of these barriers pull actors away from learning, as discussed earlier. Systems that surmount these barriers and align actors toward learning can achieve remarkable learning outcomes. Shanghai provided proof when it topped the 2012 PISA rankings, in part thanks to policies that ensured that every classroom had a prepared, supported, and motivated teacher.[113]

To shift the system toward learning, technically and politically, reformers can use three sets of tools:

- *Information and metrics.* Better information and metrics can promote learning in two ways: by catalyzing reforms and by serving as indicators of whether reforms are working to improve learning with equity. Thus they can improve both the political and technical alignment of the system.
- *Coalitions and incentives.* Good information will have a payoff only if there is enough support for prioritizing learning. Politics is often the problem, and politics must be part of the solution. This requires forming coalitions to advocate for broad-based learning and skills and to rebalance the political incentives.
- *Innovation and agility.* Schools and societies have achieved high levels of equitable learning in a variety of ways. Figuring out what approaches will work in a given context requires innovation and adaptation. This means using evidence to identify where to start and then using metrics to iterate with feedback loops.

All of these tools will be most effective when supported by strong implementation capacity within government.

Information and metrics
Better information and measurement—starting with learning metrics—are critical to creating political space for innovation and then using that space to achieve continuous improvement. As emphasized, the absence of good information on learning prevents stakeholders from judging system performance, designing the appropriate policies, and holding politicians and bureaucrats to account. Thus improving learning metrics is crucial for drawing attention to problems and building the will for action. In Tanzania in the early 2010s, poor results on school-leaving examinations—along with well-publicized results from citizen-led learning assessments and surveys showing poor service delivery in schools—motivated policy makers to launch ambitious reforms. In Germany, the shock of mediocre results on the first PISA in 2000 led to reforms that improved both learning and equity.

Efforts in this area need to go beyond just measuring learning; they should track its determinants as well. Understanding these determinants can enable reforms to grapple with the deeper causes, if there is a systemwide commitment to improving learning. Take the issue of learner preparedness. When indicators reveal that poorer children already lag far behind by the time they start primary school, this finding can build political will not only to expand preschool education in low-income areas, but also to combat stunting and educate parents about early stimulation of children. When indicators show that many teachers lack a strong command of what their students are meant to learn, this finding can spark efforts to improve the quality of teacher education.[114]

Of course, information and metrics can also be misleading, irrelevant, or politically unsustainable, so they need to be designed and used wisely. Metrics may fail to capture important dimensions of the outcomes the education system is trying to promote. For example, the Millennium Development Goal of universal primary education by 2015 embodied a crucial goal—equitable access—but it did not represent what many assumed it did: universal acquisition of foundational literacy and numeracy, let alone other life skills. Another risk is of distorting good metrics by putting high stakes on them, if potential beneficiaries can game the indicators. Thus systems will need different measures for different purposes.[115] Even if they are technically sound, metrics may prove politically unsustainable if they highlight too many problems and do not provide any reason for hope. One way to address this problem is to focus not on levels of learning, which may be very low, but on progress over time.

Coalitions and incentives
Mobilizing everyone who has a stake in learning has been an important strategy in efforts to improve learning. Many countries have used wide-ranging

consultations that have tried to bring in all interest groups to build support for proposed changes in education policy. Malaysia used a "lab" model to bring together coalitions of stakeholders and involve them in all stages of reform, from design to implementation.[116] Mobilizing citizens through regular information and communication campaigns can also be an important strategy. In Peru, reformers in the government used information on poor learning outcomes and performance of the education system to mobilize public support for reforms to strengthen teacher accountability. That information also catalyzed action by the business community, which funded a campaign highlighting the importance of quality education for economic growth. In parts of Peru, parents used this entry point to protest teacher strikes that had disrupted schooling.[117] Another tool for building coalitions is to bundle reforms, so that each actor achieves one of its top priorities. For example, a commitment to modernize vocational training—a reform that could help employers immediately—could buy their support for broader education reforms.

Where feasible, a negotiated and gradual approach to reform can provide a more promising alternative to direct confrontation. When system actors agree to collaborate and build trust around shared goals, the chances of successful reform are likely to be higher. In Chile, successive negotiations between the government and the teachers' union built broad support for a series of reforms that adjusted the working conditions of teachers to improve their overall welfare, while linking pay and career development more closely to performance.[118] One approach used by several countries has been to compensate actors who might lose out from reforms. In other cases, dual-track reforms have been introduced to phase in changes in a way that protects incumbent actors from their effects—for example, in Peru and the District of Columbia in the United States, pay-for-performance schemes were initially voluntary.[119]

Building strong partnerships between schools and their communities is also important for sustaining reforms. Where political and bureaucratic incentives for reform are weak, action at the local level can act as a substitute. In South Africa, the political and economic context constrains efforts to improve education performance. Yet progress was made in improving outcomes at the local level through strong partnerships between parents and schools.[120] Even where broader incentives exist to improve learning, community engagement at the local level is important and can complement national or subnational change efforts.[121]

Innovation and agility

To develop effective learning approaches that fit their contexts, education systems need to encourage innovation and adaptation. In many education systems, schools and other education institutions regularly adapt to changing circumstances. Through these adaptations, innovative solutions to education challenges often emerge. Exploring the well-performing parts of any education system can reveal technically and politically feasible approaches to the problems systems face in improving learning. For example, in Misiones province in Argentina high student dropout rates were widespread, but some schools seemed to buck the trend. A closer look at these "positive deviants" revealed very different relationships between teachers and parents. When other schools adopted the more constructive approach to parent-teacher relations used by the successful schools, their dropout rates fell significantly.[122] Burundi, while recovering from a civil war, used an adaptive approach to find the right way to get textbooks to schools. It reduced delivery times from over a year to 60 days—then replicated that approach in other areas.[123]

Incentives are important in determining whether systems innovate and adopt emerging solutions at scale. Systems that are closed, that limit the autonomy of teachers and schools, and that judge performance by the extent of compliance with rules governing resource use often provide little room for innovation. By contrast, more open systems that pay more attention to overall outcomes and reward progress in raising outcomes are more likely to see greater innovation and the diffusion of new approaches across the education system.[124]

To make a difference at the system level, such innovations needs to be packaged with good metrics and with system-level coalitions for learning. Without both, any improvements from innovation are likely to prove short-lived or limited to local areas. But with such support, a virtuous cycle becomes possible as systems follow these steps:

- Set learning as a clearly articulated goal and measure it.
- Build a coalition for learning that gives the political space for innovation and experimentation.
- Innovate and test approaches that seem the most promising for the given context, drawing inspiration from the evidence base and focusing on areas that promise the biggest improvements over current practice.
- Use the measure of learning, along with the other metrics of delivery, as a gauge of whether the approach is working.

Figure O.15 Coherence and alignment toward learning

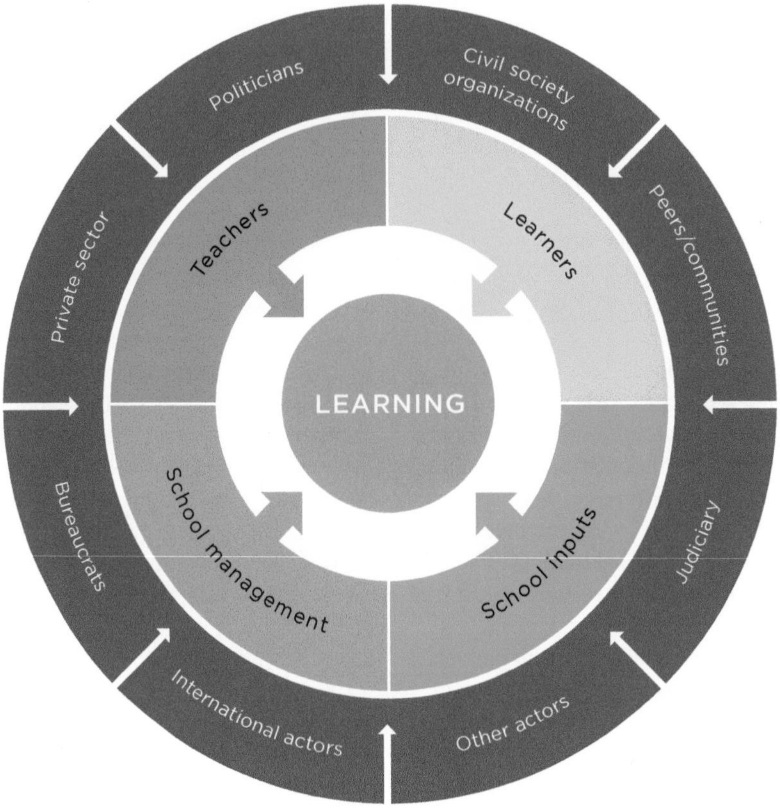

Source: WDR 2018 team.

- Build on what works, and scale back what doesn't, to deliver short-term results that strengthen the long-term resolve of the coalition for learning.
- Repeat.

The payoff to doing what needs to be done is a system in which the elements are coherent with each other and everything aligns with learning (figure O.15).

Increased financing can support this learning-for-all equilibrium, if the various key actors behave in ways that show learning matters to them. This is a big "if" because higher levels of public spending are not associated statistically with higher completion or even enrollment rates in countries with weak governance.[125] Ensuring that students learn is even more challenging, and so there is little correlation between spending and learning after accounting for national income. It is easy to see the reason for this because of the many ways in which financing can leak out—whether because money never reaches the school, or because it pays for inputs that don't affect the

teaching-learning relationship, or because the system doesn't prioritize learning for disadvantaged children and youth. More financing for business as usual will therefore just lead to the usual outcomes. But where countries seriously tackle the barriers to learning for all, spending on education is a critical investment for development, especially for those countries where overall spending is currently low, as recent major studies of global education have emphasized.[126] More children staying in school longer and learning while there will undoubtedly require more public financing for education. An injection of financing—either from domestic or international sources—can help countries escape the low-learning trap, if they are willing to take the other necessary steps laid out here.

Implications for external actors

External actors can reinforce these strategies for opening the political and technical space for learning. In the realm of information and metrics, for example, international actors can fund participation in regional learning assessments (such as PASEC in West Africa or LLECE in Latin America) or global learning assessments (such as PISA or TIMSS) to spotlight challenges and catalyze domestic efforts for reform. External actors can also develop tools for tracking the proximate determinants of learning to aid in feedback loops. Domestic financing usually makes up the bulk of education financing, so a high-leverage entry point for international actors is to fund better information that will make domestic spending more effective. In the realm of innovation and experimentation, external funders such as the World Bank can provide results-based financing that gives countries more room to innovate and iterate their way to achieving better outcomes.

Learning to realize education's promise

By showing that learning really matters to them, countries can realize education's full promise. Beyond being a basic human right, education—done right—improves social outcomes in many spheres of life. For individuals and families, education boosts human capital, improves economic opportunities, promotes health, and expands the ability to make effective choices. For societies, education expands economic opportunities, promotes social mobility, and makes institutions function more effectively. In measuring these benefits, research has only recently focused on the distinction between schooling and learning. But the evidence confirms the intuition that these benefits often depend on the skills that students acquire, not just the number of years in the classroom. Economies with higher skills grow faster than those with schooling but mediocre skills; higher literacy predicts better financial knowledge and better health, beyond the effects of schooling; and poor children are more likely to rise in the income distribution when they grow up in communities with better learning outcomes.

Taking learning seriously won't be easy. It's hard enough to work through the technical challenges of figuring out what will promote learning at the level of the student and school in any context, let alone tackle the political and technical challenges of working at scale. Many countries struggling with the learning crisis may be tempted to continue with business as usual. After all, they may reason, development will eventually improve learning outcomes: as households escape poverty and schools take advantage of better facilities, more materials, and better-trained teachers, better learning outcomes should follow.

But waiting out the learning crisis isn't a winning strategy. Even though national income and learning are somewhat correlated at lower levels of development, higher incomes do not invariably lead to better learning outcomes. And to the extent that development does bring better learning and skills, it is partly because development has been accompanied by a willingness to tackle the political impasses and governance challenges that hamper learning. Ultimately, then, those challenges are not avoidable. Furthermore, there's no need to wait for learning. At every level of income, there are countries that not only score better than others on international assessments, but also—and more important—show from the quality of their education systems and their policy making that they are committed to learning.

The future of work will place a premium on learning. Rapid technological change has led to major shifts in the nature of work, leading some to declare this a new era—the Second Machine Age or the Fourth Industrial Revolution. In the extreme versions of this vision, all but a few jobs could disappear, decreasing the value of skills for most people. But the seismic changes predicted have yet to permeate the high-income countries, let alone the low- and middle-income ones. More important, no matter how the demand for skills changes in the future, people will require a solid foundation of basic skills and knowledge. If anything, rapid change will increase the returns to learning how to learn, which requires foundational skills that allow individuals to size up new situations, adapt their thinking, and know where to go for information and how to make sense of it.

* * *

Countries have already made a tremendous start by getting so many children and youth into school. Now it's time to realize education's promise by accelerating learning. A real education—one that encourages learning—is a tool for promoting both shared prosperity and poverty elimination. That type of education will benefit many: children and families whose positive schooling experience restores their faith in government and society rather than eroding it; youth who have skills employers are seeking; teachers who can respond to their professional calling rather than to political demands; adult workers who have learned how to learn, preparing them for unforeseeable economic and social changes; and citizens who have the values and reasoning abilities to contribute to civic life and social cohesion.

Notes

1. Uwezo (2014). In all countries, the test was administered in English. In Kenya and Tanzania, it was also administered in Kiswahili, and the highest score (English or Kiswahili) was used in the assessment of proficiency. English is the language of instruction in Kenya and Uganda.
2. ASER Centre (2017).
3. WDR 2018 team, using data from the Programme for International Student Assessment (PISA), 2015 (OECD 2016).
4. WDR 2018 team, using data from the Third Regional Comparative and Explanatory Study (TERCE), 2012 (UNESCO 2013).
5. UNESCO (2016).
6. World Bank (2011).
7. Barro and Lee (2013).
8. Pritchett (2013).
9. Pritchett (2013).
10. Gove and Cvelich (2011).
11. Crouch (2006).
12. Castillo and others (2011).
13. ASER Pakistan (2015a, 2015b).
14. Southern and Eastern Africa Consortium for Monitoring Educational Quality (SACMEQ) results for grade 6 students in 15 countries in 2007 (Hungi and others 2010).
15. Programme d'Analyse des Systèmes Éducatifs de la Confemen (PASEC) results for grade 6 students in 10 francophone countries in 2014 (PASEC 2015).
16. ASER Centre (2017).
17. RTI International (2009).
18. World Bank (2016b).
19. Muralidharan and Zieleniak (2013).
20. Spaull and Kotze (2015).
21. Singh (2015).
22. *Minimum proficiency* is defined as one standard deviation below the mean of the harmonized assessment scores.
23. These numbers are based on analysis of the data in "A Global Data Set on Education Quality" (2017), a data set made available to the WDR 2018 team by Nadir Altinok, Noam Angrist, and Harry Anthony Patrinos. These averages do not include China or India because of lack of data.
24. UNESCO (2016).
25. UIS and EFA (2015).
26. Banerjee, Jacob, and Kremer (2000); Hanushek and Woessmann (2008); Rivkin, Hanushek, and Kain (2005).
27. Alderman, Orazem, and Paterno (2001); Andrabi, Das, and Khwaja (2008); Farah (1996); Kingdon (1996); Orazem (2000); Tooley and Dixon (2007).
28. Hanushek, Lavy, and Hitomi (2008).
29. STEP surveys (World Bank 2014).
30. Lupien and others (2000); McCoy and others (2016); Walker and others (2007).
31. Coe and Lubach (2007); Garner and others (2012); Nelson (2016).
32. Black and others (2017). *Stunting* is defined by the World Health Organization (WHO) as a height-for-age z-score of less than two standard deviations below the median of a healthy reference population.
33. Paxson and Schady (2007); Schady and others (2015).
34. Hanushek (1992); Rockoff (2004).
35. Bau and Das (2017).
36. Bruns and Luque (2015).
37. UIS (2006).
38. Chang and others (2013).
39. Abadzi (2009); EQUIP2 (2010).
40. Bold and others (2017).
41. Hanushek (1995); Mingat and Tan (1998); Tan and Mingat (1992); Wolf (2004).
42. Glewwe and others (2011); Hanushek (1986); Kremer (1995).
43. Sabarwal, Evans, and Marshak (2014).
44. Lavinas and Veiga (2013).
45. Robinson, Lloyd, and Rowe (2008); Waters, Marzano, and McNulty (2003).
46. Bloom and others (2015). Management areas include operations, monitoring, target setting, and people management.
47. Bruns, Filmer, and Patrinos (2011); Orazem, Glewwe, and Patrinos (2007); World Bank (2003).
48. Data extracted from U.S. Agency for International Development's Demographic and Health Survey (DHS) StatCompiler, http://www.statcompiler.com/en/.
49. Park (2016).
50. Todd and Mason (2005).
51. Chisholm and Leyendecker (2008).
52. World Bank (2003).
53. Andrews, Pritchett, and Woolcock (2017).
54. Grindle (2004).
55. Evans and Yuan (2017).
56. The team thanks Kai-Ming Cheng for suggesting this formulation.
57. Dweck (2008).
58. Save the Children (2013).
59. Guilfoyle (2006).
60. Jacob (2005).
61. Fausset (2014).
62. UIS (2016).
63. OECD (2011).
64. Jacob (2007).
65. Solano-Flores, Contreras-Niño, and Backhoff Escudero (2005).
66. Muralidharan and Sundararaman (2011).
67. De Smedt (2014); Insel and Landis (2013); Kuhl (2010).
68. Dua and others (2016).
69. Evans and Popova (2016).
70. Gertler and others (2014).
71. Calculations carried out for WDR 2018. See Evans and Yuan (2017).
72. Pritchett and Sandefur (2013).
73. Deaton and Cartwright (2016).
74. Romer (2015).

75. Duflo, Hanna, and Ryan (2012); Muralidharan and Sundararaman (2011).
76. Das and others (2013).
77. The evidence is from countries ranging from the United States to Argentina, Bangladesh, China, and Uganda, among others (Berlinski, Galiani, and Gertler 2008; Engle and others 2011).
78. Berlinski and Schady (2015); Bernal and others (2016); Grantham-McGregor and others (2014).
79. Baird and others (2014); Fiszbein and Schady (2009); Morgan, Petrosino, and Fronius (2012).
80. Snilstveit and others (2016).
81. Blimpo (2014); Kremer, Miguel, and Thornton (2009). Direct financial incentives have been less successful in high-income countries (Fryer 2011), although alternate designs that deliver incentives immediately after the test have worked (Levitt and others 2016).
82. Barrera-Osorio and Filmer (2013).
83. Avitabile and de Hoyos (2015); Nguyen (2008).
84. ILO (2015).
85. Bragg (2014).
86. Calcagno and Long (2008); Martorell and McFarlin Jr. (2011); Scott-Clayton and Rodriguez (2014).
87. Tandon and Fukao (2015); World Bank (2013, 2016a).
88. Layton (2015).
89. Bruns and Luque (2015); Mulkeen (2010).
90. Darling-Hammond and others (2009).
91. Lauwerier and Akkari (2015).
92. Banerjee and others (2007); Conn (2017).
93. Abadzi and Llambiri (2011); Ciaccio (2004); Leder (1987).
94. Banerjee and others (2016); Pritchett and Beatty (2015).
95. Banerjee and others (2007); Duflo, Dupas, and Kremer (2011); Kiessel and Duflo (2014); Muralidharan, Singh, and Ganimian (2016).
96. Andrabi, Das, and Khwaja (2015); de Hoyos, Garcia-Moreno, and Patrinos (2017).
97. Snilstveit and others (2016).
98. Linden (2008).
99. Piper and others (2015).
100. Barrera-Osorio and Linden (2009).
101. Glewwe, Kremer, and Moulin (2009); Sabarwal, Evans, and Marshak (2014).
102. McEwan (2015).
103. Muralidharan, Singh, and Ganimian (2016).
104. Cristia and others (2012); De Melo, Machado, and Miranda (2014). For Uruguay, the evaluation covers math and reading impacts in the early years of the program, when its main objective was to provide equipment and connectivity for schools; the program evolved since then to add ICT training for teachers and adaptive educational technology, and new evaluations are expected to be published in late 2017.
105. Lavinas and Veiga (2013).
106. Fryer (2017).
107. Bloom and others (2015).
108. Bruns, Filmer, and Patrinos (2011).
109. Pradhan and others (2014).
110. Bouguen and others (2013).
111. Bold and others (2013).
112. Chang and others (2013); de Ree and others (2015).
113. Liang, Kidwai, and Zhang (2016).
114. For example, in Mozambique, after the World Bank's Service Delivery Indicators revealed very low levels of teacher knowledge and very high levels of absentee-ism—results that were picked up by the local media—the government launched a program (ultimately supported through a loan from the World Bank) to address these issues.
115. Neal (2013).
116. World Bank (2017).
117. Bruns and Luque (2015).
118. Mizala and Schneider (2014); Wales, Ali, and Nicolai (2014).
119. Birnbaum (2010); Bruns and Luque (2015).
120. Levy and others (2016).
121. Mansuri and Rao (2013).
122. Green (2016); Pascale, Sternin, and Sternin (2010).
123. Campos, Randrianarivelo, and Winning (2015).
124. Andrews, Pritchett, and Woolcock (2013).
125. Rajkumar and Swaroop (2008); Suryadarma (2012).
126. See, in particular, the report of the Education Commission (2016), which emphasizes the important role of finance in complementing reforms.

References

Abadzi, Helen. 2009. "Instructional Time Loss in Developing Countries: Concepts, Measurement, and Implications." *World Bank Research Observer* 24 (2): 267–90.

Abadzi, Helen, and Stavri Llambiri. 2011. "Selective Teacher Attention in Lower-Income Countries: A Phenomenon Linked to Dropout and Illiteracy?" *Prospects* 41 (4): 491–506.

Alderman, Harold, Peter F. Orazem, and Elizabeth M. Paterno. 2001. "School Quality, School Cost, and the Public/Private School Choices of Low-Income Households in Pakistan." *Journal of Human Resources* 36 (2): 304–26.

Andrabi, Tahir, Jishnu Das, and Asim Ijaz Khwaja. 2008. "A Dime a Day: The Possibilities and Limits of Private Schooling in Pakistan." *Comparative Education Review* 52 (3): 329–55.

———. 2015. "Report Cards: The Impact of Providing School and Child Test Scores on Educational Markets." Policy Research Working Paper 7226, World Bank, Washington, DC.

Andrews, Matt, Lant Pritchett, and Michael Woolcock. 2013. "Escaping Capability Traps through Problem Driven Iterative Adaptation (PDIA)." *World Development* 51: 234–44.

———. 2017. *Building State Capability: Evidence, Analysis, Action.* New York: Oxford University Press.

ASER Centre. 2017. *Annual Status of Education Report (Rural) 2016.* New Delhi: ASER Centre. http://img.asercentre.org /docs/Publications/ASER%20Reports/ASER%202016 /aser_2016.pdf.

ASER Pakistan. 2015a. "Annual Status of Education Report: ASER Pakistan 2015 National (Rural)." Lahore, Pakistan: South Asian Forum for Education Development.

ASER Pakistan. 2015b. "Annual Status of Education Report: ASER Pakistan 2015 National (Urban)." Lahore, Pakistan: South Asian Forum for Education Development.

Avitabile, Ciro, and Rafael E. de Hoyos. 2015. "The Heterogeneous Effect of Information on Student Performance: Evidence from a Randomized Control Trial in Mexico." Policy Research Working Paper 7422, World Bank, Washington, DC.

Baird, Sarah Jane, Francisco H. G. Ferreira, Berk Özler, and Michael Woolcock. 2014. "Conditional, Unconditional and Everything in Between: A Systematic Review of the Effects of Cash Transfer Programmes on Schooling Outcomes." *Journal of Development Effectiveness* 6 (1): 1–43.

Banerjee, Abhijit Vinayak, Rukmini Banerji, James Berry, Esther Duflo, Harini Kannan, Shobhini Mukherji, Marc Shotland, et al. 2016. "Mainstreaming an Effective Intervention: Evidence from Randomized Evaluations of 'Teaching at the Right Level' in India." NBER Working Paper 22746, National Bureau of Economic Research, Cambridge, MA.

Banerjee, Abhijit Vinayak, Shawn Cole, Esther Duflo, and Leigh Linden. 2007. "Remedying Education: Evidence from Two Randomized Experiments in India." *Quarterly Journal of Economics* 122 (3): 1235–64.

Banerjee, Abhijit Vinayak, Suraj Jacob, and Michael Kremer. 2000. "Promoting School Participation in Rural Rajasthan: Results from Some Prospective Trials." With Jenny Lanjouw and Peter Lanjouw. Working paper, Massachusetts Institute of Technology, Cambridge, MA.

Barrera-Osorio, Felipe, and Deon Filmer. 2013. "Incentivizing Schooling for Learning: Evidence on the Impact of Alternative Targeting Approaches." Policy Research Working Paper 6541, World Bank, Washington, DC.

Barrera-Osorio, Felipe, and Leigh L. Linden. 2009. "The Use and Misuse of Computers in Education: Evidence from a Randomized Experiment in Colombia." Policy Research Working Paper 4836, World Bank, Washington, DC.

Barro, Robert J., and Jong Wha Lee. 2013. "A New Data Set of Educational Attainment in the World, 1950–2010." *Journal of Development Economics* 104: 184–98.

Bau, Natalie, and Jishnu Das. 2017. "The Misallocation of Pay and Productivity in the Public Sector: Evidence from the Labor Market for Teachers." Policy Research Working Paper 8050, World Bank, Washington, DC.

Berlinski, Samuel, Sebastian Galiani, and Paul J. Gertler. 2008. "The Effect of Pre-primary Education on Primary School Performance." *Journal of Public Economics* 93 (1–2): 219–34.

Berlinski, Samuel, and Norbert R. Schady, eds. 2015. *The Early Years: Child Well-Being and the Role of Public Policy.* Development in the Americas Series. Washington, DC: Inter-American Development Bank; New York: Palgrave Macmillan.

Bernal, Raquel, Orazio Pietro Attanasio, Ximena Peña, and Marcos Vera-Hernández. 2016. "The Effects of the Transition from Home-Based Community Nurseries to Child-Care Centers on Children in Colombia." Working paper, Universidad de los Andes, Bogotá, Colombia.

Birnbaum, Michael. 2010. "D.C. Schools Unveil Teacher-Pay Bonus Plan." *Washington Post,* September 12. http://www.washingtonpost.com/wp-dyn/content/article/2010/09/10/AR2010091006604.html.

Black, Maureen M., Susan P. Walker, Lia C. H. Fernald, Christopher T. Andersen, Ann M. DiGirolamo, Chunling Lu, Dana C. McCoy, et al. 2017. "Early Childhood Development Coming of Age: Science through the Life Course." *Lancet* 389 (10064): 77–90.

Blimpo, Moussa P. 2014. "Team Incentives for Education in Developing Countries: A Randomized Field Experiment in Benin." *American Economic Journal: Applied Economics* 6 (4): 90–109.

Bloom, Nicholas, Renata Lemos, Raffaella Sadun, Daniela Scur, and John Van Reenen. 2014. "JEEA-FBBVA Lecture 2013: The New Empirical Economics of Management." *Journal of the European Economic Association* 12 (4): 835–76.

Bloom, Nicholas, Renata Lemos, Raffaella Sadun, and John Van Reenen. 2015. "Does Management Matter in Schools?" *Economic Journal* 125 (584): 647–74.

Bold, Tessa, Deon Filmer, Gayle Martin, Ezequiel Molina, Brian Stacy, Christophe Rockmore, Jakob Svensson, et al. 2017. "What Do Teachers Know and Do? Does It Matter? Evidence from Primary Schools in Africa." Policy Research Working Paper 7956, World Bank, Washington, DC.

Bold, Tessa, Mwangi Kimenyi, Germano Mwabu, Alice Ng'ang'a, and Justin Sandefur. 2013. "Scaling Up What Works: Experimental Evidence on External Validity in Kenyan Education." Working Paper 321, Center for Global Development, Washington, DC.

Bouguen, Adrien, Deon Filmer, Karen Macours, and Sophie Naudeau. 2013. "Impact Evaluation of Three Types of Early Childhood Development Interventions in Cambodia." Policy Research Working Paper 6540, World Bank, Washington, DC.

Bragg, Debra D. 2014. "Career Pathways in Disparate Industry Sectors to Serve Underserved Populations." Paper presented at American Educational Research Association conference, Philadelphia, April 5.

Bruns, Barbara, Deon Filmer, and Harry Anthony Patrinos. 2011. *Making Schools Work: New Evidence on Accountability Reforms.* Human Development Perspectives Series. Washington, DC: World Bank.

Bruns, Barbara, and Javier Luque. 2015. *Great Teachers: How to Raise Student Learning in Latin America and the Caribbean.* With Soledad De Gregorio, David K. Evans, Marco Fernández, Martin Moreno, Jessica Rodriguez, Guillermo Toral, and Noah Yarrow. Latin American Development Forum Series. Washington, DC: World Bank.

Calcagno, Juan Carlos, and Bridget Terry Long. 2008. "The Impact of Postsecondary Remediation Using a Regression Discontinuity Approach: Addressing Endogenous Sorting and Noncompliance." NBER Working Paper 14194, National Bureau of Economic Research, Cambridge, MA.

Campos, Jose Edgardo, Benjamina Randrianarivelo, and Kay Winning. 2015. "Escaping the 'Capability Trap': Turning 'Small' Development into 'Big' Development." *International Public Management Review* 16 (1): 99–131.

Castillo, Melba, Vanesa Castro, José Ramón Laguna, and Josefina Vijil. 2011. *Informe de Resultados: EGMS Nicaragua.*

Research Triangle Park, NC: Centro de Investigación y Acción Educativa Social and RTI International. https://shared.rti.org/content/informe-de-resultados-egma-nicaragua.

Chang, Mae Chu, Sheldon Shaeffer, Samer Al-Samarrai, Andrew B. Ragatz, Joppe De Ree, and Ritchie Stevenson. 2013. *Teacher Reform in Indonesia: The Role of Politics and Evidence in Policy Making*. Directions in Development: Human Development Series. Washington, DC: World Bank.

Chisholm, Linda, and Ramon Leyendecker. 2008. "Curriculum Reform in Post-1990s Sub-Saharan Africa." *International Journal of Educational Development* 28 (2): 195–205.

Ciaccio, Joseph. 2004. *Totally Positive Teaching: A Five-Stage Approach to Energizing Students and Teachers*. Alexandria, VA: ASCD.

Coe, Christopher L., and Gabrielle R. Lubach. 2007. "Mother-Infant Interactions and the Development of Immunity from Conception through Weaning." In *Psychoneuro-immunology*, edited by Robert Ader, 455–74. Burlington, MA: Elsevier Academic Press.

Conn, Katharine M. 2017. "Identifying Effective Education Interventions in Sub-Saharan Africa: A Meta-Analysis of Impact Evaluations." *Review of Educational Research* (May 26). http://journals.sagepub.com/doi/abs/10.3102/0034654317712025.

Cristia, Julián P., Pablo Ibarrarán, Santiago Cueto, Ana Santiago, and Eugenio Severín. 2012. "Technology and Child Development: Evidence from the One Laptop Per Child Program." IZA Discussion Paper 6401, Institute for the Study of Labor, Bonn, Germany.

Crouch, Luis. 2006. "Education Sector: Standards, Accountability, and Support." In *A New Social Contract for Peru: An Agenda for Improving Education, Health Care, and the Social Safety Net*, edited by Daniel Cotlear, 71–106. World Bank Country Study Series. Washington, DC: World Bank.

Darling-Hammond, Linda, Ruth Chung Wei, Alethea Andree, Nikole Richardson, and Stelios Orphanos. 2009. "Professional Learning in the Learning Profession: A Status Report on Teacher Development in the United States and Abroad." National Staff Development Council, Dallas.

Das, Jishnu, Stefan Dercon, James Habyarimana, Pramila Krishnan, Karthik Muralidharan, and Venkatesh Sundararaman. 2013. "School Inputs, Household Substitution, and Test Scores." *American Economic Journal: Applied Economics* 5 (2): 29–57.

Deaton, Angus S., and Nancy Cartwright. 2016. "Understanding and Misunderstanding Randomized Controlled Trials." NBER Working Paper 22595, National Bureau of Economic Research, Cambridge, MA.

de Hoyos, Rafael E., Vicente A. Garcia-Moreno, and Harry Anthony Patrinos. 2017. "The Impact of an Accountability Intervention with Diagnostic Feedback: Evidence from Mexico." *Economics of Education Review* 58: 123–40.

De Melo, Gioia, Alina Machado, and Alfonso Miranda. 2014. "The Impact of a One Laptop Per Child Program on Learning: Evidence from Uruguay." IZA Discussion Paper 8489, Institute for the Study of Labor, Bonn, Germany.

de Ree, Joppe, Karthik Muralidharan, Menno Pradhan, and Halsey Rogers. 2015. "Double for Nothing? Experimental Evidence on the Impact of an Unconditional Teacher Salary Increase on Student Performance in Indonesia." NBER Working Paper 21806, National Bureau of Economic Research, Cambridge, MA.

De Smedt, Bert. 2014. "Advances in the Use of Neuroscience Methods in Research on Learning and Instruction." *Frontline Learning Research* 2 (4): 7–14.

Dua, Tarun, Mark Tomlinson, Elizabeth Tablante, Pia Britto, Aisha Yousfzai, Bernadette Daelmans, and Gary L. Darmstadt. 2016. "Global Research Priorities to Accelerate Early Child Development in the Sustainable Development Era." *Lancet Global Health* 4 (12): e887–e889.

Duflo, Esther, Pascaline Dupas, and Michael Kremer. 2011. "Peer Effects, Teacher Incentives, and the Impact of Tracking: Evidence from a Randomized Evaluation in Kenya." *American Economic Review* 101 (5): 1739–74.

Duflo, Esther, Rema Hanna, and Stephen P. Ryan. 2012. "Incentives Work: Getting Teachers to Come to School." *American Economic Review* 102 (4): 1241–78.

Dweck, Carol S. 2008. *Mindset, the New Psychology of Success: How We Can Learn to Fulfill Our Potential*. New York: Ballantine Books.

Education Commission. 2016. *The Learning Generation: Investing in Education for a Changing World*. New York: International Commission on Financing Global Education Opportunity.

Engle, Patrice L., Lia C. H. Fernald, Harold Alderman, Jere Behrman, Chloe O'Gara, Aisha Yousafzai, Meena Cabral de Mello, et al. 2011. "Strategies for Reducing Inequalities and Improving Developmental Outcomes for Young Children in Low-Income and Middle-Income Countries." *Lancet* 378 (9799): 1339–53.

EQUIP2 (Educational Quality Improvement Program 2). 2010. "Using Opportunity to Learn and Early Grade Reading Fluency to Measure School Effectiveness in Ethiopia, Guatemala, Honduras, and Nepal." Working paper, Educational Policy, Systems Development, and Management, U.S. Agency for International Development, Washington, DC.

Evans, David K., and Anna Popova. 2016. "What Really Works to Improve Learning in Developing Countries? An Analysis of Divergent Findings in Systematic Reviews." *World Bank Research Observer* 31 (2): 242–70.

Evans, David K., and Fei Yuan. 2017. "Economic Returns to Interventions That Increase Learning." Background paper, *World Development Report 2018*, World Bank, Washington, DC.

Farah, I. 1996. "Road to Success: Self-Sustaining Primary School Change in Rural Pakistan." With T. Mehmood, Amna, R. Jaffar, F. Ashams, P. Iqbal, S. Khanam, Z. Shah, and N. Gul-Mastoi. Institute for Educational Development, Aga Khan University, Karachi, Pakistan.

Fausset, Richard. 2014. "Trial Opens in Atlanta School Cheating Scandal." *New York Times*, September 29. https://www.nytimes.com/2014/09/30/us/racketeering-trial-opens-in-altanta-schools-cheating-scandal.html?_r=1.

Filmer, Deon. 2016. "Educational Attainment and Enrollment around the World: An International Database." World

Bank, Washington, DC. http://go.worldbank.org/3 GEREWJ0E0.

Fiszbein, Ariel, and Norbert R. Schady. 2009. *Conditional Cash Transfers: Reducing Present and Future Poverty*. With Francisco H. G. Ferreira, Margaret Grosh, Niall Keleher, Pedro Olinto, and Emmanuel Skoufias. World Bank Policy Research Report. Washington, DC: World Bank.

Fryer, Roland G., Jr. 2011. "Financial Incentives and Student Achievement: Evidence from Randomized Trials." *Quarterly Journal of Economics* 126 (4): 1755–98.

———. 2017. "Management and Student Achievement: Evidence from a Randomized Field Experiment." Working paper, Harvard University, Cambridge, MA.

Garner, Andrew S., Jack P. Shonkoff, Benjamin S. Siegel, Mary I. Dobbins, Marian F. Earls, Laura McGuinn, John Pascoe, et al. 2012. "Early Childhood Adversity, Toxic Stress, and the Role of the Pediatrician: Translating Developmental Science into Lifelong Health." *Pediatrics* 129 (1): e224-e231.

Gertler, Paul J., James J. Heckman, Rodrigo Pinto, Arianna Zanolini, Christel Vermeersch, Susan Walker, Susan M. Chang, et al. 2014. "Labor Market Returns to an Early Childhood Stimulation Intervention in Jamaica." *Science* 344 (6187): 998–1001.

Glewwe, Paul W., Eric A. Hanushek, Sarah D. Humpage, and Renato Ravina. 2011. "School Resources and Educational Outcomes in Developing Countries: A Review of the Literature from 1990 to 2010." NBER Working Paper 17554, National Bureau of Economic Research, Cambridge, MA.

Glewwe, Paul W., Michael Kremer, and Sylvie Moulin. 2009. "Many Children Left Behind? Textbooks and Test Scores in Kenya." *American Economic Journal: Applied Economics* 1 (1): 112–35.

Gove, Amber, and Peter Cvelich. 2011. "Early Reading, Igniting Education for All: A Report by the Early Grade Learning Community of Practice." Rev. ed. Research Triangle Park, NC: Research Triangle Institute.

Grantham-McGregor, Sally M., Lia C. H. Fernald, Rose M. C. Kagawa, and Susan Walker. 2014. "Effects of Integrated Child Development and Nutrition Interventions on Child Development and Nutritional Status." *Annals of the New York Academy of Sciences* 1308 (1): 11–32.

Green, Duncan. 2016. *How Change Happens*. Oxford, U.K.: Oxford University Press.

Grindle, Merilee Serrill. 2004. *Despite the Odds: The Contentious Politics of Education Reform*. Princeton, NJ: Princeton University Press.

Guilfoyle, Christy. 2006. "NCLB: Is There Life Beyond Testing?" *Educational Leadership* 64 (3): 8–13.

Hanushek, Eric A. 1986. "The Economics of Schooling: Production and Efficiency in Public Schools." *Journal of Economic Literature* 24 (3): 1141–77.

———. 1992. "The Trade-Off between Child Quantity and Quality." *Journal of Political Economy* 100 (1): 84–117.

———. 1995. "Interpreting Recent Research on Schooling in Developing Countries." *World Bank Research Observer* 10 (2): 227–46.

Hanushek, Eric A., Victor Lavy, and Kohtaro Hitomi. 2008. "Do Students Care about School Quality? Determinants of Dropout Behavior in Developing Countries." *Journal of Human Capital* 2 (1): 69–105.

Hanushek, Eric A., and Ludger Woessmann. 2008. "The Role of Cognitive Skills in Economic Development." *Journal of Economic Literature* 46 (3): 607–68.

Hungi, Njora, Demus Makuwa, Kenneth Norman Ross, Mioko Saito, Stéphanie Dolata, Frank Van Cappelle, Laura Paviot, et al. 2010. "SACMEQ III Project Results: Pupil Achievement Levels in Reading and Mathematics." Southern and Eastern Africa Consortium for Monitoring Educational Quality, Paris.

ILO (International Labor Organization). 2015. "Global Employment Trends for Youth 2015: Scaling Up Investments in Decent Jobs for Youth." ILO, Geneva.

Insel, Thomas R., and Story C. Landis. 2013. "Twenty-Five Years of Progress: The View from Nimh and Ninds." *Neuron* 80 (3): 561–67.

Jacob, Brian A. 2005. "Accountability, Incentives, and Behavior: The Impact of High-Stakes Testing in the Chicago Public Schools." *Journal of Public Economics* 89 (5): 761–96.

———. 2007. "Test-Based Accountability and Student Achievement: An Investigation of Differential Performance on NAEP and State Assessments." NBER Working Paper 12817, National Bureau of Economic Research, Cambridge, MA.

Kiessel, Jessica, and Annie Duflo. 2014. "Cost Effectiveness Report: Teacher Community Assistant Initiative (TCAI)." IPA Brief (March 26), Innovation for Poverty Action, New Haven, CT.

Kingdon, Geeta. 1996. "The Quality and Efficiency of Private and Public Education: A Case-Study of Urban India." *Oxford Bulletin of Economics and Statistics* 58 (1): 57–82.

Kremer, Michael R. 1995. "Research on Schooling: What We Know and What We Don't, a Comment on Hanushek." *World Bank Research Observer* 10 (2): 247–54.

Kremer, Michael R., Edward Miguel, and Rebecca Thornton. 2009. "Incentives to Learn." *Review of Economics and Statistics* 91 (3): 437–56.

Kuhl, Patricia K. 2010. "Brain Mechanisms in Early Language Acquisition." *Neuron* 67 (5): 713–27.

Lauwerier, Thibaut, and Abdeljalil Akkari. 2015. "Teachers and the Quality of Basic Education in Sub-Saharan Africa." ERF Working Paper 11, Education Research and Foresight, Paris.

Lavinas, Lena, and Alinne Veiga. 2013. "Brazil's One Laptop Per Child Program: Impact Evaluation and Implementation Assessment." *Cadernos de Pesquisa* 43 (149).

Layton, Lyndsey. 2015. "Study: Billions of Dollars in Annual Teacher Training Is Largely a Waste." *Washington Post*, August 4. https://www.washingtonpost.com/local/education/study-billions-of-dollars-in-annual-teacher-training-is-largely-a-waste/2015/08/03/c4e1f322-39ff-11e5-9c2d-ed991d848c48_story.html.

Leder, Gilah C. 1987. "Teacher Student Interaction: A Case Study." *Educational Studies in Mathematics* 18 (3): 255–71.

Lemos, Renata, and Daniela Scur. 2016. "Developing Management: An Expanded Evaluation Tool for Developing Countries." RISE Working Paper 16/007, Research on Improving Systems of Education, Blavatnik School of Government, Oxford University, Oxford, U.K.

Levitt, Steven D., John A. List, Susanne Neckermann, and Sally Sadoff. 2016. "The Behavioralist Goes to School: Leveraging Behavioral Economics to Improve Educational Performance." *American Economic Journal: Economic Policy* 8 (4): 183–219.

Levy, Brian, Robert Cameron, Ursula Hoadley, and Vinothan Naidoo. 2016. "The Politics of Governance and Basic Education: A Tale of Two South African Provinces." Occasional Working Paper 2, Graduate School of Development Policy and Practice, University of Cape Town, Cape Town.

Liang, Xiaoyan, Huma Kidwai, and Minxuan Zhang. 2016. *How Shanghai Does It: Insights and Lessons from the Highest-Ranking Education System in the World.* Directions in Development: Human Development Series. Washington, DC: World Bank.

Linden, Leigh L. 2008. "Complement or Substitute? The Effect of Technology on Student Achievement in India." Edited by Michael Trucano. InfoDev Working Paper 17 (June), World Bank, Washington, DC.

Lupien, Sonia J., Suzanne King, Michael J. Meaney, and Bruce S. McEwen. 2000. "Child's Stress Hormone Levels Correlate with Mother's Socioeconomic Status and Depressive State." *Biological Psychiatry* 48 (10): 976–80.

Mansuri, Ghazala, and Vijayendra Rao. 2013. *Localizing Development: Does Participation Work?* Policy Research Report Series. Washington, DC: World Bank.

Martorell, Paco, and Isaac McFarlin Jr. 2011. "Help or Hindrance? The Effects of College Remediation on Academic and Labor Market Outcomes." *Review of Economics and Statistics* 93 (2): 436–54.

McCoy, Dana Charles, Evan D. Peet, Majid Ezzati, Goodarz Danaei, Maureen M. Black, Christopher R. Sudfeld, Wafaie Fawzi, et al. 2016. "Early Childhood Developmental Status in Low- and Middle-Income Countries: National, Regional, and Global Prevalence Estimates Using Predictive Modeling." *PLOS Medicine* 13 (6): e1002034.

McEwan, Patrick J. 2015. "Improving Learning in Primary Schools of Developing Countries: A Meta-Analysis of Randomized Experiments." *Review of Educational Research* 85 (3): 353–94.

Mingat, Alain, and Jee-Peng Tan. 1998. "The Mechanics of Progress in Education: Evidence from Cross-Country Data." Policy Research Working Paper 2015, World Bank, Washington, DC.

Mizala, Alejandra, and Ben Ross Schneider. 2014. "Negotiating Education Reform: Teacher Evaluations and Incentives in Chile (1990–2010)." *Governance* 27 (1): 87–109.

Morgan, Claire, Anthony Petrosino, and Trevor Fronius. 2012. "A Systematic Review of the Evidence of the Impact of Eliminating School User Fees in Low-Income Developing Countries." Evidence for Policy and Practice Information and Co-ordinating Centre, Social Science Research Unit, Institute of Education, University of London.

Mulkeen, Aidan G. 2010. *Teachers in Anglophone Africa: Issues in Teacher Supply, Training, and Management.* Development Practice in Education Series. Washington, DC: World Bank.

Mullis, I. V. S., M. O. Martin, P. Foy, and K. T. Drucker. 2012. "PIRLS 2011 International Results in Reading." TIMSS and PIRLS International Study Center, Boston College, Chestnut Hill, MA. https://timssandpirls.bc.edu/pirls2011/international-results-pirls.html.

Mullis, I. V. S., M. O. Martin, P. Foy, and M. Hooper. 2016. "TIMSS 2015 International Results in Mathematics." TIMSS and PIRLS International Study Center, Boston College, Chestnut Hill, MA. http://timssandpirls.bc.edu/timss2015/international-results/.

Muralidharan, Karthik, Abhijeet Singh, and Alejandro Ganimian. 2016. "Disrupting Education? Experimental Evidence on Technology-Aided Instruction in India." NBER Working Paper 22923, National Bureau of Economic Research, Cambridge, MA.

Muralidharan, Karthik, and Venkatesh Sundararaman. 2011. "Teacher Performance Pay: Experimental Evidence from India." *Journal of Political Economy* 119 (1): 39–77.

Muralidharan, Karthik, and Yendrick Zieleniak. 2013. "Measuring Learning Trajectories in Developing Countries with Longitudinal Data and Item Response Theory." Paper presented at Young Lives Conference, Oxford University, Oxford, U.K., July 8–9.

Neal, Derek. 2013. "The Consequences of Using One Assessment System to Pursue Two Objectives." *Journal of Economic Education* 44 (4): 339–52.

Nelson, Charles A. 2016. "Brain Imaging as a Measure of Future Cognitive Outcomes: A Study of Children in Bangladesh Exposed to Multiple Levels of Adversity." Presentation, CMU Department of Psychology Colloquium, Department of Psychology, College of Humanities and Social Sciences, Carnegie Mellon University, Pittsburgh, September 29.

Nguyen, Trang. 2008. "Information, Role Models, and Perceived Returns to Education: Experimental Evidence from Madagascar." Economics Department, Massachusetts Institute of Technology, Cambridge, MA.

OECD (Organisation for Economic Co-operation and Development). 2011. *Strong Performers and Successful Reformers in Education: Lessons from PISA for the United States.* Paris: OECD.

———. 2016. *PISA 2015 Results: Excellence and Equity in Education.* Vol. 1. Paris: OECD.

Orazem, Peter F. 2000. "The Urban and Rural Fellowship School Experiments in Pakistan: Design, Evaluation, and Sustainability." *Economics of Education Review* 22 (3): 265–74.

Orazem, Peter F., Paul W. Glewwe, and Harry Patrinos. 2007. "The Benefits and Costs of Alternative Strategies to Improve Educational Outcomes." Department of Economics Working Paper 07028, Iowa State University, Ames.

Park, Rufina Kyung Eun. 2016. "Preparing Students for South Korea's Creative Economy: The Successes and Challenges of Educational Reform" [refers to the Republic of Korea]. Research Report, Asia Pacific Foundation of Canada, Vancouver.

Pascale, Richard T., Jerry Sternin, and Monique Sternin. 2010. *The Power of Positive Deviance: How Unlikely Innovators Solve the World's Toughest Problems.* Boston: Harvard Business Press.

PASEC (Programme d'Analyse des Systèmes Éducatifs de la Confemen). 2015. *PASEC 2014: Education System Performance* in Francophone Africa, Competencies and Learning Factors in Primary Education. Dakar, Senegal: PASEC.

Paxson, Christina H., and Norbert R. Schady. 2007. "Cognitive Development among Young Children in Ecuador: The Roles of Wealth, Health, and Parenting." *Journal of Human Resources* 42 (1): 49–84.

Piper, Benjamin, Evelyn Jepkemei, Dunston Kwayumba, and Kennedy Kibukho. 2015. "Kenya's ICT Policy in Practice: The Effectiveness of Tablets and E-readers in Improving Student Outcomes." *FIRE: Forum for International Research in Education* 2 (1): 3–18.

Pradhan, Menno, Daniel Suryadarma, Amanda Beatty, Maisy Wong, Arya Gaduh, Armida Alisjahbana, and Rima Prama Artha. 2014. "Improving Educational Quality through Enhancing Community Participation: Results from a Randomized Field Experiment in Indonesia." *American Economic Journal: Applied Economics* 6 (2): 105–26.

Pritchett, Lant. 2013. *The Rebirth of Education: Schooling Ain't Learning.* Washington, DC: Center for Global Development; Baltimore: Brookings Institution Press.

Pritchett, Lant, and Amanda Beatty. 2015. "Slow Down, You're Going Too Fast: Matching Curricula to Student Skill Levels." *International Journal of Educational Development* 40: 276–88.

Pritchett, Lant, and Justin Sandefur. 2013. "Context Matters for Size: Why External Validity Claims and Development Practice Do Not Mix." *Journal of Globalization and Development* 4 (2): 161–98.

Rajkumar, Andrew Sunil, and Vinaya Swaroop. 2008. "Public Spending and Outcomes: Does Governance Matter?" *Journal of Development Economics* 86 (1): 96–111.

Rivkin, Steven G., Eric A. Hanushek, and John F. Kain. 2005. "Teachers, Schools, and Academic Achievement." *Econometrica* 73 (2): 417–58.

Robinson, Viviane M. J., Claire A. Lloyd, and Kenneth J. Rowe. 2008. "The Impact of Leadership on Student Outcomes: An Analysis of the Differential Effects of Leadership Types." *Educational Administration Quarterly* 44 (5): 635–74.

Rockoff, Jonah E. 2004. "The Impact of Individual Teachers on Student Achievement: Evidence from Panel Data." *American Economic Review* 94 (2): 247–52.

Romer, Paul Michael. 2015. "Botox for Development." *Paul Romer's Blog*, September 13. https://paulromer.net/botox -for-development/.

RTI International. 2009. "Early Grade Reading Assessment Toolkit." Research Triangle Institute, Research Triangle Park, NC.

Sabarwal, Shwetlena, David K. Evans, and Anastasia Marshak. 2014. "The Permanent Input Hypothesis: The Case of Textbooks and (No) Student Learning in Sierra Leone." Policy Research Working Paper 7021, World Bank, Washington, DC.

Save the Children. 2013. "Ending the Hidden Exclusion: Learning and Equity in Education Post-2015." Education Global Initiative, Save the Children International, London.

Schady, Norbert R., Jere Behrman, Maria Caridad Araujo, Rodrigo Azuero, Raquel Bernal, David Bravo, Florencia

Lopez-Boo, et al. 2015. "Wealth Gradients in Early Childhood Cognitive Development in Five Latin American Countries." *Journal of Human Resources* 50 (2): 446–63.

Scott-Clayton, Judith, and Olga Rodriguez. 2014. "Development, Discouragement, or Diversion? New Evidence on the Effects of College Remediation Policy." *Education Finance and Policy* 10 (1): 4–45.

Singh, Abhijeet. 2015. "Learning More with Every Year: School Year Productivity and International Learning Divergence." CESifo Area Conference on the Economics of Education, CESifo Group, Munich, September 11–12.

Snilstveit, Birte, Jennifer Stevenson, Radhika Menon, Daniel Phillips, Emma Gallagher, Maisie Geleen, Hannah Jobse, et al. 2016. "The Impact of Education Programmes on Learning and School Participation in Low- and Middle-Income Countries: A Systematic Review Summary Report." 3ie Systematic Review Summary 7, International Initiative for Impact Evaluation, London. http:// www.3ieimpact.org/media/filer_public/2016/09/20/srs7 -education-report.pdf.

Solano-Flores, Guillermo, Luis Ángel Contreras-Niño, and Eduardo Backhoff Escudero. 2005. "The Mexican Translation of TIMSS-95: Test Translation Lessons from a Post-mortem Study." Paper presented at Annual Meeting, National Council on Measurement in Education, Montreal, April 12–14.

Spaull, Nicholas, and Janeli Kotze. 2015. "Starting Behind and Staying Behind in South Africa: The Case of Insurmountable Learning Deficits in Mathematics." *International Journal of Educational Development* 41: 13–24.

Suryadarma, Daniel. 2012. "How Corruption Diminishes the Effectiveness of Public Spending on Education in Indonesia." *Bulletin of Indonesian Economic Studies* 48 (1): 85–100.

Tan, Jee-Peng, and Alain Mingat. 1992. *Education in Asia: A Comparative Study of Cost and Financing.* World Bank Regional and Sectoral Studies Series. Washington, DC: World Bank.

Tandon, Prateek, and Tsuyoshi Fukao. 2015. *Educating the Next Generation: Improving Teacher Quality in Cambodia.* Directions in Development: Human Development Series. Washington, DC: World Bank.

Todd, Alexa, and Mark Mason. 2005. "Enhancing Learning in South African Schools: Strategies beyond Outcomes-Based Education." *International Journal of Educational Development* 25 (3): 221–35.

Tooley, James, and Pauline Dixon. 2007. "Private Education for Low-Income Families: Results from a Global Research Project." In *Private Schooling in Less Economically Developed Countries: Asian and African Perspectives*, edited by Prachi Srivastava and Geoffrey Walford, 15–39. Oxford Studies in Comparative Education Series. Oxford, U.K.: Symposium Books.

UIS (UNESCO Institute for Statistics). 2006. *Teachers and Educational Quality: Monitoring Global Needs for 2015.* Montreal: UIS.

———. 2016. "Sustainable Development Data Digest: Laying the Foundation to Measure Sustainable Development Goal 4." UIS, Montreal.

UIS (UNESCO Institute for Statistics) and EFA (Education for All). 2015. "A Growing Number of Children and

Adolescents Are Out of School as Aid Fails to Meet the Mark." Policy Paper 22/Fact Sheet 31, UIS, Montreal; EFA, Paris.

UNESCO (United Nations Educational, Scientific, and Cultural Organization). 2013. Third Regional Comparative and Explanatory Study (TERCE). UNESCO Regional Bureau for Education in Latin America and the Caribbean, Santiago, Chile. http://www.unesco.org/new/en /santiago/education/education-assessment-llece/third -regional-comparative-and-explanatory-study-terce/.

———. 2016. *Global Education Monitoring Report 2016, Education for People and Planet: Creating Sustainable Futures for All.* Paris: UNESCO. http://unesdoc.unesco.org/images/0024 /002457/245752e.pdf.

USAID (U.S. Agency for International Development). 2017. Early Grade Reading Barometer. Washington, DC. http:// www.earlygradereadingbarometer.org/.

Uwezo. 2014. "Are Our Children Learning? Literacy and Numeracy across East Africa 2013." Twaweza, Nairobi.

Wales, Joseph, Ahmed Ali, and Susan Nicolai. 2014. "Improvements in the Quality of Basic Education: Chile's Experience." With Francisca Morales and Daniel Contreras. Case Study Report: Education, Overseas Development Institute, London.

Walker, Susan P., Theodore D. Wachs, Julie Meeks Gardner, Betsy Lozoff, Gail A. Wasserman, Ernesto Pollitt, Julie A. Carter, and the International Child Development Steering Group. 2007. "Child Development: Risk Factors for Adverse Outcomes in Developing Countries." *Lancet* 369 (9556): 145–57.

Waters, Tim, Robert J. Marzano, and Brian McNulty. 2003. "Balanced Leadership: What 30 Years of Research Tells Us about the Effect of Leadership on Student Achievement." McRel Working Paper, McRel International, Denver.

Wolf, Alison. 2004. "Education and Economic Performance: Simplistic Theories and Their Policy Consequences." *Oxford Review of Economic Policy* 20 (2): 315–33.

World Bank. 2003. *World Development Report 2004: Making Services Work for Poor People.* Washington, DC: World Bank; New York: Oxford University Press.

———. 2011. *World Development Report 2012: Gender Equality and Development.* Washington, DC: World Bank.

———. 2013. Service Delivery Indicators (database). World Bank, Washington, DC. http://datatopics.worldbank.org /sdi/.

———. 2014. "STEP Skills Measurement Surveys: Innovative Tools for Assessing Skills." Social Protection and Labor Discussion Paper No. 1421. Washington, DC. http:// documents.worldbank.org/curated/en/51674146817873 6065/STEP-skills-measurement-surveys-innovative -tools-for-assessing-skills.

———. 2016a. *Assessing Basic Education Service Delivery in the Philippines: The Philippines Public Education Expenditure Tracking and Quantitative Service Delivery Study.* Report AUS6799. Washington, DC: World Bank.

———. 2016b. "Francophone Africa Results Monitor: Basic Education (Multiple Countries)." World Bank, Washington, DC. http://documents.worldbank.org/curated/en/doc search/projects/P156307.

———. 2017. "Driving Performance from the Center: Malaysia's Experience with Pemandu." Knowledge and Research: The Malaysia Development Experience Series, World Bank, Kuala Lumpur.

PART I

Education's promise

1 Schooling, learning, and the promise of education

1

Schooling, learning, and the promise of education

> "No one has yet realized the wealth of sympathy, the kindness and generosity hidden in the soul of a child. The effort of every true education should be to unlock that treasure."
>
> EMMA GOLDMAN

> "In the long run, the best way to reduce inequalities with respect to labor as well as to increase the average productivity of the labor force and the overall growth of the economy is surely to invest in education."
>
> THOMAS PIKETTY, *CAPITAL IN THE TWENTY-FIRST CENTURY*

Education is a basic human right, and it is central to unlocking human capabilities. It also has tremendous instrumental value. Education raises human capital, productivity, incomes, employability, and economic growth. But its benefits go far beyond these monetary gains: education also makes people healthier and gives them more control over their lives. And it generates trust, boosts social capital, and creates institutions that promote inclusion and shared prosperity.

Education as freedom

Since 1948, education has been recognized as a basic human right, highlighting its role as a safeguard for human dignity and a foundation of freedom, justice, and peace.[1] In the language of Amartya Sen's capability approach, education increases both an individual's assets and his or her ability to transform them into well-being—or what has been called the individual's "beings and doings" and "capabilities."[2] Education can have corresponding salutary effects on communities and societies.

Education expands freedom through many channels, both raising aspirations and increasing

the potential to reach them. These benefits are both monetary and nonmonetary for individuals, families, communities, and society as a whole (table 1.1).

Most people—whether policy makers or parents—already recognize the great value of education.[3] Families around the world make great sacrifices to keep their children in good schools, and political and opinion leaders consistently rank education among their top development priorities. For that reason, this chapter does not try to review all the evidence on the benefits of education. But before launching into the main theme of this Report—the learning crisis and what to do about it—it is worth surveying briefly the many ways in which education can contribute to progress, highlighting that these benefits often depend on learning, not just schooling.[4]

Education improves individual freedoms

Education improves economic opportunities

Education is a powerful tool for raising incomes. Education makes workers more productive by giving

Table 1.1 Examples of education's benefits

	Individual/family	Community/society
Monetary	Higher probability of employment Greater productivity Higher earnings Reduced poverty	Higher productivity More rapid economic growth Poverty reduction Long-run development
Nonmonetary	Better health Improved education and health of children/family Greater resilience and adaptability More engaged citizenship Better choices Greater life satisfaction	Increased social mobility Better-functioning institutions/service delivery Higher levels of civic engagement Greater social cohesion Reduced negative externalities

Source: WDR 2018 team.

them the skills that allow them to increase their output.[5] Each additional year of schooling typically raises an individual's earnings by 8–10 percent, with larger increases for women (figure 1.1).[6] This is not just because higher-ability or better-connected people (who would earn more regardless of their schooling) receive more education, as proposed by the signaling model of education. "Natural experiments" from a wide variety of countries—such as Honduras, Indonesia, the Philippines, the United Kingdom, and the United States—prove that schooling does drive the increased earnings (box 1.1).[7]

In well-functioning labor markets, education reduces the likelihood of unemployment. In these economies, high school graduates are less likely than less educated workers to lose their jobs, and if they do they are more likely to find another job. Educated workers are more attached to the firms they work for. They are also more effective at acquiring and processing job search information.[8] Research in Finland and the United States finds that more schooling makes it easier for unemployed people to find reemployment.[9] In less developed economies with large informal sectors and underemployment, education is associated with greater access to full-time jobs in the formal sector.[10]

Education leads to longer lives and enables better life choices

Education promotes longer, healthier lives. Around the world, there are strong links among education,

Figure 1.1 More schooling is systematically associated with higher wages

Median percentage increase in wages associated with each additional year of schooling, by country group and gender

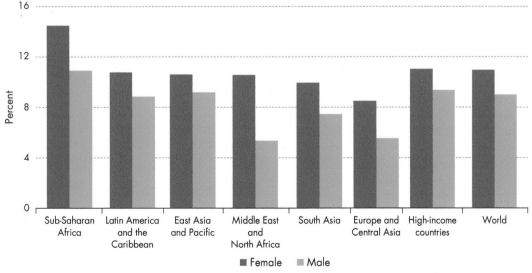

Source: WDR 2018 team, using data from Montenegro and Patrinos (2017). Data at http://bit.do/WDR2018-Fig_1-1.

Note: Figure is based on the latest available data, 1992–2012. Regions do not include high-income countries.

Why is education associated with higher earnings? Unlike the human capital model, which posits that education increases a worker's productivity, the signaling model of education states that individuals acquire education credentials to signal a high ability to potential employers. Having a university degree does signal perseverance, grit, and ability—all valuable skills for the labor market.

But the human capital acquired typically drives the link from schooling to earnings, as different types of evidence show. First, the returns to an additional year of schooling for those who drop out without a high school or university diploma are as large as for those who complete the degree. Second, the wage differentials across education levels rise with age, whereas signaling theory suggests they should

fall, because the usefulness of the signal component would presumably decline with age. Finally, education is an expensive screening strategy.

If education worked only as a screening device, individuals with the same years of schooling should have similar outcomes regardless of the skills they acquired, which is not the case.[a] In many countries, individuals with higher measured skills have been consistently shown to earn more than their lower-skilled peers who have the same amount of schooling.[b] In Mexico, those high school graduates with higher test scores are substantially less likely to be unemployed three years after leaving school (among those who did not go to university) than their lower-scoring peers.[c]

Source: WDR 2018 team.

a. Layard and Psacharopoulos (1974).
b. For example, see the results for Organisation for Economic Co-operation and Development (OECD) countries in Hanushek and others (2015) and Valerio and others (2016). For individual countries such as Ghana, see Glewwe (1991), or for South Africa, see Moll (1998).
c. de Hoyos, Estrada, and Vargas (2017).

better health outcomes, and longer lives.[11] Regardless of their race, gender, or income, more-educated individuals in Europe and the United States have a lower probability of having a chronic health condition.[12] In the United States, each additional year of schooling is associated with a lower probability of death, especially after high school (figure 1.2). One reason is that education makes people less likely to smoke, drink in excess, be overweight, or use illegal drugs.[13] In the United States, education makes people less likely to smoke; in Uganda, more-educated individuals were more responsive to HIV/AIDS information campaigns.[14]

Educated individuals have more control over the life they want to pursue—often called "agency." Increased agency manifests itself as a reduction in risky behavior, higher life satisfaction, and greater happiness. Across 52 countries at all income levels in 2010–14, only 1 in 10 university graduates felt that they had little or no control over their lives.[15] When the United Kingdom and the United States extended compulsory schooling, people who received more education were less likely to report being unhappy later in life.[16]

The positive relationship between education and agency is partly mediated by the positive effect of education on income, but there seems to be an

Figure 1.2 Mortality rates in the United States are lower for adults with more education

Relative odds (log-odds coefficient) of death for groups with different years of education, by age, gender, and race

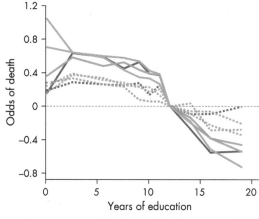

— Black female, ages 25–64 ··· Black female, ages 65+ — Black male, ages 25–64 ··· Black male, ages 65+ — White female, ages 25–64 ··· White female, ages 65+ — White male, ages 25–64 ··· White male, ages 65+

Source: WDR 2018 team, using data from Montez, Hummer, and Hayward (2012). Data at http://bit.do/WDR2018-Fig_1-2.

Note: Groups exclude Hispanic population.

independent effect as well: the effects on crime and fertility, for example, are not contingent only on income. Schooling reduces most types of crime committed by adults,[17] as well as crime during late adolescence.[18] Among 16- and 17-year-olds in the United Kingdom, school dropouts are three times more likely to commit crimes than those who have stayed in school, and this gap remains well into their early 20s. In Sweden, the United Kingdom, and the United States, completing high school makes youth less likely to commit crimes, and education is linked with lower crime rates elsewhere—such as in Mexico, where high school dropouts were more caught up in the violence of the war on drugs.[19]

As for fertility, education reduces teen pregnancy and increases the control that women have over the size of their families. Schooling reduces teenage pregnancy indirectly by increasing girls' aspirations, empowerment, and agency. In Turkey, primary school completion induced by a change in compulsory schooling laws—allowing research to isolate the causal effects—reduced teenage fertility by 0.37 children per woman.[20] School subsidies reduced teen pregnancy (and in some cases school dropout) in Brazil, Colombia, Kenya, Malawi, and Peru.[21] More generally, women with more schooling have lower fertility rates. In Brazil, increased schooling among young women explains 40–80 percent of the decline in the fertility rate that began in the late 1960s.[22] When school coverage expanded in Nigeria, each additional year of female schooling reduced fertility by at least 0.26 births per woman.[23] One reason may be that educated women earn more, making it costlier for them to leave the labor market.[24] Education also increases women's use of contraception, increases their role in family decisions on fertility, and makes them more aware of the trade-offs in having children.[25]

The benefits of education are long-lasting

Education can eliminate poverty in families. The incomes of parents and their children are highly correlated: income inequality persists, and poverty is transmitted from one generation to the next.[26] But improving education gives poor children a boost: in the United States, the children of households that moved to a (one standard deviation) better neighborhood had incomes as adults that were more than 10 percent higher, in part because the move improved learning.[27]

Better-educated mothers raise healthier and more educated children. Women's education is linked to many health benefits for their children, from higher immunization rates to better nutrition to lower mortality.[28] Improvements in women's education have been linked to better health outcomes for their children in many countries, including Brazil, Nepal, Pakistan, and Senegal.[29] Parental schooling robustly predicts higher educational attainment for children, even after controlling for other factors. And children's ability to benefit from education is shaped by their parents' education. In the United States, each additional year of a mother's schooling increases her children's math test scores by 0.1 standard deviation and significantly reduces behavioral problems.[30] In Pakistan, mothers who have one more year of schooling have children who spend an additional hour a day studying at home.[31]

Education's benefits are especially apparent in changing environments. Individuals with stronger skills can take better advantage of new technologies and adapt to changing work. Indeed, experts on technological change have long argued that the more volatile the state of technology, the more productive education is.[32] Returns to primary schooling in India increased during the Green Revolution, with the more educated farmers adopting and diffusing new technologies.[33] More generally, globalization and advances in technology are putting a premium on education and skills—both cognitive and socioemotional (see spotlight 5). New skills facilitate the adoption of technologies and promote innovation,[34] with general skills enabling individuals to adapt to the economic changes that occur over their lifetimes.[35] When the North American Free Trade Agreement (NAFTA) increased labor productivity in Mexico, the benefits were concentrated among more-skilled workers in the richer northern states.[36] In general, returns to education are higher in economically free countries with institutions that allow individuals to adjust to shocks and market forces.[37]

Education benefits all of society

Education builds human capital, which translates into economic growth. If improvements are faster among the disadvantaged, the additional growth will reduce poverty, reduce inequality, and promote social mobility. Through its effect on civic agency—meaning high levels of political engagement, trust, and tolerance—education can create the building blocks for more inclusive institutions.[38] Greater civic agency can create a political constituency for inclusive institutions, strengthening the social contract between the state and its citizens. A more engaged citizenry can also provide political support for the reforms needed to realize the promise of education.

Education promotes economic growth

At the national level, education underpins growth. Human capital can boost growth in two ways: first, by improving the capacity to absorb and adapt new technology, which will affect short- to medium-term growth, and, second, by catalyzing the technological advances that drive sustained long-term growth.[39] Widespread basic education may provide a bigger boost for countries far from the global technological frontier—a group that includes most low- and middle-income countries.[40] These countries do not need to push that frontier out through innovation, but they do need widespread basic education to absorb and adapt the technologies that are already available globally. In countries close to the technological frontier, mainly high-income countries, higher levels of education can boost growth through innovation.[41] Although data limitations make empirical analysis of this relationship challenging, many influential studies have concluded that higher levels of education do drive more rapid growth.[42] Growth accounting analyses also suggest that education can explain a significant share of growth—a share that may be even larger if unskilled workers are more productive when there are more skilled workers in an economy.[43]

But this statistical evidence is not the only—or even the most compelling—evidence on the impact of education on growth. Countries that have sustained rapid growth over decades have typically shown a strong public commitment to expanding education, as well as infrastructure and health.[44] Although the relationship flows the other way as well—in that rapid growth allows greater investment in all three sectors—research on the East Asian miracle countries in particular flags education and human capital as factors in their rapid growth.[45] Countries such as the Republic of Korea reaped the benefits of their "progressive universalism" approach to education, in which they ensured high-quality basic education for all children early on, followed by expansion of high-quality secondary and tertiary opportunities.[46] These cases reinforce the idea that strong foundational skills drive growth early in development, but also that as countries approach the global technological frontier, they need to invest more in higher education and in research and development.[47]

As education coverage expands, poor people typically benefit the most at the margin, and so income inequality should fall.[48] A review of more than 60 studies reveals that greater education coverage is associated with substantial reductions in the income gap between households across the income distribution. Specifically, going from a primary enrollment rate of 50 to 100 percent is associated with an 8 percentage point increase in the share of income going to households in the poorest decile.[49]

Education creates the building blocks for inclusive institutions

Education strengthens the political development of nations by promoting the civic engagement of their populations.[50] People with more education consistently participate more in political activities than those with less education: education increases awareness and understanding of political issues, fosters the socialization needed for effective political activity, and increases civic skills.[51] Evidence from a variety of settings shows that this relationship is causal.[52] In the United States, getting more education—for example, as a result of preschool programs, high school scholarships, or smaller class sizes—leads people to vote more often (table 1.2).[53] Using changes in compulsory school laws to identify the causal impact of education confirms these findings for the United Kingdom and the United States, while using access to community college or changes in child labor laws does so for the United States.[54] In Benin, receiving more education made people more politically active over their lifetimes. In Nigeria, too, educational

Table 1.2 More schooling leads to more voting
Percent

Program	Graduated from high school		Voted	
	Control	Treatment	Control	Treatment
Perry Preschool experiment	44	65	13	18
"I Have a Dream" scholarships	62	79	32	42
STAR Experiment	85	90	42	47

Source: Sondheimer and Green (2010).

Note: The Perry Preschool experiment was an intensive effort to enroll children from low-income families in preschool in Ypsilanti, Michigan. The "I Have a Dream" scholarships were high school scholarships targeted to fifth-grade students who qualified (because of their family's poverty status) for free or reduced-price lunch in Lafayette, Colorado. The STAR Experiment assigned some students in kindergarten through grade 3 in Tennessee to smaller class sizes. The measure of voting differs across the studies, but corresponds to a time between 2000 and 2004 when the participants would have already graduated from high school.

Figure 1.3 **People with higher education hold stronger beliefs about the importance of democracy**

Percentage of population that believes it is "absolutely important to live in a democracy," by country and level of education

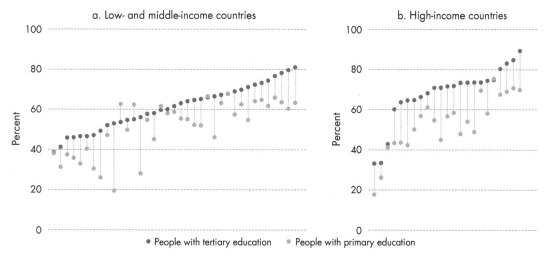

Source: WDR 2018 team, using data from World Values Survey (World Values Survey Association 2015). Data at http://bit.do/WDR2018-Fig_1-3.

expansion substantially increased the civic and political engagement of its beneficiaries decades later.[55]

As with the other effects of education, context matters in how education affects political views and engagement. In an indicator of perceptions of one common mechanism for political participation, surveys in 30 developing countries show that more-educated citizens are more likely to believe that living in a democracy is important (figure 1.3). But in Kenya, although more education caused young women to have more political knowledge, it also led them to be more disenchanted and more accepting of political violence, perhaps because democratic institutions were particularly fragile at the time of the research.[56]

Education increases trust, tolerance, and civic agency. Evidence from member countries of the Organisation for Economic Co-operation and Development (OECD), as well as from developing countries, indicates that more-educated individuals are more trusting and tolerant of people they know and even of strangers.[57] Although such cross-sectional evidence cannot prove a causal relationship, historical analysis suggests a mechanism: the spread of literacy may have contributed to a generalized decline in violence after the Middle Ages, because the ability to read others' viewpoints promoted empathy.[58] Some educational environments appear to promote trust especially well. Data for 28 countries reveal that the openness of a classroom climate, or the "degree to which students are able to discuss political and social issues in class," is positively linked to trust and tolerance.[59] Similarly,

teaching styles that encourage teamwork rather than a more top-down pedagogy appear to promote social capital: students are more likely to believe in the importance of civic life and the value of cooperation.[60]

Education makes institutions work better and improves public services. Educated parents are better able to leverage decision-making authority at the school level. In The Gambia, a school-based management program improved student learning—but only when there was a high level of literacy in the village.[61] A more educated population generally demands more transparent use of public resources, better service delivery, and government accountability. Recent cross-country research identifies citizen complaints as a primary mechanism: educated citizens complain more, inducing officials to behave better.[62] Education also appears to improve dimensions of governance: countries that had achieved mass education by 1870 had less corruption in 2010.[63]

Growth built on human capital rather than other sources (such as natural resources) may lead to fewer incentives for conflict, for three main reasons.[64] First, because human capital is difficult to appropriate, conquest of a well-educated population may be less rewarding than seizure of natural resources or even physical capital.[65] Second, education raises the opportunity cost of fighting: it is easier to recruit people who have poor job prospects.[66] Third, as discussed, education can promote tolerance and cooperation, thereby reducing the propensity to turn to violence to resolve conflicts.[67]

Learning and the promise of education

Education can be a powerful tool for individual and societal empowerment, but its benefits are not automatic. It is not just that education cannot do it alone, in that much also has to go right in other sectors of the economy and society (box 1.2). Another problem is that if an education system is managed poorly, it can promote social "bads" instead of social "goods." First, education can deepen cleavages between favored and disadvantaged groups. Young people from poor, rural, and otherwise disadvantaged households not only complete less schooling, but also learn much

---

Box 1.2 Education can't do it alone

Economics, politics, and society shape the returns to education. Education systems do not function in a vacuum; they are part of broader economic, political, and social institutions. For example, does a society uphold property rights? If not, entrepreneurs are unlikely to invest in risky new ventures, which cuts into job creation and reduces education's returns in the labor market. Are there regulations to prevent fraud? If not, those with education might find it more profitable to engage in socially unproductive but financially remunerative activities. Are women restricted from working outside the home? If so, the economic returns from education will be unavailable to them. These are all examples of how formal or informal institutions influence education's returns. In general, reliable institutions that implement the rule of law, reduce corruption, and protect property rights are associated with higher returns to human capital.[a]

Here are several examples of how problems elsewhere in the economy or society reduce education's returns:

Low demand for educated labor reduces the return to skills. Education's returns depend on the interplay between demand and supply forces in the labor market. If the demand for educated labor is low relative to supply, then the returns to education will be low or declining.[b] In urban China, the returns to education rose from 4 percent a year of schooling in 1988 to 10 percent in 2001, with most of the increase attributable to institutional reforms that increased the demand for skilled labor.[c] More generally, shifts from planned to market economies have increased the returns to human capital.[d] When the investment climate is poor,[e] both investment and demand for labor by private firms are lower, reducing the returns to education.[f]

Countries can incentivize the wrong things. Many educated youth in parts of the developing world queue for jobs in already large public sectors. In several countries, political candidates compete in terms of their ability to offer patronage or public employment to their supporters.[g] In several North African countries, for example, it was not uncommon in the past for governments to guarantee public employment opportunities for all university graduates, and the public sector remains the employer of a large share of wage earners.[h] In such situations, individual returns to

education might be high (for those who land public sector jobs), but the impact of education on growth will be low because improved cognitive skills are not used in ways that will increase productivity the most.[i]

Discriminatory norms distort the benefits of education. Prevailing norms on ethnic or gender discrimination can strongly mediate the returns to education for these groups. In many societies, social norms severely restrict women's access to economic opportunities.[j] Two studies found that nearly 90 percent of women in northern India (from the state of Uttar Pradesh) and Nigeria (of Hausa ethnicity) felt they needed their husband's permission to work. But norms vary substantially: in the Ethiopian capital, this share was only 28 percent.[k]

Such norms do not always operate through open discrimination. Labor market segregation along occupational and social lines is often covert. Occupational gender segregation is a strong feature of many labor markets across the world.[l] In Organisation for Economic Co-operation and Development (OECD) countries, women dominate the service sector, whereas men are overrepresented in industry.[m] In addition to horizontal segregation, women also face a "glass ceiling" or "vertical segregation" because they do not advance in their careers as fast or as far as men. In OECD countries, just a third of managers were women in 2013, with small variations across countries.[n] Labor market segregation may also exist along socioeconomic lines.[o] In the 1960s and 1970s, during a period of rapid economic growth in Chile, education was significant in determining occupational attainment for the middle class. For the upper class and the very poor, education was less important, and intergenerational status inheritance was much more likely.[p] In Jamaica, a country with a rigid class structure, the massive expansion of educational opportunities at the secondary level did little to increase the permeability of social structure.[q]

The very people who are constrained by social norms may become complicit in perpetuating them. A study of students newly admitted to an elite master's in business administration (MBA) program in the United States found that single women reported lower desired compensation when they believed their classmates would see their responses. No such differences were observed for men or for women

(Box continues next page)

who were not single, suggesting that single women were reluctant to signal personality traits, such as ambition, that they perceived to be undesirable in the marriage market.[r] Social norms can operate in much the same way to inhibit male access to opportunities. Case studies in Australia and Jamaica suggest that underachievement among boys is linked to notions of education being a "feminized" realm that clashes with expectations of "masculine" behavior.[s]

When getting a job depends on informal institutions, education is less useful.[t] In Kolkata (formerly Calcutta), India,

45 percent of employees reported that they helped a friend or relative get a job with their current employer.[u] Nearly 60 percent of enterprises surveyed in 14 countries in Sub-Saharan Africa report that their most recent position was filled through contacts with "family/friends."[v] This finding applies as well to places where labor markets are segmented by kinship and socioeconomic class.[w] Informal networks can also be particularly important for certain subpopulations—for example, among Mexican migrants in the United States.[x]

Source: WDR 2018 team.

a. World Bank (2011).
b. Pritchett (2001).
c. Zhang and others (2005).
d. Nee and Matthews (1996).
e. World Bank (2012).
f. Almeida and Carneiro (2005); Besley and Burgess (2004); Botero and others (2004); Djankov and others (2002); Haltiwanger, Scarpetta, and Schweiger (2008); Klapper, Laeven, and Rajan (2004); Micco and Pagés (2007); Petrin and Sivadasan (2006).
g. Cammett (2009); Kao (2012); Lust-Okar (2009); Sakai, Jabar, and Dawod (2001).
h. Bteddini (2016); Egypt Census, 2006, Egypt Data Portal, Central Agency for Public Mobilizations and Statistics, Cairo, http://egypt.opendatafor africa.org/EGSNS2006/egypt-census-2006; Ghafar (2016).
i. Pritchett (2001).
j. Chiswick (1988); Goldin and Polachek (1987); McNabb and Psacharopoulos (1981); World Bank (2011).
k. World Bank (2011).
l. Hegewisch and Hartmann (2014).
m. OECD Employment Statistics Database, http://stats.oecd.org.
n. OECD Family Database, http://www.oecd.org/els/family/database .htm.
o. First described by Blau and Duncan (1967).
p. Farrell and Schiefelbein (1985).
q. Strudwick and Foster (1991).
r. Bursztyn, Fujiwara, and Pallais (2017).
s. Jha and Kelleher (2006).
t. Granovetter (1995).
u. Beaman and Magruder (2012).
v. Filmer and Fox (2014).
w. Assaad (1997); Barsoum (2004); Brixi, Lust, and Woolcock (2015).
x. Munshi (2003).

less while in school (see part II of this Report). In such cases, education does little to enhance social mobility. Second, leaders sometimes abuse education systems for political ends and in ways that reinforce autocracy or the social exclusion of certain groups.

Finally, schooling is not the same as learning. *Education* is an imprecise word, and so it must be clearly defined. *Schooling* is the time a student spends in classrooms, whereas *learning* is the outcome—what the student takes away from schooling. This distinction is crucial: around the world, many students learn little (figure 1.4). To be sure, many students learn something, even in settings facing huge challenges. And students enjoy some benefits from education regardless of whether they are learning. When schools serve as oases of security in violent areas, or when participation in schooling keeps adolescent girls from becoming pregnant, these are real societal benefits. When graduates can use their degrees to open doors to employment, that opportunity changes their lives, even when the degree represents less learning than it should.

Intuitively, many of education's benefits depend on the skills that students develop in school. As workers,

Figure 1.4 **Learning varies widely across countries; in 6 of the 10 countries assessed, only half or fewer of primary completers can read**

Literacy rates at successive education levels, selected countries

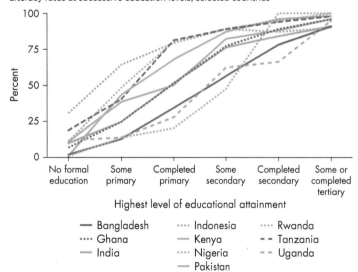

Source: Kaffenberger and Pritchett (2017). Data at http://bit.do/WDR2018-Fig_1-4.

Note: Literacy is defined as being able to read a three-sentence passage either "fluently without help" or "well but with a little help."

people need a range of skills—cognitive, socioemotional, technical—to be productive and innovative. As parents, they need literacy to read to their children or to interpret medication labels, and they need numeracy to budget for their futures. As citizens, people need literacy and numeracy, as well as higher-order reasoning abilities, to evaluate politicians' promises. As community members, they need the sense of agency that comes from developing mastery. None of these capabilities flows automatically from simply attending school; all depend on learning while in school.

Research on the benefits of education has begun to reflect this distinction between schooling and learning. In the past, most empirical research equated education with schooling—whether measured by school enrollment, number of years of schooling, or degrees acquired—in part because of lack of other good measures of education. But as the focus on learning has grown, some studies have explored the effects of the skills that students acquire. The results confirm the intuition: skills matter.

The channel by which schooling accelerates economic growth appears to be through boosting learning and skills.[68] Thanks to the growing availability of large-scale student assessments, it is now possible to explore how learning mediates the relationship from schooling to economic growth.[69] While the relationship between test scores and growth is strong even

after controlling for the years of schooling completed, years of schooling do not predict growth once test scores are taken into account (figure 1.5), or they become only marginally significant.[70] In other words, what matters is less the years of education completed than the knowledge that students acquire while in school. Simulations show that providing all students with basic cognitive skills could massively boost economic outcomes, especially in developing countries (figure 1.6).[71] This finding suggests that cross-country comparisons of the years of schooling completed—especially when used to explain economic phenomena—could be misguided if they do not account for the differences in skills acquired during those years (box 1.3).

At the micro level, too, growing evidence shows that skills acquisition determines how much individuals gain from schooling. For example, learning—not just schooling—matters in how education affects earnings. Across 23 OECD countries, as well as in a number of other countries, simple measures of foundational skills such as numeracy and reading proficiency explain hourly earnings over and above the effect of years of schooling completed.[72] These effects extend beyond the labor market. Across 10 low- and middle-income countries, schooling improved measures of financial behavior only when it was associated with increased reading ability.[73] When people

Figure 1.5 **What matters for growth is learning**

Annual average per capita growth in GDP, 1970–2015, conditional on test scores, years of schooling completed, and initial GDP per capita

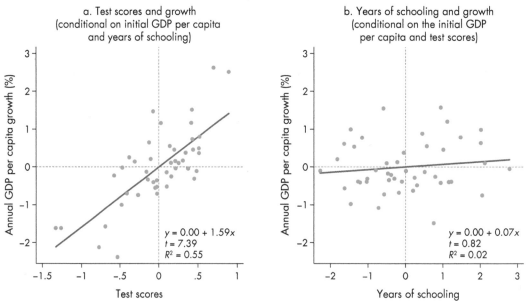

a. Test scores and growth (conditional on initial GDP per capita and years of schooling)

b. Years of schooling and growth (conditional on the initial GDP per capita and test scores)

$y = 0.00 + 1.59x$
$t = 7.39$
$R^2 = 0.55$

$y = 0.00 + 0.07x$
$t = 0.82$
$R^2 = 0.02$

Source: WDR 2018 team, using data on test scores from Hanushek and Woessmann (2012) and data on years of schooling and GDP from the World Bank's World Development Indicators (database), 2017. Data at http://bit.do/WDR2018-Fig_1-5.

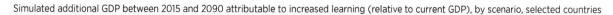

Figure 1.6 Increasing learning would yield major economic benefits

Simulated additional GDP between 2015 and 2090 attributable to increased learning (relative to current GDP), by scenario, selected countries

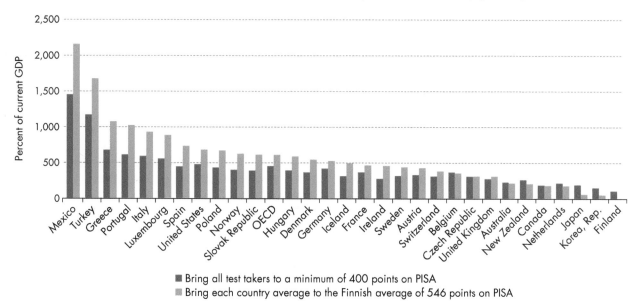

■ Bring all test takers to a minimum of 400 points on PISA
■ Bring each country average to the Finnish average of 546 points on PISA

Source: OECD (2010). Data at http://bit.do/WDR2018-Fig_1-6.

Note: PISA = Programme for International Student Assessment.

had acquired more schooling but not more literacy—which was common in these countries—financial behaviors did not change. Socioemotional skills matter as well: various measures have been shown to significantly predict earnings over and above the effects of schooling and cognitive skills.[74]

Learning matters for health, too. Numerous studies have documented the benefits of girls' schooling on outcomes such as lower fertility or better child survival, but these studies do not typically distinguish between learning and schooling. There are exceptions, however. In Morocco, research showed that maternal education improved child health through its effects on the ability of mothers to acquire health knowledge.[75] Globally, data from 48 developing countries show that learning is responsible for much of these gains. Each additional year of female primary schooling is associated with roughly six fewer deaths per 1,000 live births, but the effect is about two-thirds larger in the countries where schooling delivers the most learning (compared with the least).[76]

Even limited measures of skills explain a lot. The measures used in the studies just noted are often narrow, capturing only simple numeracy or reading proficiency. Sometimes, the measures are coarse. For example, the 48-country study of the relationship between schooling and health uses as its measure of literacy whether a woman can read a single sentence

such as "Parents love their children" or "Farming is hard work." Yet even these highly imperfect measures of skills have considerable predictive and explanatory power. If better measures of skills were available, skills would likely explain even more of the impacts of education—and the role remaining for the simple schooling measure (which typically retains predictive power in these analyses) would be further diminished.

Finally, learning promotes social mobility. The research cited earlier on intergenerational social mobility in the United States also investigated which educational mechanisms were responsible. One candidate is school quality based on inputs, such as school spending and class size, and these measures did have some predictive power. But learning outcomes turn out to be especially important: the test scores of the community in which a child lives (adjusted for the income of that community) are among the strongest predictors of social mobility later in life.[77]

The literature on the benefits of learning is still growing, with much more research needed. But both common sense and the emerging research literature make it clear that if investigators care about the benefits of education, they should focus on whether students are learning—not just on how well schools are equipped or even how long students stay in school. Part II of this Report takes up this issue.

Box 1.3 Comparing attainment across countries and economies— learning-adjusted years of schooling

A given number of years in school leads to much more learning in some economies than in others. Because they do not account for these differences, standard comparisons of schooling attainment may be misleading. But how should they be adjusted to make meaningful comparisons?

One approach is to draw on measures of student learning that are standardized across different economies to adjust for quality. International assessments such as the Trends in International Mathematics and Science Study (TIMSS) or the Programme for International Student Assessment (PISA) provide such measures. If one is willing to assume that the average learning trajectory across economies is linear—starting at no learning when learners enter school and growing at a constant rate to grade 8—then the ratio of scores across two economies would reflect the relative learning per year in one economy versus the other. For example, if economy A has twice the score of economy B in grade 8, then, on average, a year of schooling in economy A may be considered twice as effective.

Two important facts support the credibility of this analysis: first, the TIMSS score ratios across economies for grade 4 are similar to those for grade 8; and second, PISA scores tend to increase linearly across the grades in which that test is administered.

What might such an adjustment reveal? An illustration using TIMSS math scores from 2015 confirms that years of schooling are indeed very different from learning-adjusted years, and this difference varies a lot across economies. Whereas people ages 25–29 in Hong Kong SAR, China, and the United States have similar average years of schooling (14 and 13.5, respectively), the number of learning-adjusted schooling years in the United States is almost two years less (figure B1.3.1). And whereas young Singaporeans have only 30 percent more schooling than young Jordanians by the standard measure, the learning-adjusted measure shows Singapore outpaces Jordan by 109 percent in effective schooling years.

Figure B1.3.1 There can be a large gap between learning-adjusted and unadjusted years of schooling

Years of actual and learning-adjusted schooling among young people, ages 25–29, illustrated using TIMSS data

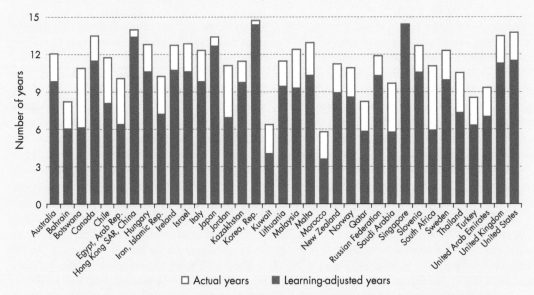

□ Actual years   ■ Learning-adjusted years

Source: WDR 2018 team, using data from Barro and Lee (2013) and TIMSS 2015 (Mullis and others 2016). Data at http://bit.do/WDR2018-Fig_B1-3-1.

Note: Years of schooling in Singapore are the same as learning-adjusted years because Singapore, which scored highest on the Trends in International Mathematics and Science Study (TIMSS) mathematics assessment in 2015, serves as the basis for comparison in this illustration. For the purposes of this illustration, data for years of education in the United Kingdom are adjusted using the TIMSS score for England. Note that for all countries and economies, the size of the adjustment will reflect the scale of the metric used to make it.

Notes

1. United Nations (1948). Article 26 of the Universal Declaration of Human Rights (1948) states: "Everybody has the right to education. . . . Education shall be directed to the full development of the human personality and to the strengthening of respect for human rights and fundamental freedoms. It shall promote understanding, tolerance and friendship among all nations, racial or religious groups, and shall further the activities for the maintenance of peace."
2. Sen (1985, 1999, 2004).
3. For example, see UNESCO (2016) for a comprehensive discussion of the role of education in the United Nations' Sustainable Development Goals.
4. Heckman and others (2014).
5. Becker (1964).
6. Montenegro and Patrinos (2017).
7. Angrist and Krueger (1992); Bedi and Gaston (1999); Card (1993); Duflo (2000); Harmon and Walker (1995); Maluccio (1998).
8. Mincer (1991).
9. Kettunen (1997); Riddell and Song (2011).
10. Filmer and Fox (2014).
11. See Cutler, Lleras-Muney, and Vogl (2008) and Vogl (2012) for a review of the evidence in developed and developing countries, respectively.
12. Cutler and Lleras-Muney (2007); Mackenbach (2006).
13. Although there is reverse causality—better health leads to more education—natural experiments such as the introduction of minimum schooling laws or military draft avoidance have identified the positive and significant causal effects of education on health.
14. de Walque (2007a, 2007b).
15. The World Values Survey 2010–14 (Wave 6) covers 57 developed and developing economies (World Values Survey Association 2015). The survey measures the beliefs, values, and motivations of 90,000 survey respondents selected in nationally representative samples, while also collecting socioeconomic data from those respondents. Estimations include average weights and consolidated categories for analysis (education level and scaled responses).
16. Oreopoulos (2007).
17. Lochner (2004); Lochner and Moretti (2004).
18. Belfield and others (2006); Cullen, Jacob, and Levitt (2006).
19. Anderson (2014); de Hoyos, Gutiérrez Fierros, and Vargas M. (2016); Hjalmarsson, Holmlund, and Lindquist (2015); Machin, Marie, and Vujić (2011). At least two possible mechanisms could explain why education reduces crime. First, because education increases potential earnings, it also drives up the opportunity costs of crime. Second, more schooling may reduce crime simply by reducing the time available to young people to commit a crime. Some U.S. data support this "incapacitation effect" (Anderson 2014).
20. Güneş (2016).
21. Azevedo and others (2012); Baird and others (2010); Duflo, Dupas, and Kremer (2014).
22. Lam, Sedlacek, and Duryea (2016).
23. Osili and Long (2008).
24. Becker, Cinnirella, and Woessmann (2013).
25. Lavy and Zablotsky (2011).
26. Solon (1999).
27. Chetty, Hendren, and Katz (2016).
28. Schultz (1975); Thomas, Strauss, and Henriques (1990); Welch (1970); World Bank (2011).
29. World Bank (2011).
30. Carneiro, Meghir, and Parey (2013).
31. Andrabi, Das, and Khwaja (2012).
32. Nelson and Phelps (1966).
33. Foster and Rosenzweig (1996).
34. Aghion and others (2009).
35. Hanushek and others (2017).
36. Hanson (2007).
37. King, Montenegro, and Orazem (2012).
38. Chong and Gradstein (2015); Dahl (1998); Dewey (1916).
39. Romer (1990); Solow (1956).
40. Aghion (2009); Madsen (2014).
41. Acemoglu, Aghion, and Zilibotti (2006); Aghion (2009); Aghion and others (2009).
42. Barro (2001); Cohen and Soto (2007); Glewwe, Maiga, and Zheng (2014); Krueger and Lindahl (2001); Mankiw, Romer, and Weil (1992).
43. Bosworth and Collins (2003); Jones (2014).
44. Commission on Growth and Development (2008).
45. World Bank (1993).
46. Education Commission (2016).
47. Aghion and Howitt (2006).
48. Lanjouw and Ravallion (1999); Younger (2003).
49. Abdullah, Doucouliagos, and Manning (2015).
50. Dewey (1916); Lipset (1959, 1960).
51. Campante and Chor (2012).
52. Chzhen (2013).
53. Sondheimer and Green (2010).
54. Dee (2004); Milligan, Moretti, and Oreopolous (2004).
55. Larreguy and Marshall (2017); Wantchekon, Klasnja, and Novta (2015).
56. Friedman and others (2011).
57. Borgonovi and Burns (2015); Chzhen (2013).
58. Pinker (2011).
59. Campbell (2006).
60. Algan, Cahuc, and Shleifer (2013).
61. Blimpo, Evans, and Lahire (2015).
62. Botero, Ponce, and Shleifer (2013).
63. Chong and others (2014).
64. de la Brière and others (2017).
65. Acemoglu and Wolitzky (2011).
66. Collier, Hoeffler, and Rohner (2009).
67. Davies (2004).
68. Glewwe, Maiga, and Zheng (2014); Hanushek and Woessmann (2008, 2012).
69. Barro (2001, 2013).
70. Barro (2013).
71. Hanushek and Woessmann (2015); OECD (2010).
72. Hanushek and others (2015); Valerio and others (2016).
73. Kaffenberger and Pritchett (2017).

74. For OECD countries, see Heckman, Stixrud, and Urzua (2006); Heineck and Anger (2010); Mueller and Plug (2006). For countries outside of OECD, see Díaz, Arias, and Tudela (2012); Valerio and others (2016).
75. Glewwe (1999).
76. Oye, Pritchett, and Sandefur (2016).
77. Chetty and others (2014).

References

Abdullah, Abdul, Hristos Doucouliagos, and Elizabeth Manning. 2015. "Does Education Reduce Income Inequality? A Meta-Regression Analysis." *Journal of Economic Surveys* 29 (2): 301–16.

Acemoglu, Daron, Philippe Aghion, and Fabrizio Zilibotti. 2006. "Distance to Frontier, Selection, and Economic Growth." *Journal of the European Economic Association* 4 (1): 37–74.

Acemoglu, Daron, and Alexander Wolitzky. 2011. "The Economics of Labor Coercion." *Econometrica* 79 (2): 555–600.

Aghion, Philippe. 2009. "Growth and Education." Working Paper 56, Commission on Growth and Development, World Bank, Washington, DC.

Aghion, Philippe, Leah Boustan, Caroline Hoxby, and Jerome Vandenbussche. 2009. "The Causal Impact of Education on Economic Growth: Evidence from U.S." Working paper, Harvard University, Cambridge, MA.

Aghion, Philippe, and Peter Howitt. 2006. "Joseph Schumpeter Lecture Appropriate Growth Policy: A Unifying Framework." *Journal of the European Economic Association* 4 (2–3): 269–314.

Algan, Yann, Pierre Cahuc, and Andrei Shleifer. 2013. "Teaching Practices and Social Capital." *American Economic Journal: Applied Economics* 5 (3): 189–210.

Almeida, Rita, and Pedro Manuel Carneiro. 2005. "Enforcement of Regulation, Informal Labor, and Firm Performance." IZA Discussion Paper 1759, Institute for the Study of Labor, Bonn, Germany.

Anderson, D. Mark. 2014. "In School and Out of Trouble? The Minimum Dropout Age and Juvenile Crime." *Review of Economics and Statistics* 96 (2): 318–31.

Andrabi, Tahir, Jishnu Das, and Asim Ijaz Khwaja. 2012. "What Did You Do All Day? Maternal Education and Child Outcomes." *Journal of Human Resources* 47 (4): 873–912.

Angrist, J. D., and A. B. Krueger. 1992. "Estimating the Payoff to Schooling Using the Vietnam-Era Draft Lottery." NBER Working Paper w4067, National Bureau of Economic Research, Cambridge, MA.

Assaad, Ragui. 1997. "Kinship Ties, Social Networks, and Segmented Labor Markets: Evidence from the Construction Sector in Egypt." *Journal of Development Economics* 52 (1): 1–30.

Azevedo, João Pedro, Marta Favara, Sarah E. Haddock, Luis F. López-Calva, Miriam Müller, and Elizaveta Perova. 2012. *Teenage Pregnancy and Opportunities in Latin America and the Caribbean: On Teenage Fertility Decisions, Poverty, and Economic Achievement.* Report 83167 v2 rev. Washington, DC: World Bank.

Baird, Sarah Jane, Ephraim Chirwa, Craig McIntosh, and Berk Özler. 2010. "The Short-Term Impacts of a Schooling Conditional Cash Transfer Program on the Sexual Behavior of Young Women." *Health Economics* 19 (S1): 55–68.

Barro, Robert J. 2001. "Human Capital and Growth." *American Economic Review* 91 (2): 12–17.

———. 2013. "Education and Economic Growth." *Annals of Economics and Finance* 14 (2): 301–28.

Barro, Robert J., and Jong Wha Lee. 2013. "A New Data Set of Educational Attainment in the World, 1950–2010." *Journal of Development Economics* 104: 184–98.

Barsoum, Ghada F. 2004. "The Employment Crisis of Female Graduates in Egypt: An Ethnographic Account." *Cairo Papers* 25 (3). Cairo: American University in Cairo Press.

Beaman, Lori, and Jeremy Magruder. 2012. "Who Gets the Job Referral? Evidence from a Social Networks Experiment." *American Economic Review* 102 (7): 3574–93.

Becker, Gary. 1964. *Human Capital.* New York: Columbia University Press.

Becker, Sashca O., Francesco Cinnirella, and Ludger Woessmann. 2013. "Does Women's Education Affect Fertility? Evidence from Pre-demographic Transition Prussia." *European Review of Economic History* 17 (1): 24–44.

Bedi, A. S., and N. Gaston. 1999. "Using Variation in Schooling Availability to Estimate Educational Returns for Honduras." *Economics of Education Review* 18 (1): 107–16.

Belfield, Clive R., Milagros Nores, Steve Barnett, and Lawrence Schweinhart. 2006. "The High/Scope Perry Preschool Program Cost-Benefit Analysis Using Data from the Age-40 Followup." *Journal of Human Resources* 41 (1): 162–90.

Besley, Timothy J., and Robin S. L. Burgess. 2004. "Can Labour Regulation Hinder Economic Performance? Evidence from India." *Quarterly Journal of Economics* 119 (1): 91–134.

Blau, Peter M., and Otis Dudley Duncan. 1967. *The American Occupational Structure.* New York: John Wiley.

Blimpo, Moussa P., David K. Evans, and Nathalie Lahire. 2015. "Parental Human Capital and Effective School Management." Policy Research Working Paper 7238, World Bank, Washington, DC.

Borgonovi, Francesca, and Tracey Burns. 2015. "The Educational Roots of Trust." OECD Education Working Paper 119, Organisation for Economic Co-operation and Development, Paris.

Bosworth, Barry P., and Susan M. Collins. 2003. "The Empirics of Growth: An Update." *Brookings Papers on Economic Activity* 2: 113–79.

Botero, Juan Carlos, Simeon Djankov, Rafael La Porta, Florencio Lopez de Silanes, and Andrei Shleifer. 2004. "The Regulation of Labor." *Quarterly Journal of Economics* 119 (4): 1339–82.

Botero, Juan Carlos, Alejandro Ponce, and Andrei Shleifer. 2013. "Education, Complaints, and Accountability." *Journal of Law and Economics* 56 (4): 959–96.

Brixi, Hana, Ellen Lust, and Michael Woolcock. 2015. *Trust, Voice, and Incentives: Learning from Local Success Stories in*

Service Delivery in the Middle East and North Africa. Washington, DC: World Bank.

Bteddini, Lida. 2016. "Middle East and North Africa: Public Employment and Governance in MENA." Report ACS18501, World Bank, Washington, DC.

Bursztyn, Leonardo, Thomas Fujiwara, and Amanda Pallais. 2017. "'Acting Wife': Marriage Market Incentives and Labor Market Investments." NBER Working Paper 23043, National Bureau of Economic Research, Cambridge, MA.

Cammett, Melani. 2009. "Democracy, Lebanese-Style." *MER: Middle East Report Online* (August 18). http://www.merip .org/mero/mero081809.

Campante, Filipe R., and Davin Chor. 2012. "Schooling, Political Participation, and the Economy." *Review of Economics and Statistics* 94 (4): 841–59.

Campbell, David E. 2006. "What Is Education's Impact on Civic and Social Engagement?" In *Measuring the Effects of Education on Health and Civic Engagement: Proceedings of the Copenhagen Symposium*, 25–126. Paris: Organisation for Economic Co-operation and Development.

Card, D. 1993. "Using Geographic Variation in College Proximity to Estimate the Return to Schooling." NBER Working Paper wp4438, National Bureau of Economic Research, Cambridge, MA.

Carneiro, Pedro, Costas Meghir, and Matthias Parey. 2013. "Maternal Education, Home Environments, and the Development of Children and Adolescents." *Journal of the European Economic Association* 11 (S1): 123–60.

Chetty, Raj, Nathaniel Hendren, and Lawrence F. Katz. 2016. "The Effects of Exposure to Better Neighborhoods on Children: New Evidence from the Moving to Opportunity Experiment." *American Economic Review* 106 (4): 855–902.

Chetty, Raj, Nathaniel Hendren, Patrick Kline, and Emmanuel Saez. 2014. "Where Is the Land of Opportunity? The Geography of Intergenerational Mobility in the United States." *Quarterly Journal of Economics* 129 (4): 1553–1623.

Chiswick, Barry R. 1988. "Differences in Education and Earnings across Racial and Ethnic Groups: Tastes, Discrimination, and Investments in Child Quality." *Quarterly Journal of Economics* 103 (3): 571–97.

Chong, Alberto, and Mark Gradstein. 2015. "On Education and Democratic Preferences." *Economics and Politics* 27 (3): 362–88.

Chong, Alberto, Rafael La Porta, Florencia Lopez-de-Silanes, and Andrei Shleifer. 2014. "Letter Grading Government Efficiency." *Journal of the European Economic Association* 12 (2): 277–99.

Chzhen, Yekaterina. 2013. "Education and Democratisation: Tolerance of Diversity, Political Engagement, and Understanding of Democracy." Background paper, Report 2014/ED/EFA/MRT/PI/03, United Nations Educational, Scientific, and Cultural Organization, Paris.

Cohen, Daniel, and Marcelo Soto. 2007. "Growth and Human Capital: Good Data, Good Results." *Journal of Economic Growth* 12 (1): 51–76.

Collier, Paul, Anke Hoeffler, and Dominic Rohner. 2009. "Beyond Greed and Grievance: Feasibility and Civil War." *Oxford Economic Papers* 61 (1): 1–27.

Commission on Growth and Development. 2008. *The Growth Report: Strategies for Sustained Growth and Inclusive Development*. Washington, DC: World Bank.

Cullen, Julie Berry, Brian A. Jacob, and Steven Levitt. 2006. "The Effect of School Choice on Participants: Evidence from Randomized Lotteries." *Econometrica* 74 (5): 1191–1230.

Cutler, David M., and Adriana Lleras-Muney. 2007. "Education and Health." Policy Brief 9, National Poverty Center, Gerald R. Ford School of Public Policy, University of Michigan, Ann Arbor.

Cutler, David M., Adriana Lleras-Muney, and Tom Vogl. 2008. "Socioeconomic Status and Health: Dimensions and Mechanisms." NBER Working Paper 14333, National Bureau of Economic Research, Cambridge, MA.

Dahl, Robert A. 1998. *On Democracy*. Yale Nota Bene Series. New Haven, CT: Yale University Press.

Davies, Lynn. 2004. *Education and Conflict: Complexity and Chaos*. New York: RoutledgeFalmer.

Dee, Thomas S. 2004. "Are There Civic Returns to Education?" *Journal of Public Economics* 88 (9–10): 1697–1720.

de Hoyos, Rafael E., Ricardo Estrada, and María José Vargas. 2017. "Predicting Well-Being through Test Scores." World Bank, Washington, DC.

de Hoyos, Rafael E., Carlos Gutiérrez Fierros, and J. Vicente Vargas M. 2016. "Idle Youth in Mexico: Trapped between the War on Drugs and Economic Crisis." Policy Research Working Paper 7558, World Bank, Washington, DC.

de la Brière, Bénédicte, Deon Filmer, Dena Ringold, Dominic Rohner, Karelle Samuda, and Anastasiya Denisova. 2017. *From Mines and Wells to Well-Built Minds: Turning Sub-Saharan Africa's Natural Resource Wealth into Human Capital*. Directions in Development: Human Development Series. Washington, DC: World Bank.

de Walque, Damien. 2007a. "Does Education Affect Smoking Behaviors? Evidence Using the Vietnam Draft as an Instrument for College Education." *Journal of Health Economics* 26 (5): 877–95.

———. 2007b. "How Does the Impact of an HIV/AIDS Information Campaign Vary with Educational Attainment? Evidence from Rural Uganda." *Journal of Development Economics* 84 (2): 686–714.

Dewey, John. 1916. *Democracy and Education: An Introduction to the Philosophy of Education*. New York: Macmillan.

Díaz, Juan José, Omar Arias, and David Vera Tudela. 2012. "Does Perseverance Pay as Much as Being Smart? The Returns to Cognitive and Non-cognitive Skills in Urban Peru." Working paper, World Bank, Washington, DC.

Djankov, Simeon, Rafael La Porta, Florencio Lopez-de-Silanes, and Andrei Shleifer. 2002. "The Regulation of Entry." *Quarterly Journal of Economics* 117 (1): 1–37.

Duflo, Esther. 2000. "Schooling and Labor Market Consequences of School Construction in Indonesia: Evidence from an Unusual Policy Experiment." NBER Working Paper wp7860, National Bureau of Economic Research, Cambridge, MA.

Duflo, Esther, Pascaline Dupas, and Michael Kremer. 2014. "Education, HIV, and Early Fertility: Experimental

Evidence from Kenya." NBER Working Paper 20784, National Bureau of Economic Research, Cambridge, MA.

Education Commission. 2016. *The Learning Generation: Investing in Education for a Changing World.* New York: International Commission on Financing Global Education Opportunity.

Farrell, Joseph P., and Ernesto Schiefelbein. 1985. "Education and Status Attainment in Chile: A Comparative Challenge to the Wisconsin Model of Status Attainment." *Comparative Education Review* 29 (4): 490–506.

Filmer, Deon, and Louise Fox. 2014. *Youth Employment in Sub-Saharan Africa.* With Karen Brooks, Aparajita Goyal, Taye Mengistae, Patrick Premand, Dena Ringold, Siddharth Sharma, and Sergiy Zorya. Report ACS8133. Africa Development Forum Series. Washington, DC: Agence Française de Développement and World Bank. http://elibrary.worldbank.org/doi/book/10.1596/978-1-4648-0107-5.

Foster, Andrew D., and Mark R. Rosenzweig. 1996. "Technical Change and Human-Capital Returns and Investments: Evidence from the Green Revolution." *American Economic Review* 86 (4): 931–53.

Friedman, Willa, Michael Kremer, Edward Miguel, and Rebecca Thornton. 2011. "Education as Liberation?" NBER Working Paper 16939, National Bureau of Economic Research, Cambridge, MA.

Ghafar, Adel Abdel. 2016. "Educated but Unemployed: The Challenge Facing Egypt's Youth." Policy briefing, Brookings Doha Center, Doha, Qatar.

Glewwe, Paul W. 1991. "Schooling, Skills, and the Returns to Government Investment in Education: An Exploration Using Data from Ghana." LSMS Working Paper 76, Living Standards Measurement Study, World Bank, Washington, DC.

———. 1999. "Why Does Mother's Schooling Raise Child Health in Developing Countries? Evidence from Morocco." *Journal of Human Resources* 34 (1): 124–59.

Glewwe, Paul W., Eugenie Maiga, and Haochi Zheng. 2014. "The Contribution of Education to Economic Growth: A Review of the Evidence, with Special Attention and an Application to Sub-Saharan Africa." *World Development* 59: 379–93.

Goldin, Claudia, and Solomon Polachek. 1987. "Residual Differences by Sex: Perspectives on the Gender Gap in Earnings." *American Economic Review* 77 (2): 143–51.

Granovetter, Mark. 1995. *Getting a Job: A Study of Contacts and Careers.* Chicago: University of Chicago Press.

Güneş, Pinar Mine. 2016. "The Impact of Female Education on Teenage Fertility: Evidence from Turkey." *B.E. Journal of Economic Analysis and Policy* 16 (1): 259–88.

Haltiwanger, John, Stefano Scarpetta, and Helena Schweiger. 2008. "Assessing Job Flows across Countries: The Role of Industry, Firm Size, and Regulations." NBER Working Paper 13920, National Bureau of Economic Research, Cambridge, MA.

Hanson, Gordon H. 2007. "Globalization, Labor Income, and Poverty in Mexico." In *Globalization and Poverty*, edited by Ann Harrison, 417–56. Chicago: University of Chicago Press.

Hanushek, Eric A., Guido Schwerdt, Simon Wiederhold, and Ludger Woessmann. 2015. "Returns to Skills around the World: Evidence from PIAAC." *European Economic Review* 73: 103–30.

Hanushek, Eric A., Guido Schwerdt, Ludger Woessmann, and Lei Zhang. 2017. "General Education, Vocational Education, and Labor-Market Outcomes over the Lifecycle." *Journal of Human Resources* 52 (1): 48–87.

Hanushek, Eric A., and Ludger Woessmann. 2008. "The Role of Cognitive Skills in Economic Development." *Journal of Economic Literature* 46 (3): 607–68.

———. 2012. "Do Better Schools Lead to More Growth? Cognitive Skills, Economic Outcomes, and Causation." *Journal of Economic Growth* 17 (4): 267–321.

———. 2015. *The Knowledge Capital of Nations: Education and the Economics of Growth.* CESifo Book Series. Cambridge, MA: MIT Press.

Harmon, C., and I. Walker. 1995. "Estimates of the Economic Return to Schooling for the United Kingdom." *American Economic Review* 85 (5): 1278–86.

Heckman, James J., John Eric Humphries, Greg Veramendi, and Sergio S. Urzua. 2014. "Education, Health, and Wages." NBER Working Paper 19971, National Bureau of Economic Research, Cambridge, MA.

Heckman, James J., Jora Stixrud, and Sergio S. Urzua. 2006. "The Effects of Cognitive and Noncognitive Abilities on Labor Market Outcomes and Social Behavior." *Journal of Labor Economics* 24 (3): 411–82.

Hegewisch, Ariane, and Heidi Hartmann. 2014. "Occupational Segregation and the Gender Wage Gap: A Job Half Done." Report, Institute for Women's Policy Research, Washington, DC.

Heineck, Guido, and Silke Anger. 2010. "The Returns to Cognitive Abilities and Personality Traits in Germany." *Labour Economics* 17 (3): 535–46.

Hjalmarsson, Randi, Helena Holmlund, and Matthew J. Lindquist. 2015. "The Effect of Education on Criminal Convictions and Incarceration: Causal Evidence from Micro-Data." *Economic Journal* 125 (587): 1290–1326.

Jha, Jyotsna, and Fatimah Kelleher. 2006. *Boys' Underachievement in Education: An Exploration in Selected Commonwealth Countries.* London: Commonwealth Secretariat.

Jones, Benjamin F. 2014. "The Human Capital Stock: A Generalized Approach." *American Economic Review* 104 (11): 3752–77.

Kaffenberger, Michelle, and Lant Pritchett. 2017. "The Impact of Education versus the Impact of Schooling: Schooling, Reading Ability, and Financial Behavior in 10 Countries." Background paper, World Bank, Washington, DC.

Kao, Kristen. 2012. "Jordan's Ongoing Election Law Battle." SADA Middle East Analysis, Carnegie Endowment for International Peace, Washington, DC. http://carnegieendowment.org/sada/48781.

Kettunen, Juha. 1997. "Education and Unemployment Duration." *Economics of Education Review* 16 (2): 163–70.

King, Elizabeth M., Claudio E. Montenegro, and Peter F. Orazem. 2012. "Economic Freedom, Human Rights, and the Returns to Human Capital: An Evaluation of the Schultz Hypothesis." *Economic Development and Cultural Change* 61 (1): 39–72.

Klapper, Leora F., Luc Laeven, and Raghuram Rajan. 2004. "Business Environment and Firm Entry: Evidence from

International Data." NBER Working Paper 10380, National Bureau of Economic Research, Cambridge, MA.

Krueger, Alan B., and Mikael Lindahl. 2001. "Education for Growth: Why and for Whom?" *Journal of Economic Literature* 39 (4): 1101–36.

Lam, David, Guilherme Sedlacek, and Suzanne Duryea. 2016. "Increases in Women's Education and Fertility Decline in Brazil." *Anais do VIII Encontro Nacional de Estudos Populacionais*, Vol. 1, 89–118. Belo Horizonte, Brazil: Associação Brasileira de Estudos Populacionais.

Lanjouw, Peter F., and Martin Ravallion. 1999. "Benefit Incidence, Public Spending Reforms, and the Timing of Program Capture." *World Bank Economic Review* 15 (2): 257–73.

Larreguy, Horacio A., and John Marshall. 2017. "The Effect of Education on Civic and Political Engagement in Non-consolidated Democracies: Evidence from Nigeria." *Review of Economics and Statistics*. http://www.mitpressjournals.org/doi/abs/10.1162/REST_a_00633.

Lavy, Victor, and Alexander Zablotsky. 2011. "Mother's Schooling and Fertility under Low Female Labor Force Participation: Evidence from a Natural Experiment." NBER Working Paper 16856, National Bureau of Economic Research, Cambridge, MA.

Layard, Richard, and George Psacharopoulos. 1974. "The Screening Hypothesis and the Returns to Education." *Journal of Political Economy* 82 (5): 985–98.

Lipset, Seymour Martin. 1959. "Some Social Requisites of Democracy: Economic Development and Political Legitimacy." *American Political Science Review* 53 (01): 69–105.

———. 1960. *Political Man: The Social Basis of Modern Politics*. Garden City, NY: Doubleday.

Lochner, Lance. 2004. "Education, Work, and Crime: A Human Capital Approach." *International Economic Review* 45 (3): 811–43.

Lochner, Lance, and Enrico Moretti. 2004. "The Effect of Education on Crime: Evidence from Prison Inmates, Arrests, and Self-Reports." *American Economic Review* 94 (1): 155–89.

Lust-Okar, Ellen. 2009. "Legislative Elections in Hegemonic Authoritarian Regimes: Competitive Clientelism and Resistance to Democratization." *Democratization by Elections: A New Mode of Transition*, edited by Staffan I. Lindberg, 226–45. Baltimore: Johns Hopkins University Press.

Machin, Stephen, Olivier Marie, and Sunčica Vujić. 2011. "The Crime Reducing Effect of Education." *Economic Journal* 121 (552): 463–84.

Mackenbach, Johan P. 2006. "Health Inequalities: Europe in Profile." Department of Health, London.

Madsen, Jakob B. 2014. "Human Capital and the World Technology Frontier." *Review of Economics and Statistics* 96 (4): 676–92.

Maluccio, J. 1998. "Endogeneity of Schooling in the Wage Function: Evidence from the Rural Philippines." Food Consumption and Nutrition Division Discussion Paper 54, International Food Policy Research Institute, Washington, DC.

Mankiw, N. Gregory, David Romer, and David N. Weil. 1992. "A Contribution to the Empirics of Economic Growth." *Quarterly Journal of Economics* 107 (2): 407–37.

McNabb, Robert, and George Psacharopoulos. 1981. "Racial Earnings Differentials in the UK." *Oxford Economic Papers* 33 (3): 413–25.

Micco, Alejandro, and Carmen Pagés. 2007. "The Economic Effects of Employment Protection: Evidence from International Industry-Level Data." Working Paper 592, Research Department, Inter-American Development Bank, Washington, DC.

Milligan, Kevin, Enrico Moretti, and Philip Oreopolous. 2004. "Does Education Improve Citizenship? Evidence from the United States and the United Kingdom." *Journal of Public Economics* 88 (9): 1667–95.

Mincer, Jacob. 1991. "Education and Unemployment." NBER Working Paper 3838, National Bureau of Economic Research, Cambridge, MA.

Moll, Peter G. 1998. "Primary Schooling, Cognitive Skills, and Wages in South Africa." *Economica* 65 (258): 263–84.

Montenegro, Claudio E., and Harry Anthony Patrinos. 2017. "Comparable Estimates of Returns to Schooling around the World." Policy Research Working Paper 7020, World Bank, Washington, DC.

Montez, Jennifer Karas, Robert A. Hummer, and Mark D. Hayward. 2012. "Educational Attainment and Adult Mortality in the United States: A Systematic Analysis of Functional Form." *Demography* 49 (1): 315–36.

Mueller, Gerrit, and Erik Plug. 2006. "Estimating the Effect of Personality on Male and Female Earnings." *ILR Review* 60 (1): 3–22.

Mullis, I. V. S., M. O. Martin, P. Foy, and M. Hooper. 2016. "TIMSS 2015 International Results in Mathematics." TIMSS and PIRLS International Study Center, Boston College, Chestnut Hill, MA. http://timssandpirls.bc.edu/timss2015/international-results/.

Munshi, Kaivan. 2003. "Networks in the Modern Economy: Mexican Migrants in the US Labor Market." *Quarterly Journal of Economics* 118 (2): 549–99.

Nee, Victor, and Rebecca Matthews. 1996. "Market Transition and Societal Transformation in Reforming State Socialism." *Annual Review of Sociology* 22 (August): 401–35.

Nelson, Richard R., and Edmund S. Phelps. 1966. "Investment in Humans, Technological Diffusion, and Economic Growth." *American Economic Review* 56 (1/2): 69–75.

OECD (Organisation for Economic Co-operation and Development). 2010. "The High Cost of Low Educational Performance: The Long-Run Economic Impact of Improving PISA Outcomes." Programme for International Student Assessment, OECD, Paris.

Oreopoulos, Philip. 2007. "Do Dropouts Drop Out Too Soon? Wealth, Health, and Happiness from Compulsory Schooling." *Journal of Public Economics* 91 (11): 2213–29.

Osili, Una Okonkwo, and Bridget Terry Long. 2008. "Does Female Schooling Reduce Fertility? Evidence from Nigeria." *Journal of Development Economics* 87 (1): 57–75.

Oye, Mari, Lant Pritchett, and Justin Sandefur. 2016. "Girls' Schooling Is Good, Girls' Schooling with Learning Is Better." Education Commission, Center for Global Development, Washington, DC.

Petrin, Amil, and Jagadeesh Sivadasan. 2006. "Job Security Does Affect Economic Efficiency: Theory, a New Statistic, and Evidence from Chile." NBER Working Paper

12757, National Bureau of Economic Research, Cambridge, MA.

Pinker, Steven. 2011. *The Better Angels of Our Nature: The Decline of Violence in History and Its Causes.* New York: Viking.

Pritchett, Lant. 2001. "Where Has All the Education Gone?" *World Bank Economic Review* 15 (3): 367–91.

Riddell, Craig W., and Xueda Song. 2011. "The Impact of Education on Unemployment Incidence and Re-Employment Success: Evidence from the US Labour Market." *Labour Economics* 18 (4): 453–63.

Romer, Paul Michael. 1990. "Endogenous Technological Change." *Journal of Political Economy* 98 (5): 71–102.

Sakai, Keiko, Faleh Abdul Jabar, and Hosham Dawod. 2001. "Tribalism and the State: Remarks on the Army, Cabinets, and the National Assembly, 1980–1990." *In Tribes and Power: Nationalism and Ethnicity in the Middle East*, edited by Faleh Abdul Jabar and Hosham Dawod, 136–64. London: Saqi Books.

Schultz, Theodore W. 1975. "The Value of the Ability to Deal with Disequilibria." *Journal of Economic Literature* 13 (3): 827–46.

Sen, Amartya. 1985. *Commodities and Capabilities.* Amsterdam: North-Holland.

———. 1999. *Development as Freedom.* New York: Oxford University Press.

———. 2004. "Capabilities, Lists, and Public Reason: Continuing the Conversation." *Feminist Economics* 10 (3): 77–80.

Solon, Gary. 1999. "Intergenerational Mobility in the Labor Market." In *Handbook of Labor Economics*, Vol. 3A, edited by Orley Ashenfelter and David Card, 1761–800. Handbooks in Economics Series. Amsterdam: Elsevier.

Solow, Robert M. 1956. "A Contribution to the Theory of Economic Growth." *Quarterly Journal of Economics* 70 (1): 65–94.

Sondheimer, Rachel Milstein, and Donald P. Green. 2010. "Using Experiments to Estimate the Effects of Education on Voter Turnout." *American Journal of Political Science* 54 (1): 174–89.

Strudwick, Jeremy, and Philip Foster. 1991. "Origins and Destinations in Jamaica." *International Journal of Educational Development* 11 (2): 149–59.

Thomas, Duncan, John Strauss, and Maria-Helena Henriques. 1990. "Child Survival, Height for Age, and Household Characteristics in Brazil." *Journal of Development Economics* 33 (2): 197–234.

UNESCO (United Nations Educational, Scientific, and Cultural Organization). 2016. *Global Education Monitoring Report 2016, Education for People and Planet: Creating Sustainable Futures for All.* Paris: UNESCO. http://unesdoc.unesco.org/images/0024/002457/245752e.pdf.

United Nations. 1948. "Universal Declaration of Human Rights." Document A/RES/3/217 A, New York.

Valerio, Alexandria, María Laura Sánchez Puerta, Namrata Raman Tognatta, and Sebastián Monroy-Taborda. 2016. "Are There Skills Payoffs in Low- and Middle-Income Countries? Empirical Evidence Using Step Data." Policy Research Working Paper 7879, World Bank, Washington, DC.

Vogl, Tom S. 2012. "Education and Health in Developing Economies." Working Paper 1453, Research Program in Development Studies, Woodrow Wilson School of Public and International Affairs, Princeton University, Princeton, NJ.

Wantchekon, Leonard, Marko Klasnja, and Natalija Novta. 2015. "Education and Human Capital Externalities: Evidence from Colonial Benin." *Quarterly Journal of Economics* 130 (2): 703–57.

Welch, Finis. 1970. "Education in Production." *Journal of Political Economy* 78 (1): 35–59.

World Bank. 1993. *The East Asian Miracle: Economic Growth and Public Policy.* Policy Research Report Series. Washington, DC: World Bank; New York: Oxford University Press.

———. 2011. *World Development Report 2012: Gender Equality and Development.* Washington, DC: World Bank.

———. 2012. *World Development Report 2013: Jobs.* Washington, DC: World Bank.

———. 2017. World Development Indicators (database). World Bank, Washington, DC. http://data.worldbank.org/data-catalog/world-development-indicators.

World Values Survey Association. 2015. World Values Survey Wave 6 2010-2014 Official Aggregate V.20150418. King's College, Old Aberdeen, U.K. http://www.worldvaluessurvey.org/WVSDocumentationWV6.jsp.

Younger, Stephen D. 2003. "Benefits on the Margin: Observations on Marginal Benefit Incidence." *World Bank Economic Review* 17 (1): 89–106.

Zhang, Junsen, Yaohui Zhao, Albert Park, and Xiaoqing Song. 2005. "Economic Returns to Schooling in Urban China, 1988 to 2001." *Journal of Comparative Economics* 33 (4): 730–52.

PART II

The learning crisis

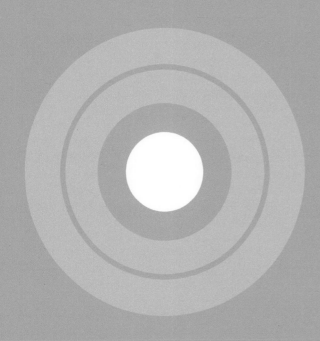

The great schooling expansion—and those it has left behind

In 1945, when Indonesia declared independence, only 5 percent of its people could read and write. In 2015, 95 percent could (UIS 2016).

In Nepal in 1981, only one in five adults were literate. In 2015, nearly two-thirds were (UIS 2016).

Over the last 50 years, schooling has expanded dramatically in most low- and middle-income countries. In some countries, this expansion has been at historically unprecedented rates. Another pattern is the rapid expansion of postprimary education, though many young people remain excluded from even primary education. So even in countries with strong schooling expansions, exclusions due to poverty, gender, ethnicity, disability, and location persist. Fragile and postconflict countries also remain glaring exceptions to the global boom in schooling.

Most children have access to basic education

Schooling has expanded almost universally. In 1970 the gross primary enrollment rate was 68 percent in Sub-Saharan Africa and 47 percent in South Asia. By 2010, that rate was above 100 percent in both regions.[1] These numbers reflect the progress made in nearly all countries regardless of regime type, rate of economic growth, or quality of governance.[2] As a result, most children today enroll in primary school—and every new cohort of young people spends more time in school than previous ones.[3]

The recent expansion in schooling in low-income countries is especially remarkable in its scope and speed. The years of schooling completed by the average adult in the developing world more than tripled between 1950 and 2010—from 2.0 to 7.2 years.[4] This rate is historically unprecedented. In Zambia, secondary enrollment increased by nearly 75 percentage points between 2000 and 2010, faster than the rate experienced by any high-income country during its fastest phase of secondary expansion.[5] It took the United States 40 years—from 1870 to 1910—to increase girls' enrollments from 57 percent to 88 percent. Morocco achieved a similar increase in just 11 years.[6] Accordingly, the enrollment gaps between low- and high-income countries are closing. By 2008 the average low-income country was enrolling students in primary school at nearly the same rate as the average high-income country (figure 2.1). Despite these gains, there is a large stock of uneducated adults—322 million in South Asia alone (figure 2.2).

Previously marginalized groups, especially girls, are now much more likely to start primary school. Between 2000 and 2014, the number of out-of-school children fell by about 112 million.[7] At the same time,

Figure 2.1 School enrollments have shot up in developing countries

Net enrollment rates, by country group (1820–2010)

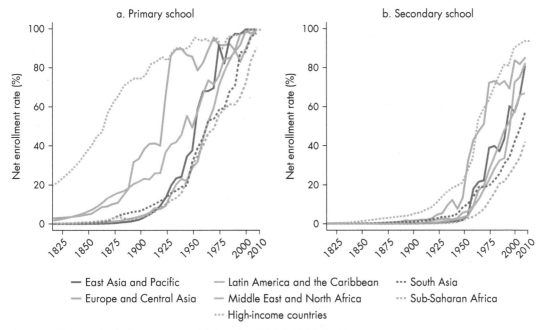

Source: WDR 2018 team, using data from Lee and Lee (2016). Data at http://bit.do/WDR2018-Fig_2-1.

the share of girls enrolled in basic education reached a historic high.[8] In primary and secondary schools in the developing world, the ratio of girls to boys jumped from 0.84 to 0.96 between 1991 and 2007.[9] Indeed, girls outnumber boys in secondary school in 38 developing countries (out of 121 for which data are available).[10] Gender parity, however, has yet to be achieved; 62 million girls between the ages of 6 and 15 years are still out of school,[11] with the highest concentrations in West and South Asia and Sub-Saharan Africa.[12] Although many girls start primary school, their likelihood of completing it remains low in some countries. By 2014 the primary enrollment rate of girls in low-income countries was at 78 percent, but their completion rate was only 63 percent.[13]

The strongest schooling expansions have occurred at the primary level, leading to a sharp increase in the demand for secondary education. Secondary enrollment rates have risen above 50 percent in every region except parts of Sub-Saharan Africa. But at that level there remain big gaps between low- and high-income countries, especially for completion. In 2016 the secondary completion rate was 96 percent in high-income Organisation for Economic Cooperation and

Figure 2.2 Most of the world's population with less than a primary education is in South Asia, but rates are similar in Sub-Saharan Africa

Stock of educational attainment (ages 15–64), by country group (2010)

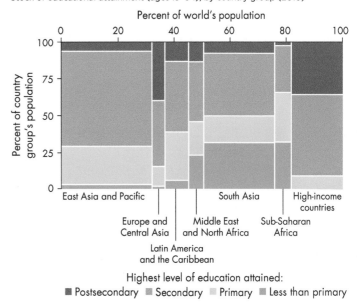

Source: WDR 2018 team, using data from Lee and Lee (2016). Data at http://bit.do/WDR2018-Fig_2-2.

Figure 2.3 National income is correlated with the gap between primary and lower secondary completion rates

Distribution of completion rates across countries, by country group and level of schooling

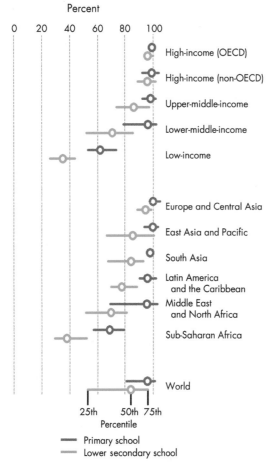

Source: WDR 2018 team, using data from UIS (2016). Data at http://bit.do/WDR2018-Fig_2-3.

Note: Geographic regions exclude high-income countries. The data presented are the latest available, by country, for the period 2010–16. Completion rates include students whose age exceeds the official age group for a particular education level, and so the rate may exceed 100 percent.

Development (OECD) countries, but only 35 percent in low-income countries (figure 2.3).[14]

Developing countries are following a very different path to schooling expansion than developed countries did. Low-income countries are leapfrogging the progress experienced by high-income countries—with strong expansion in postprimary education even while primary education remains inaccessible to many young people (figure 2.4).

Poverty, gender, ethnicity, disability, and location explain most remaining schooling disparities

Mawut, a refugee from South Sudan, lived in a refugee camp in Kenya for years so he could finish primary school. "In 2010 my sister [decided to return] to Sudan and I decided not to follow her because I knew if I did so, that would be the end of my education. I went to Kakuma Refugee Camp with my brother, where I completed the two remaining years of my primary course. I passed very well despite the problems that I had experienced" (Kelland 2016).

Nadya is a 25-year-old from Mashkhail, a remote district in southeastern Afghanistan. "I am the only literate woman in this heavily populated province working outside home and, more important, the only female teacher in this traditional province.... When the elders of Mashkhail found out I was literate ... [they asked] my husband if I could volunteer teaching their daughters, mostly those older girls who were not allowed to be taught by a male teacher" (IRIN 2003).

Conflict-affected countries remain a glaring exception to the global schooling expansion (box 2.1). The net primary enrollment rate in conflict-affected South Sudan was 41 percent in 2011; the enrollment rate in neighboring Ethiopia was 78 percent.[15] Conflict-affected countries are home to more than a third of out-of-school children.[16] Children in these countries are less likely to complete school—30 percent less likely for primary, 50 percent less likely for lower secondary.[17] They have higher dropout rates, lower completion rates, higher gender disparities, lower literacy levels, and disproportionately high out-of-school numbers.[18] Conflict can also erase past gains. The Syrian Arab Republic had achieved universal primary enrollment in 2000. But in 2013, 1.8 million children were out of school due to conflict.[19]

Exclusions based on poverty, location, gender, and ethnicity persist (figure 2.5). In 2014 an estimated 61 million primary school-age children and 202 million secondary school-age youth—with a disproportionate share from poor households—were out of school.[20] Only about a quarter of the poorest children in low-income countries—compared with three-quarters in the richest—complete primary school.[21]

These gaps are even larger when disaggregating by gender, where the double exclusions from gender and poverty mean that only 25 percent of the poorest girls in low-income countries complete primary school.[22] In some contexts, ethnicity can be an important predictor of education access. In 2011 only 10 percent of adult Roma had completed secondary education in Romania, compared with 58 percent of non-Roma living nearby.[23] Children of indigenous groups in Latin America are more than twice as likely as other children to be working.[24]

Children from the poorest families are less likely to start school. Those who do start school are more likely to drop out early, though at varying rates across countries. In some countries, such as Mali and Pakistan, the effect of poverty on education levels is already visible at the start of primary school. In Indonesia and Peru, gaps emerge later (figure 2.6). In nearly every country, parents' wealth and education attainment are the main determinants of their children's education.[25] On average, in developing countries there is a 32 percentage point gap between the chances of children in the poorest and richest quintiles completing primary school—with these wealth-related inequalities increasing in 10 of 25 such countries for which data are available.[26] The poorest people are the most affected by any marginal increase in or contraction of public spending on education.[27] Not surprisingly, then, making school more

Figure 2.4 Lower-income countries are rapidly expanding secondary education at a time when much of their population has not yet completed primary school

Evolution in the stock of educational attainment (ages 15–64), by present-day income group (1890–2010)

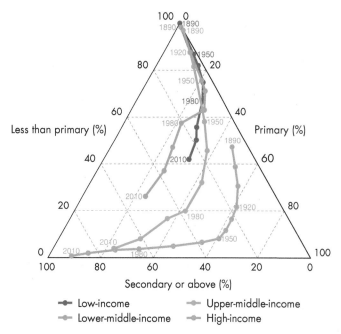

Source: WDR 2018 team, using data from Lee and Lee (2016). Data at http://bit.do/WDR2018-Fig_2-4.

Box 2.1 Access denied: The effects of fragility, conflict, and violence

Children living in the most fragile contexts make up about 20 percent of the world's primary school-age population. Yet they constitute about 50 percent of those not in school, an increase from 42 percent in 2008.[a] Children in fragile states are up to three times more likely to be out of school than those living in nonconflict contexts, and they are far more likely to drop out of primary school before completion. Even when fragility, conflict, and violence do not directly disrupt access, they can affect learning by changing the pedagogical experience, such as through lack of teachers and resources or trauma from violence. Conflict tends to exacerbate exclusions based on ethnicity, religion, or gender.

Education systems can exacerbate conflict through, for example, ethnic, religious, or gender stereotyping in

textbooks. Other manifestations include the singular use of a nonindigenous language as part of noninclusive "nation building," the denial of education to marginalized groups, the manipulation of history for political purposes, and the use of geography lessons to promote a particular ideological view.

Displaced children face significant obstacles to learning. Only one out of every two refugee children has access to primary education; a refugee child is five times more likely than the average child to be out of school.[b] Education for these vulnerable children can provide a sense of normalcy and structure, with high returns.[c] But the challenge of equipping these children with the necessary skills and knowledge has often fallen to host governments, some

(Box continues next page)

Box 2.1 Access denied: The effects of fragility, conflict, and violence (continued)

of which are already struggling to provide quality education for their own populations. Lebanon, for example, has increased the size of its public education system by almost 50 percent since 2011, largely because of the conflict in the Syrian Arab Republic. In Lebanon, refugees make up almost a third of the total enrollment in education.[d]

In addition to conflict and violence at the societal level, school-level violence hinders learning. Physical and psychological violence are common forms of so-called discipline, with students in many parts of the world routinely subjected to corporal punishment. Across three major

cities in one large country, for example, more than half of all students had been subjected to some form of violent punishment at school.[e] One-quarter of the children who were physically punished said they sustained injuries as a result. Children already discriminated against based on disability, poverty, caste, class, ethnicity, or sexual orientation are more likely than their peers to suffer corporal punishment. In some contexts, sexual violence in schools is also an issue—for example, authority figures may abuse their power by demanding sex in return for better grades or for waiving school fees.

Source: Commins (2017).

a. UNESCO (2013).
b. UNHCR (2016).
c. Burde and others (2015).
d. World Bank (2016a).
e. NCCM and UNICEF (2015).

affordable—both in terms of defraying direct costs and compensating for opportunity costs—increases the school participation of children from poorer families.[28]

Globally, girls are twice as likely as boys never to start school, which results in lower school completion rates.[29] In Sub-Saharan Africa, poor rural girls are seven times less likely than nonpoor urban boys to complete school; less than 1 in 20 of these girls is on

track to complete secondary school.[30] Even in regions where gender parity has been achieved at the primary level, such as North Africa and West Asia, gender disparities in enrollment exist at the lower secondary school level and become more pronounced in upper secondary school.[31]

Gender reinforces other disadvantages. It often compounds disadvantages related to socioeconomic

Figure 2.5 School completion is higher for richer and urban families, but gender gaps are more context-dependent

Gaps in grade 6 completion rates (percent) for 15- to 19-year-olds, by wealth, location, and gender

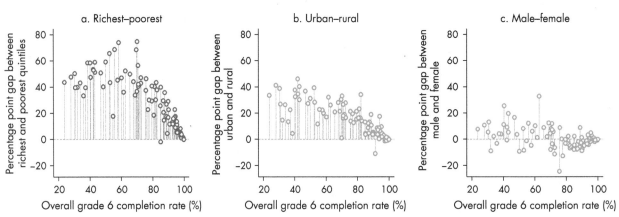

Source: WDR 2018 team, using data from Filmer (2016). Data at http://bit.do/WDR2018-Fig_2-5.

Note: The data presented are the latest available by country, 2005–14. Each vertical line indicates the size and direction of the gap for a country.

Figure 2.6 Multiple exclusions: Girls from poor households often have the lowest rates of education attainment

Percentage of youth (ages 15–19) who have completed each grade, by wealth quintile and gender, selected countries (2012)

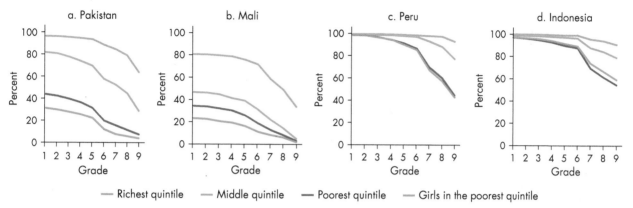

a. Pakistan b. Mali c. Peru d. Indonesia

—— Richest quintile —— Middle quintile —— Poorest quintile —— Girls in the poorest quintile

Source: WDR 2018 team, using data from U.S. Agency for International Development's Demographic and Health Surveys for 2012 (http://www.dhsprogram.com). Data at http://bit.do/WDR2018-Fig_2-6.

status, ethnicity, location, religion, sexual orientation, disability, age, and race.[32] Across 44 countries, boys in the poorer half of the population were almost 75 percent more likely to complete grade 5 than girls; by contrast, in the richer half of the population the boys' advantage was less than 20 percent.[33] Nearly 70 percent of all girls who were not enrolled in primary school in 2006 came from socially excluded groups.[34]

Children with disabilities face substantial obstacles to education—and substantially lower participation in school.[35] In Burkina Faso, having a disability increases the probability of a child never attending school by about two times.[36] Even in countries with high overall primary school enrollments, children with disabilities are still significantly less likely to attend school. In Moldova, 97 percent of children without disabilities between the ages of 7 and 15 years are enrolled in primary school, whereas only 58 percent of children with disabilities are in school.[37] At the same time, quality education for children with disabilities has significant economic and social returns. Across 12 developing countries, each additional year of schooling for people with a disability decreased their probability of being in the poorest two quintiles by between 2 and 5 percentage points.[38]

For poor parents, schooling requires trade-offs

Millions of poor parents make difficult choices about whether to educate their children. This cost-benefit assessment—where costs include both the direct cost of school and the opportunity cost of a child's time

outside it—determines their children's enrollment, grade completion, and learning outcomes.[39] In some contexts, this calculus might involve sending just some—but not all—children to school. For example, only about a quarter of rural households in Burkina Faso enroll all their children in school.[40] Cutting the cost of schooling, therefore, significantly raises school participation by children from poorer families.[41] The removal of direct costs to schooling through universal primary education in Uganda increased primary enrollment by over 60 percent and lowered cost-related dropouts by over 33 percentage points.[42] In Malawi, free primary education increased enrollment by half, favoring girls and poor people.[43]

For some poor households, distance to the nearest school is a predictor of school participation, especially where social norms or safety concerns make it difficult for children—particularly girls—to travel far from home.[44] In Indonesia, each school built for every 1,000 children increased education by an average of 0.12 years.[45] But school availability matters most when starting from a point of low availability, and school construction by itself can only do so much.[46]

Perceived returns, whether in the labor market or in realms such as the marriage "market," often determine how willing poor parents are to send their children to school.[47] Thus the demand for education is likely to be lower if parents underestimate the returns to education.[48] Parents might also misunderstand how the returns to education vary by level. If they believe the returns from secondary education are significantly higher than the returns from primary, it might make more sense to focus on sending their brightest child to secondary school rather than sending all their children to primary school.[49] In the face of extreme poverty and perceived low returns to schooling, poor people might restrict their overall aspirations for education.[50]

Parents' perceptions about whether their children are learning affect their decisions about whether to continue schooling. In most low-income countries, students who have to repeat grades or who exceed the average age of their classmates by several years are more likely to drop out before completing primary school.[51] In the Philippines, a child's perceived educational ability is a key determinant of whether parents choose to keep him or her in school, or in the workplace instead.[52] Similarly, adolescents in Burkina Faso are far more likely to be enrolled when they score high on an intelligence test, but much less likely if their sibling scores higher.[53]

When parents perceive the education available to be of low quality, it also affects their choices about schooling.[54] Although parental perceptions of school quality depend on a variety of factors—from the physical condition of the school to teacher punctuality—student learning outcomes are a critical aspect.[55] Holding student ability and achievement constant,

families in the Arab Republic of Egypt could differentiate schools by their quality of education—and students attending lower-quality schools were more likely to drop out.[56] Indeed, parents seem willing to bypass lower-quality public schools in favor of higher-quality, more remote public ones, or better-quality private ones with higher fees.[57]

* * *

Worldwide, parents and students have incredible faith in the power of education. People everywhere know that education can transform lives, including the lives of their children. The rapid growth in schooling in poor rural areas around the world is indicative of this demand.[58] Almost all parents say they want their children to complete school—even parents who did not attend school themselves.[59] The last 50 years have generated high hopes of strong returns to education and a great drive toward universal school enrollment. But much remains to be done. Achieving this promise means addressing gaps in school participation and ensuring that education leads to learning. As chapter 3 shows, the great schooling expansion has not translated into commensurate gains in learning. Attention must now shift to ensuring learning for all.

Notes

1. UIS (2016). Gross enrollment includes students whose age exceeds the official age group for a particular education level, and so the rate may exceed 100 percent.
2. Pritchett (2013).
3. United Nations (2015).
4. Barro and Lee (2013).
5. WDR 2018 team calculations using data from Lee and Lee (2016).
6. World Bank (2011b).
7. UNESCO (2016).
8. UNESCO (2015).
9. World Bank (2011a).
10. World Bank (2017). Data used are the latest available between 2010 and 2015.
11. World Bank (2016b).
12. UNESCO (2015).
13. UIS (2016).
14. UIS (2016).
15. World Bank (2016c).
16. UNESCO (2016).
17. Education Commission (2016).
18. UNESCO (2011).
19. UIS and UNESCO (2015).
20. UNESCO (2016).
21. UIS (2016).
22. UIS (2016).
23. World Bank (2014).
24. López-Calva and Patrinos (2015).
25. Alderman, Orazem, and Paterno (2001); Bailey and Dynarski (2011); Lincove (2015).
26. Education Commission (2016).
27. Lanjouw and Ravallion (1999).
28. Kremer and Holla (2009); Orazem and King (2008).
29. Education Commission (2016).
30. Education Commission (2016).
31. UNESCO (2016).
32. Kabeer (2015); Lewis and Lockheed (2006).
33. Filmer (2005).
34. Lockheed (2010).
35. World Bank (2007).
36. Kobiané and Bougma (2009).
37. Mete (2008).
38. Filmer (2008).
39. Becker (2009); Glewwe (2002); Hanushek and Woessmann (2008).
40. Akresh and others (2012).
41. Kremer and Holla (2009); Orazem and King (2008).
42. Deininger (2003).
43. Bentaouet-Kattan and Burnett (2004).
44. Burde and Linden (2012).
45. Duflo (2001).
46. Filmer (2007).

47. Behrman, Rosenzweig, and Taubman (1994); Jensen (2010); Nguyen (2008).
48. Banerjee and Duflo (2011); Murnane and Ganimian (2014).
49. Banerjee and Duflo (2011).
50. Dalton, Ghosal, and Mani (2016); Genicot and Ray (2014).
51. Glick and Sahn (2010); UNESCO and UNICEF (2015).
52. Bacolod and Ranjan (2008).
53. Akresh and others (2012).
54. Banerjee, Jacob, and Kremer (2000); Rivkin, Hanushek, and Kain (2005).
55. Alderman, Orazem, and Paterno (2001); Andrabi, Das, and Khwaja (2008); Tooley and Dixon (2007).
56. Hanushek, Lavy, and Hitomi (2006).
57. Andrabi, Das, and Khwaja (2008); He and Giuliano (2017).
58. Tooley and Dixon (2006).
59. Mukerji and Walton (2013).

References

Akresh, Richard, Emilie Bagby, Damien de Walque, and Harounan Kazianga. 2012. "Child Ability and Household Human Capital Investment Decisions in Burkina Faso." *Economic Development and Cultural Change* 61 (1): 157–86.

Alderman, Harold, Peter F. Orazem, and Elizabeth M. Paterno. 2001. "School Quality, School Cost, and the Public/Private School Choices of Low-Income Households in Pakistan." *Journal of Human Resources* 36 (2): 304–26.

Andrabi, Tahir, Jishnu Das, and Asim Ijaz Khwaja. 2008. "A Dime a Day: The Possibilities and Limits of Private Schooling in Pakistan." *Comparative Education Review* 52 (3): 329–55.

Bacolod, Marigee P., and Priya Ranjan. 2008. "Why Children Work, Attend School, or Stay Idle: The Roles of Ability and Household Wealth." *Economic Development and Cultural Change* 56 (4): 791–828.

Bailey, Martha J., and Susan M. Dynarski. 2011. "Inequality in Postsecondary Education." In *Whither Opportunity? Rising Inequality, Schools, and Children's Life Chances*, edited by Greg J. Duncan and Richard J. Murnane, 117–32. Chicago: Spencer Foundation; New York: Russell Sage Foundation.

Banerjee, Abhijit Vinayak, and Esther Duflo. 2011. *Poor Economics: A Radical Rethinking of the Way to Fight Global Poverty*. Philadelphia: Public Affairs.

Banerjee, Abhijit Vinayak, Suraj Jacob, and Michael Kremer. 2000. "Promoting School Participation in Rural Rajasthan: Results from Some Prospective Trials." With Jenny Lanjouw and Peter F. Lanjouw. Working paper, Massachusetts Institute of Technology, Cambridge, MA.

Barro, Robert J., and Jong-Wha Lee. 2013. "A New Data Set of Educational Attainment in the World, 1950–2010." *Journal of Development Economics* 104: 184–98.

Becker, Gary. 2009. *A Treatise on the Family (Enlarged Edition)*. Cambridge, MA: Harvard University Press.

Behrman, Jere R., Mark R. Rosenzweig, and Paul Taubman. 1994. "Endowments and the Allocation of Schooling in the Family and in the Marriage Market: The Twins Experiment." *Journal of Political Economy* 102 (6): 1131–74.

Bentaouet-Kattan, Raja, and Nicholas Burnett. 2004. "User Fees in Primary Education." Education for All Working Paper, World Bank, Washington, DC.

Burde, Dana, Ozen Guven, Jo Kelcey, Heddy Lahmann, and Khaled Al-Abbadi. 2015. "What Works to Promote Children's Educational Access, Quality of Learning, and Well-Being in Crisis-Affected Contexts." Education Rigorous Literature Review, U.K. Department for International Development, London.

Burde, Dana, and Leigh L. Linden. 2012. "The Effect of Village-Based Schools: Evidence from a Randomized Controlled Trial in Afghanistan." NBER Working Paper 18039, National Bureau of Economic Research, Cambridge, MA.

Commins, Stephen. 2017. "Fragility, Conflict and Violence." Background paper, WDR 2018, World Bank, Washington, DC.

Dalton, Patricio S., Sayantan Ghosal, and Anandi Mani. 2016. "Poverty and Aspirations Failure." *Economic Journal* 126 (590): 165–88.

Deininger, Klaus. 2003. "Does Cost of Schooling Affect Enrollment by the Poor? Universal Primary Education in Uganda." *Economics of Education Review* 22 (3): 291–305.

Duflo, Esther. 2001. "Schooling and Labor Market Consequences of School Construction in Indonesia: Evidence from an Unusual Policy Experiment." *American Economic Review* 91 (4): 795–813.

Education Commission. 2016. *The Learning Generation: Investing in Education for a Changing World*. New York: International Commission on Financing Global Education Opportunity.

Filmer, Deon. 2005. "Gender and Wealth Disparities in Schooling: Evidence from 44 Countries." *International Journal of Education Research* 43 (6): 351–69.

———. 2007. "If You Build It, Will They Come? School Availability and School Enrolment in 21 Poor Countries." *Journal of Development Studies* 43 (5): 901–28.

———. 2008. "Disability, Poverty, and Schooling in Developing Countries: Results from 14 Household Surveys." *World Bank Economic Review* 22 (1): 141–63.

———. 2016. "Education Attainment and Enrollment around the World: An International Database." World Bank, Washington, DC. http://go.worldbank.org/3GEREWJ0E0.

Genicot, Garance, and Debraj Ray. 2014. "Aspirations and Inequality." NBER Working Paper 19976, National Bureau of Economic Research, Cambridge, MA.

Glewwe, Paul W. 2002. "Schools and Skills in Developing Countries: Education Policies and Socioeconomic Outcomes." *Journal of Economic Literature* 40 (2): 436–82.

Glick, Peter, and David E. Sahn. 2010. "Early Academic Performance, Grade Repetition, and School Attainment in Senegal: A Panel Data Analysis." *World Bank Economic Review* 24 (1): 93–120.

Hanushek, Eric A., Victor Lavy, and Kohtaro Hitomi. 2006. "Do Students Care about School Quality? Determinants of Dropout Behavior in Developing Countries." NBER Working Paper 12737, National Bureau of Economic Research, Cambridge, MA.

Hanushek, Eric A., and Ludger Woessmann. 2008. "The Role of Cognitive Skills in Economic Development." *Journal of Economic Literature* 46 (3): 607–68.

He, Sylvia Y., and Genevieve Giuliano. 2017. "School Choice: Understanding the Trade-Off between Travel Distance and School Quality." *Transportation.* DOI 10.1007/s11116 -017-9773-3.

IRIN. 2003. "Interview with Nadya, Rural Teacher." Interview: Human Rights (October 13), IRIN, Geneva. http:// www.irinnews.org/report/20764/afghanistan-interview -nadya-rural-teacher.

Jensen, Robert. 2010. "The (Perceived) Returns to Education and the Demand for Schooling." *Quarterly Journal of Economics* 125 (2): 515–48.

Kabeer, Naila. 2015. "Tracking the Gender Politics of the Millennium Development Goals: Struggles for Interpretive Power in the International Development Agenda." *Third World Quarterly* 36 (2): 377–95.

Kelland, Zoe. 2016. "Education: 4 Children Explain How Education Has Changed Their Lives." *Global Citizen* (February 25), Global Poverty Project, New York. https://www .globalcitizen.org/en/content/4-children-explain-how -education-has-changed-their/.

Kobiané, Jean-François, and Moussa Bougma. 2009. *Burkina Faso, RGPH 2006, Rapport d'analyse du thème IV: Instruction, Alphabétisation et Scolarisation.* Ouagadougou, Burkina Faso: Institut National de la Statistique et de la Démographie.

Kremer, Michael R., and Alaka Holla. 2009. "Improving Education in the Developing World: What Have We Learned from Randomized Evaluations?" *Annual Review of Economics* 1: 513–45.

Lanjouw, Peter F., and Martin Ravallion. 1999. "Benefit Incidence, Public Spending Reforms, and the Timing of Program Capture." *World Bank Economic Review* 13 (2): 257–73.

Lee, Jong-Wha, and Hanol Lee. 2016. "Human Capital in the Long Run." *Journal of Development Economics* 122 (September): 147–69.

Lewis, Maureen A., and Marlaine E. Lockheed. 2006. *Inexcusable Absence: Why 60 Million Girls Still Aren't in School and What to Do about It.* Washington, DC: Center for Global Development.

Lincove, Jane Arnold. 2015. "Improving Identification of Demand-Side Obstacles to Schooling: Findings from Revealed and Stated Preference Models in Two SSA Countries." *World Development* 66 (February): 69–83.

Lockheed, Marlaine. 2010. *"Gender and Social Exclusion."* Paris: United Nations Educational, Scientific, and Cultural Organization.

López-Calva, Luis F., and Harry Anthony Patrinos. 2015. "Exploring the Differential Impact of Public Interventions on Indigenous People: Lessons from Mexico's Conditional Cash Transfer Program." *Journal of Human Development and Capabilities* 16 (3): 452–67.

Mete, Cem, ed. 2008. *Economic Implications of Chronic Illness and Disability in Eastern Europe and the Former Soviet Union.* Report 42851 rev. Washington, DC: World Bank.

Mukerji, Shobhini, and Michael Walton. 2013. "Learning the Right Lessons: Measurement, Experimentation and

the Need to Turn India's Right to Education Act Upside Down." In *India Infrastructure Report 2012: Private Sector in Education,* edited by IDFC Foundation, 109–26. New Delhi: Routledge.

Murnane, Richard J., and Alejandro Ganimian. 2014. "Improving Educational Outcomes in Developing Countries: Lessons from Rigorous Evaluations." NBER Working Paper 20284, National Bureau of Economic Research, Cambridge, MA.

NCCM (National Council for Childhood and Motherhood) and UNICEF (United Nations Children's Fund). 2015. *Violence against Children in Egypt: A Quantitative Survey and Qualitative Study in Cairo, Alexandria and Assiut.* Cairo: NCCM and UNICEF.

Nguyen, Trang. 2008. "Information, Role Models, and Perceived Returns to Education: Experimental Evidence from Madagascar." MIT working paper, Massachusetts Institute of Technology, Cambridge, MA.

Orazem, Peter F., and Elizabeth M. King. 2008. "Schooling in Developing Countries: The Roles of Supply, Demand, and Government Policy." In *Handbook of Development Economics,* Vol. 4, edited by T. Paul Schultz and John A. Strauss, 3475–559. Handbooks in Economics Series 9. Amsterdam: North-Holland.

Pritchett, Lant. 2013. *The Rebirth of Education: Schooling Ain't Learning.* Washington, DC: Center for Global Development; Baltimore: Brookings Institution Press.

Rivkin, Steven G., Eric A. Hanushek, and John F. Kain. 2005. "Teachers, Schools, and Academic Achievement." *Econometrica* 73 (2): 417–58.

Tooley, James, and Pauline Dixon. 2006. " 'De Facto' Privatisation of Education and the Poor: Implications of a Study from Sub-Saharan Africa and India." *Compare* 36 (4): 443–62.

———. 2007. "Private Education for Low-Income Families: Results from a Global Research Project." In *Private Schooling in Less Economically Developed Countries: Asian and African Perspectives,* edited by Prachi Srivastava and Geoffrey Walford, 15–39. Oxford Studies in Comparative Education Series. Oxford, U.K.: Symposium Books.

UIS (UNESCO Institute for Statistics). 2016. Education (database). Montreal. http://data.uis.unesco.org/.

UIS (UNESCO Institute for Statistics) and UNESCO (United Nations Educational, Scientific, and Cultural Organization). 2015. "A Growing Number of Children and Adolescents Are Out of School as Aid Fails to Meet the Mark." Policy Paper 22/Fact Sheet 31, UIS, Montreal; UNESCO, Paris.

———. 2016. "Leaving No One Behind: How Far on the Way to Universal Primary and Secondary Education?" Policy Paper 27/Fact Sheet 37, UIS, Montreal; UNESCO, Paris.

UNESCO (United Nations Educational, Scientific, and Cultural Organization). 2011. *EFA Global Monitoring Report 2011, The Hidden Crisis: Armed Conflict and Education.* Paris: UNESCO.

———. 2013. *Children Still Battling to Go to School.* Paris: UNESCO.

———. 2015. *EFA Global Monitoring Report 2015, Education for All 2000–2015: Achievements and Challenges.* Paris: UNESCO.

———. 2016. *Global Education Monitoring Report 2016, Education for People and Planet: Creating Sustainable Futures for All.* Paris: UNESCO.

UNESCO (United Nations Educational, Scientific, and Cultural Organization) and UNICEF (United Nations Children's Fund). 2015. "Fixing the Broken Promise of Education for All: Findings from the Global Initiative on Out-of-School Children." UNESCO Institute for Statistics, Montreal.

UNHCR (United Nations High Commissioner for Refugees). 2016. "Missing Out: Refugee Education in Crisis." Geneva. http://www.unhcr.org/57d9d01d0.

United Nations. 2015. *The Millennium Development Goals Report.* New York: United Nations.

World Bank. 2007. "People with Disabilities from India: From Commitments to Outcomes." Report 41585, World Bank, Washington, DC.

———. 2011a. "Learning for All: Investing in People's Knowledge and Skills to Promote Development; World Bank Group Education Strategy 2020." World Bank, Washington, DC.

———. 2011b. *World Development Report 2012: Gender Equality and Development.* Washington, DC: World Bank.

———. 2014. *Diagnostics and Policy Advice for Supporting Roma Inclusion in Romania.* Report 89621. Washington, DC: World Bank.

———. 2015. *World Development Report 2015: Mind, Society, and Behavior.* Washington, DC: World Bank.

———. 2016a. "Lebanon: Support to Reaching All Children with Education (Race 2) Program-for-Results." Program Appraisal Document, Report 108014-LB, International Development Association, World Bank, Washington, DC.

———. 2016b. "Reaching Girls, Transforming Lives." Snapshot, Education Global Practice, World Bank, Washington, DC.

———. 2016c. World Development Indicators (database). World Bank, Washington, DC. http://data.worldbank.org/data-catalog/world-development-indicators.

———. 2017. EdStats (database). Washington, DC. http://datatopics.worldbank.org/education/.

The biology of learning

Research has dramatically expanded our understanding of how the brain works—and therefore how people learn. The brain is very malleable: it adapts to its surroundings. This phenomenon is called *neuroplasticity*, which means the ability to learn is dictated not only by genetic endowments, but also by how genes interact with experiences and environmental inputs. Genes govern when specific brain circuits are formed, but experiences can turn those genes on or off, as well as determine which neural connections—synapses— survive over the life cycle. Environmental inputs such as caregivers' or teachers' stimulation, or nutrition, or violence shape the architecture of the brain from the formative years on.[1]

The brain is malleable throughout life, even if most brain development is completed by late adolescence or early adulthood. The fastest synaptic growth (thus malleability) occurs between the prenatal period and age 3 (1 million new neural connections a second), with growth then gradually slowing.[2] Because different parts of the brain develop at different times, and because neuroplasticity is highest during developmental stages, not all areas of the brain are equally malleable at the same time (figure S1.1). The periods of greatest plasticity, or "sensitive periods," whose length varies widely by brain region, are characterized by an initial stage in which the brain develops far more synapses than it needs. That stage is followed by synaptic pruning in which, to maximize efficiency in brain functionality, the neural connections used more often grow more permanent, while those used less are discarded to reach optimal levels of synapses (that is, the adult level of synapses in figure S1.1).[3] Because most sensitive periods take place early in life, a 3-year-old has, in total, far more brain synapses (about 1 quadrillion) than an adult (100–500 trillion).

Although different parts of the brain have different sensitive periods, their development is interdependent. Neural circuits (series of synapses) form sequentially and cumulatively: simpler networks develop first, more complex ones later. Just as with the construction of a house, the robustness of progressively more complex brain structures depends on the robustness of foundational ones. For example, the development of increasingly complex skills and functions builds on circuits formed earlier: linguistic development relies on visual and auditory functions that are dependent on neural circuits lower in the hierarchy, which are most malleable earlier in life; neural circuits that support higher cognitive functions, most malleable until as late as adolescence, build on sensorial stimuli as well as linguistic development.[4] Moreover, physical, sensory-motor, cognitive, and socioemotional development are interdependent, constituting a web of dynamic links that ultimately determine a person's ability to thrive. For example, higher levels of health promote learning; emotional security fosters child exploration, which leads to learning; and higher self-regulation reduces health risks.[5]

A range of enriching experiences leads to more complex synapses, but cumulative exposure to risk factors (such as neglect or violence) either eliminates synapses associated with healthy brain development, or it consolidates those associated with unhealthy development. Experiences affect the architecture of the brain in part because of the hormonal response they trigger. Hormones such as dopamine (triggered when the brain encounters novelty) stimulate information absorption,[6] whereas hormones such as cortisol (associated with stress as well as negative emotions) can shut off learning.[7]

Figure S1.1 Synapse development over the first 20 years of life

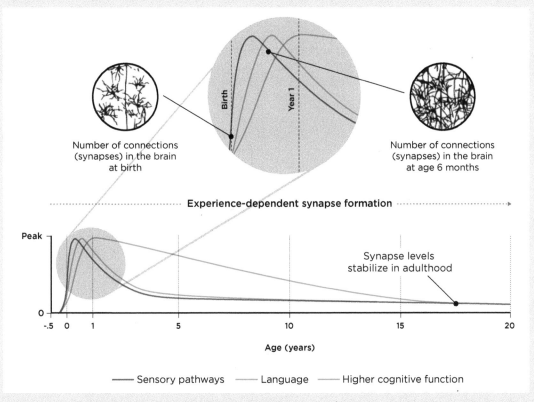

Number of connections (synapses) in the brain at birth

Birth

Year 1

Number of connections (synapses) in the brain at age 6 months

Experience-dependent synapse formation

Peak

Synapse levels stabilize in adulthood

0

-.5 0 1 5 10 15 20

Age (years)

—— Sensory pathways —— Language —— Higher cognitive function

Sources: Parker (2015); Thompson and Nelson (2001). Adapted with permission from Lawson Parker/National Geographic Creative; further permission required for reuse. Synapse drawings based on Golgi stain preparations (1939–1967) by J. L. Conel.

Note: The figure is a representation of synapse development for selected brain functions over the life course. Not drawn to scale.

The available insights on brain development have implications for investments in learning and skill formation. Because brain malleability is much greater earlier in life and brain development is sequential and cumulative, establishing sound foundations can lead to a virtuous cycle of skill acquisition. Moreover, investment in experiences and environmental inputs that foster learning at the very earliest stages increases the impact of investments at later stages: *skills beget skills.*[8] Weak foundations, by contrast, result in the accumulation of learning gaps, as well as higher risks of poor biological development that hamper skill formation—with repercussions over the life cycle (see chapter 5). Yet the optimal periods for cultivating higher-order cognitive and socioemotional skills occur throughout childhood, adolescence, and early adulthood.[9] Furthermore, the brain's ability to adapt to its environment, learn, and acquire new skills continues throughout life (that is, the experience-dependent synapse formation in figure S1.1). Thus investments in environmental inputs are needed well beyond early childhood to sustain learning along with skills development.

Interventions to improve learning and skills should place a greater emphasis on the areas of the brain that are the most malleable over the life course. Children's brains are most efficient at incorporating new information through exploration, play, and interactions with caring adults or peers. Because of this receptivity, preschool programs should concentrate on building foundational skills through developmentally appropriate program structures that emphasize play and interaction.[10] Although foundational cognitive skills become less malleable after age 10, some areas associated with socioemotional development remain highly malleable through early adulthood. Accordingly, interventions that aim to improve the school-to-work transition, as well as social inclusion for youth with weak foundational skills, may prove most effective when they emphasize socioemotional skills.[11]

Teaching strategies can deeply influence how students approach challenges in and out of school. Because the brain thrives when exposed to novelty, incorporating enriching opportunities for learning along with exploration may lead to better learning outcomes. Finally, intense stress or sustained nega-tive emotions—such as those associated with crises or acute deprivation, where multiple stressors coexist—interfere with the brain's ability to learn, retain, and use information. Extended exposure to stressors is toxic for biological systems, particularly for develop-ing brains, and it may impede disadvantaged children from flourishing in the classroom (see spotlight 2 on the effects of poverty). Consequently, programs that increase the availability of protective factors to shel-ter children from stress (such as nurturing care from at least one meaningful relationship that teaches chil-dren how to cope) can improve not only schooling, but also overall life outcomes.

Notes

1. Knudsen (2004).
2. Shonkoff and Phillips (2000).
3. Knudsen and others (2006).
4. Center on the Developing Child (2009).
5. Heckman (2007); Knudsen and others (2006).
6. Hong and Hikosaka (2011).
7. McEwen and Gianaros (2010).
8. Cunha and Heckman (2007); Cunha and others (2006).
9. Guerra, Modecki, and Cunningham (2014).
10. Whitebread and Bingham (2011).
11. Kautz and others (2014).

References

Center on the Developing Child. 2009. "In Brief: The Science of Early Childhood Development." Center on the Devel-oping Child, Harvard University, Cambridge, MA. http://developingchild.harvard.edu/resources/inbrief-science -of-ecd.

Cunha, Flavio, and James J. Heckman. 2007. "The Technology of Skill Formation." American Economic Review 97 (2): 31–47.

Cunha, Flavio, James J. Heckman, Lance Lochner, and Dimi-triy V. Masterov. 2006. "Interpreting the Evidence on Life Cycle Skill Formation." In Handbook of the Economics of Education, Vol. 1, edited by Eric A. Hanushek and Finis Welch, 697–812. Handbooks in Economics Series 26. Amsterdam: North-Holland.

Guerra, Nancy, Kathryn Modecki, and Wendy Cunningham. 2014. "Developing Social-Emotional Skills for the Labor Market: The Practice Model." Policy Research Working Paper 7123, World Bank, Washington, DC.

Heckman, James J. 2007. "The Economics, Technology, and Neuroscience of Human Capital Formation." Proceedings of the National Academy of Sciences 104 (33): 13250–55.

Hong, Simon, and Okihide Hikosaka. 2011. "Dopamine-Mediated Learning and Switching in Cortico-Striatal Circuit Explain Behavioral Changes in Reinforcement Learning." Frontiers in Behavioral Neuroscience 5 (15).

Kautz, Tim, James J. Heckman, Ron Diris, Bas Ter Weel, and Lex Borghans. 2014. "Fostering and Measuring Skills: Improving Cognitive and Non-cognitive Skills to Pro-mote Lifetime Success." NBER Working Paper 20749, National Bureau of Economic Research, Cambridge, MA.

Knudsen, Eric I. 2004. "Sensitive Periods in the Development of the Brain and Behavior." Journal of Cognitive Neuro-science 16 (8): 1412–25.

Knudsen, Eric I., James J. Heckman, Judy L. Cameron, and Jack P. Shankoff. 2006. "Economic, Neurobiological, and Behavioral Perspectives on Building America's Future Workforce." Proceedings of the National Academy of Sciences 103 (27): 10155–62.

McEwen, Bruce S., and Peter J. Gianaros. 2010. "Central Role of the Brain in Stress and Adaptation: Links to Socioeco-nomic Status, Health, and Disease." Annals of the New York Academy of Sciences 1186 (1): 190–222.

Parker, Lawson. 2015. "Neural Network." Graphic in Yudhijit Bhattacharjee, "Baby Brains: The First Year," National Geo-graphic, January. http://ngm.nationalgeographic.com/2015 /01/baby-brains/bhattacharjee-text.

Shonkoff, Jack P., and Deborah A. Phillips, eds. 2000. From Neurons to Neighborhoods: The Science of Early Childhood Development. Washington, DC: National Academies Press.

Thompson, Ross A., and Charles A. Nelson. 2001. "Develop-mental Science and the Media: Early Brain Develop-ment." American Psychologist 56 (1): 5–15.

Whitebread, David, and Sue Bingham. 2011. "School Readi-ness: A Critical Review of Perspectives and Evidence." TACTYC Occasional Paper 2, Association for the Profes-sional Development of Early Years Educators, University of Cambridge, Cambridge, U.K.

The many faces of the learning crisis

Rabia Nura, a 16-year-old girl from Kano in northern Nigeria, goes to school despite ever-present threats from Boko Haram. She is determined to become a doctor (Smith 2014). But 37 million African children will learn so little in school that they will not be much better off than kids who never attend school (van Fleet 2012).

The global schooling expansion hides another statistic: for millions, schooling is not producing enough learning. Learning outcomes in basic education are so low, in so many contexts, that the developing world is facing a learning crisis. In many low-income countries, learning levels are low in an absolute sense, while in many middle-income countries average learning levels remain far behind those in high-income countries. The learning crisis disproportionately affects children from poor households: they are far more likely to leave school without acquiring basic skills like literacy or numeracy. Ultimately, the learning crisis translates into severe shortcomings in the skills of the workforce.

For too many, learning isn't happening

In South Africa, 27 percent of 12-year-olds were enrolled in grade 6 but were functionally illiterate; in Zambia that share was 44 percent (Hungi and others 2010).

Globally, 125 million children are not acquiring functional literacy or numeracy, even after spending at least four years in school.[1] In Malawi and Zambia in 2012, more than 89 percent of students could not

read a single word by the end of grade 2.[2] In Guyana in 2008 (when the most recent data were collected), that share was 29 percent at the start of grade 3.[3] A similar picture emerges for numeracy. In rural India in 2016, less than 28 percent of students in grade 3 could master double-digit subtraction.[4] Emerging data on student achievement show that, for millions, schooling is producing little learning in crucial early grades.[5]

Millions complete primary education without acquiring the basic competencies needed for further learning. According to a 2014 regional assessment, among grade 6 students in West and Central Africa, nearly 58 percent are not sufficiently competent in reading or mathematics to continue schooling (figure 3.1).[6] Similarly, the most recently available regional assessment of grade 6 students in southern and East Africa (from 2007) shows that 37 percent are not competent in reading, and more than 60 percent are not competent in mathematics (figure 3.2).[7] This lack of basic competency is systematically lower for students from poorer families. In Honduras, half of the grade 6 students from the poorest quintile scored at the lowest reading competency level in a 2013 regional Latin American assessment; only 7 percent of those from the richest quintile did (figure 3.3).

Low-performing education systems are failing to meet their own curriculum standards (box 3.1).

Figure 3.1 Most grade 6 students in West and Central Africa are not sufficiently competent in reading or mathematics

Competency levels from PASEC (2014), by subject, participating countries

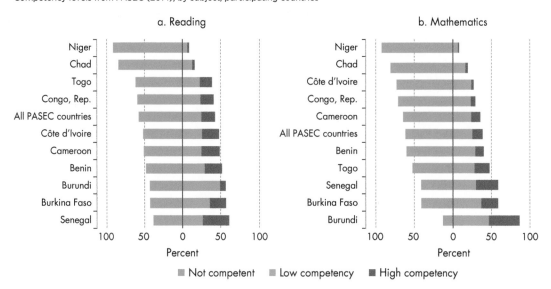

Source: WDR 2018 team, using data from Programme d'Analyse des Systèmes Éducatifs de la Confemen (PASEC 2015) and World Bank's World Development Indicators (World Bank 2016c). Data at http://bit.do/WDR2018-Fig_3-1.

Note: For the PASEC reading exam, "not competent" refers to levels 0–2 in the original coding, "low competency" to level 3, and "high competency" to level 4. For the PASEC mathematics exam, "not competent" refers to levels 0–1 in the original coding, "low competency" to level 2, and "high competency" to level 3.

Figure 3.2 Most grade 6 students in southern and East Africa are not sufficiently competent in mathematics, and several countries score poorly in reading as well

Competency levels from SACMEQ (2007), by subject, participating countries

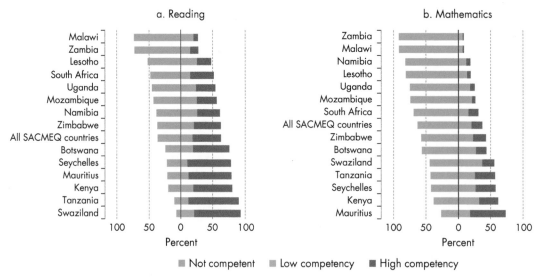

Source: WDR 2018 team, using data from Southern and Eastern Africa Consortium for Monitoring Educational Quality (SACMEQ 2007) and World Bank's World Development Indicators (World Bank 2016c). Data at http://bit.do/WDR2018-Fig_3-2.

Note: "Not competent" refers to levels 1–3 in the original SACMEQ coding, "low competency" to level 4, and "high competency" to levels 5–8.

Figure 3.3 Learning outcomes are substantially lower for poor children in Latin America

Competency levels for TERCE (2013) grade 6, by subject, for students in poorest and richest socioeconomic quintiles, participating countries

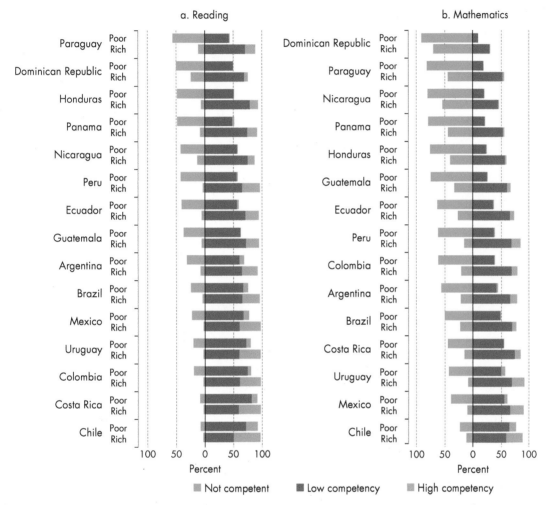

Source: WDR 2018 team, using data from Third Regional Comparative and Explanatory Study (TERCE), 2013 (UNESCO 2013). Data at http://bit.do /WDR2018-Fig_3-3.

Note: Socioeconomic quintiles are defined nationally. "Not competent" refers to level 1 in the original coding, "low competency" to levels 2–3, and "high competency" to level 4.

While test scores on international assessments may be worryingly low, similar patterns emerge when assessing students against national standards. In urban Pakistan in 2015, only three-fifths of grade 3 students could correctly perform a subtraction like 54 – 25; in rural areas only two-fifths could.[8] Across 51 countries, only about half of women who completed grade 6 (but no higher) could read a single sentence.[9] It is hard to imagine that these women are reaping the full potential economic or social returns from their years of schooling.

These low learning levels are not an inevitable by-product of rapidly expanding education. Starting in the 1950s, the Republic of Korea focused on ensuring quality primary education for the vast majority of its population before shifting to a similar emphasis on secondary and ultimately higher education—with excellent learning results. The success of this strategy shows it is possible to ensure quality education even while rapidly expanding schooling. The key ingredient is a persistent emphasis on the needs of the poor and disadvantaged.[10] The more recent experience

Box 3.1 Those who can't read by the end of grade 2 struggle to catch up

Illiteracy at the end of grade 2 has long-term consequences for two reasons. First, learning is cumulative. Education systems around the world expect students to acquire foundational skills such as reading by grades 1 or 2. By grade 3, students need to read to access their curriculum. Students who master these foundational skills early are at an advantage: skills from early grades are strongly positively associated with later school performance (see spotlight 1).[a] Children who cannot read by grade 3 fall behind and struggle to catch up, perhaps irreparably.[b]

Second, schools do not offer struggling students a chance to catch up. In many contexts, the pace of classroom instruction is determined by the need to cover an overly ambitious curriculum rather than by the pace of student learning.[c] This means teachers have no choice but to ignore students who are falling behind. In India and Kenya, for example, the curriculum has been designed for the elite.[d] Teachers and textbooks focus on advanced topics that are of little use in helping struggling students.[e] These students then fall even further behind—eventually so far that no learning whatsoever takes place.[f]

Source: WDR 2018 team.

a. Glick and Sahn (2010).
b. Muralidharan and Zieleniak (2013).
c. Pritchett and Beatty (2012).
d. Banerjee and Duflo (2012); Glewwe, Kremer, and Moulin (2009).
e. Pritchett and Beatty (2012).
f. Pritchett and Beatty (2012).

of Vietnam reinforces that lesson; it, too, has maintained education quality during rapid expansion by ensuring that disadvantaged students receive relatively equitable access to quality schooling.[11]

Even in middle-income countries, millions of students are lagging behind. In Brazil, internationally comparable assessments reveal that more than three-quarters of youth are reaching the age of 15 without being able to perform at the lowest level of competence on the Programme for International Student Assessment (PISA) tests.[12] Similarly, a third of students in Paraguay have only a basic grasp of reading skills ("reading for meaning") by grade 6.[13] These students are therefore ill-equipped to participate in their economy and society.[14] These numbers also show interesting gender-based differences (box 3.2).

However, some countries are doing better. Albania, Peru, and Portugal have made impressive progress in improving average student achievement relative to countries with similar incomes.[15] Latvia outperforms several countries in eastern Europe; Vietnam is a positive outlier in Southeast Asia. Although it is not always possible to clearly isolate the factors responsible for systemwide improvements in student learning, a policy focus on education quality appears to be important. For example, a major component of Vietnam's strong performance has been a convergence in school quality within the country. The share of schools that meet the national

standards of quality has steadily increased over the last 25 years.[16]

Low student achievement in some middle-income countries relative to their economic competitors signals a failure to live up to their own expectations. According to the leading international assessments of literacy and numeracy, the average student in low-income countries performs worse than 95 percent of the students in Organisation for Economic Co-operation and Development (OECD) countries—meaning that student would be singled out for remedial attention in a class in a wealthier country.[17] In Colombia, Indonesia, and Peru, student performance at the 75th percentile on the PISA math test is barely above that at the 25th percentile of the OECD average. In Algeria, the Dominican Republic, Kosovo, and Tunisia, it is below the 25th percentile of the OECD average (figure 3.4). The disparity between the average PISA score for Latin American countries and OECD countries is equivalent to over two full years of math education. Based on its rate of progress in average PISA scores from 2003 to 2015, it would take Tunisia over 180 years to reach the OECD average in math. This slow rate of improvement is especially problematic for middle-income countries trying to position themselves as important players in the global economic landscape.

The mapping between schooling and workforce skills varies dramatically across countries. For example, the working-age population in Colombia reaches

Box 3.2 Gender-based differences in learning depend on the subject

Data from internationally benchmarked tests show that boys lag behind girls on test averages. In all but 6 of the 72 countries and economies participating in the Programme for International Student Assessment (PISA), 15-year-old boys are more likely than girls of the same age to be low achievers on the composite average of the three subjects tested.[a] Whether on UNESCO's Third Regional Comparative and Explanatory Study (TERCE), the Scholastic Aptitude Test (SAT) in the United States, or an array of national assessments, girls outperform boys on total test averages in most countries and economies.[b]

Figure B3.2.1 Girls outperform boys on reading in all countries and economies, but boys typically do better in mathematics and science

Distribution across countries and economies of gap between mean score for girls and mean score for boys

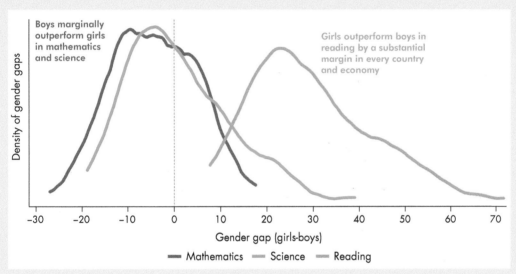

Source: WDR 2018 team, using data from Programme for International Student Assessment (PISA) collected in 2015 (OECD 2016a). Data at http://bit.do/WDR2018-Fig_B3-2-1.

Note: Distribution based on data from 72 countries and economies that participated in PISA 2015.

This higher average performance by girls masks important variations across subjects (figure B3.2.1). Girls consistently score higher in reading and writing; boys tend to perform better on mathematics and science in most countries and economies where these tests—and others, such as the Programme d'Analyse des Systèmes Éducatifs de la Confemen (PASEC) and Southern and Eastern Africa Consortium for Monitoring Educational Quality (SACMEQ)—are administered.[c]

Whereas girls and boys perform at equal levels in both mathematics and reading from kindergarten through grade 2, boys score slightly better in mathematics and worse in reading starting in grade 3. This subject-specific gender gap continues to grow through secondary school.[d]

But the mathematics and science gap in favor of boys may be shrinking. Results from the 2015 Trends in International Mathematics and Science Study (TIMSS) assessment were much more mixed than for previous years: in about half the countries and economies tested, there were no statistically significant differences in gender performance in these subjects.[e]

Source: WDR 2018 team.

a. OECD (2015).
b. TERCE: UNESCO (2016); SAT: Fryer and Levitt (2010); national assessments: Bharadwaj and others (2015); Cornwell, Mustard, and Van Parys (2013); Uwezo (2014, 2015).
c. Dickerson, McIntosh, and Valente (2015).
d. Fryer and Levitt (2010); Singh (2016); UNESCO (2016).
e. Mullis, Martin, and Loveless (2016).

Figure 3.4 Learning outcomes vary greatly across countries and economies—in several countries, the 75th percentile of PISA test takers performs below the 25th percentile of the OECD average

Performance of 25th, 50th, and 75th percentiles in 2015 PISA assessment, participating non-OECD economies and selected OECD economies

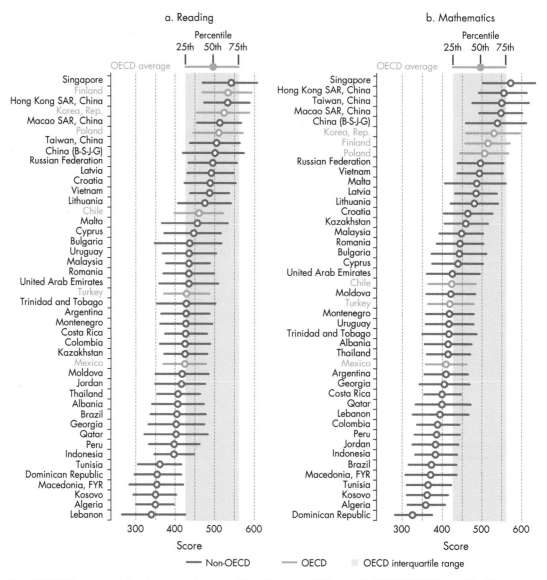

Source: WDR 2018 team, using data from Programme for International Student Assessment (PISA) collected in 2015 (OECD 2016a). Data at http://bit.do /WDR2018-Fig_3-4.

Note: PISA 2015 defines baseline levels of proficiency at a score of 407 for reading and 420 for mathematics. China (B-S-J-G) = China (Beijing-Shanghai-Jiangsu-Guangdong).

basic literacy proficiency by the lower secondary level, whereas the population of Bolivia needs six more years to attain even close to the same proficiency. Similarly, among 18- to 37-year-olds in Nigeria, only 19 percent of primary completers can read; in Tanzania, 80 percent can.[18]

In some countries, large proportions of "educated" working adults are effectively low-skilled. Nearly 80

percent of Ghana's working-age population and over 60 percent of Kenya's have just level 1 literacy or below—that is, their literacy proficiency is limited to understanding basic texts, but they are not able to integrate, evaluate, or interpret information from a variety of text materials (figure 3.5).[19] This contrasts with the average for high-income countries, where only 15 percent of the working-age population is at level 1 or below. Individuals

Figure 3.5 Middle-income countries tend to have lower rates of literacy proficiency than high-income countries (HICs)

Percentage of working-age population relative to minimal level of foundational literacy (2011–14)

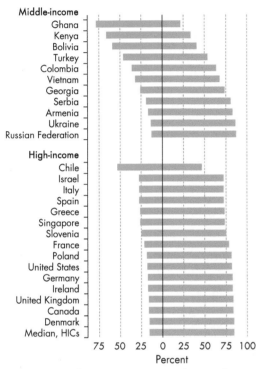

Literacy proficiency: ■ Low ■ Medium–High

Source: WDR 2018 team, using data from Programme for the International Assessment of Adult Competencies (PIAAC) collected between 2011 and 2014 (OECD 2016b, 2016c) and STEP Skills Measurement Program, 2011–14 (http://microdata.worldbank.org/index.php/catalog/step/about). Data at http://bit.do/WDR2018-Fig_3-5.

Note: Data are the latest available by country. PIAAC is representative at the national level for adults, ages 16–65. STEP is representative for urban populations, ages 15–64. Low proficiency is defined as level 1 and below on the assessments and indicates limited understanding of basic texts. Medium to high proficiency is defined as level 2 and above and indicates the ability to integrate, evaluate, and interpret information from a variety of text materials.

with low literacy proficiency are poorly prepared for the labor market, further education, and on-the-job training. In rapidly modernizing labor markets, most high-quality jobs—and even job training—require reading competency beyond minimum proficiency.[20]

Low skills continue to undermine career opportunities—and earnings—long after students leave school. Gaps in foundational skills affect not only the starting points of new workers entering the labor market but also their growth trajectories. Good foundational skills are essential for further skills accumulation. Worldwide, many students leave school without mastering the key cognitive skills that

underpin the development of higher-order cognitive, technical, and specialized skills. This skills deficit limits opportunities for further education or training because the capacity to make up for lost skills shrinks over time: second-chance adult education programs have limited success, and on-the-job training usually favors workers with more education and skills.[21] The consequences are dead-end jobs with relatively flat lifetime income growth for students leaving school with poor foundational skills, a situation that will only get worse as technology affects the demand for skills (see spotlight 5).

Estimates based on 41 countries where skill measures are available suggest that, globally, more than 2.1 billion of 4.6 billion working-age adults (ages 15–64) lack crucial foundational skills.[22] Among younger adults (ages 15–24), the number is 418 million. While these skills gaps exist in all countries, their magnitude is greater in developing countries (figure 3.6), with an estimated 92 million 15- to 24-year-olds affected in East Asia and Pacific, 120 million in South Asia, and 47 million in Latin America and the Caribbean. The implications, already profound, will be felt more acutely as jobs continue to shift from physical to more cognitive or socioemotional tasks. Progress in

Figure 3.6 Reading proficiency is low in many parts of the developing world

Estimated population ages 15–24, by country group and level of reading proficiency

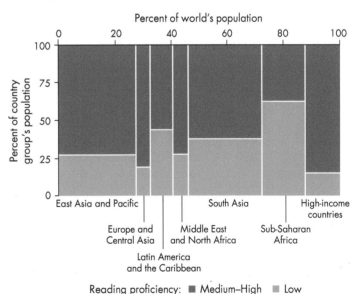

Reading proficiency: ■ Medium–High ■ Low

Source: WDR 2018 team, using data from Larson and Valerio (2017). Data at http://bit.do/WDR2018-Fig_3-6.

Note: Model predicts proportion of working-age adults scoring at level 1 or below on the PIAAC-STEP scale based on 41 countries; then projects to world population. PIAAC = Programme for the International Assessment of Adult Competencies; STEP = STEP Skills Measurement Program.

meeting global development goals will be limited as long as the dimensions of this problem, its origins, and its implications remain unrecognized.

Poor children learn the least, which hurts them the most

Learning deficits are largest for poor people. In nearly all countries, students' family backgrounds—including parental education, socioeconomic status, and conditions at home (such as access to books)—remain the largest predictors of learning outcomes (figure 3.7).[23] In France, the difference in science performance on the 2015 PISA between the richest and the poorest students was 115 points.[24] In Hungary, this difference was 202 points.[25] A 100-point difference in PISA scores is roughly equivalent to three years of schooling.[26]

The learning gap between rich and poor students grows as students move to higher grades. In South Africa, children in grade 3 from the poorest households are three years' worth of learning behind children from the richest households. This gap grows to four years' worth of learning by grade 9.[27] In Andhra Pradesh, India, testing the same set of students each year reveals that this gap increases every year after grade 2.[28]

Are learning gaps between rich and poor students simply a matter of household characteristics? Recent evidence suggests not. In Pakistan, rich-poor learning gaps are smaller than learning gaps between children from good and bad schools. In tests of English language, the difference in learning between a high-performing and a low-performing public school is 24 times the difference between children from poor and nonpoor backgrounds, after controlling for observed child-level differences.[29] Analysis of the 2009 PISA found that "the best performing school systems [in Canada; Finland; Hong Kong SAR, China; Japan; the Republic of Korea; and Shanghai, China] manage to provide high-quality education to all students" rather than only to students from privileged groups.[30]

What is causing the learning crisis?

A simple framework can be used to organize the proximate (or immediate) determinants of the learning crisis.[31] Proximate determinants are those most directly linked to learning outcomes and are themselves the result of deeper determinants. The framework identifies four proximate determinants: learner preparation, teacher skills and motivation, the availability of relevant inputs, and the school management and governance that bring these together (figure 3.8). This approach provides a simple tool for

Figure 3.7 Family socioeconomic status significantly affects students' average PISA scores

Distribution of scores on PISA 2015 across 69 countries (pooled) for students from the bottom and top quintiles of socioeconomic status, by subject

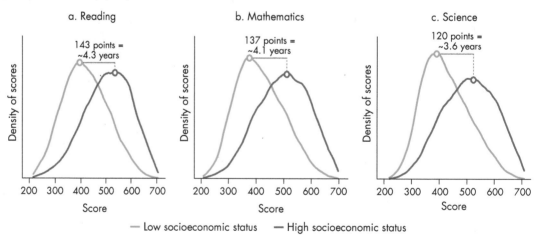

Source: WDR 2018 team, using data from Programme for International Student Assessment (PISA) collected in 2015 (OECD 2016a). Data at http://bit.do /WDR2018-Fig_3-7.

Note: A year of education is assumed to equal roughly 33 points on the PISA exam in this analysis, and the gap is calculated as the difference between modal averages of the top and bottom quintiles for each subject.

systematically integrating a wide range of actors and factors in determining the learning process.

Children do not arrive ready to learn

Children from disadvantaged backgrounds tend to exhibit learning deficits years before they start school; these deficits leave them ill-prepared for the demands of formal education. Acquiring foundational skills in early childhood is essential for learning, and robust early childhood development can launch children on higher learning trajectories (see spotlight 1). But for children from disadvantaged backgrounds, adversities begin to accumulate before they are born. Chronic malnutrition, illness, the cumulative effects of material deprivation, low parental support, and the unpredictable, chaotic, or violent environments that can be associated with poverty all undermine early childhood development learning (see spotlight 2).[32]

Steep socioeconomic gradients in cognitive, linguistic, and early literacy development help determine school outcomes. Language and cognitive gaps are evident before a child's first birthday.[33] In a wide range of countries, from the Democratic Republic of Congo to the United States,[34] children from poor households lag behind their more affluent peers by age 3, with gaps widening as children age (figure 3.9). Gaps in early

Figure 3.8 The proximate determinants of learning

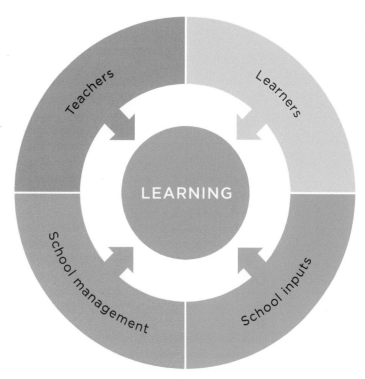

Source: WDR 2018 team.

Figure 3.9 Socioeconomic gaps in cognitive achievement grow with age—even in preschool years

Percentage of children (ages 3–5) who can recognize 10 letters of the alphabet, by wealth quintile, selected countries

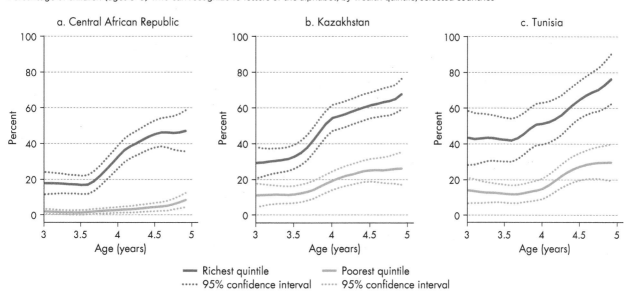

Source: WDR 2018 team, using data from Multiple Indicator Cluster Surveys (http://mics.unicef.org). Data are for 2010 for the Central African Republic, 2010–11 for Kazakhstan, and 2012 for Tunisia. Data at http://bit.do/WDR2018-Fig_3-9.

language and cognitive abilities are very alarming because they are important predictors of performance throughout school and into early adulthood.[35]

Poor foundations are evident in other crucial determinants of school performance such as socioemotional and executive functions. Socioemotional skills include teamwork, motivation, and confidence, while executive functions (which rely on both socioemotional and cognitive skills) include planning, organizing, implementing, and multitasking, among others.[36] The evidence on these developmental dimensions is more limited because of measurement difficulties. Still, gaps in working memory and sustained attention (executive functions) for poorer children are evident starting at 6 months of age and through the preschool years.[37] Even in Madagascar, a very poor country, wealth gradients are apparent after accounting for maternal education and household inputs—gaps that widen with age.[38] There are wealth gradients of socioemotional development as well. One in every three children between the ages of 3 and 4 in a range of countries fails to meet basic milestones in socioemotional development, such as the ability to control aggressive behaviors, avoid distractions, and get along with peers.[39]

Because learning is cumulative and skills beget skills (see spotlight 1), the cognitive and socioemotional developmental gaps that emerge at young ages worsen over time. So do learning gaps: poor developmental foundations and lower preschool skills mean disadvantaged children arrive at school late and unprepared to benefit fully from learning opportunities. As these children get older, it becomes harder and harder for them to break out of lower learning trajectories.

Teachers often lack the needed skills and motivation

Teachers are the most important determinant of student learning. Estimates suggest that in the United States, students with great teachers advance 1.5 grade levels or more over a single school year, whereas those with a poor teacher advance just 0.5 grade levels.[40] Across kindergartens in Ecuador, differences in learning outcomes for language, math, and executive function are strongly associated with differences in teacher behaviors and practices.[41] No other school-level factor has an impact nearly this large on student achievement.[42]

But high-quality teachers are in short supply in low-income countries.[43] Less than 25 percent of Sub-Saharan Africans currently complete secondary education.[44] Thus there are simply not enough qualified candidates to meet the growing demand for teachers. In some countries, teacher training colleges have had to lower their entry requirements to ensure an adequate supply of teachers. These colleges also push trainees through the programs in two years or less to try to fill the need for primary school teachers.[45] In Latin America, there is evidence that candidates entering the teaching profession are academically weaker than the pool of higher education students. Fifteen-year-olds who identified themselves as interested in a teaching career had much lower PISA math scores than students interested in engineering in every country in the region, and they scored below the national average in nearly all countries.[46] Teachers may also not always have the necessary pedagogical skills; classroom observations in six countries in Sub-Saharan Africa found that few public primary school teachers are able to assess children's abilities and evaluate students' progress, and few engage in the practices typically associated with good teaching.[47]

As a result, teachers often do not have sufficient mastery of concepts they are expected to teach. In several Sub-Saharan countries, the average teacher does not perform much better on reading tests than the highest-performing grade 6 students.[48] Across six countries in the region, 40 percent of primary school teachers are not as knowledgeable as their students should be (table 3.1).[49] In Bihar, India, only 10.5 percent

Table 3.1 Few teachers reach minimum thresholds of performance on knowledge assessments

Percentage of teachers who score at least 80 percent on a test of grade 4 material

Subject	Average	Kenya (2012)	Mozambique (2014)	Nigeria (2013)[a]	Tanzania (2014)	Togo (2013)	Uganda (2013)
Equivalent to student language curriculum	61	66	77	24	41	54	90
Equivalent to student mathematics curriculum	56	82	26	31	62	24	55

Source: Bold and others (2017).

a. Data based on four states in Nigeria.

Figure 3.10 A lot of official teaching time is lost

Percentage of time officially allocated to schooling that a teacher is scheduled to teach, is present in the classroom, and is actually teaching

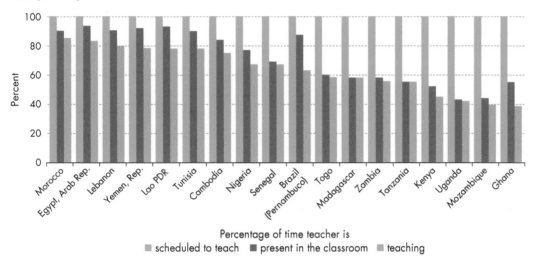

Percentage of time teacher is
■ scheduled to teach ■ present in the classroom ■ teaching

Sources: WDR 2018 team, using data from Abadzi (2009): Brazil (Pernambuco state), Ghana, Morocco, and Tunisia; Benveniste, Marshall, and Araujo (2008): Cambodia; Benveniste, Marshall, and Santibañez (2007): Lao People's Democratic Republic; Millot and Lane (2002): Arab Republic of Egypt, Lebanon, and Republic of Yemen; World Bank (2016a): Madagascar; World Bank (2016b): Zambia; World Bank's Service Delivery Indicators, 2012–13 (http://www.worldbank.org/sdi): Kenya, Mozambique, Nigeria, Senegal, Tanzania, Togo, and Uganda. Data at http://bit.do/WDR2018-Fig_3-10.

Note: For Brazil, Cambodia, Ghana, Lao PDR, Senegal, Tanzania, and Tunisia, data include public schools. For all other countries, data include both public and private schools.

of tested public school teachers are able to solve a three-digit by one-digit division problem and show the steps correctly.[50]

Many developing countries suffer significant losses of instructional time (figure 3.10). Unannounced visits to primary schools in six countries found that in public schools, on average, about one teacher in five was absent on a typical school day.[51] Even when teachers are present in school, they may not be teaching. In seven Sub-Saharan countries, students receive only about two and a half hours of teaching a day—less than half the scheduled time.[52] Teacher absenteeism and low time on task when in class—combined with other factors such as informal school closures or student absenteeism—mean that only about one-third of the total instructional time is used in Ethiopia, Ghana, and Guatemala.[53] Even in middle-income countries in Latin America, about 20 percent of potential instructional time is lost—the equivalent of one less day of instruction a week.[54] There are many reasons for this loss of instructional time, including poor training and other demands on teachers, and some teachers may perceive it as justified (box 3.3). But whatever the cause, lost teaching time reduces student learning.

This problem is particularly concerning because the bulk of national education budgets goes to teacher salaries. In Latin America and the Caribbean, teacher salaries absorb nearly 4 percent of the regional gross domestic product (GDP).[55] Staff compensation accounts for 80 percent of public spending on education in some countries (figure 3.11). If one in five government primary school teachers is absent from school, developing countries are wasting considerable resources.

According to recent data on 1,300 villages in India, nearly 24 percent of teachers were absent during unannounced visits, at an associated fiscal cost of US$1.5 billion a year.[56] Reducing absenteeism in these schools would be over 10 times more cost-effective at increasing student-teacher contact time than hiring additional teachers.

School management skills are low

The effective management of schools relies on capacity and autonomy for decision making at the school level, which are often lacking. Higher management quality[57] and school leadership are associated with better education outcomes.[58] Yet in many developing countries effective school management is missing

Box 3.3 Teachers may perceive low effort as being justified

Teachers across a variety of countries justify certain types of service delivery gaps. Consider teacher perceptions of two basic aspects of teacher performance, based on teacher surveys administered in 2017 (figure B3.3.1).

Figure B3.3.1 Teachers' beliefs about their effort and its effects

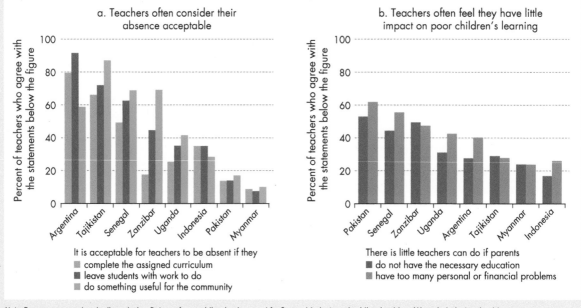

Note: Responses are not mutually exclusive. Data are from public schools, except for Senegal (private and public schools) and Uganda (private schools).

Source: Sabarwal and Abu-Jawdeh (2017). Data at http://bit.do/WDR2018-Fig_B3-3-1.

Figure 3.11 Staff compensation consumes the largest share of resources available for public education

Staff compensation as percentage of total expenditure on public education, by country and income group

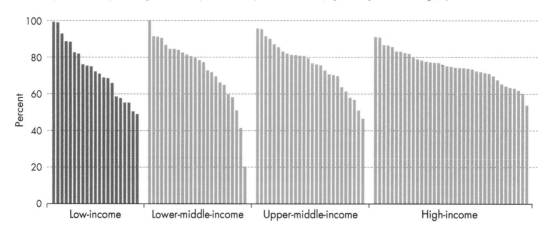

Source: WDR 2018 team, using data from UNESCO Institute for Statistics (UIS 2017). Data at http://bit.do/WDR2018-Fig_3-11.

Note: Figure includes all countries with populations of over 500,000 for which spending data are available at the primary or secondary levels. Latest data available.

Figure 3.12 Management capacity is low in schools in low- and middle-income countries

Distribution of management scores by sector, participating countries

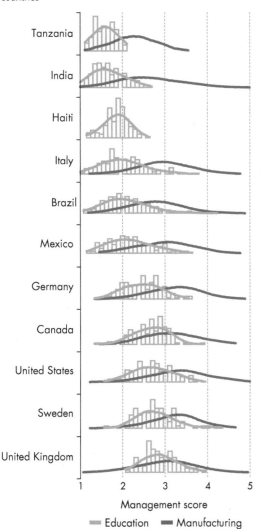

Management score

— Education   — Manufacturing

Sources: Bloom and others (2014, 2015); Lemos and Scur (2016), with updates. Data at http://bit.do/WDR2018-Fig_3-12.

Note: The underlying distributions for the education data are shown as bars; for both sectors, the smoothed distributions are shown as curves. The indexes are constructed from the nine items that are comparable across sectors. Data on manufacturing are not available for Haiti.

(figure 3.12). Moreover, lack of autonomy prevents head teachers or school management committees from improving service delivery.[59] Even when the requisite autonomy exists, it may not be enough. Schools may choose not to exercise the provided authority or may lack the will and capacity to do so.[60] For example, a survey in Uganda found that only 57 percent of school management committee members reported having read their committee's handbook.[61] In Uttar Pradesh, India, a quarter of village education committee members surveyed did not even know they were members.[62]

School inputs have not kept pace

In many developing countries, the expansion of inputs has not kept pace with the explosion in enrollments. Governments have built classrooms and recruited teachers at unprecedented levels. But these efforts may not have kept up with rising enrollments, leading to a decline in per capita input availability. In Malawi between 2008 and 2015, as the gross enrollment rate in primary schools increased from 131 to 146 percent, the average number of students per class increased from 85 to 126.[63] Uganda introduced universal primary education in 1997. The 68 percent increase in primary school enrollment that followed increased the student-teacher ratio from 38:1 in 1996 to 80:1 in 1997 and the student-to-classroom ratio from 68:1 in 1996 to 105:1 in 1997.[64]

* * *

The learning crisis is real, but too often education systems operate as if it is not. Many policy makers do not realize how low learning levels are. Others do not acknowledge them or simply equate low learning with low resources. Still, there are reasons for optimism. First, learning is increasingly in the spotlight. Second, learning metrics are generating irrefutable evidence of the learning crisis, thereby creating pressure for action (see chapter 4).[65] Third, promising new insights on how to tackle the crisis are becoming available (see parts III and IV of this Report).

Notes

1. UNESCO (2014).
2. RTI International (2015).
3. Gove and Cvelich (2011).
4. ASER Centre (2017).
5. Muralidharan and Zieleniak (2013); Pritchett (2013).
6. Programme d'Analyse des Systèmes Éducatifs de la Confemen (PASEC) results for grade 6 students in 10 francophone countries in 2015 (PASEC 2015).
7. Southern and Eastern Africa Consortium for Monitoring Educational Quality (SACMEQ) results for grade 6 students in 15 countries in 2007 (Hungi 2010).
8. ASER Pakistan (2015a, 2015b).
9. Pritchett and Sandefur (2017).
10. Lee and Hong (2016).
11. Dang and Glewwe (2017).
12. Filmer, Hasan, and Pritchett (2006).

13. UNESCO (2015).
14. Filmer, Hasan, and Pritchett (2006).
15. OECD (2016a).
16. Dang and Glewwe (2017).
17. Crouch and Gove (2011), which is based on the Progress in International Reading Literacy Study (PIRLS) and Trends in International Mathematics and Science Study (TIMSS).
18. Kaffenberger and Pritchett (2017).
19. The literacy skills proficiency construct covers a range of skills from the decoding of written words and sentences to the comprehension, interpretation, and evaluation of complex texts. It takes into account workplace, personal, society, and community. To facilitate the interpretation of individual scores, described proficiency scales are available to articulate the requisite skills and knowledge needed to perform specific tasks along a 500-point scale. The tasks move progressively in complexity from level 0 to level 5. See ETS (2014) and OECD (2016c).
20. Desjardins and Rubenson (2011); OECD (2016b).
21. di Gropello (2011); Fouarge, Schils, and de Grip (2013); Heckman (2000); O'Connell and Jungblut (2008); Windisch (2015).
22. WDR 2018 team estimates using literacy proficiency as a proxy for foundational skills.
23. Bruns and Luque (2015); Filmer and Pritchett (1999).
24. OECD (2016a).
25. OECD (2016a).
26. OECD (2016a).
27. Spaull and Kotze (2015).
28. Muralidharan and Zieleniak (2013).
29. Das, Pandey, and Zajonc (2006).
30. OECD (2010).
31. Hanushek (1979).
32. Lupien and others (2000); McCoy and others (2016); Walker and others (2007).
33. Rubio-Codina and others (2015).
34. Countries where these outcomes have been evaluated include Cambodia, Chile, the Democratic Republic of Congo, Ethiopia, India, Madagascar, Mozambique, Nigeria, Sierra Leone, Togo, the United States, and Vietnam.
35. Fernald, Marchman, and Weisleder (2013).
36. Galasso, Weber, and Fernald (2017); McCoy and others (2016).
37. Fernald and others (2012); Lipina and others (2005); Noble, Norman, and Farah (2005).
38. Galasso, Weber, and Fernald (2017).
39. McCoy and others (2016).
40. Hanushek (1992); Rockoff (2004).
41. Araujo and others (2016).
42. Bruns and Luque (2015).
43. UIS (2006).
44. UNESCO Institute for Statistics, 2016 (UIS 2017).
45. Mulkeen (2010).
46. Bruns and Luque (2015).
47. Bold and others (2017).
48. UIS (2006).
49. Bold and others (2017).
50. Sinha, Banerji, and Wadhwa (2016).
51. Chaudhury and others (2006).
52. Bold and others (2017).
53. Informal school closures may stem from strikes, inclement weather, or ad hoc holidays. For Ethiopia and Guatemala see EQUIP2 (2010); for Ghana, see Abadzi (2009).
54. Bruns and Luque (2015).
55. Bruns and Luque (2015).
56. Muralidharan and others (2017).
57. Bloom and others (2015); Fryer (2017).
58. Robinson, Lloyd, and Rowe (2008).
59. Bruns, Filmer, and Patrinos (2011); Orazem, Glewwe, and Patrinos (2007).
60. King, Özler, and Rawlings (1999).
61. Najjumba, Habyarimana, and Bunjo (2013).
62. Banerjee and others (2010).
63. MoEST (2008, 2015); World Bank (2016c). Gross enrollment includes students whose age exceeds the official age group for a particular education level, so the rate may exceed 100 percent.
64. Bentaouet-Kattan (2006).
65. The World Bank's 2020 sector strategy and the U.K. Department for International Development's 2010 strategy are learning for all; the U.S. Agency for International Development's strategy is opportunity through learning; and AusAID is also adopting learning goals.

References

Abadzi, Helen. 2009. "Instructional Time Loss in Developing Countries: Concepts, Measurement, and Implications." *World Bank Research Observer* 24 (2): 267–90.

Araujo, María Caridad, Pedro Carneiro, Yyannú Cruz-Aguayo, and Norbert R. Schady. 2016. "Teacher Quality and Learning Outcomes in Kindergarten." *Quarterly Journal of Economics* 131 (3): 1415–53.

ASER Centre. 2017. *Annual Status of Education Report (Rural)*. New Delhi: ASER Centre.

ASER Pakistan. 2015a. "Annual Status of Education Report: ASER Pakistan 2015 National (Rural)." Lahore, Pakistan: South Asian Forum for Education Development.

———. 2015b. "Annual Status of Education Report: ASER Pakistan 2015 National (Urban)." Lahore, Pakistan: South Asian Forum for Education Development.

Banerjee, Abhijit Vinayak, Rukmini Banerji, Esther Duflo, Rachel Glennerster, and Stuti Khemani. 2010. "Pitfalls of Participatory Programs: Evidence from a Randomized Evaluation in Education in India." *American Economic Journal: Economic Policy* 2 (1): 1–30.

Banerjee, Abhijit Vinayak, and Esther Duflo. 2012. *Poor Economics: A Radical Rethinking of the Way to Fight Global Poverty*. New York: PublicAffairs.

Bentaouet-Kattan, Raja. 2006. "Implementation of Free Basic Education Policy." Education Working Paper 7 (December), World Bank, Washington, DC.

Benveniste, Luis, Jeffrey Marshall, and M. Caridad Araujo. 2008. "Teaching in Cambodia." Human Development Sector, East Asia and the Pacific Region, World Bank, Washington, DC, and Ministry of Education, Youth and Sport, Phnom Penh, Cambodia.

Benveniste, Luis, Jeffrey Marshall, and Lucrecia Santibañez. 2007. "Teaching in the Lao PDR." Human Development

Sector, East Asia and the Pacific Region, World Bank, Washington, DC, and Ministry of Education, Vientiane, Lao People's Democratic Republic.

Bharadwaj, Prashant, Giacomo De Giorgi, David R. Hansen, and Christopher Neilson. 2015. "The Gender Gap in Mathematics: Evidence from a Middle-Income Country." Staff Report 721 (March 2), Federal Reserve Bank of New York, New York.

Bloom, Nicholas, Renata Lemos, Raffaella Sadun, Daniela Scur, and John Van Reenen. 2014. "JEEA-FBBVA Lecture 2013: The New Empirical Economics of Management." *Journal of the European Economic Association* 12 (4): 835–76.

Bloom, Nicholas, Renata Lemos, Raffaella Sadun, and John Van Reenen. 2015. "Does Management Matter in Schools?" *Economic Journal* 125 (584): 647–74.

Bold, Tessa, Deon Filmer, Gayle Martin, Ezequiel Molina, Brian Stacy, Christophe Rockmore, Jakob Svensson, et al. 2017. "What Do Teachers Know and Do? Does It Matter? Evidence from Primary Schools in Africa." Policy Research Working Paper 7956, World Bank, Washington, DC.

Bruns, Barbara, Deon Filmer, and Harry Anthony Patrinos. 2011. *Making Schools Work: New Evidence on Accountability Reforms.* Human Development Perspectives Series. Washington, DC: World Bank.

Bruns, Barbara, and Javier Luque. 2015. *Great Teachers: How to Raise Student Learning in Latin America and the Caribbean.* With Soledad De Gregorio, David K. Evans, Marco Fernández, Martin Moreno, Jessica Rodriguez, Guillermo Toral, and Noah Yarrow. Latin American Development Forum Series. Washington, DC: World Bank.

Chaudhury, Nazmul, Jeffrey Hammer, Michael R. Kremer, Karthik Muralidharan, and F. Halsey Rogers. 2006. "Missing in Action: Teacher and Health Worker Absence in Developing Countries." *Journal of Economic Perspectives* 20 (1): 91–116.

Cornwell, Christopher, David B. Mustard, and Jessica Van Parys. 2013. "Noncognitive Skills and the Gender Disparities in Test Scores and Teacher Assessments: Evidence from Primary School." *Journal of Human Resources* 48 (1): 236–64.

Crouch, Luis, and Amber K. Gove. 2011. "Leaps or One Step at a Time: Skirting or Helping Engage the Debate? The Case of Reading." In *Policy Debates in Comparative, International, and Development Education*, edited by John N. Hawkins and W. James Jacob, 155–74. New York: Springer.

Dang, Hai-Anh H., and Paul W. Glewwe. 2017. "Well Begun, but Aiming Higher: A Review of Vietnam's Education Trends in the Past 20 Years and Emerging Challenges." Policy Research Working Paper 8112, World Bank, Washington, DC.

Das, Jishnu, Priyanka Pandey, and Tristan Zajonc. 2006. "Learning Levels and Gaps in Pakistan." Policy Research Working Paper 4067, World Bank, Washington, DC.

Desjardins, Richard, and Kjell Rubenson. 2011. "An Analysis of Skill Mismatch Using Direct Measures of Skills." OECD Education Working Paper 63, Organisation for Economic Co-operation and Development, Paris.

Dickerson, Andy, Steven McIntosh, and Christine Valente. 2015. "Do the Maths: An Analysis of the Gender Gap in Mathematics in Africa." *Economics of Education Review* 46: 1–22.

di Gropello, Emanuela. 2011. *Skills for the Labor Market in Indonesia: Trends in Demand, Gaps, and Supply.* With Aurelien Kruse and Prateek Tandon. Directions in Development: Human Development Series. Washington, DC: World Bank.

EQUIP2 (Educational Quality Improvement Program 2). 2010. "Using Opportunity to Learn and Early Grade Reading Fluency to Measure School Effectiveness in Ethiopia, Guatemala, Honduras, and Nepal." Working Paper, Educational Policy, Systems Development, and Management, U.S. Agency for International Development, Washington, DC.

ETS (Educational Testing Service). 2014. "A Guide to Understanding the Literacy Assessment of the STEP Skills Measurement Surveys." ETS, Princeton, NJ.

Fernald, Anne, Virginia A. Marchman, and Adriana Weisleder. 2013. "SES Differences in Language Processing Skill and Vocabulary Are Evident at 18 Months." *Developmental Science* 16 (2): 234–48.

Fernald, Lia C. H., Patricia Kariger, Melissa Hidrobo, and Paul J. Gertler. 2012. "Socioeconomic Gradients in Child Development in Very Young Children: Evidence from India, Indonesia, Peru, and Senegal." *Proceedings of the National Academy of Sciences* 109 (Supplement 2): 17273–80.

Filmer, Deon, Amer Hasan, and Lant Pritchett. 2006. "A Millennium Learning Goal: Measuring Real Progress in Education." Working Paper 97 (August), Center for Global Development, Washington, DC.

Filmer, Deon, and Lant Pritchett. 1999. "The Effect of Household Wealth on Educational Attainment: Evidence from 35 Countries." *Population and Development Review* 25 (1): 85–120.

Fouarge, Didier, Trudie Schils, and Andries de Grip. 2013. "Why Do Low-Educated Workers Invest Less in Further Training?" *Applied Economics* 45 (18): 2587–601.

Fryer, Roland G., Jr. 2017. "Management and Student Achievement: Evidence from a Randomized Field Experiment." NBER Working Paper 23437, National Bureau of Economic Research, Cambridge, MA.

Fryer, Roland G., Jr., and Steven D. Levitt. 2010. "An Empirical Analysis of the Gender Gap in Mathematics." *American Economic Journal: Applied Economics* 2 (2): 210–40.

Galasso, Emanuela, Ann Weber, and Lia C. H. Fernald. 2017. "Dynamics of Child Development: Analysis of a Longitudinal Cohort in a Very Low Income Country." Policy Research Working Paper 7973, World Bank, Washington, DC.

Glewwe, Paul W., Michael R. Kremer, and Sylvie Moulin. 2009. "Many Children Left Behind? Textbooks and Test Scores in Kenya." *American Economic Journal: Applied Economics* 1 (1): 112–35.

Glick, Peter, and David E. Sahn. 2010. "Early Academic Performance, Grade Repetition, and School Attainment in Senegal: A Panel Data Analysis." *World Bank Economic Review* 24 (1): 93–120.

Gove, Amber, and Peter Cvelich. 2011. "Early Reading, Igniting Education for All: A Report by the Early Grade

Learning Community of Practice." Rev. ed. Research Triangle Institute, Research Triangle Park, NC.

Hanushek, Eric A. 1979. "Conceptual and Empirical Issues in the Estimation of Educational Production Functions." *Journal of Human Resources* 14 (3): 351–88.

———. 1992. "The Trade-Off between Child Quantity and Quality." *Journal of Political Economy* 100 (1): 84–117.

Heckman, James J. 2000. "Policies to Foster Human Capital." *Research in Economics* 54 (1): 3–56.

Hungi, Njora. 2010. "What Are the Levels and Trends in Grade Repetition?" SACMEQ Policy Issues 5 (September), Southern and Eastern Africa Consortium for Monitoring Educational Quality, Paris.

Hungi, Njora, Demus Makuwa, Kenneth Ross, Mioko Saito, Stephanie Dolata, Frank van Cappelle, Laura Paviot, et al. 2010. "SACMEQ III Project Results: Pupil Achievement Levels in Reading and Mathematics." Working Document Number 1, Southern and Eastern Africa Consortium for Monitoring Educational Quality, Paris.

Kaffenberger, Michelle, and Lant Pritchett. 2017. "More School or More Learning? Evidence from Learning Profiles from the Financial Inclusion Insights Data." Background paper, World Bank, Washington, DC.

King, Elizabeth M., Berk Özler, and Laura B. Rawlings. 1999. "Nicaragua's School Autonomy Reform: Fact or Fiction?" Working Paper 19, Impact Evaluation of Education Reforms, World Bank, Washington, DC.

Larson, Bradley, and Alexandria Valerio. 2017. "Estimating the Stock of Skills around the World: A Technical Note." World Bank, Washington, DC.

Lee, Ju-Ho, and Song-Chang Hong. 2016. "Accumulating Human Capital for Sustainable Development in Korea." Paper presented at the Korea Development Institute's International Conference on More and Better Investment in Global Education, Seoul, June 14.

Lemos, Renata, and Daniela Scur. 2016. "Developing Management: An Expanded Evaluation Tool for Developing Countries." RISE Working Paper 16/007, Research on Improving Systems of Education, Blavatnik School of Government, Oxford University, Oxford, U.K.

Lipina, Sebastián J., María I. Martelli, Beatriz Vuelta, and Jorge A. Colombo. 2005. "Performance on the A-Not-B Task of Argentinean Infants from Unsatisfied and Satisfied Basic Needs Homes." *Interamerican Journal of Psychology* 39 (1): 46–60.

Lupien, Sonia J., Suzanne King, Michael J. Meaney, and Bruce S. McEwen. 2000. "Child's Stress Hormone Levels Correlate with Mother's Socioeconomic Status and Depressive State." *Biological Psychiatry* 48 (10): 976–80.

McCoy, Dana Charles, Evan D. Peet, Majid Ezzati, Goodarz Danaei, Maureen M. Black, Christopher R. Sudfeld, Wafaie Fawzi, et al. 2016. "Early Childhood Developmental Status in Low- and Middle-Income Countries: National, Regional, and Global Prevalence Estimates Using Predictive Modeling." *PLOS Medicine* 13 (6): e1002034.

Millot, Benoît, and Julia Lane. 2002. "The Efficient Use of Time in Education." *Education Economics* 10 (2): 209–28.

MoEST (Malawi, Ministry of Education, Science, and Technology). 2008. "Education Management Information System." Report, MoEST, Lilongwe, Malawi.

———. 2015. "Education Management Information System." Report, MoEST, Lilongwe, Malawi.

Mulkeen, Aidan G. 2010. *Teachers in Anglophone Africa: Issues in Teacher Supply, Training, and Management.* Development Practice in Education Series. Washington, DC: World Bank.

Mullis, Ina V. S., Michael O. Martin, and Tom Loveless. 2016. "20 Years of TIMSS: International Trends in Mathematics and Science Achievement, Curriculum, and Instruction." International Association for the Evaluation of Educational Achievement, TIMSS and PIRLS International Study Center, Lynch School of Education, Boston College, Chestnut Hill, MA.

Muralidharan, Karthik, Jishnu Das, Alaka Holla, and Aakash Mohpal. 2017. "The Fiscal Cost of Weak Governance: Evidence from Teacher Absence in India." *Journal of Public Economics* 145: 116–35.

Muralidharan, Karthik, and Yendrick Zieleniak. 2013. "Measuring Learning Trajectories in Developing Countries with Longitudinal Data and Item Response Theory." Paper presented at the Young Lives Conference, Oxford University, Oxford, U.K., July 8–9.

Najjumba, Innocent Mulindwa, James Habyarimana, and Charles Lwanga Bunjo. 2013. *School-Based Management: Policy and Functionality.* Vol. 3 of *Improving Learning in Uganda.* World Bank Study Series. Washington, DC: World Bank.

Noble, Kimberly G., M. Frank Norman, and Martha J. Farah. 2005. "Neurocognitive Correlates of Socioeconomic Status in Kindergarten Children." *Developmental Science* 8 (1): 74–87.

O'Connell, Philip J., and Jean-Marie Jungblut. 2008. "What Do We Know about Training at Work?" In *Skill Formation: Interdisciplinary and Cross-National Perspectives,* edited by Karl Ulrich Mayer and Heike Solga, 109–25. New York: Cambridge University Press.

OECD (Organisation for Economic Co-operation and Development). 2010. *PISA 2009 Results, What Students Know and Can Do: Student Performance in Reading, Mathematics, and Science.* Vol. 1. Paris: OECD.

———. 2015. *The ABC of Gender Equality in Education: Aptitude, Behaviour, Confidence.* Paris: OECD.

———. 2016a. *PISA 2015 Results: Excellence and Equity in Education.* Vol. 1. Paris: OECD.

———. 2016b. *Skills Matter: Further Results from the Survey of Adult Skills.* OECD Skills Studies Series. Paris: OECD.

———. 2016c. *The Survey of Adult Skills: Reader's Companion.* 2d ed. OECD Skills Studies Series. Paris: OECD.

Orazem, Peter F., Paul W. Glewwe, and Harry Anthony Patrinos. 2007. "The Benefits and Costs of Alternative Strategies to Improve Educational Outcomes." Department of Economics Working Paper 07028 (November), Iowa State University, Ames.

PASEC (Programme d'Analyse des Systèmes Éducatifs de la Confemen). 2015. *PASEC 2014: Education System Performance in Francophone Africa, Competencies and Learning Factors in Primary Education.* Dakar, Senegal: PASEC.

Pritchett, Lant. 2013. *The Rebirth of Education: Schooling Ain't Learning.* Washington, DC: Center for Global Development; Baltimore: Brookings Institution Press.

Pritchett, Lant, and Amanda Beatty. 2012. "The Negative Consequences of Overambitious Curricula in Developing Countries." CGD Working Paper 293, Center for Global Development, Washington, DC.

Pritchett, Lant, and Justin Sandefur. 2017. "Girls' Schooling and Women's Literacy: Schooling Targets Alone Won't Reach Learning Goals." CGD Policy Paper 104, Center for Global Development, Washington, DC.

Robinson, Viviane M. J., Claire A. Lloyd, and Kenneth J. Rowe. 2008. "The Impact of Leadership on Student Outcomes: An Analysis of the Differential Effects of Leadership Types." *Educational Administration Quarterly* 44 (5): 635–74.

Rockoff, Jonah E. 2004. "The Impact of Individual Teachers on Student Achievement: Evidence from Panel Data." *American Economic Review* 94 (2): 247–52.

RTI International. 2015. *Status of Early Grade Reading in Sub-Saharan Africa*. Washington, DC: U.S. Agency for International Development.

Rubio-Codina, Marta, Orazio Attanasio, Costas Meghir, Natalia Varela, and Sally Grantham-McGregor. 2015. "The Socioeconomic Gradient of Child Development: Cross-Sectional Evidence from Children 6–42 Months in Bogota." *Journal of Human Resources* 50 (2): 464–83.

Sabarwal, Shwetlena, and Malek Abu-Jawdeh. 2017. "Understanding Teacher Effort: Insights from Cross-Country Data on Teacher Perceptions." Background paper, World Bank, Washington, DC.

SACMEQ (Southern and Eastern Africa Consortium for Monitoring Educational Quality). Various years. University of Botswana, Gaborone. http://www.sacmeq.org/.

Singh, Abhijeet. 2016. "Starting Together, Growing Apart: Gender Gaps in Learning from Preschool to Adulthood in Four Developing Countries." Paper presented at the Association for Public Policy Analysis and Management's International Conference, "Inequalities: Addressing the Growing Challenge for Policymakers Worldwide," London School of Economics, London, June 13–14.

Sinha, Shabnam, Rukmini Banerji, and Wilima Wadhwa. 2016. *Teacher Performance in Bihar, India: Implications for Education*. Directions in Development: Human Development Series. Washington, DC: World Bank.

Smith, David. 2014. "Nigerian Schoolchildren Defiant in City That Defied Boko Haram." *Guardian* (May 17). https://www.theguardian.com/world/2014/05/18/nigeria-kano-schoolchildren-boko-haram.

Spaull, Nicholas, and Janeli Kotze. 2015. "Starting Behind and Staying Behind in South Africa: The Case of Insurmountable Learning Deficits in Mathematics." *International Journal of Educational Development* 41: 13–24.

UIS (UNESCO Institute for Statistics). 2006. *Teachers and Educational Quality: Monitoring Global Needs for 2015*. Montreal: UIS.

———. 2017. Education (database). Montreal. http://data.uis.unesco.org/.

UNESCO (United Nations Educational, Scientific, and Cultural Organization). 2013. Third Regional Comparative and Explanatory Study (TERCE). UNESCO Regional Bureau for Education in Latin America and the Caribbean, Santiago, Chile. http://www.unesco.org/new/en/santiago/education/education-assessment-llece/third-regional-comparative-and-explanatory-study-terce/.

———. 2014. *EFA Global Monitoring Report 2013/4, Teaching and Learning: Achieving Quality for All*. Paris: UNESCO.

———. 2015. *Informe de resultados, TERCE: Logros de aprendizaje*. Paris: UNESCO. Santiago, Chile: UNESCO Regional Office for Education in Latin America and the Caribbean; Paris: UNESCO.

———. 2016. "Gender Inequality in Learning Achievement in Primary Education: What Can TERCE Tell Us?" Third Regional Comparative and Explanatory Study, UNESCO Regional Office for Education in Latin America and the Caribbean, Santiago, Chile; UNESCO, Paris.

Uwezo. 2014. "Are Our Children Learning? Literacy and Numeracy in Kenya 2014." Twaweza East Africa, Nairobi.

———. 2015. "Are Our Children Learning? Five Stories on the State of Education in Uganda in 2015 and Beyond." Twaweza East Africa, Kampala, Uganda.

van Fleet, Justin W. 2012. "Africa's Education Crisis: In School but Not Learning." *Up Front* (blog), September 17. https://www.brookings.edu/blog/up-front/2012/09/17/africas-education-crisis-in-school-but-not-learning/.

Walker, Susan P., Theodore D. Wachs, Julie Meeks Gardner, Betsy Lozoff, Gail A. Wasserman, Ernesto Pollitt, Julie A. Carter, et al. 2007. "Child Development: Risk Factors for Adverse Outcomes in Developing Countries." *Lancet* 369 (9556): 145–57.

Windisch, Hendrickje Catriona. 2015. "Adults with Low Literacy and Numeracy Skills: A Literature Review on Policy Intervention." OECD Education Working Paper 123, Organisation for Economic Co-operation and Development, Paris.

World Bank. 2016a. *"Africa Education Service Delivery in Madagascar: Results of 2016 Service Delivery Indicator Survey."* Washington, DC: World Bank.

———. 2016b. *"Education Sector Public Expenditure Tracking and Service Delivery Survey in Zambia."* Washington, DC: World Bank.

———. 2016c. World Development Indicators (database). World Bank, Washington, DC. http://data.worldbank.org/data-catalog/world-development-indicators.

Poverty hinders biological development and undermines learning

Life outcomes are hugely influenced by a child's development during the early years. Biological systems develop sequentially and cumulatively, so what happens early in life lays the foundation for future development. Between the time of gestation and a child's sixth birthday, the brain matures faster than at any other time of life. This period is also when the brain, along with its supporting systems, is most malleable. This malleability is a double-edged sword: high susceptibility to early environmental influence serves as both a window of opportunity and a source of vulnerability, because it means experiences can shape how development unfolds.[1] The environment children grow up in is a key determinant of their developmental trajectories toward outcomes later in life.

Growing up in poverty usually exposes children to many risk factors. In poor households, low levels of parental education exacerbate material deprivation by undermining investment choices for children's development, in terms of how parents use both their financial resources and their time. Moreover, parents' limited mental bandwidth, as well as the psychological stress imposed by poverty (including working many hours in often precarious conditions to make ends meet), further undermine the time, energy, and care they can give their children.[2] For the child, this often results in poor physical inputs starting in the womb, such as insufficient nutrition or extreme deprivation. It also results in poor social inputs, such as insufficient stimulation (not being held, responded to, talked to, or played with), neglect, abuse, exposure to violence, displacement, or maternal depression.

Acute adversity during the early years becomes embedded in children's bodies. In the face of deprivation, disease, or noxious environments, developing systems direct resources toward survival rather than promoting growth—physical or mental. For example, one in four children worldwide is stunted due to chronic malnutrition.[3] Stunting between gestation and a child's second birthday is associated with late school enrollment, lower cognition, poorer executive function, and less school attainment.[4] Some catch-up is possible after a child's second birthday, but previously stunted bodies remain highly sensitive to disease and infection. Children born with low birth weight (suggesting fetal undernutrition) are at higher risk of chronic adult diseases such as hypertension, diabetes, obesity, and coronary artery disease ("metabolic syndrome"). The extent to which the associated earlier cognitive impairment can be reversed is uncertain.

Exposure to multiple risk factors without the buffering support of available, well-informed, responsive caregivers can cause toxic stress.[5] Stress triggers the flight-or-fight response, an intense physiological reaction that puts the body in a state of alertness to deal with potential threats. Continual activation of the flight-or-fight response in early life endangers developing systems, because the brain focuses on addressing the perceived danger to the detriment of further development of biological systems not essential for survival.

Toxic stress in the early years can undermine lifelong health, learning, and behavior. Hormones associated with the flight-or-fight response, such as cortisol, can inhibit physical growth as well as weaken immune systems and metabolic regulatory mechanisms, all of which permanently increase an individual's susceptibility to illness.[6] Moreover, toxic stress during the early years can impair the development of neural connections in parts of the brain that are critical for learning—such as those associated with

Figure S2.1 Severe deprivation affects brain structure and function from early in life

Total white and gray matter in infants, by stunting status

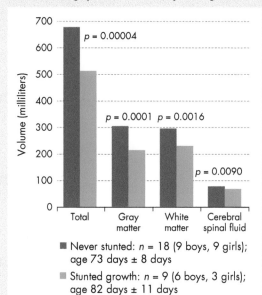

p = 0.00004
p = 0.0001 p = 0.0016
p = 0.0090

■ Never stunted: *n* = 18 (9 boys, 9 girls); age 73 days ± 8 days

■ Stunted growth: *n* = 9 (6 boys, 3 girls); age 82 days ± 11 days

Source: WDR 2018 team, using data from Nelson and others (2017). Data at http://bit.do/WDR2018-Fig_S2-1.

Note: Data obtained from infants 2–3 months old in Dhaka, Bangladesh, using magnetic resonance imaging (MRI). Graph depicts two groups of infants: 18 not stunted (not malnourished) and 9 stunted (malnourished). Graph shows (from left to right) total amount of brain volume; total amount of gray matter, where most neural computations are performed; total amount of white matter, which transmits electrical signals between gray matter and affects brain function and learning (that is, the information pathways of the brain); and cerebral spinal fluid, which protects the brain and spinal cord from injury and infection and is generally involved in many aspects of brain health.

socioemotional outcomes and executive functions, the biological foundations of learning.[7]

Severe deprivation, along with the associated stress, can impair healthy brain development.[8] Neuroimaging data from studies in Bangladesh, The Gambia, Romania, the United Kingdom, and the United States reveal differences in brain development (both structural and functional) linked to socioeconomic status. The studies confirm reduced brain connectivity as well as smaller brain volumes in areas associated with language, memory, executive function, and decision-making skills, on the one hand (figure S2.1),[9] and high activation of regions associated with emotional reactivity, on the other.[10] Such connectivity patterns and associated biological maladaptations are very difficult to reverse.

These biologically embedded responses lead to worse developmental trajectories and impaired learning, hurting foundational skills from the earliest stages of life. Because early childhood development outcomes are interdependent (see spotlight 1), subpar development in any one dimension is likely to affect the others. Children with stunted bodies and brains attempting to compensate for developmental gaps face daunting odds as they start formal schooling because of the sequential nature of development, coupled with the sharp decrease in brain malleability after a child's sixth birthday. Investments in early childhood development enable the normal, timely development of biological systems, shaping children's long-term ability to learn (figure S2.2). Well-designed

Figure S2.2 Risk and protective factors affect developmental trajectories

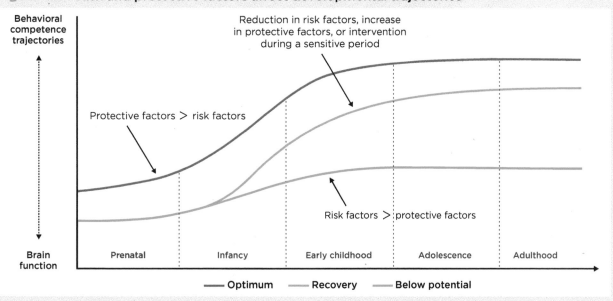

Source: Walker and others (2011).

early childhood interventions that increase poor children's access to protective factors (nutrition, stimulation, care, protection from stress) can enable those children's normal, timely biological development, thereby strengthening their long-term ability to learn (see chapter 5).

Notes

1. Knudsen (2004).
2. Mullainathan and Shafir (2013).
3. UNICEF, WHO, and World Bank (2016). *Stunting* is defined as a height-for-age z-score of less than two standard deviations below the median of a healthy reference population.
4. Black and others (2013); Christian and others (2014).
5. Center on the Developing Child (2016).
6. McEwen (2007).
7. Evans and Kim (2013); McCoy and Raver (2014).
8. Center on the Developing Child (2016).
9. Bright Project (http://www.globalfnirs.org/the-bright-project); Nelson and others (2017); Noble and others (2015); Vanderwert and others (2010).
10. Pavlakis and others (2015).

References

Black, Robert E., Cesar G. Victora, Susan P. Walker, Zulfiqar A. Bhutta, Parul Christian, Mercedes de Onis, Majid Ezzati, et al. 2013. "Maternal and Child Undernutrition and Overweight in Low-Income and Middle-Income Countries." *Lancet* 382 (9890): 427–51.

Center on the Developing Child. 2016. "From Best Practices to Breakthrough Impacts: A Science-Based Approach to Building a More Promising Future for Young Children and Families." Center on the Developing Child, Harvard University, Cambridge, MA.

Christian, Parul, Laura E. Murray-Kolb, James M. Tielsch, Joanne Katz, Steven C. LeClerq, and Subarna K. Khatry. 2014. "Associations between Preterm Birth, Small-for-Gestational Age, and Neonatal Morbidity and Cognitive Function among School-Age Children in Nepal." *BMC Pediatrics* 14 (1): 1–15.

Evans, Gary W., and Pilyoung Kim. 2013. "Childhood Poverty, Chronic Stress, Self-Regulation, and Coping." *Child Development Perspectives* 7 (1): 43–48.

Knudsen, Eric I. 2004. "Sensitive Periods in the Development of the Brain and Behavior." *Journal of Cognitive Neuroscience* 16 (8): 1412–25.

McCoy, Dana Charles, and C. Cybele Raver. 2014. "Household Instability and Self-Regulation among Poor Children." *Journal of Children and Poverty* 20 (2): 131–52.

McEwen, Bruce S. 2007. "Physiology and Neurobiology of Stress and Adaptation: Central Role of the Brain." *Physiological Reviews* 87 (3): 873–904.

Mullainathan, Sendhil, and Eldar Shafir. 2013. *Scarcity: Why Having Too Little Means So Much.* New York: Macmillan.

Nelson, Charles A., Nadine Gaab, Yingying Wang, Swapna Kumar, Danielle Sliva, Meaghan Mauer, Alissa Westerlund, et al. 2017. "Atypical Brain Development in Bangladeshi Infants Exposed to Profound Early Adversity." Paper presented at Society for Research in Child Development Biennial Meeting, Austin, TX, April.

Noble, Kimberly G., Suzanne M. Houston, Natalie H. Brito, Hauke Bartsch, Eric Kan, Joshua M. Kuperman, Natacha Akshoomoff, et al. 2015. "Family Income, Parental Education, and Brain Structure in Children and Adolescents." *Nature Neuroscience* 18 (5): 773–78.

Pavlakis, Alexandra E., Kimberly Noble, Steven G. Pavlakis, Noorjahan Ali, and Yitzchak Frank. 2015. "Brain Imaging and Electrophysiology Biomarkers: Is There a Role in Poverty and Education Outcome Research?" *Pediatric Neurology* 52 (4): 383–88.

UNICEF (United Nations Children's Fund), WHO (World Health Organization), and World Bank. 2016. "Levels and Trends in Child Malnutrition: UNICEF/WHO/World Bank Group Joint Child Malnutrition Estimates, Key Findings of the 2016 Edition." UNICEF, New York; WHO, Geneva; World Bank, Washington, DC. http://www.who.int/nutgrowthdb/estimates2015/en/.

Vanderwert, Ross E., Peter J. Marshall, Charles A. Nelson III, Charles H. Zeanah, and Nathan A. Fox. 2010. "Timing of Intervention Affects Brain Electrical Activity in Children Exposed to Severe Psychosocial Neglect." *PLoS One* 5 (7): e11415.

Walker, Susan P., Susan M. Chang, Marcos Vera-Hernández, and Sally M. Grantham-McGregor. 2011. "Early Childhood Stimulation Benefits Adult Competence and Reduces Violent Behavior." *Pediatrics* 127 (5): 849–57.

To take learning seriously, start by measuring it

Why does the learning crisis persist? How can children attend school for years but remain functionally illiterate? Why don't the people in education systems fix this? One big reason is that, for many, the learning crisis is invisible. Education systems have little systematic information on who is learning and who is not. As a result, it is impossible to generate an impetus for action—let alone a plan.

To tackle the crisis, it is necessary—though not enough—to measure learning. But learning metrics must facilitate action, be adapted to country needs, and consist of a range of tools to meet the needs of the system, including at the classroom level.

The learning crisis is often hidden—but measurement makes it visible

"Almost no low-income countries have standardized (equated over time) national assessment systems to track learning and provide a feedback mechanism to national education policies and programs" (Birdsall, Bruns, and Madan 2016, 2).

Education systems routinely report on enrollment—but not on learning. Because learning is missing from official education management data, it is missing from the agendas of politicians and bureaucrats. This is evident in how politicians often talk about education only in terms of inputs—number of schools, number of teachers, teacher salaries, school grants—but rarely in terms of actual learning. Lack of data on learning means that governments can ignore or obscure the poor quality of education, especially for disadvantaged groups.

Without objective information on learning, parents may be unaware of the poor quality of education. This prevents them from demanding better services from schools and governments. In Kenya, one study found that less than half of the children in grade 4 could pass basic proficiency tests in literacy or numeracy, yet more than two-thirds of adults were broadly satisfied with the government's performance in education.[1] The realization that learning outcomes are poor may come only when children face poor labor market prospects, but by then it is too late. If parents have no real information on how much (or little) their children are learning, how can they hold schools or governments accountable?

Without clear information on what students do not know, how can schools improve instruction? Teachers may find it hard to judge to what extent students understand what is being taught. This is particularly true in low-income countries, where teachers face large classrooms that mix students of very different abilities. For example, a study from Delhi, India, found that the same grade may contain students whose achievement level spans the equivalent of five to six grades.[2] In such contexts, learning measures provide teachers with timely feedback about which students may need additional support. More broadly, these measures provide school management with information about which areas need attention to improve instruction. If the information is shared with parents or students, it can help them direct their own efforts toward improving learning.

Yet concerted action is often derailed by concerns about the possible pitfalls of learning metrics. These metrics generate much debate on, for example, the outsize impacts of international assessments on local policy, the limited use of national assessments for improving classroom practice, or the potential gaming of high-stakes testing.[3] But *measurement of learning* is not shorthand for international testing such as the Programme for International Student Assessment (PISA) or for the high-stakes accountability approach implemented through the U.S. No Child Left Behind policy. Instead, the term covers a range of assessments, including formative classroom assessments (box 4.1). Even in this form, measures of learning provide information on only some of the skills students acquire as they develop (see spotlight 3 on multidimensionality of skills). Thus metrics are

complements of, not substitutes for, careful, context-specific analysis to determine how to improve learning.[4]

Measures *for* learning guide action

Testing in Rio de Janeiro, Brazil, happens at two levels. First, every two years all students in grades 5 and 9 take a national test (the Prova Brasil) designed to assess public education. Second, students are tested at the end of each two-month curriculum block. These tests, given by municipal education departments, aim to provide quick feedback to teachers and principals, allowing schools and the broader system to provide more support to struggling students (Elwick and McAleavy 2015).

Identifying learning gaps in the classroom is the first step toward resolving them. In environments of low learning, there is often a gap between the level of students and the level at which classes are being taught.[5] This might be because teachers are unaware of students' levels. Fostering a culture of classroom-based assessments can address this problem. In Singapore, students are given screening tests at the start of grade 1, which helps teachers identify those who require additional instruction to learn to read.[6]

Learning metrics help highlight where support is most needed. School districts and schools are then

Box 4.1 Good measures of learning illuminate all parts of the education system

Formative classroom assessments facilitate instruction by providing real-time feedback to support teaching and learning. This feedback allows teachers to identify struggling students, thereby enabling them to adjust instruction to meet the learning needs of different students. Classroom assessments also generate valuable feedback for students and parents.

National assessments provide information on the overall education system by highlighting achievements along with challenges, such as inequalities. They are useful for education management, policy, and reform.

National examinations certify student achievement, with a focus on transparently selecting students for more

advanced placements in the education system or job market. Because of their role in determining labor market outcomes, these examinations are high-stakes for students. They significantly affect what is taught and how, and they are critical for managing the flow of students through the system.

International assessments benchmark student performance by evaluating education systems across countries and over time using representative samples of children. There has also been a steady increase in the use of citizen-led assessments. These can be important for fostering public awareness, showing what is possible, advocating for change, and informing research.

Source: WDR 2018 team.

better able to target resources to improve service delivery. In Brazil, national assessments have been widely adopted by states and municipalities to strengthen school performance.[7] Learning metrics have also guided big-banner education reforms. In Chile, PISA's reading framework guided national curriculum reform.[8] Similarly, findings from the Southern and Eastern Africa Consortium for Monitoring Educational Quality (SACMEQ) I, 1995–99, underpinned a review of Mauritius's education master plan.[9] In some cases, learning metrics have been instrumental in making education reform data-driven. In Germany, lower than expected results—especially for students from poorer backgrounds—on the 2000 PISA led to the development of more support for disadvantaged students, especially those from immigrant backgrounds.[10]

For learning metrics to guide action effectively, they need to be used as a range of tools to serve different needs, from classroom practice to system management. Measures of learning come in various forms, with different measures serving different purposes for different actors. These range from simple oral questions posed by a teacher to national assessments that help policy makers prioritize action (box 4.1). In well-functioning systems, these different tools complement one another to form a coherent whole.[11]

Policy makers should rely on a broad range of information instead of any one measure. When a single metric becomes the sole basis for big policy triggers, the corresponding stakes may become dangerously high. A striking example is the U.S. No Child Left Behind policy enacted in 2001. This policy had strong negative repercussions for schools that performed poorly on annual statewide standardized tests. Though the policy led some poorly performing schools to improve, it also generated various undesirable strategic responses by teachers and school administrators.[12] These included reclassifying students as requiring special education, exempting certain students from testing, reallocating resources to students at the margin of passing, and suspending low-scoring students near test dates.[13] Even in the case of PISA, some studies have suggested that the performance in some places—Argentina, Malaysia, Vietnam, Shanghai (China)—could be tied in part to (perhaps inadvertent) "selective samples" that may exclude some poorly performing schools or students.[14]

Education systems also routinely underuse the information generated by learning metrics—making for a lot of measurement that leads to little action.[15] Often, findings are simply not communicated in a timely way to relevant audiences.[16] There may also be credibility issues. If teachers or schools do not feel heard or acknowledged in a national assessment process, they will likely reject its findings. For example, teachers are more likely to resist quantitative forms of evaluation when metrics do not take into account context.[17] This is particularly the case for measures of learning disseminated as rankings, which are susceptible to being taken out of context. In some education systems, such friction is heightened by the use of technology, which raises questions about privacy and transparency. Approaches using technology also involve limited social interaction, which is associated with less impact.[18]

For measurement to guide action, it must be actionable. It also needs to be available to stakeholders. At the design stage, stakeholders have to ask themselves how learning data will be used. In Chile, all students in grades 4 and 8 take the Sistema de Medición de la Calidad de la Educación (SIMCE) each year. After the test identifies the 900 schools scoring in the lowest 10 percent on the tests in their province, these schools receive special resources. The data, then, are clearly linked to action. Many assessment systems measure outcomes too infrequently or too broadly to be of practical use. The most recent publicly available data from the SACMEQ are for 2007. Another constraint is the lag between when data are collected and when they are made available, as well as how data are made available. Many ministries produce only hard copies of summary reports, which make them difficult to use.

Measures *of* learning spur action

"Shock as 60 [Percent] of Tanzania Students Fail National Exam" (East African, 2013)

In the United States since 2001, information on different schools' performance on standardized tests has notably increased turnout in local school board elections (Holbein 2016).

Measures of learning motivate action through three channels:[19]

• *Participation.* Learning outcomes are often far worse than stakeholders realize. In Uganda, nearly three-quarters of parents said they were satisfied with the quality of education—yet only a quarter of grade 4 students could pass a math test based on grade 2 questions.[20] By documenting service delivery shortfalls, learning metrics can motivate parents to hold their schools accountable for learning.

In such contexts, learning metrics can correct information failures, which are especially severe for the poor. This correction can in turn rebalance the relationship between users and providers. This channel operates via the direct or short route of accountability running from parents directly to schools.

- *Choice.* Providing parents with hard evidence about learning outcomes at alternative schools can encourage schools to improve learning by increasing competitive pressures. When parents have objective information about learning outcomes across schools, they can punish poorly performing schools by "voting with their feet." Public schools care about such outcomes because their resources are often tied to the number of students they enroll.[21] But this channel may also disproportionately penalize schools that serve poor children.
- *Voice.* Learning metrics can facilitate lobbying for reform by providing information on what needs fixing. Lack of reliable metrics, by contrast, undermines accountability for results.[22] This channel operates via the long route of accountability, where learning metrics may help citizens use the political process to hold politicians accountable for learning.

That said, the links from measurement to action are neither automatic nor straightforward. India's citizen-led assessment, the Annual Status of Education Report (ASER), has documented low proficiency scores since it was introduced in 2004. However, clear or sustained improvements are not yet visible for the country as a whole.[23] At the same time, some Indian states have shown significant improvements in grade 3 reading levels between ASER 2010 and 2016.[24] This shows that it is not just the information but action that matters. For learning to improve, not only do learning assessments need to be available, but also someone needs to act on them. In fact, an evaluation of the impact of citizen-led assessments in Kenya finds that for information on learning to spur action, those who receive the information must understand it, see it as actionable, care about the topic, and believe that their actions will improve outcomes.[25]

Political pressures may limit the extent to which measures of learning spur positive action. Where education quality is low, politicians have an incentive to hide or obscure learning outcomes.[26] They may also try to evade blame for poor performance by setting low standards, trying to limit year-to-year comparability, or restricting access to outcome information.[27] For example, Argentina amended its standardized test so that year-to-year comparisons are not possible,

decreased the frequency with which the test is administered, and delayed the publication of results by two years to obscure the poor performance of students.[28] Teachers, too, might resist learning assessments to minimize opportunities for blame.[29] In Chile, teacher training institutions have shown resistance to the national assessment.[30] Assessments are also political because they can affect the flow of resources or prestige in an education system—as in the United States under the No Child Left Behind policy.[31] Underlying politics can make student assessment systems particularly hard to reform (see part IV of this Report).

When does measurement mobilize citizens to demand accountability for learning? Because of limited attention, information is often ignored, especially if it is complex or provides unwelcome news.[32] Therefore, for measurement to spur action, information must be available in an easily digestible way. But this in itself may not be enough. Learning metrics can galvanize communities to hold their schools accountable for learning only when collective action problems are resolved.[33] A participatory approach—where schools and communities have a say in what type of "learning metrics" are generated at the school level—may be likely to work better here.[34] In addition, for citizens to be able to act on information, fear of reprisals must be low. Finally, for citizens to act in behalf of change, they must believe that their own individual actions can make a difference.[35]

Efforts to benchmark country performance through international or regional assessments have in some cases galvanized action because international comparisons make learning politically salient. Release of the Trends in International Mathematics and Science Study (TIMSS) or PISA rankings often triggers intense media interest, inserting learning into political and economic debates.[36] This increase in interest often generates momentum for government action—an effect known as "PISA shock"—thereby unleashing targeted reforms. About half the countries participating in the PISA assessments under the aegis of the Organisation for Economic Co-operation and Development (OECD) have launched reforms because of the results.[37] Learning assessments also spur action by making learning a tangible goal. Whereas the United Nations' Millennium Development Goals (MDGs), which inspired efforts by governments and donors, focused on enrollment, the current Sustainable Development Goals (SDGs) place greater emphasis on learning.[38] The success of the SDGs will depend on countries' ability to turn rhetoric into action by tracking learning.

Choose learning metrics based on what the country needs

When choosing which measures of learning to invest in, policy makers must consider the context. If assessment systems are nascent, priority should be given to fostering classroom assessment. Once that piece is in place, countries can develop relatively quick, sample-based, low-cost national assessments. When classroom and national assessments are established, much can be gained from participating in regional or global assessments that enable performance benchmarking. The ultimate goal is to build assessment systems in which different parts are aligned but serve different needs.

Not every student needs to be tested in national assessments. Sample-based assessments can accurately measure a system's performance. These assessments still require capable administrators, but they are much less expensive than census-based assessments. They can also be administered more often. Schools participating in these assessments do not have to be identified. This helps lower the stakes, making the assessments less susceptible to perverse responses by teachers or schools.

Assessment systems should test students at an age when effective remedial action remains possible. Of 121 countries in four regions, a third lack any reporting data on the reading and mathematics proficiency levels of children at the end of primary school.[39] Only

half of the countries surveyed produce data or participate in any regional or international tests to assess mathematics at the end of lower secondary school. Just under half assess reading. This means that comparable information about learning is missing for most children and youth outside of high-income countries (figure 4.1).[40]

Will learning metrics narrow the vision for education?

Putting emphasis on measurable learning does not mean ignoring other outcomes of education, such as physical, moral, civic, or artistic development. Indeed, focusing on learning—and on the educational quality that drives it—is more likely to crowd in these other desirable outcomes. Conditions that allow children to spend two or three years in school without learning to read a single word or to reach the end of primary school without learning two-digit subtraction are not conducive to reaching the higher goals of education. An experiment in Andhra Pradesh, India, that rewarded teachers for gains in measured learning in math and language led to improved outcomes not just in those subjects, but also in science and social studies—even though there were no rewards for improvement in the latter two subjects.[41] A study of ninth graders in the United States found that behavioral factors correlate positively with test scores.[42] Another U.S. study revealed that teachers who improve test scores also improve broad outcomes into adulthood.[43]

Figure 4.1 No internationally comparable data on learning are available for most children outside of high-income countries

Percentage of children in countries that have reported mathematics and reading scores since 2000 for ASER, EGRA, LLECE, PASEC, PIRLS, PISA, SACMEQ, and TIMSS, by income group

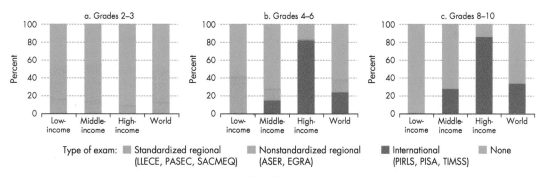

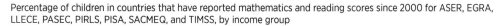

Source: WDR 2018 team, using data from Sandefur (2017). Data at http://bit.do/WDR2018-Fig_4-1.

Note: ASER = Annual Status of Education Report; EGRA = Early Grade Reading Assessment; LLECE = Latin American Laboratory for Assessment of the Quality of Education; PASEC = Programme d'Analyse des Systèmes Éducatifs de la Confemen; PIRLS = Progress in International Reading Literacy Study; PISA = Programme for International Student Assessment; SACMEQ = Southern and Eastern Africa Consortium for Monitoring Educational Quality; TIMSS = Trends in International Mathematics and Science Study.

Learning assessments of key foundational subjects such as language and mathematics are likely to be good proxies for whether an education system is delivering on its broad promise.

That said, cognitive skills are not the only skills that matter. Socioemotional skills (sometimes called noncognitive skills) such as grit, self-control, self-management, effective communication, and prosocial behavior can be central to not just economic outcomes but life outcomes more broadly.[44] Evidence from high-income countries suggests that such skills strongly affect employment status, work experience, occupational choice, and wages.[45] They also reduce risky behaviors such as crime, violence, or drug use.[46] For example, a study from the United Kingdom found that even after controlling for cognitive skills, socioemotional skills were important for predicting whether individuals stayed in school, obtained a degree, were employed, smoked, or were involved in a crime.[47] An understanding of how to measure these skills, along with how to influence them, is growing rapidly.[48] Like cognitive skills, socioemotional skills develop early in life but are malleable.[49] In fact, socioemotional skills help build cognitive skills and vice versa, with current skill levels dependent on investments made earlier in life (see spotlight 3).[50]

Lower-performing countries probably do not face the same sharp trade-offs faced by high-performing countries on the education frontier. Economists use the concept of the production possibilities frontier to understand how producers—or in this case, countries—make trade-offs between production of different goods (figure 4.2). For example, in recent years many stakeholders in the Republic of Korea have argued that their high-performing education system places too much emphasis on test scores (shown in figure 4.2 as "measured learning") and not enough on creativity or certain socioemotional skills such as teamwork ("other outputs"). Implicitly, this Korean debate is about whether to try to move up and to the left on the frontier—that is, from A toward B. But in the low-learning trap, represented by "low-performing country C" in the figure, there is so much slack that this OECD-driven debate is not relevant. Country C has an opportunity to improve on both measured learning and other education outputs at the same time.

Six tips for effective learning measurement

Tip 1: Measure gaps. The learning crisis will be truly salient politically only when vulnerable subpopulations, who are disproportionately likely to suffer from learning gaps, are adequately covered by national assessment systems. To ensure that happens, assessments should be deployed in a way that shines a light on all children. Measurement must allow for the disaggregation of data around important dimensions such as socioeconomic status, gender, location, or disability status. In particular, groups at risk for social or economic exclusion may need to be oversampled to ensure adequate representation.[51]

Tip 2: Track progress. The use of uniform methodologies, approaches, and psychometrics across years is crucial for education systems to discern trends in learning over time and changes in learning gaps across tests. Year-on-year comparisons of learning progress should also be ensured for vulnerable subpopulations.

Tip 3: Test students when effective action is still possible. Returns from student assessments will be maximized if they focus on ensuring that students attain basic skills—literacy, numeracy, critical thinking—early in their schooling. Systems should also consider household-based testing, which would allow assessments to cover students not currently in school, making the resulting measurement more useful for universal learning targets. Household testing would also allow more nuanced understanding of all the different influences on a child's school access and learning outcomes. To that end, standardized learning modules can be included at little additional cost

Figure 4.2 Low-performing countries don't face sharp trade-offs between learning and other education outputs

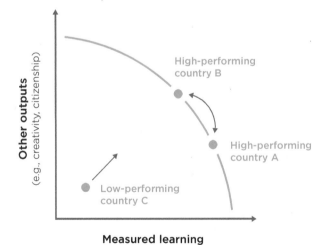

Source: WDR 2018 team.

in surveys conducted both nationally (such as income and consumption surveys) and internationally (such as Living Standards Measurement Study surveys or Demographic and Health Surveys).

Tip 4: Balance the stakes. No single measure should be misused or overused. One way to avoid that outcome is to frame learning measures that guide policy as low-stakes diagnostic tools—not as one summary number that determines sanctions and rewards. Again, "learning metrics" should be considered a system of tools, each with its own place and purpose.[52]

Tip 5: Good design is not enough—facilitate action. Learning measures should be used explicitly not just for tracking progress, but also for policy making.[53] One way to ensure that happens is to devote resources (including effort) to the timely distribution of understandable results to key stakeholders. Another factor is an open, collaborative process for instrument design. Student assessments developed with the collaboration of various stakeholders are more likely to be considered valid and relevant at local levels.

Tip 6: Exploit global public goods on learning. Leveraging international assessments can yield high returns. For example, there is considerable advantage to forging common links between international and regional assessments so they can be put on the same scale. This not only increases harmonization between international assessments such as PISA and TIMSS, but also allows ties to national and citizen-led assessments, enabling meaningful global tracking (box 4.2). Researchers have tried to link various assessments after the fact, but these attempts have faced severe

Box 4.2 A global learning metric?

A global learning metric could help bring learning center stage, making it more salient. Such a metric would use an internationally comparable scale to consistently track progress and identify gaps across contexts. It would enable comparisons across children, households, schools, and locations.

Beyond its technical dividends, a global metric would motivate action and generate accountability for learning. By showing what is possible, it could point to what countries should be aspiring to—and create pressure to meet those aspirations. By benchmarking learning gaps among disadvantaged groups, a global metric could also create pressures for social mobility within countries. Furthermore, comparable learning data could increase the effectiveness of global research, international partnerships, and global aid for learning. Such data could also help countries develop their capacity for analyzing results to drive policy.

To be sure, there are technical and political challenges that would go hand in hand with adopting a global metric. The first is how to generate a global consensus on the metric's scope. A global metric would require making choices about approach, target sample, and interpretation, which could prove controversial. In addition, challenges would arise with financing, implementation capacity, and political will. Many developing countries lack infrastructure for data collection, organization, analysis, and mechanisms to provide feedback to educators, parents, or communities. These are all necessary ingredients for turning metrics into action.

But most of these problems are surmountable. Global advocacy is generating sound technical recommendations on what a global metric could look like. Although there are no agreed-on standards of proficiency and no agreed-on tests to ensure that countries' measures of learning are comparable to each other and over time, several global initiatives—such as the Global Alliance to Monitor Learning, the Assessment for Learning (A4L) initiative, and the International Commission on Financing Global Education Opportunity—are generating momentum. Other challenges could be overcome through clear goals and quality thresholds. A global metric can succeed only if it is explicitly framed as a complement to national assessment systems—not as a substitute for them. In fact, information from the global metric could be used to strengthen the capacity of national systems.

The political will needed for a global metric might be easier to mobilize if the needs of developing countries are prioritized and the metric's advantages are clearly communicated. Estimates suggest that only 3 percent of official development assistance for education is spent on global public goods such as data and research; for health, that share is 20 percent.[a] Returns from investing more on education data could be enormous if they help focus attention on ensuring that students attain basic skills in their early years.

Source: WDR 2018 team.

a. Schäferhoff and Burnett (2016).

technical challenges.[54] Ex ante linking of measurements through common items is likely to prove much more technically sound and cost-effective.

* * *

Education systems are unlikely to tackle the learning crisis unless it becomes clearly visible. This is possible only through well-designed measures of learning. To be effective, "learning metrics" must overcome two important challenges: ensuring that information leads to action, and minimizing the potential perverse impacts of measurement. Alarm at the rise of a "testing" culture has dominated recent discourse. But in most low-learning contexts there is too little assessment and, consequently, too little accountability for learning in the system.

Notes

1. Pritchett, Banerji, and Kenny (2013).
2. Muralidharan, Singh, and Ganimian (2016).
3. Eggen and Stobart (2014); Sellar and Lingard (2013).
4. Carnoy and others (2016).
5. Pritchett (2013).
6. OECD (2011).
7. Guimarães de Castro (2012).
8. Breakspear (2012).
9. Kulpoo (1998).
10. Ertl (2006).
11. Greaney and Kellaghan (2008).
12. Dee and Jacob (2011).
13. Booher-Jennings (2005); Cullen and Reback (2006); Figlio and Getzler (2006); Jacob (2005); Jennings and Beveridge (2009); Neal and Schanzenbach (2010); Reback (2008).
14. Carnoy and others (2016); Glewwe and others (2017); OECD (2016); Xu and Dronkers (2016).
15. Székely (2011).
16. Greaney and Kellaghan (2008).
17. Baker and others (2010); Dixon and others (2013).
18. Bellamy and Raab (2005); Meijer (2009).
19. Bruns, Filmer, and Patrinos (2011).
20. Afrobarometer (2015); Uwezo (2014).
21. World Bank (2003).
22. Pritchett, Banerji, and Kenny (2013).
23. R4D (2015).
24. ASER Centre (2016).
25. Lieberman, Posner, and Tsai (2014).
26. Michener and Ritter (2016); Tanaka (2001).
27. Nicolai and others (2014).
28. Ganimian (2015).
29. Fox (2007); Hood (2010); Worthy (2015).
30. Meckes and Carrasco (2006).
31. Benveniste (2002); Peterson and West (2003).
32. Loewenstein, Sunstein, and Golman (2014).
33. Björkman and Svensson (2010).
34. Barr and others (2012); Björkman and Svensson (2010).
35. Barr and others (2012); Lieberman, Posner, and Tsai (2014).
36. Breakspear (2012).
37. Figazzolo (2009).
38. Tawil and others (2016).
39. UIS (2016).
40. By linking items across assessments—and including national assessments—coverage might be increased. But the fact that several large low- and middle-income countries still lack measures of learning means that comparable information remains missing for many children and youth outside of high-income countries.
41. Muralidharan and Sundararaman (2011).
42. Jackson (2016).
43. Chetty and others (2010).
44. Durlak and others (2011); Heckman, Pinto, and Savelyev (2013); Murnane and others (2001).
45. Heckman, Stixrud, and Urzua (2006).
46. Durlak, Weissberg, and Pachan (2010).
47. Carneiro, Crawford, and Goodman (2007).
48. Carneiro, Crawford, and Goodman (2007); Heckman, Pinto, and Savelyev (2013).
49. Heckman, Stixrud, and Urzua (2006).
50. Cunha and Heckman (2007, 2008); OECD (2015).
51. Sandefur (2016).
52. Neal (2013).
53. Guimarães de Castro (2012).
54. Altinok, Diebolt, and Demeulemeester (2014); Altinok and Murseli (2007); Sandefur (2017).

References

Afrobarometer. 2015. "Uganda, Round 6 Data (2015)." Democracy in Africa Research Unit, Center for Social Science Research, University of Cape Town, Rondebosch, South Africa. http://afrobarometer.org/data/uganda-round-6 -data-2015.

Altinok, Nadir, Claude Diebolt, and Jean-Luc Demeulemeester. 2014. "A New International Database on Education Quality: 1965–2010." *Applied Economics* 46 (11): 1212–47.

Altinok, Nadir, and Hatidje Murseli. 2007. "International Database on Human Capital Quality." *Economics Letters* 96 (2): 237–44.

ASER Centre. 2016. "Annual Status of Education Report 2016." New Delhi. http://www.asercentre.org/p/289.html.

Baker, Eva L., Paul E. Barton, Linda Darling-Hammond, Edward Haertel, Helen F. Ladd, Robert L. Linn, Diane Ravitch, et al. 2010. "Problems with the Use of Student Test Scores to Evaluate Teachers." EPI Briefing Paper #278, Economic Policy Institute, Washington, DC.

Barr, Abigail, Frederick Mugisha, Pieter Serneels, and Andrew Zeitlin. 2012. "Information and Collective Action in Community-Based Monitoring of Schools: Field and

Lab Experimental Evidence from Uganda." Working paper, Georgetown University, Washington, DC.

Bellamy, Christine, and Charles Raab. 2005. "Joined-Up Government and Privacy in the United Kingdom: Managing Tensions between Data Protection and Social Policy, Part II." *Public Administration* 83 (2): 393–415.

Benveniste, Luis. 2002. "The Political Structuration of Assessment: Negotiating State Power and Legitimacy." *Comparative Education Review* 46 (1): 89–118.

Birdsall, Nancy, Barbara Bruns, and Janeen Madan. 2016. "Learning Data for Better Policy: A Global Agenda." CGD Policy Paper, Center for Global Development, Washington, DC. http://www.cgdev.org/sites/default/files /learning-data-better-policy.pdf.

Björkman, Martina, and Jakob Svensson. 2010. "When Is Community-Based Monitoring Effective? Evidence from a Randomized Experiment in Primary Health in Uganda." *Journal of the European Economic Association* 8 (2–3): 571–81.

Booher-Jennings, Jennifer. 2005. "Below the Bubble: 'Educational Triage' and the Texas Accountability System." *American Educational Research Journal* 42 (2): 231–68.

Breakspear, Simon. 2012. "The Policy Impact of PISA: An Exploration of the Normative Effects of International Benchmarking in School System Performance." OECD Education Working Paper 71, Organisation for Economic Co-operation and Development, Paris.

Bruns, Barbara, Deon Filmer, and Harry Anthony Patrinos. 2011. *Making Schools Work: New Evidence on Accountability Reforms*. Human Development Perspectives Series. Washington, DC: World Bank.

Carneiro, Pedro, Claire Crawford, and Alissa Goodman. 2007. "The Impact of Early Cognitive and Non-cognitive Skills on Later Outcomes." CEE Discussion Paper 0092, Centre for the Economics of Education, London School of Economics.

Carnoy, Martin, Tatiana Khavenson, Prashant Loyalka, William H. Schmidt, and Andrey Zakharov. 2016. "Revisiting the Relationship between International Assessment Outcomes and Educational Production: Evidence from a Longitudinal PISA-TIMSS Sample." *American Educational Research Journal* 53 (4): 1054–85.

Chetty, Raj, John N. Friedman, Nathaniel Hilger, Emmanuel Saez, Diane Whitmore Schanzenbach, and Danny Yagan. 2010. "How Does Your Kindergarten Classroom Affect Your Earnings? Evidence from Project Star." NBER Working Paper 16381, National Bureau of Economic Research, Cambridge, MA.

Cullen, Julie Berry, and Randall Reback. 2006. "Tinkering toward Accolades: School Gaming under a Performance Accountability System." In *Improving School Accountability*, edited by Timothy J. Gronberg and Dennis W. Jansen, 1–34. Advances in Applied Microeconomics Series 14. Bingley, U.K.: Emerald Publishing Limited.

Cunha, Flavio, and James J. Heckman. 2007. "The Technology of Skill Formation." IZA Discussion Paper 2550, Institute for the Study of Labor, Bonn, Germany. http://nbn -resolving.de/urn:nbn:de:101:1-20080425464.

———. 2008. "Formulating, Identifying and Estimating the Technology of Cognitive and Noncognitive Skill Formation." *Journal of Human Resources* 43 (4): 738–82.

Dee, Thomas S., and Brian Jacob. 2011. "The Impact of No Child Left Behind on Student Achievement." *Journal of Policy Analysis and Management* 30 (3): 418–46.

Dixon, Ruth, Christiane Arndt, Manuel Mullers, Jarmo Vakkuri, Kristiina Engblom-Pelkkala, and Christopher Hood. 2013. "A Lever for Improvement or a Magnet for Blame? Press and Political Responses to International Educational Rankings in Four EU Countries." *Public Administration* 91 (2): 484–505.

Durlak, Joseph A., Roger P. Weissberg, Allison B. Dymnicki, Rebecca D. Taylor, and Kriston B. Schellinger. 2011. "The Impact of Enhancing Students' Social and Emotional Learning: A Meta-Analysis of School-Based Universal Interventions." *Child Development* 82 (1): 405–32.

Durlak, Joseph A., Roger P. Weissberg, and Molly Pachan. 2010. "A Meta-Analysis of After-School Programs That Seek to Promote Personal and Social Skills in Children and Adolescents." *American Journal of Community Psychology* 45 (3–4): 294–309.

Eggen, Theo J. H. M., and Gordon Stobart, eds. 2014. *High-Stakes Testing in Education: Value, Fairness, and Consequences.* New York: Routledge.

Elwick, Alex, and Tony McAleavy. 2015. *Interesting Cities: Five Approaches to Urban School Reform.* Reading, U.K.: CfBT Education Trust.

Ertl, Hubert. 2006. "Educational Standards and the Changing Discourse on Education: The Reception and Consequences of the PISA Study in Germany." *Oxford Review of Education* 32 (5): 619–34.

Figazzolo, Laura. 2009. "Impact of PISA 2006 on the Education Policy Debate." Working paper, Education International, Brussels.

Figlio, David N., and Lawrence S. Getzler. 2006. "Accountability, Ability, and Disability: Gaming the System?" In *Improving School Accountability*, edited by Timothy J. Gronberg and Dennis W. Jansen, 35–49. Advances in Applied Microeconomics Series 14. Bingley, U.K.: Emerald Publishing Limited.

Fox, Jonathan. 2007. "The Uncertain Relationship between Transparency and Accountability." *Development in Practice* 17 (4–5): 663–71.

Ganimian, Alejandro J. 2015. *El Termómetro Educativo: Informe Sobre el Desempeño de Argentina en los Operativos Nacionales de Evaluación (One) 2005-2013.* Buenos Aires: Proyecto Educar 2050.

Glewwe, Paul W., Jongwook Lee, Khoa Vu, and Hai-Anh H. Dang. 2017. "What Explains Vietnam's Exceptional Performance in Education Relative to Other Countries? Analysis of the 2012 PISA Data." Paper presented at the RISE Annual Conference, Center for Global Development, Washington, DC, June 15–16.

Greaney, Vincent, and Thomas Kellaghan. 2008. *Assessing National Achievement Levels in Education.* Vol. 1, *National Assessments of Educational Achievement.* Washington, DC: World Bank.

Guimarães de Castro, Maria Helena. 2012. "Developing the Enabling Context for Student Assessment in Brazil." SABER Student Assessment Working Paper 7, Systems Approach for Better Education Results, World Bank, Washington, DC.

Heckman, James J., Rodrigo Pinto, and Peter Savelyev. 2013. "Understanding the Mechanisms through Which an Influential Early Childhood Program Boosted Adult Outcomes." *American Economic Review* 103 (6): 2052–86.

Heckman, James J., Jora Stixrud, and Sergio Urzua. 2006. "The Effects of Cognitive and Noncognitive Abilities on Labor Market Outcomes and Social Behavior." *Journal of Labor Economics* 24 (3): 411–82.

Holbein, John. 2016. "Left Behind? Citizen Responsiveness to Government Performance Information." *American Political Science Review* 110 (2): 353–68.

Hood, Christopher. 2010. *The Blame Game: Spin, Bureaucracy, and Self-Preservation in Government.* Princeton, NJ: Princeton University Press.

Jackson, C. Kirabo. 2016. "What Do Test Scores Miss? The Importance of Teacher Effects on Non-test Score Outcomes." NBER Working Paper 22226, National Bureau of Economic Research, Cambridge, MA.

Jacob, Brian A. 2005. "Accountability, Incentives, and Behavior: The Impact of High-Stakes Testing in the Chicago Public Schools." *Journal of Public Economics* 89 (5): 761–96.

Jennings, Jennifer L., and Andrew A. Beveridge. 2009. "How Does Test Exemption Affect Schools' and Students' Academic Performance?" *Educational Evaluation and Policy Analysis* 31 (2): 153–75.

Kulpoo, Dhurumbeer. 1998. "The Quality of Education: Some Policy Suggestions Based on a Survey of Schools: Mauritius." SACMEQ Policy Research Report No. 1, United Nations Educational, Scientific, and Cultural Organization, Port Louis, Mauritius.

Lieberman, Evan S., Daniel N. Posner, and Lily L. Tsai. 2014. "Does Information Lead to More Active Citizenship? Evidence from an Education Intervention in Rural Kenya." *World Development* 60: 69–83.

Loewenstein, George, Cass R. Sunstein, and Russell Golman. 2014. "Disclosure: Psychology Changes Everything." *Annual Review of Economics* 6 (1): 391–419.

Meckes, Lorena, and Rafael Carrasco. 2006. "SIMCE: Lessons from the Chilean Experience in National Assessment Systems of Learning Outcomes." Paper presented at World Bank and Inter-American Development Bank's Conference, "Lessons from Best Practices in Promoting Education for All: Latin America and the Caribbean," Cartagena de Indias, Colombia, October 9–11.

Meijer, Albert. 2009. "Understanding Modern Transparency." *International Review of Administrative Sciences* 75 (2): 255–69.

Michener, Gregory, and Otavio Ritter. 2016. "Comparing Resistance to Open Data Performance Measurement: Public Education in Brazil and the UK." *Public Administration* 95 (1): 4–21.

Muralidharan, Karthik, Abhijeet Singh, and Alejandro J. Ganimian. 2016. "Disrupting Education? Experimental Evidence on Technology-Aided Instruction in India." NBER Working Paper 22923, National Bureau of Economic Research, Cambridge, MA.

Muralidharan, Karthik, and Venkatesh Sundararaman. 2011. "Teacher Performance Pay: Experimental Evidence from India." *Journal of Political Economy* 119 (1): 39–77.

Murnane, Richard J., John B. Willett, M. Jay Braatz, and Yves Duhaldeborde. 2001. "Do Different Dimensions of Male High School Students' Skills Predict Labor Market Success a Decade Later? Evidence from the NLSY." *Economics of Education Review* 20 (4): 311–20.

Neal, Derek. 2013. "The Consequences of Using One Assessment System to Pursue Two Objectives." *Journal of Economic Education* 44 (4): 339–52.

Neal, Derek, and Diane Whitmore Schanzenbach. 2010. "Left Behind by Design: Proficiency Counts and Test-Based Accountability." *Review of Economics and Statistics* 92 (2): 263–83.

Nicolai, Susan, Leni Wild, Joseph Wales, Sébastien Hine, and Jakob Engel. 2014. "Unbalanced Progress: What Political Dynamics Mean for Education Access and Quality." ODI Development Progress Working Paper 5, Overseas Development Institute, London.

OECD (Organisation for Economic Co-operation and Development). 2011. *Strong Performers and Successful Reformers in Education: Lessons from PISA for the United States.* Paris: OECD.

———. 2015. *Skills for Social Progress: The Power of Social and Emotional Skills.* Paris: OECD.

———. 2016. *PISA 2015 Results: Excellence and Equity in Education.* Vol. 1. Paris: OECD.

Peterson, Paul E., and Martin R. West. 2003. *No Child Left Behind? The Politics and Practice of School Accountability.* Washington, DC: Brookings Institution Press.

Pritchett, Lant. 2013. *The Rebirth of Education: Schooling Ain't Learning.* Washington, DC: Center for Global Development; Baltimore: Brookings Institution Press.

Pritchett, Lant, Rukmini Banerji, and Charles Kenny. 2013. "Schooling Is Not Education! Using Assessment to Change the Politics of Non-learning." CGD Report, Center for Global Development, Washington, DC.

R4D (Results for Development Institute). 2015. "Bringing Learning to Light: The Role of Citizen-Led Assessments in Shifting the Education Agenda." R4D, Washington, DC.

Reback, Randall. 2008. "Teaching to the Rating: School Accountability and the Distribution of Student Achievement." *Journal of Public Economics* 92 (5): 1394–1415.

Sandefur, Justin. 2016. "Internationally Comparable Mathematics Scores for Fourteen African Countries." CGD Working Paper 444 (December), Center for Global Development, Washington, DC.

———. 2017. "The Case for Global Standardized Testing." *Views from the Center: Education, Education Reform* (blog), April 27. https://www.cgdev.org/blog/case-global-standardized-testing.

Schäferhoff, Marco, and Nicholas Burnett. 2016. "Rethinking the Financing and Architecture of Global Education." Background Paper: The Learning Generation (April 29), International Commission on Financing Global Education Opportunity, New York.

Sellar, Sam, and Bob Lingard. 2013. "The OECD and Global Governance in Education." *Journal of Education Policy* 28 (5): 710–25.

Székely, Miguel. 2011. "Toward Results-Based Social Policy Design and Implementation." CGD Working Paper 249, Center for Global Development, Washington, DC.

Tanaka, Shinichiro. 2001. "Corruption in Education Sector Development: A Suggestion for Anticipatory Strategy." *International Journal of Educational Management* 15 (4): 158–66.

Tawil, Sobhi, Margarete Sachs-Israel, Huong Le Thu, and Matthias Eck. 2016. *Unpacking Sustainable Development Goal 4 Education 2030—Guide.* Paris: United Nations Educational, Scientific, and Cultural Organization.

UIS (UNESCO Institute for Statistics). 2016. "Laying the Foundation to Measure Sustainable Development Goal 4." Sustainable Development Data Digest, UIS, Montreal.

Uwezo. 2014. "Are Our Children Learning? Literacy and Numeracy across East Africa 2013." Twaweza, Nairobi.

World Bank. 2003. *World Development Report 2004: Making Services Work for Poor People.* Washington, DC: World Bank; New York: Oxford University Press.

Worthy, Ben. 2015. "The Impact of Open Data in the UK: Complex, Unpredictable, and Political." *Public Administration* 93 (3): 788–805.

Xu, Duoduo, and Jaap Dronkers. 2016. "Migrant Children in Shanghai: A Research Note on the PISA-Shanghai Controversy." *Chinese Sociological Review* 48 (3): 271–95.

SPOTLIGHT 3

The multidimensionality of skills

Having knowledge is not the same as being able to apply it.[1] Having a skill means having the ability to do something well. Having a skill requires knowledge, but having knowledge does not necessarily imply having skills.[2] Knowing how a wind turbine works does not mean a person has the skill to fix one.

Skills are multidimensional, dynamic, and interactive

Promoting a breadth of skills means "educating for a mastery of a wide range of competencies that will help mitigate the challenges posed by our changing world context."[3] This Report uses three broad categories of skills (figure S3.1):

Cognitive skills refers to the "ability to understand complex ideas, to adapt effectively to the environment, to learn from experience, to engage in various forms of reasoning, to overcome obstacles by taking thought."[4] Cognitive skills are needed for learning, personal and professional development, and the development of other types of skills. They can be broken down into *foundational skills*—which include basic literacy, numeracy, critical thinking, and problem-solving—and *higher-order skills* such as more advanced versions of these cognitive skills and others like adaptive learning.

Socioemotional skills are the behaviors, attitudes, and values that a person needs to "navigate interpersonal and social situations effectively,"[5] as well as to "deal effectively and ethically with daily tasks and challenges."[6] Self-awareness, leadership, teamwork, self-control, and motivation are socioemotional skills.[7] Sometimes referred to as *noncognitive skills*, socioemotional skills include so-called personality traits, which reflect enduring patterns in how individuals respond to various situations. Socioemotional skills are transversal skills, meaning they are relevant to a broad range of disciplines. They work together with cognitive skills, in that success in meeting many workplace and life challenges depends on both types of skills.

Technical skills are the acquired knowledge, expertise, and interactions needed by a worker for competent performance of the duties associated with a specific job. Technical skills require mastery of the knowledge, materials, tools, and technologies needed to do a job.[8]

Cognitive skills and socioemotional skills reinforce each other. Individuals with characteristics such as drive, diligence, perseverance, or good social skills are more likely to apply themselves to acquiring cognitive skills, as well as to have positive relationships in their lives. Yet cognitive skills are distinct from socioemotional skills.[9] Acquiring an early solid base of both is critical because both set the course of lifetime trajectories. Individuals with early advantages tend to gain more skills over their lifetimes, and it is difficult for others to close widening gaps over time.

Skills can be acquired

Different types of skills can be developed over time, depending on an individual's neurobiological and psychological development.[10]

Most cognitive skills are acquired during childhood, but they can be reinforced through young adulthood. Early childhood is an optimal period to acquire foundational cognitive skills because they are a prerequisite to developing further cognitive and socioemotional skills during later developmental periods.[11]

Figure S3.1 Cognitive, socioemotional, and technical skills interact

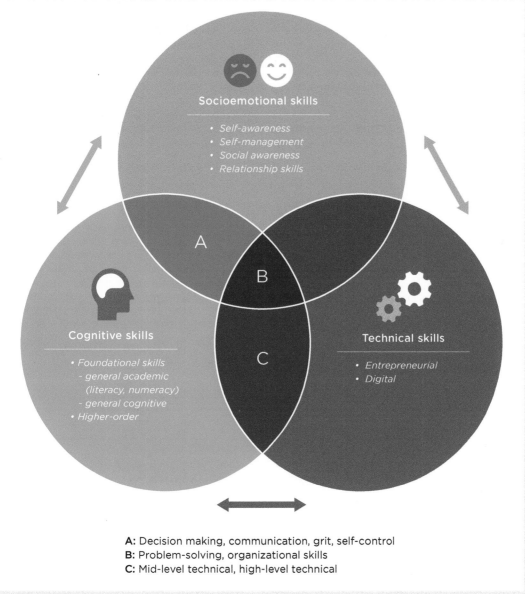

A: Decision making, communication, grit, self-control
B: Problem-solving, organizational skills
C: Mid-level technical, high-level technical

Source: WDR 2018 team.

Higher-order cognitive skills are regularly developed in late adolescence and early adulthood, in parallel with technical skills that are relevant for the labor market.[12] Given the ages that correspond to optimal skills development periods, foundational cognitive skills are usually learned in school and at home.

Similarly, socioemotional skills can be acquired through adulthood, though the optimal period is in early childhood, while the best stage to reinforce them is early adulthood. But unlike cognitive skills, certain socioemotional skills—such as self-esteem,

positive identity, or leadership—are better acquired in middle childhood and during adolescence.[13] Even though the neurobiological and psychosocial bases are already well established at this stage, socioemotional skills can also be learned well during early adulthood through new experiences.[14]

Technical skills can be learned at ages and in settings that correspond to the fields of study or jobs that a person chooses. Thus these skills can be acquired throughout life, in school and the workplace, as well as through specific training and education.[15]

Notes

1. Schönfeld (2017).
2. For a discussion of alternative definitions of the term *skills*, see Green (2011) and Warhurst and others (2017).
3. Winthrop and McGivney (2016, 14).
4. Neisser and others (1996, 77).
5. Guerra, Modecki, and Cunningham (2014, 5).
6. "Core SEL Competencies," CASEL, http://www.casel.org /core-competencies/. Also see Pierre and others (2014) and Taylor and others (2017).
7. Duckworth and Yeager (2015); Durlak and others (2011); John and DeFruyt (2015); Kautz and others (2014); Payton and others (2008).
8. Pierre and others (2014).
9. Kautz and others (2014).
10. Cunha, Heckman, and Schennach (2010); Guerra, Modecki, and Cunningham (2014).
11. Cunha and others (2006).
12. Handel, Valerio, and Sánchez Puerta (2016).
13. Cunningham, Acosta, and Muller (2016).
14. Sánchez Puerta, Valerio, and Gutiérrez Bernal (2016); Taylor and others (2017).
15. Handel and others (2016).

References

Cunha, Flavio, James J. Heckman, Lance Lochner, and Dimitriy V. Masterov. 2006. "Interpreting the Evidence on Life Cycle Skill Formation." In *Handbook of the Economics of Education*, Vol. 1, edited by Eric A. Hanushek and Finis Welch, 697–812. Handbooks in Economics Series 26. Amsterdam: North-Holland.

Cunha, Flavio, James J. Heckman, and Susanne M. Schennach. 2010. "Estimating the Technology of Cognitive and Noncognitive Skill Formation." *Econometrica* 78 (3): 883–931.

Cunningham, Wendy V., Pablo Acosta, and Noël Muller. 2016. *Minds and Behaviors at Work: Boosting Socioemotional Skills for Latin America's Workforce*. Directions in Development: Human Development Series. Washington, DC: World Bank.

Duckworth, Angela L., and David Scott Yeager. 2015. "Measurement Matters: Assessing Personal Qualities Other Than Cognitive Ability for Educational Purposes." *Educational Researcher* 44 (4): 237–51.

Durlak, Joseph A., Roger P. Weissberg, Allison B. Dymnicki, Rebecca D. Taylor, and Kriston B. Schellinger. 2011. "The Impact of Enhancing Students' Social and Emotional Learning: A Meta-Analysis of School-Based Universal Interventions." *Child Development* 82 (1): 405–32.

Green, Francis. 2011. "What Is Skill? An Inter-Disciplinary Synthesis." LLAKES Research Paper 20, Centre for Learning and Life Chances in Knowledge Economies and Societies, Institute of Education, University of London.

Guerra, Nancy, Kathryn Modecki, and Wendy V. Cunningham. 2014. "Developing Social-Emotional Skills for the Labor Market: The Practice Model." Policy Research Working Paper 7123, World Bank, Washington, DC.

Handel, Michael J., Alexandria Valerio, and María Laura Sánchez Puerta. 2016. *Accounting for Mismatch in Low- and Middle-Income Countries*. Directions in Development: Human Development Series. Washington, DC: World Bank.

John, Oliver P., and Filip DeFruyt. 2015. "Education and Social Progress: Framework for the Longitudinal Study of Social and Emotional Skills in Cities." Report EDU/CERI /CD, Organisation for Economic Co-operation and Development, Paris.

Kautz, Tim, James J. Heckman, Ron Diris, Bas Ter Weel, and Lex Borghans. 2014. "Fostering and Measuring Skills: Improving Cognitive and Non-cognitive Skills to Promote Lifetime Success." NBER Working Paper 20749, National Bureau of Economic Research, Cambridge, MA.

Neisser, Ulric, Gwyneth Boodoo, Thomas J. Bouchard Jr., A. Wade Boykin, Nathan Brody, Stephen J. Ceci, Diane F. Halpern, et al. 1996. "Intelligence: Knowns and Unknowns." *American Psychologist* 51 (2): 77–101.

Payton, John, Roger P. Weissberg, Joseph A. Durlak, Allison B. Dymnicki, Rebecca D. Taylor, Kriston B. Schellinger, and Molly Pachan. 2008. "The Positive Impact of Social and Emotional Learning for Kindergarten to Eighth-Grade Students: Findings from Three Scientific Reviews." Technical Report, Collaborative for Academic, Social, and Emotional Learning, Chicago.

Pierre, Gaëlle, María Laura Sánchez Puerta, Alexandria Valerio, and Tania Rajadel. 2014. "STEP Skills Measurement Surveys: Innovative Tools for Assessing Skills." Social Protection and Labor Discussion Paper 1421, World Bank, Washington, DC.

Sánchez Puerta, María Laura, Alexandria Valerio, and Marcela Gutiérrez Bernal. 2016. *Taking Stock of Programs to Develop Socioemotional Skills: A Systematic Review of Program Evidence*. Directions in Development: Human Development Series. Washington, DC: World Bank.

Schönfeld, Manuel. 2017. "Work Readiness Assessment Tools in Comparison: From Administration to Z-scores." World Bank, Washington, DC.

Taylor, R.D., E. Oberle, J. A. Durlak, and R. P. Weissberg. 2017. "Promoting Positive Youth Development through School-Based Social and Emotional Learning Interventions: A Meta-Analysis of Follow-Up Effects." *Child Development* 88 (4): 1156–71.

Warhurst, Chris, Ken Mayhew, David Finegold, and John Buchanan, eds. 2017. *The Oxford Handbook of Skills and Training*. Oxford, U.K.: Oxford University Press.

Winthrop, Rebecca, and Eileen McGivney. 2016. "Skills for a Changing World: Advancing Quality Learning for Vibrant Societies." Center for Universal Education, Brookings Institution, Washington, DC.

PART III

Innovations and evidence for learning

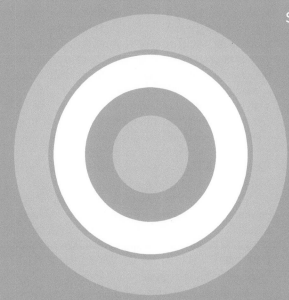

SPOTLIGHT 4

Learning about learning

Identifying gaps between evidence and practice helps set priorities for action.

As evidence of the learning crisis has grown, so has understanding of what produces learning. Cognitive neuroscience has evolved dramatically, with brain imaging revealing new insights into how children learn.[1] Over the last two decades, neuroscience has been instrumental to understanding early child brain development and the crucial nature of the early years.[2] Schools in many parts of the world are innovating in approaches to pedagogy, professional development, and the use of new technologies.[3] Governments and nonprofits are trying out innovative programs to upgrade teachers' skills on the job.[4]

At the same time, evidence on which programs most effectively boost learning is mushrooming. One example of that growth: the number of impact evaluations of interventions intended to improve learning outcomes in developing countries rose from 19 in 2000 to 299 by 2016 (figure S4.1).[5] This evidence

Figure S4.1 The number of experimental and quasi-experimental studies of interventions to improve learning has mushroomed in recent decades

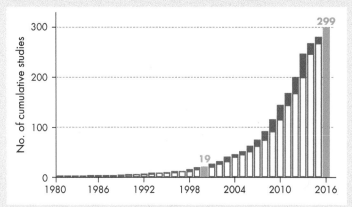

Sources: WDR 2018 team, using data from 3ie (2016) and Evans and Popova (2016b). Data at http://bit .do/WDR2018-Fig_S4-1.

Note: The blue segment on the white bars represents the increment from the previous year.

translates into clearer insights into how to improve learning at the level of the student, the classroom, and the school. Beyond the increase in their number, these impact evaluations have also grown more sophisticated over time, making them more useful for policy making. They are now more likely to compare multiple interventions, more likely to study a wide range of interventions overall, and more likely to study interventions on a large scale. The evaluations show that many of these interventions have sizable impacts. Several pedagogical interventions, for example, deliver learning gains greater than what students would learn in a year of business-as-usual schooling.[6]

Making better use of evidence

Not all evidence is created equal, but many different kinds of evidence can be credible. Scientific evidence demonstrates the pathways of brain development and functioning. Social science evidence can effectively answer the question of what would have happened in the absence of a reform or intervention (often called a counterfactual). Randomized controlled trials or analyses of "natural experiments" are useful tools for determining such a counterfactual. Implementation science and case studies can provide a detailed picture of how an intervention or a phenomenon works. The best evidence of what improves learning draws from a range of methods.

Even when an intervention in one education system has a positive impact, it may not work everywhere. Effects may differ when translating from one location to another or from a pilot study to a large-scale program. What works in Peru may not work in Burundi because the education systems and societies are different. A common intervention that has been tested in a range of settings is to reduce class size. But increasing class size by 10 students reduced test scores by four times as much in Israel as it did in Kenya.[7] A pilot intervention may allow for more controlled conditions than an at-scale intervention. In Kenya, an intervention to hire contract teachers was effective on a small scale, but when it was implemented at scale through government systems, salaries were delayed and ultimately the contract teachers were converted to civil servants.[8] The scaled-up program no longer resembled the successful pilot, and the learning gains failed to materialize.

To make sense of the evidence, policy makers should consider the likely principles behind effective programs rather than fixating on results (or "point estimates") from individual studies.[9] For example, programs that provide financial incentives for teachers have had mixed effects. Rather than taking a simple average of the effects, a nuanced assessment would reveal that these programs tend to work better when improving quality is relatively simple and within a teacher's control—for example, when they increase teacher attendance or teaching time while at school.[10]

Viewing evidence through models of human behavior is one way to focus on principles. This means examining patterns of results and using models to infer why results vary across settings. The first step would be a nuanced synthesis, bringing together the results of a range of studies and examining empirical patterns. The second step would be using theory—models of human behavior—to explain why some proposed solutions work and others do not, as well as why the same solution may work in one locale or time but not in another.

Producing learning is complex, but investments that change what happens in the classroom are a good bet

Many actors contribute to the learning process, and they all face their own incentives. The direct inputs to the learning process include the choices made by learners themselves, as well as by their parents, teachers, and other school leaders, interacting with the available infrastructure and materials. Less immediate but still important, bureaucrats, politicians, and nonstate players make decisions that influence education quality. Understanding these relationships is crucial to interpreting evidence.

Each actor in the learning process reacts to the others, so changing one element of the process does not guarantee more learning. Many of the inputs to the learning process are choices made by the actors—choices made in reaction to the actual and anticipated choices of other actors (figure S4.2). Teachers react to

Figure S4.2 It's more complicated than it looks: People act in reaction to the choices of others throughout the system

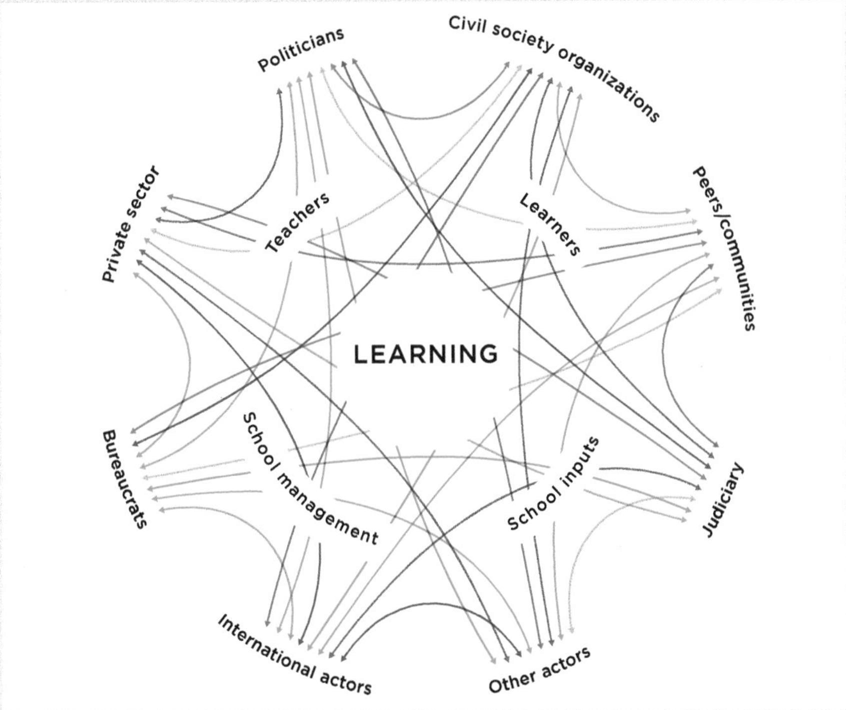

Source: WDR 2018 team.

changes in school leadership, school directors react to community demands, and parents react to changes in government policy. In India and Zambia, grants to schools led parents to reduce their own investments in their children's schooling.[11] In a household with few resources, if the government begins providing textbooks, a parent may well reallocate education resources to other needs, such as health.

How can we make sense of all of these complex, dynamic relationships? Models of human behavior illuminate the motives for choices and actions, and they can help guide solutions. Simple optimizing behavior models—in which actors maximize their well-being subject to limited budgets and other constraints—explain why parents reduce their contributions when schools increase theirs. Principal-agent models that incorporate multiple actors with different objectives explain why teachers may fail to teach when not sufficiently motivated or monitored. Behavioral models also play a role: student learning and educational aspirations can be affected by the salience of stereotypes. Economic phenomena such as information, market, and coordination failures play a role in these models. The models can also illuminate why a gap is often observed between evidence on how to improve learning and actual practice.

Focusing where the gaps between evidence and practice are largest

Gaps between evidence and actual practice provide entry points for efforts to improve education. These gaps come to light when evidence shows that certain approaches or interventions can improve outcomes, but the approaches used in practice are different.[12] For example, the accumulated research evidence demonstrates high returns to early investments in children, yet families and governments in low-income environments do not prioritize these investments. Evidence shows that certain types of teacher professional development deliver much higher learning gains than others, but outdated training methods persist.[13] Because the gap between evidence

and practice requires good information on what the evidence says, as well as what current practice is, it is likely that many opportunities for improvement have yet to be discovered.

Intuition and common sense are not enough. One fundamental lesson from the growing evidence base is that intuition is not always a trustworthy guide. It may miss the complexity of motivations and reactions in the real world, as can happen when teacher financial incentives induce cheating rather than more effort.[14] Intuition may fail to capture the net effect of conflicting forces, such as when separating students by ability allows teachers to target teaching more specifically to students' level—which should increase their learning—but also distances them from their high-performing peers—which may decrease their learning.

Knowledge about improving learning must take both the costs and the benefits of learning interventions into account. A computer-assisted learning intervention in India increased learning more than employing contract teachers in Kenya, but hiring contract teachers was so much cheaper that it delivered a higher return on investment.[15] The evidence base on costs is much thinner than that on benefits, with a tiny fraction of studies examining both.[16] But some programs have been evaluated on both effectiveness and cost-effectiveness.[17] This evidence on costs—adapted to local contexts—should qualify policy recommendations.[18]

The gaps between evidence and practice signal promising places to start, rather than the end of learning how to improve learning. Interventions cannot simply be exported from one country to another. Indeed, at times the effectiveness of an apparently similar intervention can vary even within a country, depending on how the program is implemented.[19] The cost of implementation will also vary dramatically across contexts.[20] But this does not mean that evidence from other contexts is without value. On the contrary, successes in other environments—coupled with a careful analysis of why the programs work—provide a starting point. Policy makers can draw on this evidence and experiment in their own policy environment.

Notes

1. De Smedt (2014); Insel and Landis (2013); Kuhl (2010).
2. Dua and others (2016).
3. Chisholm and Leyendecker (2008); Schweisfurth (2011).
4. Popova, Evans, and Arancibia (2016).
5. Evans and Popova (2016b).
6. Evans and Yuan (2017).
7. Pritchett and Sandefur (2013).
8. Bold and others (2016); Duflo, Dupas, and Kremer (2015).
9. Muralidharan (2017).
10. Muralidharan and Sundararaman (2011).

11. Das and others (2013).
12. Montagu and Goodman (2016); Pakenham-Walsh (2004).
13. Lauwerier and Akkari (2015).
14. Glazerman, McKie, and Carey (2009); Jacob and Levitt (2003).
15. Kremer, Brannen, and Glennerster (2013).
16. McEwan (2015).
17. Kremer, Brannen, and Glennerster (2013).
18. Evans and Popova (2016a).
19. Bold and others (2016); Kerwin and Thornton (2015).
20. Evans and Popova (2016a).

References

3ie (International Initiative for Impact Evaluation). 2016. "Impact Evaluation Repository." 3ie, London. http://www.3ieimpact.org/en/evidence/impact-evaluations/impact-evaluation-repository/.

Bold, Tessa, Mwangi Kimenyi, Germano Mwabu, Alice Ng'ang'a, and Justin Sandefur. 2016. "Experimental Evidence on Scaling Up Education Reforms in Kenya." Economic Development and Institutions Project Working Paper, Institute for International Economic Studies, Stockholm University.

Chisholm, Linda, and Ramon Leyendecker. 2008. "Curriculum Reform in Post-1990s Sub-Saharan Africa." International Journal of Educational Development 28 (2): 195–205.

Das, Jishnu, Stefan Dercon, James Habyarimana, Pramila Krishnan, Karthik Muralidharan, and Venkatesh Sundararaman. 2013. "School Inputs, Household Substitution, and Test Scores." American Economic Journal: Applied Economics 5 (2): 29–57.

De Smedt, Bert. 2014. "Advances in the Use of Neuroscience Methods in Research on Learning and Instruction." Frontline Learning Research 2 (4): 7–14.

Dua, Tarun, Mark Tomlinson, Elizabeth Tablante, Pia Britto, Aisha Yousfzai, Bernadette Daelmans, and Gary L. Darmstadt. 2016. "Global Research Priorities to Accelerate Early Child Development in the Sustainable Development Era." Lancet Global Health 4 (12): e887–e889.

Duflo, Esther, Pascaline Dupas, and Michael R. Kremer. 2015. "School Governance, Teacher Incentives, and Pupil-Teacher Ratios: Experimental Evidence from Kenyan Primary Schools." Journal of Public Economics 123 (March): 92–110.

Evans, David K., and Anna Popova. 2016a. "Cost-Effectiveness Analysis in Development: Accounting for Local Costs and Noisy Impacts." World Development 77: 262–76.

———. 2016b. "What Really Works to Improve Learning in Developing Countries? An Analysis of Divergent Findings in Systematic Reviews." World Bank Research Observer 31 (2): 242–70.

Evans, David K., and Fei Yuan. 2017. "Economic Returns to Interventions That Increase Learning." Background paper, World Bank, Washington, DC.

Glazerman, Steven, Allison McKie, and Nancy Carey. 2009. "An Evaluation of the Teacher Advancement Program (TAP) in Chicago: Year One Impact Report, Final Report." Mathematica Policy Research, Princeton, NJ.

Insel, Thomas R., and Story C. Landis. 2013. "Twenty-Five Years of Progress: The View from Nimh and Ninds." Neuron 80 (3): 561–67.

Jacob, Brian A., and Steven D. Levitt. 2003. "Rotten Apples: An Investigation of the Prevalence and Predictors of Teacher Cheating." Quarterly Journal of Economics 118 (3): 843–78.

Jinnai, Yusuke. 2016. "To Introduce or Not to Introduce Monetary Bonuses: The Cost of Repealing Teacher Incentives." Economics and Management Series EMS-2016-08 (January), IUJ Research Institute, International University of Japan, Minamiuonuma, Niigata Prefecture, Japan. http://www.iuj.ac.jp/research/workingpapers/EMS_2016_08.pdf.

Kerwin, Jason T., and Rebecca L. Thornton. 2015. "Making the Grade: Understanding What Works for Teaching Literacy in Rural Uganda." PSC Research Report 15-842, Population Studies Center, Institute for Social Research, University of Michigan, Ann Arbor.

Kremer, Michael R., Conner Brannen, and Rachel Glennerster. 2013. "The Challenge of Education and Learning in the Developing World." Science 340 (6130): 297–300.

Kuhl, Patricia K. 2010. "Brain Mechanisms in Early Language Acquisition." Neuron 67 (5): 713–27.

Lauwerier, Thibaut, and Abdeljalil Akkari. 2015. "Teachers and the Quality of Basic Education in Sub-Saharan Africa." ERF Working Paper 11, Education Research and Foresight, Paris.

McEwan, Patrick J. 2015. "Improving Learning in Primary Schools of Developing Countries: A Meta-Analysis of Randomized Experiments." Review of Educational Research 85 (3): 353–94.

Montagu, Dominic, and Catherine Goodman. 2016. "Prohibit, Constrain, Encourage, or Purchase: How Should We Engage with the Private Health-Care Sector?" Lancet 388 (10044): 613–21.

Muralidharan, Karthik. 2017. "Field Experiments in Education in Developing Countries." In Handbook of Field Experiments, edited by Abhijit Vinayak Banerjee and Esther Duflo, Vol. 2, 323–88. Handbooks in Economics Series. Amsterdam: North-Holland.

Muralidharan, Karthik, and Venkatesh Sundararaman. 2011. "Teacher Performance Pay: Experimental Evidence from India." Journal of Political Economy 119 (1): 39–77.

Pakenham-Walsh, Neil. 2004. "Learning from One Another to Bridge the 'Know-Do Gap.'" BMJ 329 (7475): 1189.

Popova, Anna, David K. Evans, and Violeta Arancibia. 2016. "Training Teachers on the Job: What Works and How to Measure It." Policy Research Working Paper 7834, World Bank, Washington, DC.

Pritchett, Lant, and Justin Sandefur. 2013. "Context Matters for Size: Why External Validity Claims and Development Practice Do Not Mix." Journal of Globalization and Development 4 (2): 161–98.

Schweisfurth, Michele. 2011. "Learner-Centred Education in Developing Country Contexts: From Solution to Problem?" International Journal of Educational Development 31 (5): 425–32.

5

There is no learning without prepared, motivated learners

Strong foundations underpin all learning and skills development. Learning depends on students who are prepared, present, and motivated—but getting students there will often require policy change within and beyond education systems.

Schools cannot produce learning without prepared, present, motivated learners. Around the world, many children receive too little investment in nutrition and stimulation during their early years, and many lack access to quality early learning opportunities that can prepare them for first grade. The one in four children worldwide who are stunted cannot achieve their potential in school.[1] Nor can the 263 million young people who do not make it to school at all. Among those who do attend, motivation to learn often suffers when the quality of education is low. A poor-quality basic education also means that learners who should be gaining advanced skills from tertiary education or technical training lack the preparation to do so.[2] Thus, just as the fundamental investments needed for primary education must be made before a child enters school, the same is true for skills training. In many cases, the failure to invest effectively can be understood through models of human behavior, which also point the way to solutions (table 5.1). A synthesis of the evidence in these areas reveals three key principles for improving learning:

- To set children on high-development trajectories, foster cognitive and socioemotional development through early child nutrition, care, stimulation, and learning opportunities.
- To get children into school—an essential first step to learning—lower school costs and then use other tools to boost motivation for learning.

- To address the fact that so many youth leave basic education lacking skills, recognize that remediation often needs to be the first step in further education and training.

Investing in their early years prepares children for school

Children's early years offer a rare window for societies to make investments in their children with extremely high returns (figure 5.1). Efforts to improve children's lives can significantly increase individual and societal productivity while reducing inequality.[3] Children cannot thrive with stunted bodies and brains, and early gaps in learning and skills trap them in lower developmental trajectories from which it becomes increasingly difficult to escape (spotlight 2). Though children's bodies are resilient, and catch-up after early childhood may be possible when inputs improve, it is extremely difficult to reverse the effects of exposure to risk factors in the first few years of a child's life. Doing so entails costly, high-quality interventions that typically need to happen at a sufficiently young age to be effective.

Recognizing the dangers that poverty poses to children's development and learning

Children need quality environmental inputs to grow in a healthy, timely fashion. Essential physical inputs

Table 5.1 Models of human behavior can guide actions to improve learner preparation: Some examples

Synthesis principle	Where this fails	Models that identify a mechanism behind this failure	Approaches that address the modeled mechanism
Provide early child nutrition, care, stimulation, and learning opportunities.	Just one in five children in low-income countries attend preschool. One in four children worldwide are stunted.	*Information failure:* Stakeholders may not be aware of relative returns to early investments or how to support early development.	In Jamaica, a program taught caregivers to provide psychosocial stimulation that improved stunted children's developmental scores and later life outcomes.
		Simple optimization with liquidity and credit constraints: Parents are aware but lack the resources to invest.	In Mexico, a conditional cash transfer program improved cognitive and motor development.
		Behavioral (mental bandwidth): Stress of poverty undermines parenting capacity.	In Argentina, Bangladesh, China, and Uganda, center-based programs improved children's outcomes.
Lower school costs; boost motivation and effort.	263 million children remain out of school. Many countries still charge fees for lower secondary school, and primary school, while usually tuition-free, still entails cash outlays in many settings.	*Simple optimization with liquidity and credit constraints:* Parents are aware but lack the resources to invest in any or all children.	In Cambodia, providing scholarships to girls dramatically increased enrollment.
		Information failure: Youth and parents may underestimate the returns to education.	In the Dominican Republic and Madagascar, providing information on the returns to education improved enrollment and learning.
		Behavioral (hyperbolic discounting): Youth may recognize the value of education but plan to invest later (yet "later" never comes).	In Pakistan, reporting child test scores to parents increased enrollment and learning outcomes.
Ensure that, where needed, remediation is the first step in further education and training.	Many skills training programs assume prerequisite skills that youth do not have.	*Information failure:* Training programs receive imperfect signals about the quality of incoming learners.	In U.S. community colleges, improving course placement accuracy and support services helped increase students' long-term performance.
		Simple optimization (on the part of training centers): Remedial students are highly likely to drop out.	In the United States, bridge programs help learners move past remediation quickly.

Source: WDR 2018 team.

include quality pre- and postnatal nutrition, health care, and safe physical environments.[4] Equally crucial are social inputs, including nurturing, protection, and stimulation.[5] Interactions between children and their caregivers—who are often, but not always, their parents—leave a significant imprint, literally shaping the developing brain.[6] Yet poor children's access to these inputs—along with caregivers' awareness of their importance—is often limited. So are programs that invest in children's early development and the policies that guide them.

Poor children are more exposed to health shocks and less likely to receive stimulation, care, and protection from stress. Nutrient deprivation, infectious diseases, and chemically toxic or physically dangerous environments affect many poor children not only after birth, but also in the womb. Exposure to any of these factors during sensitive periods can inhibit normal biological development (spotlight 1), but poor children often encounter these factors in tandem and over time.[7] At the same time, the strains associated with poverty can disrupt parents' decision making and limit their availability, sensitivity, and responsiveness.[8] As a result, poorer children not only have fewer resources such as books or toys, but also receive less stimulation, direction, and support.[9] Poor children are also more likely to experience neglect and harsher discipline, which disrupts early

Figure 5.1 Investments in high-quality programs during children's early years pay off

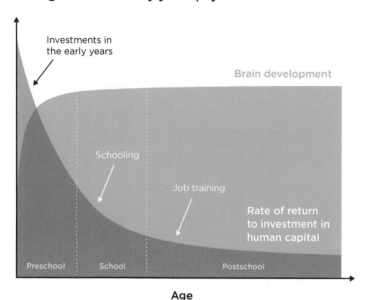

Source: WDR 2018 team, based on Carneiro, Cunha, and Heckman (2003); Martin (2012).

emotional organization—the keystone of socioemotional abilities—and is associated with worse school performance.[10]

Early childhood development programs are insufficient in number and quality to compensate for poor children's disadvantages, especially in the developing world. In poor communities, resources that stimulate early development outside the home—including quality child care, libraries, recreation centers, and preschool programs—tend to be limited and low in quality.[11] Only half of 3- to 6-year-olds have access to preprimary education. Coverage is strongly associated with income, ranging from 19 percent in low-income countries to 86 percent in high-income countries, with poorer children enrolled at the lowest rates in every country.[12] Children under 3 are widely underserved, with access to services for this age group especially inequitable and uncoordinated.[13] Moreover, reliance on poorly compensated child care workers who receive little to no training, mentoring, or monitoring undermines sustainability, retention, and quality.[14]

Governments do not invest enough in young children. Insufficient understanding of the high payoffs to early interventions, budget constraints, and the challenges of delivering wide-ranging early childhood interventions—health, nutrition, early learning—result in low public investment in young children in most regions. In Sub-Saharan Africa, on average just 2 percent of the education budget goes to preprimary education.[15] In Latin America, the average per capita government spending on children under 5 is a third of that for children ages 6–11.[16] Investments in the early years have increased in developing countries, but strategies often focus on building preschools, neglecting children who have not yet reached preschool age. Though preschool can help, foundations across developmental dimensions are set before age 3. Yet this age group typically receives little government coverage beyond health and nutrition checkups—not enough for healthy overall development.

Early exposure to risks associated with poverty may prevent children from realizing the promise of education. Intense deprivation can result in poor developmental outcomes—such as stunted growth or impaired brain development—that are difficult to address (figure 5.2; spotlight 2). Children who have fallen behind in their physical, cognitive, linguistic, or socioemotional development are more likely to enter grade 1 late, score poorly in school, repeat grades, drop out before they complete primary school, experience poor health throughout their lives, engage in high-risk behavior (particularly in adolescence), be less productive, and have lower earnings.[17] The scale of the problem is vast: nearly half of children under 5 in developing countries are stunted or live in extreme poverty, threatening their prospects of benefiting from the opportunities education can provide.[18]

Strengthening children's ability to learn with well-designed interventions

Effective early childhood interventions can significantly improve poor children's ability to learn. In the United States, at-risk children who participated in well-designed interventions—Perry Preschool, Abecedarian, the Nurse-Family Partnership—benefited well beyond their early years: their school performance, employment, income, overall welfare, and social integration all improved. Such interventions have substantial potential in developing countries because of their lower baselines. In Jamaica, the Reach Up and Learn program, which promoted early child stimulation, led to lower crime rates, better mental health, and 25 percent higher earnings two decades later. There is a consensus on what children need: nutrition, care, stimulation, nurturing, and protection. The evidence on when to implement programs is in line with biological evidence: prevention and early remediation are most cost-effective at specific points in development because adjustments beyond sensitive periods are difficult, costly, and usually incomplete. But identifying the most effective approaches to improving poor children's developmental outcomes has proven challenging because of the enormous heterogeneity in interventions as well as contexts. Still, several approaches show promise.

Health and nutrition interventions during the first 1,000 days of life (starting at conception) improve children's development. Programs that increase access to maternal health services improve maternal nutrition through diet, supplements, and fortification, while reducing child mortality and early health problems.[19] In isolation, nutritional interventions for children have only modest effects on height or stunting.[20] But when combined with improved sanitation, along with access to child health services, nutritional interventions can yield significant benefits.[21] Breastfeeding and micronutrient supplements are associated with better health and greater cognitive ability, leading to better educational outcomes in developing countries.[22] Deworming, iodine supplements, and immunizations have also led to major improvements in children's ability to learn.[23]

Programs that build caregivers' capacity to support healthy development can substantially improve children's outcomes. Interventions include coaching caregivers at home on positive discipline, as well as promoting increased frequency of quality interventions through nurturing, protection, and stimulating activities (storytelling, singing, playing with household objects). Such interventions have been delivered in diverse ways, including home visits, community meetings, and health checkups.[24] The most effective programs have systematic training and curriculums, as well as opportunities for caregivers to practice and receive feedback.[25] An emerging generation of programs is offering parents incentives through positive reinforcements, with indirect "nudges" when providing information is insufficient or when beliefs or norms are detrimental.[26]

Programs that provide caregivers with cash or psychosocial support complement interventions to improve parenting. Cash transfer programs can address acute material deprivation in households and improve developmental outcomes, particularly when provided alongside—or conditional on—prenatal care and child services. For example, conditional cash transfer (CCT) programs in Ecuador, Mexico, and Nicaragua have reduced stunting, improved cognitive development, and promoted better parenting practices.[27] In Mexico, parenting support programs integrated with CCT programs improved

Figure 5.2 Intense deprivation can impair brain development

Brain structure and wiring by stunting status

a. Infant representative of never-stunted growth

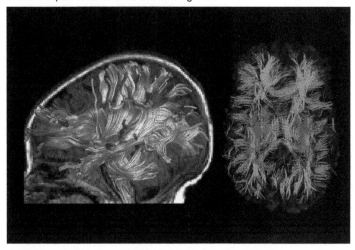

b. Infant representative of stunted growth

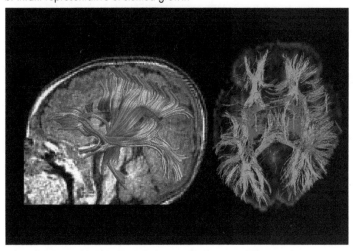

Source: Nelson and others (2017). © Nadine Gaab and Charles A. Nelson. Used with the permission of Charles A. Nelson; further permission required for reuse.

Note: The images illustrate two infants, 2–3 months old. The growth of one infant was stunted (panel b); the growth of the other infant was not (panel a). The images were obtained in Dhaka, Bangladesh, using magnetic resonance imaging (MRI). The left side of each panel shows the left side of the head. Each gold line represents a fiber tract—the long, thin fibers (axons) in the brain that transmit information to different neurons, muscles, and glands. It is apparent how much denser and more elaborate the connections are in the nonstunted infant. The colored images on the right side of each panel illustrate the same principles (neural connections) from a different orientation—a cross-section of the brain, from front to back.

child outcomes beyond the direct effects of the transfers.[28] Also important, transfer programs can alleviate parental time and psychological constraints. In addition, interventions delivered by supervised, nonspecialist health or community workers to address acute maternal stress, depression, and anxiety have led to better cognitive development, more physical growth, less diarrhea, and higher immunization rates.[29]

Center-based care can promote foundational skills. In countries from Ethiopia to the United States, high-quality, center-based programs have shown substantial benefits in developing children's language, cognitive, motor, and socioemotional skills.[30] By contrast, attending a low-quality, center-based program can be worse than attending none at all.[31] The quality of child-caregiver interactions is a key determinant of such programs' impacts, as Indonesia and Mozambique demonstrated with effective center-based preschool programs for children ages 3 to 6. These programs included minimal infrastructure investments but improved children's cognitive abilities thanks to their interactions with well-trained caregivers (box 5.1).[32] Delivering quality, center-based interventions for children under 3 is harder because they require costlier structural investments (such as lower child-to-staff ratios). Consequently, programs to build parenting capacity might be most cost-effective for children under 3 in resource-constrained environments or to reach marginalized populations.[33]

Bringing it all together

Integrating programs can lead to better development outcomes. Poor children are exposed to multiple risk factors that cannot be adequately addressed by any single intervention. Multifactor programs capture the complex, complementary nature of early childhood development and exploit complementarities (figure 5.3).[34] To be effective, interventions must be delivered during specific stages of development.[35] Packaging interventions to address sequential or related developmental goals can increase effectiveness, especially if intervention packages incorporate benefits for caregivers as well. Integrated intervention packages can build on existing platforms such as community-based strategies or social safety nets, though the effectiveness of any specific strategy will depend on contextual factors.[36] Quality should not be diluted in the effort to increase investments in the early years— say, by relying on volunteers or unqualified workers to deliver services, which is common.[37]

Providing demand-side support can get kids to school, but not necessarily to learn

School is a key input to at-scale learning. Despite major gains in access, many children still don't attend school. Even though school is not the only place that

---

Box 5.1 Early childhood education prepares young children for school

Preschool programs targeting children ages 3–6 can foster foundational skills and boost children's ability to learn. Children who attend preschool have higher attendance and better achievement in primary school. Moreover, they are less likely to repeat, drop out, or need remedial or special education, all of which benefit not only students but also education systems because efficiency is increased.[a] Across countries at all income levels, the most disadvantaged children benefit most from quality early child education programs.[b] But early child education programs are not all equally effective; overly academic and structured programs for children under 5 may undermine their cognitive and socioemotional skills, as well as their motivation to learn, because young children learn best through exploration,

play, and interaction with others.[c] Key elements of programs that have led to strong preschool outcomes include curriculums that foster crucial pre-academic abilities (emotional security, curiosity, language, self-regulation) through play; professional development plus coaching that enable teachers to effectively implement relevant curriculums; and positive, engaging classrooms that promote children's innate drive to learn.[d] For early child education gains to be sustained, the content, budget, and capacity of providers of preschool programs should be integrated into formal education systems. In addition, the quality of subsequent learning environments in primary school is an important determinant of the long-term effects of preschool programs.[e]

Source: WDR 2018 team.

a. Klees (2017).
b. Britto and others (2016).
c. Whitebread, Kuvalja, and O'Connor (2015).
d. Phillips and others (2017).
e. Johnson and Jackson (2017).

Figure 5.3 Integrated programs through the early years are necessary for proper child development

Key interventions for young children and their families

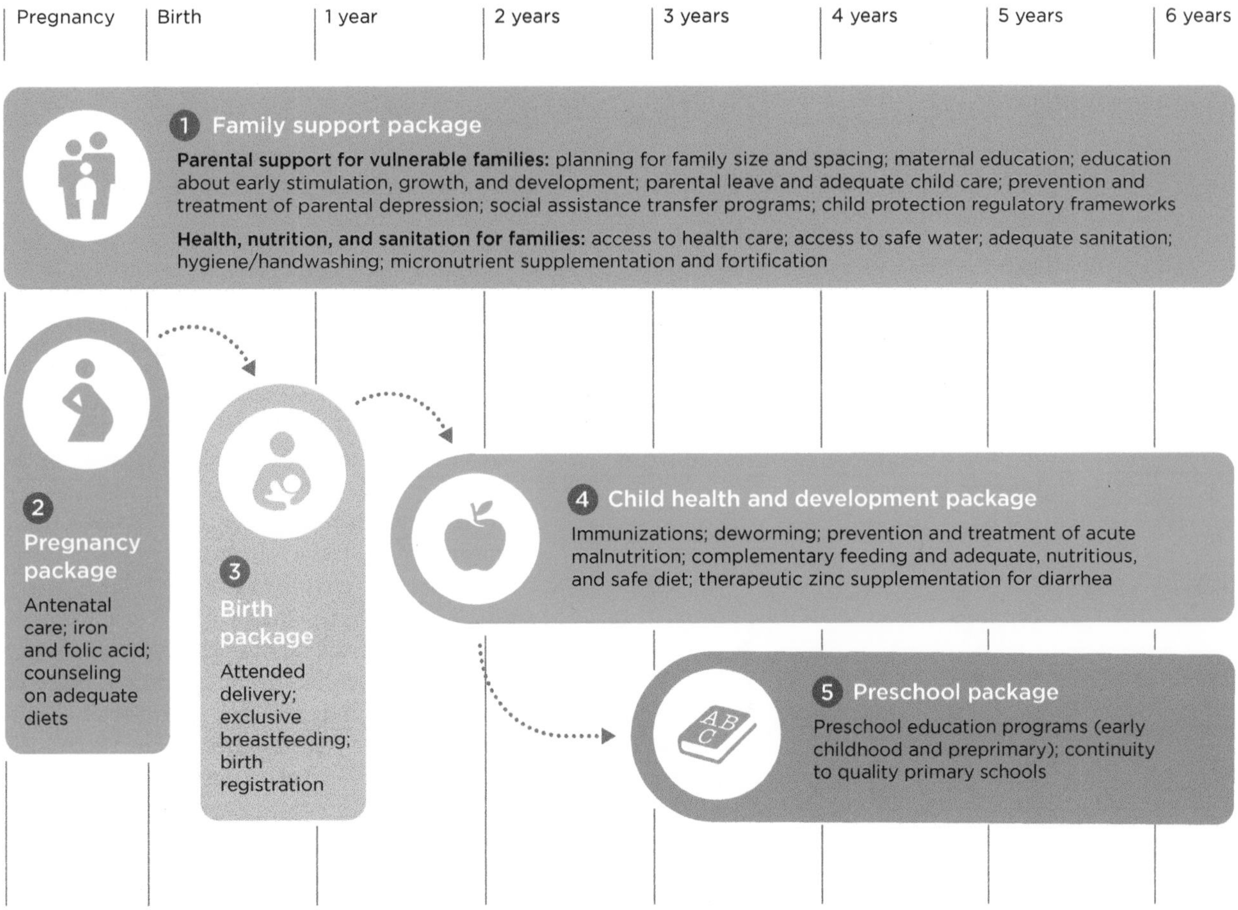

| Pregnancy | Birth | 1 year | 2 years | 3 years | 4 years | 5 years | 6 years |

1 Family support package

Parental support for vulnerable families: planning for family size and spacing; maternal education; education about early stimulation, growth, and development; parental leave and adequate child care; prevention and treatment of parental depression; social assistance transfer programs; child protection regulatory frameworks

Health, nutrition, and sanitation for families: access to health care; access to safe water; adequate sanitation; hygiene/handwashing; micronutrient supplementation and fortification

2 Pregnancy package

Antenatal care; iron and folic acid; counseling on adequate diets

3 Birth package

Attended delivery; exclusive breastfeeding; birth registration

4 Child health and development package

Immunizations; deworming; prevention and treatment of acute malnutrition; complementary feeding and adequate, nutritious, and safe diet; therapeutic zinc supplementation for diarrhea

5 Preschool package

Preschool education programs (early childhood and preprimary); continuity to quality primary schools

Source: Denboba and others (2014).

children learn (box 5.2), most parents want their children to go to school. Moreover, most children want to go. In a survey of Indian mothers with an average of less than three years of education, 94 percent hoped their children would complete at least grade 10.[38] In Kenya, among parents with no education at all, more than half wanted a university education for their children.[39]

Significant costs—both formal fees and a wide array of other expenses—prevent children, especially the most vulnerable, from learning. Nearly 90 percent of the world's low-income countries proclaim free primary education. But for lower secondary education, more than 40 percent of the countries charge fees, along with 10 percent of middle-income countries.[40] In Africa, almost half the expenditures that households incur to send their children to school—for

school supplies, learning materials, transportation— are in addition to formal fees.[41] These costs of schooling widen the gaps in school participation separating poorer children from their wealthier peers.

High aspirations for schooling among children and their parents explain why initiatives that ease constraints to schooling for households—so-called demand-side interventions—have been so effective at getting children to school. In many countries, the elimination of school fees has raised enrollments, suggesting that parents simply did not have the resources to pay the fees (figure 5.4).[42] The interventions, which have sought to reduce other costs associated with school, have consistently improved access in the form of enrollment as well as attendance.[43] Nonmerit scholarships—which reduce fees on a smaller scale—have increased enrollment at the

Box 5.2 Communities can leverage the many hours spent outside the classroom to boost learning

Much learning happens outside the classroom, including from tutoring and at-home programs. Across Africa and Asia, the Literacy Boost program has implemented community reading activities to leverage the many hours that learners spend outside school. These include pairing struggling readers with stronger readers ("reading buddies"), implementing read-a-thons (in which all the books that children read during a specific period are recorded), and providing mini-libraries. Children who participate in such activities have better reading outcomes. In Rwandese communities, implementing Literacy Boost led to better reading skills and school advancement.[a]

Source: WDR 2018 team.

a. Dowd and others (2017); Friedlander and Goldenberg (2016).

Figure 5.4 What happens when school fees are eliminated? Evidence from eight countries

Gross enrollment in years before and after elimination of school fees, selected countries

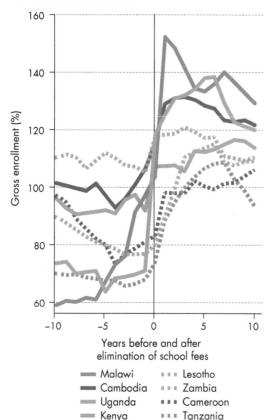

Source: WDR 2018 team, using data from World Bank (2017); year of policy change from Bentaouet Kattan (2006). Data at http://bit.do/WDR2018 -Fig_5-4.
Note: Vertical line indicates last year with fees. Gross enrollment rates include students whose age exceeds the official age group for a particular education level, and so the rate may exceed 100 percent.

primary level in Kenya and at the secondary level in Ghana.[44] The flip side of reducing school fees is increasing household income, which cash transfer programs do. These programs have increased both primary and secondary enrollments.[45]

Information interventions are particularly promising because they cost little.[46] In some cases, demand for education remains low because students and their families underestimate the returns to education. In the Dominican Republic and Madagascar, simply providing information on the returns to education led to improved educational outcomes, though a similar intervention in rural China had no impact.[47] In India, providing job recruiting services for women in their 20s increased school enrollment for teenage girls. Gender leadership quotas in Indian villages eliminated the gender gap in educational attainment.[48]

Though interventions that reduce the cost of schooling are highly effective at increasing school participation for most children, especially at young ages, some children do require additional incentives to attend school. In some countries, parents give priority to sending to school their children with the highest cognitive ability or higher perceived—not necessarily actual—returns to schooling (such as boys).[49] In Burkina Faso, beginning in 2008, some families received unconditional cash transfers, while others received cash transfers conditional on children's school enrollment. Boys and children who scored better on tests were equally likely to be enrolled in school under both schemes, but transfers with conditions were significantly more beneficial for girls and children who started out at lower levels of learning.[50] This finding suggests that the most vulnerable children may need more than simple cost reductions to guarantee enrollment in school.

Demand-side interventions can improve learning when programs increase either capacity to learn or student effort. Targeted cash transfers have led to more learning when framed to induce more effort, as have some information interventions.[51] Even in low-quality education systems, students learn more in school than out of it: there is a learning crisis, but the positive relationship between schooling and literacy persists (figure 5.5). When individuals with similar literacy and numeracy levels are compared, those with more schooling have higher earnings, most likely because of other benefits of schooling, including improved socio-emotional skills such as discipline.[52] Getting learners into school is beneficial in its own right.

In addition to getting to school, learners must be motivated. One way to increase motivation is to ensure that learners' skills are rewarded, whether by a labor market that offers high returns or by a higher education system that admits students based on merit rather than connections. Perhaps the most immediate way to motivate students is to provide relevant, quality education that reaches them at their current level of learning. In Kenya, students who drop out of school say their inability to perform well, rather than costs or parental pressures, caused them to leave.[53] Some systems seek to further motivate students with merit-based scholarships or prizes. Such incentives can improve effort as students strive to qualify—whether for a direct financial prize, such as in Benin and Mexico, or a scholarship for girls, such as in Kenya.[54] Direct financial incentives have been less successful in high-income countries, though alternate designs that deliver incentives immediately after tests have raised test scores.[55] Providing caregivers with information about learner performance can also have a large impact, helping caregivers to translate motivation into action (box 5.3). But in general, a positive overall educational experience is likely the backbone of student motivation.

Remedial education can prepare learners for further education and training

Many young people leave formal education with weak foundational skills, and thus they are unprepared for further education and training. Globally, of every 100 students entering primary education, 61 complete lower secondary education, and just 35 complete upper secondary (figure 5.6).[56] About a third of youth leave school between lower and upper secondary. This problem is especially pronounced in several developing countries, where sizable shares of 15- to 24-year-olds score below the minimum level of literacy proficiency—23 percent in Chile, 29 percent in urban Bolivia, 34 percent in urban Ghana.[57] Improving foundational skills early can alter workers' labor market trajectories. Employed adults ages 15–64 who score at level 2[58] or above in literacy proficiency have significantly higher probabilities of holding high-skill, better-paid white-collar jobs (figure 5.7).[59]

Youth vary greatly in skills and maturity, putting them on a range of different pathways. Some young school leavers enroll in second-chance programs seeking to obtain formal education equivalency diplomas so they can gain access to further education or training.[60] Others pursue remedial coursework to fulfill admission requirements for postsecondary education or training institutions.[61] Another group—usually those with the most serious skills gaps—goes into unstable, low-wage, low-productivity jobs, while some youth remain out of both school and the labor force.[62] It is difficult to reach all these young people.

Figure 5.5 Not all education systems are equally productive, but even the least productive deliver some learning to some learners

Percentage of women ages 25–34, by highest grade completed, who can read all of a single sentence in their chosen language, selected countries

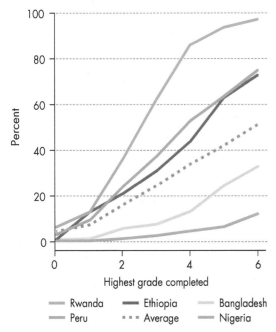

Source: Oye, Pritchett, and Sandefur (2016). Data at http://bit.do/WDR2018-Fig_5-5.

Note: The average is calculated across 51 countries.

Box 5.3 Providing information on children's school performance can help parents to motivate their children

Most parents want their children to succeed in school. Promising interventions in several countries show that providing parents with information about their children's performance can lead to better educational outcomes. In the United States, text messages sent to parents when secondary school students missed assignments led not only to more assignment completion but also to higher test scores.[a] Sending letters to parents about student absences also reduced absenteeism.[b] In Malawi, providing parents with information about their children's academic ability enabled them to buy the appropriate books for their children.[c] In Chile, low-income families received text messages each week detailing their child's attendance record along with a monthly message on behavior and test performance. Students whose parents received the texts were less likely to behave poorly in school, had better grades, and were more likely to move up to the next grade. After receiving the messages, parents expressed a willingness to pay for the service, suggesting that they saw real value to it.[d] But simply providing information to parents is no guarantee of success: a program in Kenya that provided parents with information on their children's literacy levels and suggested strategies to improve them did not lead to change.[e] The programs that have been effective have provided parents with regular updates on the inputs to learning—attendance and performance on individual assignments—rather than just on learning levels. Such information interventions can be automated, making them extremely cost-effective because they leverage the intrinsic motivation of families.

Source: WDR 2018 team.

a. Bergman (2015).
b. Rogers and Feller (2016).
c. Dizon-Ross (2016).
d. Berlinski and others (2016).
e. Lieberman, Posner, and Tsai (2014).

Figure 5.6 Young people follow different paths in their education

Completion and attrition rates (percent), by cohort and region

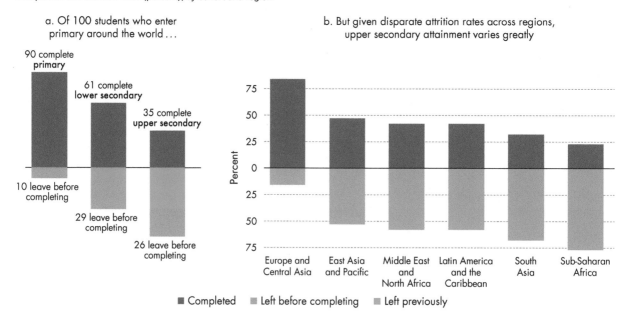

a. Of 100 students who enter primary around the world ...

90 complete primary

61 complete lower secondary

35 complete upper secondary

10 leave before completing

29 leave before completing

26 leave before completing

b. But given disparate attrition rates across regions, upper secondary attainment varies greatly

Percent

Europe and Central Asia | East Asia and Pacific | Middle East and North Africa | Latin America and the Caribbean | South Asia | Sub-Saharan Africa

■ Completed   ■ Left before completing   ■ Left previously

Source: WDR 2018 team, using data from UIS (2017); UNESCO (2015); WIDE (2017). Data at http://bit.do/WDR2018-Fig_5-6.

Note: Estimates are for circa 2010.

Figure 5.7 Workers with higher literacy proficiency are more likely to enter white-collar jobs

Marginal probability of entering high-skill white-collar jobs relative to blue-collar jobs when scoring at level 2 or above in literacy proficiency, for all workers in urban areas of participating countries (2011–14)

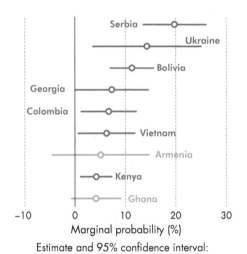

Estimate and 95% confidence interval:
–◯– Significant   –◯– Not significant

Source: WDR 2018 team, using data from World Bank's STEP Skills Measurement Program (http://microdata.worldbank.org/index.php/catalog/step /about). Data at http://bit.do/WDR2018-Fig_5-7.

Motivating them to join second-chance or remedial programs is not easy, especially if they have been out of the education system for some time. Many are uncertain about the benefits of remedial courses, and returning to school settings can stir up negative feelings. In Uganda, early school leavers said they suffered from diminished self-worth, limited life opportunities, and social exclusion associated with early departure from formal education.[63]

Remedial education interventions can work—if they reach the right people using the right approach.[64] Effective remedial education interventions meet young people where they are, helping them transition into careers. Remedial programs are more likely to support students' interests when they are short, relevant to students' lives, delivered by experienced teachers, and part of a long-term plan for career growth.[65] Most evidence to date comes from programs in high-income countries, with three main types of interventions standing out as promising:

- Remedial prevention programs support academically weak students by strengthening their foundational skills and encouraging them to complete a formal education.

- Second-chance programs offer early school leavers, many of whom are low-skilled, an opportunity to reengage with education and training.
- Remedial coursework at the onset of postsecondary education and training increases young people's chances of completing their programs of study.

Remedial prevention programs can help low-performing students and keep them in school

Remedial prevention programs can help at-risk youth who are in the formal education system to prepare for rigorous academic work in further education or training.[66] Three remedial prevention approaches show promise.[67] The first offers support to primary and secondary students willing to stay in school and master foundational skills. Programs in India and Mexico City that offer additional instruction for disadvantaged students have shown positive impacts on foundational skills (especially in India).[68] The second approach offers students early assessments of their academic standing, along with extra instruction to improve performance. A statewide early assessment program in California that supports academically at-risk students shows declining needs for remediation at later stages of education and training.[69] The third approach gives secondary school students the option of registering concurrently in postsecondary courses. Participants in such programs in the United States are less likely to require remediation and more likely to persist in tertiary education and improve academic outcomes.[70]

Second-chance programs offer a way to return to education and obtain training

Second-chance programs give youth who have dropped out of school a path to reengage in nontraditional learning environments, obtain secondary education equivalency qualifications, and enter job training.[71] These programs offer a learning experience that signals a level of achievement to participants, their families, and employers. In Australia and the United States, early school leavers are encouraged to enroll in programs that provide an equivalent to an upper secondary diploma.[72] Though equivalency programs can improve employment, wages, and other education indicators (relative to outcomes for individuals with no credentials), such impacts are often smaller than those for individuals holding traditional educational credentials.[73] Across second-chance interventions, socioemotional skills play an important role in student success—with skills such as the ability to work toward long-term goals sometimes mattering more than the equivalency certificate itself.

The demand for second-chance programs is high and the evidence is promising, but keeping youth engaged in further education and training requires an integrated policy approach. In Sub-Saharan Africa, there is a demand for programs to reengage early school leavers, especially in low-income or conflict regions.[74] But in practice, programs tend to be small, and few operate within a policy framework that integrates them into the formal education and training systems.[75] For low-income students, who usually make up a disproportionate number of early school leavers around the world, second-chance programs like the Open Basic Programme in India can provide important pathways to educational opportunities.[76] In India, Indonesia, the Philippines, and Thailand, equivalency programs for early school leavers improve students' self-development, especially when programs are aligned with the formal education system.[77] Similarly, second-chance programs in Latin America and the Caribbean yield better results when they take into account the multidimensional needs of young people, connect students to pathways for further education and training opportunities, and provide support to help participants return to productive adulthood.[78]

Postsecondary remedial education programs can help youth succeed in their programs of study

Many students enrolling in postsecondary education and training are not prepared for the rigor of their programs of study. In Chile and Mexico, several postsecondary institutions offer remedial support to academically underprepared students, but impact evaluations of such interventions are rare.[79] In the United States, participation in postsecondary remedial education is widespread, often at great cost to individuals and institutions.[80] About 42 percent of incoming students in two-year institutions and 20 percent in four-year institutions enroll in remedial courses at an annual cost of $1–$7 billion, depending on how the estimates are calculated. Due to this high cost, U.S. institutions have been experimenting with new approaches. There are three main types of remedial models that show promise: accelerated remediation, contextualized instruction, and intensive student support.[81]

Accelerated remediation models reduce the time students spend on remedial coursework. Conventional remedial education programs are often designed as a series of sequential courses that can take multiple semesters to complete, which often

leads students to drop out.[82] New accelerated remedial models addressing this problem include fast-track courses, self-paced modularized courses, and efforts to mainstream students directly into postsecondary courses while providing additional instructional support. In the U.S. state of Indiana, a study of two fast-track programs found participants achieve better course pass rates and fewer course withdrawals than students in longer remedial programs.[83] Similarly, evidence on self-paced modularized and mainstreaming programs indicates that participants have higher postsecondary pass rates in math, complete more rigorous course requirements, and attempt tertiary courses at higher rates than nonparticipants.[84]

Contextualized instruction improves the effectiveness of remedial education interventions, because learners benefit most when they engage, interpret, and generate meaning from instructional content relevant to their background.[85] These models are designed to reinforce foundational skills, while emphasizing learners' career aspirations.[86] New approaches include contextualized vocational learning. An example that blends foundational skills upgrading with occupational training is the I-BEST (Integrated Basic Education and Skills Training) program in the U.S. state of Washington. An evaluation of the program finds that participation has positive effects on student learning, including course credit accumulation, persistence in tertiary education, and earning of occupational certificates.[87] Learning community approaches, which emphasize multisubject instruction, project-based work, and learner social interactions, also are showing promising results. In the United States, participation in these programs has a significantly positive relationship with a number of factors associated with student success, such as level of course engagement, student and faculty interactions, or continuation to advanced courses.[88]

Intensive student support can provide an institutional safety net for at-risk youth. New approaches showing promising results include intensive tutoring with supplemental instruction, intensive advising, and student success courses. Intensive tutoring programs range from providing general academic counseling and tutoring to offering special skills training.[89] Evaluations of programs offering sustained tutoring show improvements in course completion and academic standing.[90] Intensive personalized advising services help students navigate course selection and develop career plans. These services can help students take advantage of other forms of support; beneficiaries are also more likely to complete their remedial coursework and stay on in school after program completion.[91] Student success courses are usually stand-alone, credit-bearing courses for new students that emphasize the development of study skills. Experimental evidence from the United States shows promising results on participants' number of credits earned, classes passed, and class standing.[92]

Finally, recent developments in self-directed technology models are opening new opportunities for youth to work independently to meet their learning needs and upgrade their skills, but this remains a new area for remedial education research, and evidence on their impacts is still sparse.[93]

Notes

1. UNICEF, WHO, and World Bank (2016).
2. Hungi (2010).
3. Cunha and others (2006).
4. Black and others (2008); Horton, Alderman, and Rivera (2008); Thompson and Nelson (2001).
5. Coe and Lubach (2007); Garner and others (2012).
6. Center on the Developing Child (2016).
7. Walker and others (2007).
8. Bendini (2015).
9. Black and others (2017).
10. Bradley and Corwyn (2005); McCoy and Raver (2014); Shonkoff and others (2010).
11. Farah and others (2006); McLoyd (1998).
12. These numbers likely overestimate global preschool coverage because many low-income countries do not report access data (Save the Children 2017).
13. Black and others (2017).
14. Devercelli, Sayre, and Denboba (2016).
15. ACPF (2011).
16. Berlinski and Schady (2015).
17. Naudeau and others (2011).
18. Black and others (2017). This is likely an underestimate of the true number of young children who are at risk of not reaching their developmental potential, given the multiple risk factors associated with poverty.
19. Bhutta and others (2013); Britto and others (2016).
20. Galasso and Wagstaff (2016).
21. Galasso and Wagstaff (2016); Skoufias (2016).
22. Eilander and others (2010); Horta, Loret de Mola, and Victora (2015).
23. Galasso and Wagstaff (2016).
24. Almond and Currie (2011); Baker-Henningham and López Bóo (2010).
25. Aboud and Yousafzai (2015); Britto and others (2016).
26. For a review, see World Bank (2015).
27. Britto and others (2016); World Bank (2015).
28. Denboba and others (2014).
29. Rahman and others (2013).
30. Berlinski, Galiani, and Gertler (2008); Engle and others (2011); Favara and others (2017); García and others (2016); Rao and others (2014).
31. Bouguen and others (2013); Rosero and Oosterbeek (2011).
32. Martinez, Naudeau, and Pereira (2012); Nakajima and others (2016).
33. However, center-based care can have the important added benefit of increasing labor force participation or further skills acquisition among parents, especially mothers.
34. Attanasio and others (2014); Denboba and others (2014).
35. Britto and others (2016).
36. Richter and others (2016).
37. Devercelli, Sayre, and Denboba (2016).
38. Serneels and Dercon (2014).
39. Oketch, Mutisya, and Sagwe (2012).
40. World Policy Analysis Center (various years).
41. Foko, Tiyab, and Husson (2012).
42. Al-Samarrai and Zaman (2007); Bold, Kimenyi, and Sandefur (2013); Deininger (2003); Grogan (2009); Lucas and Mbiti (2012); Nishimura, Yamano, and Sasaoka (2008).
43. Morgan, Petrosino, and Fronius (2012); Zuilkowski, Jukes, and Dubeck (2016).
44. Duflo, Dupas, and Kremer (2017); Kremer, Miguel, and Thornton (2009).
45. Filmer and Schady (2008); Fiszbein and Schady (2009).
46. J-PAL (2013).
47. Avitabile and de Hoyos (2015); Jensen (2010); Loyalka and others (2013); Nguyen (2008).
48. Beaman and others (2012); Jensen (2012).
49. Akresh and others (2012); Garg and Morduch (1998); Parish and Willis (1993).
50. Akresh, de Walque, and Kazianga (2013).
51. Avitabile and de Hoyos (2015); Barrera-Osorio and Filmer (2013); Nguyen (2008).
52. Valerio and others (2016).
53. Zuilkowski, Jukes, and Dubeck (2016).
54. Benin: Blimpo (2014); Kenya: Kremer, Miguel, and Thornton (2009); Mexico: Behrman and others (2015).
55. Fryer (2011); Levitt and others (2016).
56. The primary completion cohort is approximated by estimating the net intake rate to last grade in primary, and the lower secondary completion rate is modeled as a function of three components: primary completion rate, effective primary-to-lower-secondary transition rate, and net intake rate to last grade in lower secondary. The regional upper secondary completion rates are estimates from UNESCO's World Inequality Database on Education (WIDE 2017), and the global upper secondary completion rate estimate is based on UNESCO's 2015 projection (UNESCO 2015).
57. OECD (2016); Roseth, Valerio, and Gutiérrez (2016).
58. Low proficiency is defined as level 1 and below on OECD's Programme for the International Assessment of Adult Competencies (PIAAC) and the World Bank's Skills Measurement Program (STEP) literacy assessments, and indicates limited understanding of basic texts. Medium to high proficiency is defined as level 2

and above and indicates the ability to integrate, evaluate, and interpret information from a variety and complexity of text materials.

59. Estimates are based on marginal effect of literacy skills at or above level 2 on the predicted probabilities of entry into high-skill white-collar and blue-collar and other jobs (base outcome). The full specification includes background control variables such as sex, age, education attainment, and proxies for family endowment.

60. Zachry and Schneider (2010).

61. Almeida, Johnson, and Steinberg (2006); NCES (2004).

62. de Hoyos, Rogers, and Székely (2016).

63. Black, Polidano, and Tseng (2012); Tukundane and others (2014); Windisch (2015).

64. The terms "remedial education" and "developmental education" are often used interchangeably to describe programs aimed at supporting low-performing students to enter and complete postsecondary and training programs. The Report uses the term "remedial education" because it is a more widely recognized concept in low- and middle-income countries. (See Bailey and others 2010; Bailey, Bashford, and others 2016; Long and Boatman 2013.)

65. Post (2016).

66. "At-risk" students are defined here as having a higher propensity of dropping out of formal education or of not completing post-basic education and training programs.

67. The typology used is from a systematic review of remedial (developmental) education by Rutschow and Crary-Ross (2014); Tukundane and others (2015); Wilson and Tanner-Smith (2013); and Zachry Rutschow and Schneider (2011).

68. Gutiérrez and Rodrigo (2014); Lakshminarayana and others (2013).

69. Howell, Kurlaender, and Grodsky (2010).

70. Karp and others (2008).

71. Jepsen, Mueser, and Troske (2012).

72. De Witte and others (2013).

73. Tyler and Lofstrom (2009).

74. Inoue and others (2015).

75. Tukundane and others (2015).

76. UNESCO (2010).

77. UNESCO (2010).

78. Cunningham and others (2008).

79. Cabrera (2013); Figueroa and others (2015); Micin and others (2015).

80. Bailey (2009); Clotfelter and others (2015); Scott-Clayton and Rodriguez (2014).

81. Bailey, Jaggars, and Scott-Clayton (2013); Clotfelter and others (2015); Moss, Kelcey, and Showers (2014); Scott-Clayton and Rodriguez (2014).

82. Bailey (2009); Scott-Clayton and Rodriguez (2014).

83. Brown and Ternes (2009).

84. Epper and Baker (2009); "Tennessee Board of Regents: Developmental Studies Redesign Initiative, Jackson State Community College," National Center for Academic Transformation, Saratoga Springs, NY. http://www.thencat.org/States/TN/Abstracts/JSCC%20Algebra_Abstract.htm#FinalRpt.

85. CSS (2007).

86. California Basic Skills Initiative (2009).

87. Jenkins, Zeidenberg, and Kienzl (2009).

88. Engstrom and Tinto (2008); Visher and others (2010); Zhao and Kuh (2004).

89. Zachry Rutschow and Schneider (2011).

90. Scrivener and others (2008); Zachry (2008).

91. Bahr (2008); Visher, Butcher, and Cerna (2010).

92. Scrivener and others (2008); Scrivener, Sommo, and Collado (2009).

93. Zachry Rutschow and Schneider (2011).

References[a]

Aboud, Frances, and Aisha Yousafzai. 2015. "Global Health and Development in Early Childhood." *Annual Review of Psychology* 66: 433–57.

ACPF (African Child Policy Forum). 2011. *The African Report on Child Wellbeing: Budgeting for Children*. Addis Ababa: ACPF. http://resourcecentre.savethechildren.se/sites/default/files/documents/3764.pdf.

Akresh, Richard, Emilie Bagby, Damien de Walque, and Harounan Kazianga. 2012. "Child Ability and Household Human Capital Investment Decisions in Burkina Faso." *Economic Development and Cultural Change* 61 (1): 157–86.

Akresh, Richard, Damien de Walque, and Harounan Kazianga. 2013. "Cash Transfers and Child Schooling: Evidence from a Randomized Evaluation of the Role of Conditionality." Policy Research Working Paper 6340, World Bank, Washington, DC.

Almeida, Cheryl, Cassius Johnson, and Adria Steinberg. 2006. "Making Good on a Promise: What Policymakers Can Do to Support the Educational Persistence of Dropouts." Double the Numbers Series (April), Jobs for the Future, Boston.

Almond, Douglas, and Janet Currie. 2011. "Human Capital Development before Age Five." In *Handbook of Labor Economics*, Vol. 4, Part B, edited by Orley Ashenfelter and David Card, 1315–1486. Amsterdam: North-Holland.

Al-Samarrai, Samer, and Hassan Zaman. 2007. "Abolishing School Fees in Malawi: The Impact on Education Access and Equity 1." *Education Economics* 15 (3): 359–75.

Attanasio, Orazio P., Camila Fernández, Emla O. A. Fitzsimons, Sally M. Grantham-McGregor, Costas Meghir, and Marta Rubio-Codina. 2014. "Using the Infrastructure of a Conditional Cash Transfer Program to Deliver a Scalable Integrated Early Child Development Program in Colombia: Cluster Randomized Controlled Trial." *BMJ* 349 (September 29): g5785.

Avitabile, Ciro, and Rafael E. de Hoyos. 2015. "The Heterogeneous Effect of Information on Student Performance: Evidence from a Randomized Control Trial in Mexico." Policy Research Working Paper 7422, World Bank, Washington, DC.

Bahr, Peter Riley. 2008. "Cooling Out in the Community College: What Is the Effect of Academic Advising on Students' Chances of Success?" *Research in Higher Education* 49 (8): 704–32.

Bailey, Thomas R. 2009. "Challenge and Opportunity: Rethinking the Role and Function of Developmental

a. References to titles of publications that include Taiwan refer to Taiwan, China.

Education in Community College." *New Directions for Community Colleges* 2009 (145): 11–30.

Bailey, Thomas, Dong Wook Jeong, and Sung-Woo Cho. 2010. "Referral, Enrollment, and Completion in Developmental Education Sequences in Community Colleges." *Economics of Education Review* 29 (2): 255–70.

Bailey, Thomas, Joanne Bashford, Angela Boatman, John Squires, and Michael Weiss. 2016. *Strategies for Postsecondary Students in Developmental Education: A Practice Guide for College and University Administrators, Advisors, and Faculty.* Washington, DC: U.S. Department of Education, National Center for Education Evaluation and Regional Assistance, What Works Clearinghouse, Institute of Education Sciences. Available at http://ies.ed.gov/ncee /wwc/Docs/PracticeGuide/wwc_dev_ed_112916.pdf.

Bailey, Thomas R., Shanna Smith Jaggars, and Judith Scott-Clayton. 2013. "Commentary: Characterizing the Effectiveness of Developmental Education: A Response to Recent Criticism." *Journal of Developmental Education* 36 (3): 18–22, 24–25.

Baker-Henningham, Helen, and Florencia López Bóo. 2010. "Early Childhood Stimulation Interventions in Developing Countries: A Comprehensive Literature Review." IDB Working Paper 213, Inter-American Development Bank, Washington, DC.

Barrera-Osorio, Felipe, and Deon Filmer. 2013. "Incentivizing Schooling for Learning: Evidence on the Impact of Alternative Targeting Approaches." Policy Research Working Paper 6541, World Bank, Washington, DC.

Beaman, Lori, Esther Duflo, Rohini Pande, and Petia Topalova. 2012. "Female Leadership Raises Aspirations and Educational Attainment for Girls: A Policy Experiment in India." *Science* 335 (6068): 582–86.

Behrman, Jere R., Susan W. Parker, Petra E. Todd, and Kenneth I. Wolpin. 2015. "Aligning Learning Incentives of Students and Teachers: Results from a Social Experiment in Mexican High Schools." *Journal of Political Economy* 123 (2): 325–64.

Bendini, Maria Magdalena. 2015. "The Effect of Stress on Developmental Trajectories: Empirical Evidence from Peru." Dissertation, University of Maryland, College Park, MD.

Bentaouet Kattan, Raja. 2006. "Implementation of Free Basic Education Policy." Education Working Paper 7, World Bank, Washington, DC.

Bergman, Peter. 2015. "Parent-Child Information Frictions and Human Capital Investment: Evidence from a Field Experiment." CESifo Working Paper 5391, Center for Economic Studies and Ifo Institute, Munich.

Berlinski, Samuel, Matias Busso, Taryn Dinkelman, and Claudia Martinez. 2016. "Reducing Parent-School Information Gaps and Improving Education Outcomes: Evidence from High Frequency Text Messaging in Chile." Working paper, Abdul Latif Jameel Poverty Action Lab, Massachusetts Institute of Technology, Cambridge, MA.

Berlinski, Samuel, Sebastian Galiani, and Paul J. Gertler. 2008. "The Effect of Pre-primary Education on Primary School Performance." *Journal of Public Economics* 93 (1–2): 219–34.

Berlinski, Samuel, and Norbert R. Schady, eds. 2015. *The Early Years: Child Well-Being and the Role of Public Policy.* Development in the Americas Series. Washington, DC: Inter-American Development Bank; New York: Palgrave Macmillan.

Bhutta, Zulfiqar A., Jai K. Das, Arjumand Rizvi, Michelle F. Gaffey, Neff Walker, Susan Horton, Patrick Webb, et al. 2013. "Evidence-Based Interventions for Improvement of Maternal and Child Nutrition: What Can Be Done and at What Cost?" *Lancet* 382 (9890): 452–77.

Black, David, Cain Polidano, and Yi-Ping Tseng. 2012. "The Re-engagement in Education of Early School Leavers." *Economic Papers* 31 (2): 202–15.

Black, Maureen M., Susan P. Walker, Lia C. H. Fernald, Christopher T. Andersen, Ann M. DiGirolamo, Chunling Lu, Dana Charles McCoy, et al. 2017. "Early Childhood Development Coming of Age: Science through the Life Course." *Lancet* 389 (10064): 77–90.

Black, Robert E., Lindsay H. Allen, Zulfiqar A. Bhutta, Laura E. Caulfield, Mercedes de Onis, Majid Ezzati, Colin Mathers, et al. 2008. "Maternal and Child Undernutrition: Global and Regional Exposures and Health Consequences." *Lancet* 371 (9608): 243–60.

Blimpo, Moussa P. 2014. "Team Incentives for Education in Developing Countries: A Randomized Field Experiment in Benin." *American Economic Journal: Applied Economics* 6 (4): 90–109.

Bold, Tessa, Mwangi S. Kimenyi, and Justin Sandefur. 2013. "Public and Private Provision of Education in Kenya." *Journal of African Economies* 22 (supplement 2): ii39–ii56.

Bouguen, Adrien, Deon Filmer, Karen Macours, and Sophie Naudeau. 2013. "Impact Evaluation of Three Types of Early Childhood Development Interventions in Cambodia." Policy Research Working Paper 6540, World Bank, Washington, DC.

Bradley, Robert H., and Robert F. Corwyn. 2005. "Caring for Children around the World: A View from Home." *International Journal of Behavioral Development* 29 (6): 468–78.

Britto, Pia Rebello, Stephen J. Lye, Kerrie Proulx, Aisha K. Yousafzai, Stephen G. Matthews, Tyler Vaivada, Rafael Perez-Escamilla, et al. 2016. "Nurturing Care: Promoting Early Childhood Development." *Lancet* 389 (10064): 91–102.

Brown, R., and R. Ternes. 2009. "Final Report to the Lilly Endowment Grant: Grant for Targeted and Accelerated Remediation." Ivy Tech Community College, Indianapolis, IN.

Cabrera, Gabriela. 2013. "Programas de Apoyo a Transiciones Académicas del Sistema Escolarizado en la UNAM." Paper presented at Tercera Conferencia Latinoamericana sobre el Abandono en la Educación Superior, Mexico City, November 13–15.

California Basic Skills Initiative. 2009. "Contextualized Teaching and Learning, a Faculty Primer: A Review of Literature and Faculty Practices with Implications for California Community College Practitioners." Research and Planning Group, Academic Senate for California Community Colleges, and Bay Area Workforce Funding Collaborative, San Rafael, CA.

Carneiro, Pedro, Flavio Cunha, and James J. Heckman. 2003. "Interpreting the Evidence of Family Influence on Child Development." Paper presented at Federal Reserve Bank of Minneapolis and McKnight Foundation's conference, "Economics of Early Childhood Development: Lessons for Economic Policy," Minneapolis, October 17.

Center on the Developing Child. 2016. "From Best Practices to Breakthrough Impacts: A Science-Based Approach to Building a More Promising Future for Young Children and Families." Center on the Developing Child, Harvard University, Cambridge, MA.

Clotfelter, Charles T., Helen F. Ladd, Clara Muschkin, and Jacob L. Vigdor. 2015. "Developmental Education in North Carolina Community Colleges." *Educational Evaluation and Policy Analysis* 37 (3): 354–75.

Coe, Christopher L., and Gabrielle R. Lubach. 2007. "Mother-Infant Interactions and the Development of Immunity from Conception through Weaning." In *Psychoneuroimmunology*, edited by Robert Ader, 455–74. Burlington, MA: Elsevier Academic Press.

CSS (Center for Student Success). 2007. *Basic Skills as a Foundation for Student Success in California Community Colleges.* San Rafael, CA: CSS, Research and Planning Group.

Cunha, Flavio, James J. Heckman, Lance J. Lochner, and Dimitriy V. Masterov. 2006. "Interpreting the Evidence on Life Cycle Skill Formation." In *Handbook of the Economics of Education*, Vol. 1, edited by Eric A. Hanushek and Finis Welch, 697–812. Handbooks in Economics Series 26. Amsterdam: North-Holland.

Cunningham, Wendy V., Linda McGinnis, Rodrigo García Verdú, Cornelia Tesliuc, and Dorte Verner. 2008. *Youth at Risk in Latin America and the Caribbean: Understanding the Causes, Realizing the Potential.* Directions in Development: Human Development Series. Washington, DC: World Bank.

de Hoyos, Rafael E., Halsey Rogers, and Miguel Székely. 2016. "Out of School and Out of Work: Risk and Opportunities for Latin America's *Ninis*." World Bank, Washington, DC.

Deininger, Klaus. 2003. "Does Cost of Schooling Affect Enrollment by the Poor? Universal Primary Education in Uganda." *Economics of Education Review* 22 (3): 291–305.

Denboba, Amina D., Rebecca K. Sayre, Quentin T. Wodon, Leslie K. Elder, Laura B. Rawlings, and Joan Lombardi. 2014. "Stepping Up Early Childhood Development: Investing in Young Children for High Returns." October, Children's Investment Fund Foundation and World Bank, Washington, DC.

Devercelli, Amanda E., Rebecca K. Sayre, and Amina D. Denboba. 2016. "What Do We Know about Early Childhood Development Policies in Low and Middle Income Countries?" SABER-ECD Brief Note 1, World Bank, Washington, DC.

De Witte, Kristof, Sofie Cabus, Geert Thyssen, Wim Groot, and Henriëtte Maassen van den Brink. 2013. "A Critical Review of the Literature on School Dropout." *Educational Research Review* 10: 13–28.

Dizon-Ross, Rebecca. 2016. "Parents' Beliefs and Children's Education: Experimental Evidence from Malawi." Working paper, Booth School of Business, University of Chicago.

Dowd, Amy Jo, Elliott Friedlander, Christine Jonason, Jane Leer, Lisa Zook Sorensen, Jarrett Guajardo, Nikhit D'Sa, et al. 2017. "Lifewide Learning for Early Reading Development." *New Directions for Child and Adolescent Development* 155: 31–49.

Duflo, Esther, Pascaline Dupas, and Michael R. Kremer. 2017. "The Impact of Free Secondary Education: Experimental Evidence from Ghana." Paper presented at Ghana Education Evidence Summit 2017, "Towards Quality Education in Ghana: Using Evidence to Achieve Better Learning Outcomes," Accra, Ghana, March 28.

Eilander, Ans, Tarun Gera, Harshpal S. Sachdev, Catherine Transler, Henk C. M. van der Knaap, Frans J. Kok, and Saskia J. M. Osendarp. 2010. "Multiple Micronutrient Supplementation for Improving Cognitive Performance in Children: Systematic Review of Randomized Controlled Trials." *American Journal of Clinical Nutrition* 91 (1): 115–30.

Engle, Patrice L., Lia C. H. Fernald, Harold Alderman, Jere R. Behrman, Chloe O'Gara, Aisha Yousafzai, Meena Cabral de Mello, et al. 2011. "Strategies for Reducing Inequalities and Improving Developmental Outcomes for Young Children in Low-Income and Middle-Income Countries." *Lancet* 378 (9799): 1339–53.

Engstrom, Cathy McHugh, and Vincent Tinto. 2008. "Learning Better Together: The Impact of Learning Communities on the Persistence of Low-Income Students." *Opportunity Matters* 1: 5–21.

Epper, Rhonda M., and Elaine D. Baker. 2009. "Technology Solutions for Developmental Math: An Overview of Current and Emerging Practices." *Journal of Developmental Education* 26 (2): 4–23.

Farah, Martha J., David M. Shera, Jessica H. Savage, Laura Betancourt, Joan M. Giannetta, Nancy L. Brodsky, Elsa K. Malmud, et al. 2006. "Childhood Poverty: Specific Associations with Neurocognitive Development." *Brain Research* 1110 (1): 166–74.

Favara, Marta, Martin Woodhead, Juan Francisco Castro, Grace Chang, and Patricia Espinoza. 2017. "Pre-school Education and Skills Development in Peru, Vietnam, Ethiopia, and India: Evidence from Young Lives." World Bank, Washington, DC.

Figueroa, Lorna, Bernardita Maillard, Nelson Veliz, Samara Toledo, and Máximo González. 2015. "La Experiencia de los Programas Propedéuticos y su Articulación con la Escuela." Paper presented at Quinta Conferencia Latinoamericana sobre el Abandono en la Educación Superior, Talca, Chile, November 11–13.

Filmer, Deon, and Norbert R. Schady. 2008. "Getting Girls into School: Evidence from a Scholarship Program in Cambodia." *Economic Development and Cultural Change* 56 (3): 581–617.

Fiszbein, Ariel, and Norbert R. Schady. 2009. *Conditional Cash Transfers: Reducing Present and Future Poverty.* With Francisco H. G. Ferreira, Margaret E. Grosh, Niall Keleher, Pedro Olinto, and Emmanuel Skoufias. World Bank Policy Research Report. Washington, DC: World Bank.

Foko, Borel, Beifith Kouak Tiyab, and Guillaume Husson. 2012. "Household Education Spending: An Analytical and Comparative Perspective for 15 African Countries."

Working paper, Pôle de Dakar for Education Sector Analysis, Regional Bureau for Education in Africa, United Nations Educational, Scientific, and Cultural Organization, Dakar, Senegal.

Friedlander, Elliott, and Claude Goldenberg, eds. 2016. *Literacy Boost in Rwanda: Impact Evaluation of a Two Year Randomized Control Trial.* Stanford, CA: Stanford University.

Fryer, Roland G. 2011. "Financial Incentives and Student Achievement: Evidence from Randomized Trials." *Quarterly Journal of Economics* 126 (4): 1755–98.

Galasso, Emanuela, and Adam Wagstaff. 2016. "The Economic Costs of Stunting and How to Reduce Them." With Sophie Naudeau and Meera Shekar. Policy Research Note 5, World Bank, Washington, DC.

García, Jorge Luis, James J. Heckman, Duncan Ermini Leaf, and María José Prados. 2016. "The Life-Cycle Benefits of an Influential Early Childhood Program." NBER Working Paper 22993, National Bureau of Economic Research, Cambridge, MA.

Garg, Ashish, and Jonathan Morduch. 1998. "Sibling Rivalry and the Gender Gap: Evidence from Child Health Outcomes in Ghana." *Journal of Population Economics* 11 (4): 471–93.

Garner, Andrew S., Jack P. Shonkoff, Benjamin S. Siegel, Mary I. Dobbins, Marian F. Earls, Laura McGuinn, John Pascoe, et al. 2012. "Early Childhood Adversity, Toxic Stress, and the Role of the Pediatrician: Translating Developmental Science into Lifelong Health." *Pediatrics* 129 (1): e224–e231.

Grogan, Louise. 2009. "Universal Primary Education and School Entry in Uganda." *Journal of African Economies* 18 (2): 183–211.

Gutiérrez, Emilio, and Rodmiro Rodrigo. 2014. "Closing the Achievement Gap in Mathematics: Evidence from a Remedial Program in .Mexico City." *Latin American Economic Review* 23 (14): 1–30.

Horta, Bernardo L., Christian Loret de Mola, and Cesar G. Victora. 2015. "Breastfeeding and Intelligence: A Systematic Review and Meta-Analysis." *Acta Paediatrica* 104 (S467): 14–19.

Horton, Sue, Harold Alderman, and Juan A. Rivera. 2008. "The Challenge of Hunger and Malnutrition." Copenhagen Consensus 2008 Challenge Paper, Copenhagen Consensus Center, Tewksbury, MA.

Howell, Jessica S., Michal Kurlaender, and Eric Grodsky. 2010. "Postsecondary Preparation and Remediation: Examining the Effect of the Early Assessment Program at California State University." *Journal of Policy Analysis and Management* 29 (4): 726–48.

Hungi, Njora. 2010. "What Are the Levels and Trends in Grade Repetition?" SACMEQ Policy Issues 5, Southern and Eastern Africa Consortium for Monitoring Educational Quality, Paris.

Inoue, Keiko, Emanuela di Gropello, Yesim Sayin Taylor, and James Gresham. 2015. *Out-of-School Youth in Sub-Saharan Africa: A Policy Perspective.* Directions in Development: Human Development Series. Washington, DC: World Bank.

Jenkins, Davis, Matthew Zeidenberg, and Gregory S. Kienzl. 2009. "Educational Outcomes of I-BEST, Washington State Community and Technical College System's Integrated Basic Education and Skills Training Program: Findings from a Multivariate Analysis." CCRC Working Paper 16, Community College Research Center, Teachers College, Columbia University, New York.

Jensen, Robert T. 2010. "The (Perceived) Returns to Education and the Demand for Schooling." *Quarterly Journal of Economics* 125 (2): 515–48.

———. 2012. "Do Labor Market Opportunities Affect Young Women's Work and Family Decisions? Experimental Evidence from India." *Quarterly Journal of Economics* 127 (2): 753–92.

Jepsen, Christopher, Peter R. Mueser, and Kenneth R. Troske. 2012. "Labor-Market Returns to the GED Using Regression Discontinuity Analysis." IZA Discussion Paper 6758, Institute for the Study of Labor, Bonn, Germany.

Johnson, Rucker C., and C. Kirabo Jackson. 2017. "Reducing Inequality through Dynamic Complementarity: Evidence from Head Start and Public School Spending." NBER Working Paper 23489, National Bureau of Economic Research, Cambridge, MA.

J-PAL (Abdul Latif Jameel Poverty Action Lab). 2013. "Informing Future Choices." J-PAL Policy Briefcase, J-PAL, Massachusetts Institute of Technology, Cambridge, MA.

Karp, Melinda Jane Mechur, Juan Carlos Calcagno, Katherine Lee Hughes, Dong Wook Jeong, and Thomas R. Bailey. 2008. "Dual Enrollment Students in Florida and New York City: Postsecondary Outcomes." CCRC Brief 37, Community College Research Center, Teachers College, Columbia University, New York.

Klees, Steven J. 2017. "Will We Achieve Education for All and the Education Sustainable Development Goal?" *Comparative Education Review* 61 (2): 425–40.

Kremer, Michael R., Edward Miguel, and Rebecca L. Thornton. 2009. "Incentives to Learn." *Review of Economics and Statistics* 91 (3): 437–56.

Lakshminarayana, Rashmi, Alex Eble, Preetha Bhakta, Chris Frost, Peter Boone, Diana Elbourne, and Vera Mann. 2013. "The Support to Rural India's Public Education System (STRIPES) Trial: A Cluster Randomised Controlled Trial of Supplementary Teaching, Learning Material and Material Support." *PLoS ONE* 8 (7): e65775.

Levitt, Steven D., John A. List, Susanne Neckermann, and Sally Sadoff. 2016. "The Behavioralist Goes to School: Leveraging Behavioral Economics to Improve Educational Performance." *American Economic Journal: Economic Policy* 8 (4): 183–219.

Lieberman, Evan S., Daniel N. Posner, and Lily L. Tsai. 2014. "Does Information Lead to More Active Citizenship? Evidence from an Education Intervention in Rural Kenya." *World Development* 60: 69–83.

Long, Bridget T., and Angela Boatman. 2013. "The Role of Remedial and Developmental Courses in Access and Persistence." In *The State of College Access and Completion: Improving College Success for Students from Underrepresented Groups,* edited by Laura W. Perna and Anthony P. Jones, 77–95. New York: Routledge.

Loyalka, Prashant, Chengfang Liu, Yingquan Song, Hongmei Yi, Xiaoting Huang, Jianguo Wei, Linxiu Zhang, et al. 2013. "Can Information and Counseling Help Students from Poor Rural Areas Go to High School? Evidence from China." *Journal of Comparative Economics* 41 (4): 1012–25.

Lucas, Adrienne M., and Isaac M. Mbiti. 2012. "Access, Sorting, and Achievement: The Short-Run Effects of Free Primary Education in Kenya." *American Economic Journal: Applied Economics* 4 (4): 226–53.

Martin, Paul. 2012. "Responsabilidad Social Corporativa y Primera Infancia." Paper presented at Ministry of Development and Social Inclusion's Semana de la Inclusión, Lima, October 21–24.

Martinez, Sebastian, Sophie Naudeau, and Vitor Pereira. 2012. "The Promise of Preschool in Africa: A Randomized Impact Evaluation of Early Childhood Development in Rural Mozambique." Save the Children, Fairfield, CT, February 14. World Bank, Washington, DC. http://site resources.worldbank.org/INTAFRICA/Resources/The_Promise_of_Preschool_in_Africa_ECD_REPORT.pdf.

McCoy, Dana Charles, and C. Cybele Raver. 2014. "Household Instability and Self-Regulation among Poor Children." *Journal of Children and Poverty* 20 (2): 131–52.

McLoyd, Vonnie C. 1998. "Socioeconomic Disadvantage and Child Development." *American Psychologist* 53 (2): 185–204.

Micin, Sonia, Natalia Farías, Beatriz Carreño, and Sergio Urzúa. 2015. "Beca Nivelación Académica: La Experiencia de una Política Pública Aplicada en una Universidad Chilena." *Calidad en la Educación* 42: 189–208.

Morgan, Claire, Anthony Petrosino, and Trevor Fronius. 2012. "A Systematic Review of the Evidence of the Impact of Eliminating School User Fees in Low-Income Developing Countries." Evidence for Policy and Practice Information and Co-ordinating Centre, Social Science Research Unit, Institute of Education, University of London, London.

Moss, Brian G., Ben Kelcey, and Nancy Showers. 2014. "Does Classroom Composition Matter? College Classrooms as Moderators of Developmental Education Effectiveness." *Community College Review* 42 (3): 201–20.

Nakajima, Nozomi, Amer Hasan, Haeil Jung, Sally Anne Brinkman, Menno Prasad Pradhan, and Angela Kinnell. 2016. "Investing in School Readiness: An Analysis of the Cost-Effectiveness of Early Childhood Education Pathways in Rural Indonesia." Policy Research Working Paper 7832, World Bank, Washington, DC.

Naudeau, Sophie, Naoko Kataoka, Alexandria Valerio, Michelle J. Neuman, and Leslie Kennedy Elder. 2011. *Investing in Young Children: An Early Childhood Development Guide for Policy Dialogue and Project Preparation.* Directions in Development: Human Development Series. Washington, DC: World Bank.

NCES (National Center for Education Statistics). 2004. "Educational Attainment of High School Dropouts 8 Years Later." Issue Brief NCES 2005-026, NCES, Institute of Education Sciences, U.S. Department of Education, Washington, DC.

Nelson, Charles A., Nadine Gaab, Yingying Wang, Swapna Kumar, Danielle Sliva, Meaghan Mauer, Alissa Westerlund, et al. 2017. "Atypical Brain Development in Bangladeshi Infants Exposed to Profound Early Adversity." Presented at conference of Society for Research in Child Development, Austin, TX, April.

Nguyen, Trang. 2008. "Information, Role Models, and Perceived Returns to Education: Experimental Evidence from Madagascar." MIT working paper, Massachusetts Institute of Technology, Cambridge, MA.

Nishimura, Mikiko, Takashi Yamano, and Yuichi Sasaoka. 2008. "Impacts of the Universal Primary Education Policy on Educational Attainment and Private Costs in Rural Uganda." *International Journal of Educational Development* 28 (2): 161–75.

OECD (Organisation for Economic Co-operation and Development). 2016. *Skills Matter: Further Results from the Survey of Adult Skills.* OECD Skills Studies Series. Paris: OECD.

Oketch, Moses, Maurice Mutisya, and Jackline Sagwe. 2012. "Parental Aspirations for Their Children's Educational Attainment and the Realisation of Universal Primary Education (UPE) in Kenya: Evidence from Slum and Non-slum Residences." *International Journal of Educational Development* 32 (6): 764–72.

Oye, Mari, Lant Pritchett, and Justin Sandefur. 2016. "Girls' Schooling Is Good, Girls' Schooling with Learning Is Better." Education Commission, Center for Global Development, Washington, DC.

Parish, William L., and Robert J. Willis. 1993. "Daughters, Education, and Family Budgets: Taiwan Experiences" [refers to Taiwan, China]. *Journal of Human Resources* 28 (4): 863–98.

Phillips, Deborah A., Mark W. Lipsey, Kenneth A. Dodge, Ron Haskins, Daphna Bassok, Margaret R. Burchinal, Greg J. Duncan, et al. 2017. "Puzzling It Out: The Current State of Scientific Knowledge on Pre-kindergarten Effects, a Consensus Statement." Center for Child and Family Policy, Duke University, Durham, NC; Brookings Institution, Washington, DC.

Post, David. 2016. "Adult Literacy Benefits? New Opportunities for Research into Sustainable Development." *International Review of Education* 62 (6): 751–70.

Rahman, Atif, Jane Fisher, Peter Bower, Stanley Luchters, Thach Tran, M. Taghi Yasamy, Shekhar Saxena, et al. 2013. "Interventions for Common Perinatal Mental Disorders in Women in Low- and Middle-Income Countries: A Systematic Review and Meta-Analysis." *Bulletin of the World Health Organization* 91 (8): 593–601.

Rao, Nirmala, Jin Sun, Jessie M. S. Wong, Brendan Weekes, Patrick Ip, Sheldon Shaeffer, Mary Young, et al. 2014. "Early Childhood Development and Cognitive Development in Developing Countries: Education Rigorous Literature Review." Faculty of Education, University of Hong Kong, Hong Kong SAR, China.

Richter, Linda M., Bernadette Daelmans, Joan Lombardi, Jody Heymann, Florencia López Bóo, Jere R. Behrman, Chunling Lu, et al. 2016. "Investing in the Foundation of Sustainable Development: Pathways to Scale Up for Early Childhood Development." *Lancet* 389 (10064): 103–18.

Rogers, Todd, and Avi Feller. 2016. "Intervening through Influential Third Parties: Reducing Student Absences at Scale via Parents." Working paper, Harvard University, Cambridge, MA.

Rosero, José, and Hessel Oosterbeek. 2011. "Trade-Offs between Different Early Childhood Interventions: Evidence from Ecuador." Tinbergen Institute Discussion Paper TI 2011-102/3, Faculty of Economics and

Business, University of Amsterdam; Tinbergen Institute, Amsterdam.

Roseth, Viviana V., Alexandria Valerio, and Marcela Gutiérrez. 2016. *Education, Skills, and Labor Market Outcomes: Results from Large-Scale Adult Skills Surveys in Urban Areas in 12 Countries*. STEP Skills Measurement Series. Washington, DC: World Bank.

Rutschow, Elizabeth Zachry, and Shane Crary-Ross. 2014. "Beyond the GED: Promising Models for Moving High School Dropouts to College." MDRC, New York.

Save the Children. 2017. "Windows into Early Learning and Development: Cross Country IDELA Findings Fueling Progress on ECD Access, Quality, and Equity." Save the Children International, London.

Scott-Clayton, Judith, and Olga Rodriguez. 2014. "Development, Discouragement, or Diversion? New Evidence on the Effects of College Remediation Policy." *Education Finance and Policy* 10 (1): 4–45.

Scrivener, Susan, Dan Bloom, Allen LeBlanc, Christina Paxson, Cecilia Elena Rouse, and Colleen Sommo. 2008. "A Good Start: Two-Year Effects of a Freshmen Learning Community Program at Kingsborough Community College." With Jenny Au, Jedediah J. Teres, and Susan Yeh. Opening Doors Project, MDRC, New York, March.

Scrivener, Susan, Colleen Sommo, and Herbert Collado. 2009. "Getting Back on Track: Effects of a Community College Program for Probationary Students." Opening Doors Project, MDRC, New York.

Serneels, Pieter, and Stefan Dercon. 2014. "Aspirations, Poverty, and Education: Evidence from India." Young Lives Working Paper 125, Young Lives, Oxford Department of International Development, University of Oxford, Oxford, U.K.

Shonkoff, Jack, Pat Levitt, W. T. Boyce, Judy Cameron, Greg Duncan, N. A. Fox, Megan Gunnar, et al. 2010. "Persistent Fear and Anxiety Can Affect Young Children's Learning and Development." Working Paper 9, Center on the Developing Child, Harvard University, Cambridge, MA.

Skoufias, Emmanuel. 2016. "Synergies in Child Nutrition: Interactions of Food Security, Health and Environment, and Child Care." Policy Research Working Paper 7794, World Bank, Washington, DC.

Thompson, Ross A., and Charles A. Nelson. 2001. "Developmental Science and the Media: Early Brain Development." *American Psychologist* 56 (1): 5–15.

Tukundane, Cuthbert, Alexander Minnaert, Jacques Zeelen, and Peter Kanyandago. 2015. "A Review of Enabling Factors in Support Intervention Programmes for Early School Leavers: What Are the Implications for Sub-Saharan Africa?" *Children and Youth Services Review* 52: 54–62.

Tukundane, Cuthbert, Jacques Zeelen, Alexander Minnaert, and Peter Kanyandago. 2014. "'I Felt Very Bad, I Had Self-Rejection': Narratives of Exclusion and Marginalisation among Early School Leavers in Uganda." *Journal of Youth Studies* 17 (4): 475–91.

Tyler, John H., and Magnus Lofstrom. 2009. "Finishing High School: Alternative Pathways and Dropout Recovery." *Future of Children* 19 (1): 77–103.

UIS (UNESCO Institute of Statistics). 2017. Education indicators. http://data.uis.unesco.org.

UNESCO (United Nations Educational, Scientific, and Cultural Organization). 2010. "Achieving EFA through Equivalency Programmes in Asia-Pacific: A Regional Overview with Highlights from India, Indonesia, Thailand, and the Philippines." Asia and Pacific Regional Bureau for Education, UNESCO, Bangkok.

————. 2015. "How Long Will It Take to Achieve Universal Primary and Secondary Education?" Technical background note for the Framework for Action on the post-2015 education agenda. http://en.unesco.org/gem-report/how-long-will-it-take-achieve-universal-primary-and-secondary-education.

UNICEF (United Nations Children's Fund), WHO (World Health Organization), and World Bank. 2016. "Levels and Trends in Child Malnutrition: UNICEF/WHO/World Bank Group Joint Child Malnutrition Estimates, Key Findings of the 2016 Edition." UNICEF, New York; WHO, Geneva; World Bank, Washington, DC. http://www.who.int/nutgrowthdb/estimates2015/en/.

Valerio, Alexandria, María Laura Sánchez Puerta, Namrata Raman Tognatta, and Sebastián Monroy-Taborda. 2016. "Are There Skills Payoffs in Low- and Middle-Income Countries? Empirical Evidence Using STEP Data." Policy Research Working Paper 7879, World Bank, Washington, DC.

Visher, Mary G., Kristin F. Butcher, and Oscar S. Cerna. 2010. "Guiding Developmental Math Students to Campus Services: An Impact Evaluation of the Beacon Program at South Texas College." With Dan Cullinan and Emily Schneider. Report, MDRC, New York.

Visher, Mary G., Emily Schneider, Heather Wathington, and Herbert Collado. 2010. "Scaling Up Learning Communities: The Experience of Six Community Colleges." Report, National Center for Postsecondary Research, Teachers College, Columbia University, New York.

Walker, Susan P., Theodore D. Wachs, Julie Meeks Gardner, Betsy Lozoff, Gail A. Wasserman, Ernesto Pollitt, Julie A. Carter, et al. 2007. "Child Development: Risk Factors for Adverse Outcomes in Developing Countries." *Lancet* 369 (9556): 145–57.

Whitebread, David, Martina Kuvalja, and Aileen O'Connor. 2015. "Quality in Early Childhood Education: An International Review and Guide for Policy Makers." With contributions from Qatar Academy. WISE 20, World Innovation Summit for Education, Qatar Foundation, Doha.

WIDE (World Inequality Database on Education). 2017. Completion indicators. http://www.education-inequalities.org.

Wilson, Sandra Jo, and Emily E. Tanner-Smith. 2013. "Dropout Prevention and Intervention Programs for Improving School Completion among School-Aged Children and Youth: A Systematic Review." *Journal of the Society for Social Work and Research* 4 (4): 357–72.

Windisch, Hendrickje Catriona. 2015. "Adults with Low Literacy and Numeracy Skills: A Literature Review on Policy Intervention." OECD Education Working Paper 123, Organisation for Economic Co-operation and Development, Paris.

World Bank. 2015. *World Development Report 2015: Mind, Society, and Behavior*. Washington, DC: World Bank.

———. 2017. World Development Indicators (database). World Bank, Washington, DC. http://data.worldbank.org/data-catalog/world-development-indicators.

World Policy Analysis Center. Various years. Is Education Tuition-Free? (database). World Policy Analysis Center, Fielding School of Public Health, University of California, Los Angeles. http://www.worldpolicycenter.org/policies/is-education-tuition-free/is-beginning-secondary-education-tuition-free.

Zachry, Elizabeth M. 2008. "Promising Instructional Reforms in Developmental Education: A Case Study of Three Achieving the Dream Colleges." With Emily Schneider. MDRC, New York.

Zachry, Elizabeth M., and Emily Schneider. 2010. "Building Foundations for Student Readiness: A Review of Rigorous Research and Promising Trends in Developmental Education." NCPR working paper, National Center for Postsecondary Research, Teachers College, Columbia University, New York.

Zachry Rutschow, Elizabeth M., and Emily Schneider. 2011. "Unlocking the Gate: What We Know About Improving Developmental Education." MDRC, New York, June.

Zhao, Chun-Mei, and George D. Kuh. 2004. "Adding Value: Learning Communities and Student Engagement." *Research in Higher Education* 45 (2): 115–38.

Zuilkowski, Stephanie Simmons, Matthew C. H. Jukes, and Margaret M. Dubeck. 2016. "'I Failed, No Matter How Hard I Tried': A Mixed-Methods Study of the Role of Achievement in Primary School Dropout in Rural Kenya." *International Journal of Educational Development* 50: 100–07.

Teacher skills and motivation both matter (though many education systems act like they don't)

For students to learn, teachers have to teach effectively—but many education systems pay little attention to what teachers know or what they do in the classroom. Focusing on teachers' skills and motivation can pay off.

After prepared and motivated learners, equipped and motivated teachers are the most fundamental ingredient of learning. Teachers are also the largest budget item, with their salaries accounting for over three-quarters of the education budget at the primary level in low- and middle-income countries.[1] Yet many education systems put in classrooms teachers who have little mastery of the subjects they are to teach—especially in classrooms serving poor children.[2] Once in place, most teachers take part in some professional development, but much of it is inconsistent and overly theoretical. Meanwhile, education systems often lack effective mechanisms to mentor and motivate teachers.[3] Such failures can be illuminated through models of human behavior—which also point to solutions (table 6.1). A synthesis of the evidence in these areas reveals three principles that are key to achieving learning success through teachers:

- To be effective, teacher training needs to be individually targeted and repeated, with follow-up coaching, often around a specific pedagogical technique.
- To avoid learners falling behind to the point where they cannot catch up, teaching needs to be pitched to the level of the student.
- Increasing teacher motivation with incentives can increase learning if the incentivized actions are within teachers' capacity and if the failure to perform those actions has impeded learning.

Most teacher training is ineffective, but some approaches work

In-service professional development requires significant time and resources. A survey of 38 developed and developing countries found that 91 percent of teachers had participated in professional development in the previous 12 months.[4] Two-thirds of World Bank projects with an education component in the last decade incorporated teacher professional development. Developing countries spend many millions a year to strengthen teachers.[5]

But a lot of teacher professional development goes unevaluated—and much of it may be ineffective. One team of teacher training experts in the United States characterized professional development in the country as "episodic, myopic, and often meaningless."[6] Teacher training in low- and middle-income countries is often short and of low quality.[7] Countries often have many training programs under way at the same time—in some cases dozens—with little to show for them (box 6.1).

Though preservice teacher training is important in providing basic skills (box 6.2), evidence on teacher training credentials is mixed. Much of the limited evidence on teacher credentials, generally from high-income countries, indicates they have no or extremely

Table 6.1 Models of human behavior can guide actions to improve teaching: Some examples

Synthesis principle	Where this fails	Models that identify a mechanism behind this failure	Approaches that address the modeled mechanism
Provide individually targeted and repeated teacher training, with follow-up coaching.	Much teacher training is one-off, with little to no follow-up coaching in the classroom.	*Simple optimization (by government) with information failure:* Follow-up coaching is more costly than centrally delivered training, and centrally delivered training may give the impression of effectiveness by changing teacher knowledge but not practice. General pedagogical training may be cheaper than training in specific techniques, and evidence on relative effectiveness is recent.	In India, a program with limited preservice but repeated follow-up for community teachers led to sizable learning gains. In the United States, programs associated with a specific pedagogical technique were twice as effective as general pedagogical training.
Pitch teaching to the level of the student.	In many countries, most students fall far behind the curriculum, and, facing large, heterogeneous classes, teachers have difficulty teaching at a level that allows students to learn.	*Information failure:* Policy makers may have an imperfect understanding of how little many students are learning. *Behavioral (mental models):* Teachers may believe that lower-performing learners cannot succeed; curriculums may be optimistically pitched higher than most students can keep up with.	In India and Kenya, reorganizing classes by ability improved learning. In India, complementing teachers with dynamic computer-assisted learning programs that adapt to learners' ability levels improved math ability. Teachers receive explicit guidance to teach students at their level.
Strengthen teacher motivation by incentivizing actions that are within teachers' capacity and that are essential to learning.	In many systems, teachers have few incentives (financial or professional) for good performance beyond their intrinsic motivation.	*Principal-agent:* If the education system signals that learning is not valued, teachers will not have the same incentives as students and parents have.	Teacher financial incentives have been effective in countries with high absenteeism, such as India and Kenya.

Source: WDR 2018 team.

small effects on student learning.[8] Simple statistical associations across francophone Africa suggest a positive relationship between teacher preparation and student performance, but that relationship could be driven by other factors, such as strategic placement of good teachers in desirable areas (where students would perform well in any case).[9] Preparing teachers better is crucial, but the political economy challenges to doing so may be greater than for in-service training, and the evidence is more limited. The same principles that lead to effective in-service training serve as useful starting points for improving preservice training.

Is there hope for in-service training or professional development? Decidedly yes. Experience from high-income countries shows that practicality, specificity, and continuity are key to effective teacher professional development.[10] Practicality means teachers are trained using concrete methods as opposed to theoretical constructs, and the training is classroom-based.[11]

Specificity means teacher training programs are most effective when they teach pedagogy specific to a subject area (say, how to effectively teach a mathematics class). Continuity means teachers receive significant continual support—not one-off workshops.[12]

In teacher training programs, the inclusion of follow-up visits in school leads to higher learning gains. To bridge the gap between learning new methods in training and implementing them in practice, developing countries should make more use of follow-up visits in which trainers observe and support teachers in the classroom.[13] In Africa, a range of programs with long-term teacher mentoring and coaching has shown sizable learning effects.[14] In India, a program that provided little initial training to teachers but then provided support throughout the year significantly increased both math and language ability, with the largest gains for those students who were performing poorly at the outset.[15] Teachers in Shanghai,

Box 6.1 The landscape of in-service teacher training

The quality of in-service teacher training varies dramatically across countries, but much of the training does not align with practices that are associated with better student performance.[a] One good practice of in-service teacher training involves follow-up visits to teachers' classrooms to provide ongoing support. Among 100 teacher training programs across five regions, the median number of follow-up visits is fewer than one per teacher. Many in-service training programs (50 percent among a sample of programs) evaluate their success based on teacher knowledge at the end of the training; far fewer (25 percent) seek to assess their impact on student learning.[b]

Source: WDR 2018 team.

a. Popova, Evans, and Arancibia (2016).
b. Popova, Breeding, and Evans (2017).

Box 6.2 What works in preservice teacher training?

In New York City, teachers who participated in teacher education programs that focused on practical classroom work and on the curriculum of the first year produced significantly better results among first-year teachers than programs that did not.[a] At the same time, systems that have introduced alternative routes to teaching—routes such as Teach for America or community-teacher programs that skip regular preservice education—have not reduced learning for students.[b] This finding calls into question the value of preservice training. However, the alternative routes often replace preservice education with more careful selection of teachers (such as in Teach for America) or with more performance-oriented contracts (such as those for contracted community teachers). Thus preservice education remains important for most education systems and will likely yield better results with more practical training.

Source: WDR 2018 team.

a. Boyd and others (2009).
b. Duflo, Dupas, and Kremer (2015); Glazerman, Mayer, and Decker (2006).

China—where performance is high by global standards—participate in ongoing Teaching-Research Groups, which provide development, mentoring, and peer evaluation based on classroom observation.[16]

Likewise, training associated with a specific pedagogical technique tends to be more effective. Across educational interventions in the United States, programs teaching a specific pedagogical method have more than twice the impact of programs focused on general pedagogy.[17] Globally, specific guidance is crucial for low-skilled teachers, who may lack the ability to be effective even when motivated.[18] At times, in settings where teachers have limited skills, this involves providing lesson plans that are highly scripted, outlining concrete steps for teachers.[19] Many countries will protest that high-quality in-service professional development—repeated, with follow-up visits in school, often around a specific technique—is beyond their budget to deliver at scale. But teachers will not learn without receiving high-quality teaching themselves. A country facing this conundrum may be better served by delivering high-quality training in stages rather than ineffective training to all in the short run.

Helping teachers teach to the level of the student has proven effective

In many countries facing the learning crisis, it may be that only students who start at the highest levels of learning are able to keep learning. This is in part because teachers tend to teach to the most advanced students in a class.[20] These students are the easiest to teach, and when teachers solicit answers from students, the high performers are the most likely

Figure 6.1 Only a small fraction of learners keeps up with the curriculum

Probability of a correct answer on a math test, by grade, relative to curriculum standards, Andhra Pradesh, India

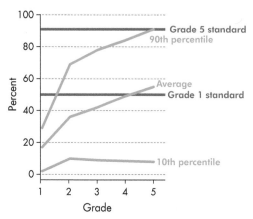

Source: WDR 2018 team, using data from Muralidharan and Zieleniak (2013). Data at http://bit.do/WDR2018-Fig_6-1.

teaching the students in the lower-performing group, and higher-quality teachers may be assigned to the higher-performing classes because these students may be easier to teach and so the assignment appears to be a reward.

In school systems with very low learning levels, ability grouping has had positive impacts on both lower- and higher-performing students. In Kenya, grouping students into classes by ability led to improved outcomes across the board, with the highest impacts among learners with more motivated teachers.[25] In India, schools reorganized classes by group for just an hour a day and observed major gains in learning.[26] Much of the rest of the evidence comes from the United States. Studies that relied on a credible counterfactual found that grouping students by ability either helps some students or at least has no adverse impact.[27] In low-performing education systems, the lowest-performing students learn little to nothing (figure 6.1), so allowing teachers to target pedagogy may have a positive net effect.

Another way to help teachers teach to the level of the student is to help them conduct better diagnostics. In Liberia, an intervention that taught teachers to better evaluate their students was effective, especially when combined with training and additional materials. So was a similar program in Malawi.[28] In Singapore, students take screening tests at the beginning of grade 1, and those who are behind in reading receive additional support daily.[29] By contrast, an intervention in India that merely provided formative evaluation was not effective; nor was another program in India that provided diagnostic reports and written suggestions on how to use the reports to strengthen teaching.[30] Clearly, helping teachers to better understand their students' ability levels is worthwhile, but if teachers lack the tools to respond effectively or the incentives to do so—given that teaching students at multiple levels is challenging—then it may not be sufficient. The diagnostics can work where a system is in place to follow up, as well as where teacher motivation is less of a binding constraint (box 6.4).

New technologies offer promising ways to help with teaching to the level of the student. Computer-assisted learning programs can permit students to go at their own pace or adjust the level of instruction based on an initial screening test.[31] More advanced software can not only screen students initially but also dynamically adjust questions based on ongoing performance. Although the overall evidence on computer-assisted instruction is markedly mixed, such a dynamic learning program among secondary school students in Delhi, India, led to striking gains in both mathematics

to volunteer them. That leaves behind the students who entered the class with less knowledge. Indeed, Kenyan school dropouts identified that problem as a primary reason for leaving school.[21] Another reason that many students fall behind is that in many countries the curriculum may simply be too ambitious.[22] Teachers feel constrained to teach to the curriculum even when students have trouble keeping up.[23]

A key principle in leaving no learner behind is to help teachers teach to the level of their students. This technique has been successful in different formats across a range of scenarios, whether by using community teachers to provide remedial lessons to the lowest performers, reorganizing classes by ability, or using technology to adapt lessons.[24] In many cases, it does not require a significantly greater teacher effort, but rather relies on restructuring classes or providing remedial lessons for the lowest performers. A related principle of effective instruction is to reach students by teaching them in their mother tongue (box 6.3).

Grouping students by ability may allow teachers to more effectively target teaching to the levels of students in their classes. The theoretical effects of such grouping are mixed. The positive effects of better-targeted teaching have a potential downside: the adverse effect for lower-performing students of no longer learning from their higher-performing peers. Furthermore, in early grades in particular, student ability is not always easy to measure, so separating students by ability can put students on the wrong track. Teachers may also reduce their efforts when

Box 6.3 Reaching learners in their own language

Children learn to read most effectively in the language they speak at home—their mother tongue. In Kenya, students in early grades had higher reading comprehension when their teachers had training and materials in mother tongue instruction.[a] Students participating in a pilot in rural Philippines, where they received instruction in their local language, showed significantly higher reading and math scores than students in traditional schools, which used English and Filipino.[b] In Ethiopia, students in schools affected by a reform to implement mother tongue instruction were subsequently more likely to be in the appropriate grade for their age.[c] Beyond its direct learning impacts on them, students receiving instruction in their mother tongue are more likely to attend and persist in school, as demonstrated by data from 26 countries.[d]

The increased skill from learning to read in mother tongue can translate into greater skill in a second language. Parents and policy makers sometimes object to mother tongue instruction on the grounds that the mother tongue is not a practical language for the labor market. Yet in South Africa, students instructed in their mother tongue in early grades actually performed better in English proficiency in later grades.[e] Likewise in pilot interventions in Malawi and the Philippines, students instructed in their mother tongue

also performed better in English reading later on.[f] On the other hand, results from a first-language program in Kenya do not show better outcomes in the second language compared with a second-language literacy program only (though the program lasted only one year).[g]

But in countries with many languages, mother tongue instruction can be overwhelming to implement, and a language "mismatch" can result in learners being left behind. Filipinos speak more than 180 different languages, Kenyans speak more than 70, and Peruvians speak nearly 100. In 98 countries worldwide, the chance that two randomly selected individuals speak the same mother tongue is under 50 percent (map B6.3.1).[h] In communities with a dominant language group, the choice of that language for mother tongue instruction may marginalize minority children. Even in countries with few languages, teachers generally have little training in mother tongue instruction, and the materials available for mother tongue instruction may be limited and of lower quality than materials in the lingua franca.[i] In communities with multiple mother tongues, schools may divide classes by mother tongue, but this division can act as segregation.[j] Mother tongue instruction may be an unambiguous benefit for countries with a limited number of mother tongues, such as Burundi or Haiti, but the initiative still involves a major

Map B6.3.1 Linguistic diversity around the world

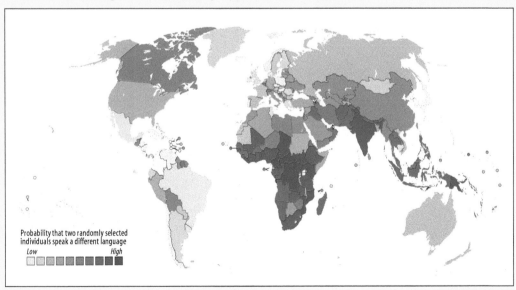

Probability that two randomly selected individuals speak a different language

Low　　　High

Source: WDR 2018 team, using data from Ethnologue (2015). Data at http://bit.do/WDR2018-Map_B6-3-1.　　IBRD 43166 | SEPTEMBER 2017

(Box continues next page)

investment in materials and teacher training. In more diverse locales, governments will need to weigh the gains and the costs associated with mother tongue instruction against those of competing investments in higher-quality education

overall. In some cases, they may opt for better-selected and better-trained teachers who receive more support in teaching students at their level, regardless of the language they speak.

Source: WDR 2018 team.

a. Piper, Zuilkowski, and Ong'ele (2016).
b. Walter and Dekker (2011).
c. Seid (2016).
d. Smits, Huisman, and Kruijff (2008).
e. Taylor and von Fintel (2016).

f. Shin and others (2015); Walter and Dekker (2011).
g. Piper, Zuilkowski, and Ong'ele (2016).
h. Ethnologue (2015).
i. Ong'uti, Aloka, and Raburu (2016); RTI International (2016).
j. Metila, Pradilla, and Williams (2016).

Box 6.4 **Using diagnostic data to deliver better learning in Latin America**

Mexico's Colima state implemented a learning improvement program in low-performing public schools using student performance on a national exam. Each school was assigned a technical adviser who visited schools three times a month to train teachers on analyzing the test information, as well as on understanding the reasons for poor performance. Based on the analysis, the adviser—working with school directors and teachers—developed a school-specific plan to address identified problems and provided follow-up support during

implementation of the plan. Student performance improved in both language and math, but only several months after the program was launched.[a] A similar program in Argentina—distributing reports on the learning outcomes of students to public primary schools to inform teachers of the strengths and weaknesses of their students—also increased learning. Students in those schools reported that their teachers were more active in interacting with students in their classrooms and were less likely to leave early.[b]

Source: WDR 2018 team.

a. de Hoyos, Garcia-Moreno, and Patrinos (2017).
b. de Hoyos, Ganimian, and Holland (2016).

---

and language.[32] Teaching at the level of the student is not a novel idea, but a range of new evidence is showing how it can be implemented—even at scale—in developing countries.

Teacher motivation and incentives make a difference, even with few inputs

No amount of training or inputs can substitute for teacher motivation. Because of high teacher absenteeism in many countries, fostering effort is a serious challenge. Moreover, even when they are in school, teachers are often not in class teaching. Yet education systems in many countries neither reward

teachers for performing well nor penalize them for performing poorly. Teachers need to be treated as professionals—and good professionals receive support and respect, but are also held to high expectations. A system that does not pay attention to what its teachers are doing does not afford teachers the respect they deserve (box 6.5).

Over the long run, the best way to strengthen teacher ability and motivation may be to attract capable, intrinsically motivated people into the profession. In many countries and economies, the youth who plan to go into teaching are not among the highest academic performers (figure 6.2). In Finland, teaching is a coveted profession, largely because teachers receive great respect, are well trained, are reasonably paid, and have autonomy to implement teaching standards.[33] Across

Box 6.5 Would raising teachers' salaries increase their motivation?

In many countries, teachers are paid less than other comparably educated professionals.[a] Would raising their salaries lead to higher motivation and better performance? Indonesia doubled pay for certified teachers, using a randomized controlled trial to evaluate the impact. Doubling pay increased teacher satisfaction, but it had no effect on either measurable effort or student performance for existing teachers.[b] Though higher salaries could attract more capable candidates to the profession over time, raising salaries is no quick fix for shortcomings in motivation or effort.

Source: WDR 2018 team.

a. Mizala and Ñopo (2016); OECD (2016a).
b. de Ree and others (forthcoming).

many countries, average teacher pay has fallen relative to that of other professions. At the same time, the wage distribution in teaching has narrowed. High-ability candidates may be less attracted by a narrow pay structure because it gives them little opportunity to reap professional rewards from high performance.[34] Restructuring teacher pay both to remunerate competitively and to provide returns to good performance—whether directly through pay or indirectly through promotion or retention—may improve the quality of candidates entering the teaching profession. But this is a long-term solution, not a quick fix, and even the best candidates need a supportive system to maintain their skills and effort over time.

Better selection and retention policies will result in better teachers. More meritocratic hiring—say, based on a test instead of patronage—could improve student learning.[35] One proposal would be to introduce a teaching apprenticeship of three to five years, allowing systems to identify effective teachers.[36] The least effective teachers could then be transitioned out of the teaching force. In the United States, proposals to phase out the least effective teachers suggest that the gains to learners over time would be substantial: replacing the least effective 7–12 percent of teachers could bridge the gap between U.S. student performance and that of Finland.[37] Estimates of teacher value added in other countries are

Figure 6.2 Prospective engineers typically score higher than prospective teachers on PISA tests

PISA 2015 scores for participating countries and economies, by subject and self-identified prospective occupation

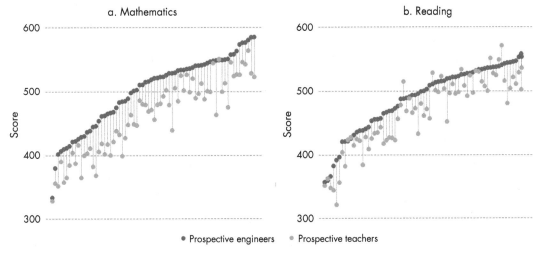

Source: WDR 2018 team, using data from OECD (2016b). Data at http://bit.do/WDR2018-Fig_6-2.

Note: PISA = Programme for International Student Assessment.

comparable, suggesting similarly large gains around the world to improved teacher selection.[38]

Education systems need to build accountability to align incentives between teachers and others. Teachers have incentives and information that are distinct from those of students, parents, and administrators, and mental models and social expectations affect the decisions of all actors. In the absence of accountability to provide motivation, teachers may minimize their efforts even as learners and parents wish for them to exert more. In Argentina and Uganda, more than one-third of teachers surveyed do not see themselves as responsible for their students' learning; in Senegal, the share is more than half.[39]

Teacher motivation works through various behavioral mechanisms and comes in multiple forms.[40] The fact that another person may observe their performance offers a form of professional motivation. So do evaluations, where teachers expect their performance to be assessed, with the associated consequences.[41] Financial incentives for successful teachers and firing of neglectful ones are just two important parts of a broader spectrum of accountability interventions. At the same time, teachers in many environments face multiple demands beyond teaching, as well as risks such as late payment of salaries and even physical danger (box 6.6). It can be tempting, in light of data on high teacher absenteeism and low teacher skills, to blame teachers for many of the faults of education systems. But these systems often ask far more of teachers than teaching—and at times offer relatively little in return.[42]

Financial and nonfinancial incentives are one possible mechanism for teacher motivation. In India, students performed better in primary schools that provided teachers with financial incentives for higher reading and mathematics scores.[43] Students also scored higher in science and social studies, despite no financial incentives being offered in those areas. Other financial incentive programs were successful in two districts of Kenya and elsewhere in India.[44] In the United States, by contrast, teacher

---

Box 6.6 One factor undermining teaching: Poor working conditions

Analyses of the proximate causes of lack of learning in low- and middle-income countries often point to teachers. Evidence suggests that in many countries teachers are absent for an astonishing number of school days and know too little about the subjects they are to teach. For this reason, students and other stakeholders may want and deserve more from teachers—but teachers also deserve more from the systems that employ them.[a] Over the last few decades, the status of the teaching profession has declined across the world in terms of pay, respect, and working conditions.[b] Because of the rapid expansion in access to education, teachers in developing countries often lead oversized, multigrade classes.[c] The teacher shortage increases workloads and requires long working hours, sometimes including double shifts.[d] Moreover, teachers often have duties outside classrooms, such as coordinating the activities of parent-teacher associations, running extracurricular activities, and performing administrative tasks.[e]

Teachers in developing countries also face difficult working and living conditions. A lack of school infrastructure and equipment often handicaps their efforts.[f] Many teachers take on other jobs to support themselves and their families.[g] The situation is even worse for teachers in remote and rural areas, who have to travel long distances to work and collect their salary.[h]

And then there are the widely implemented curriculum reforms that require teachers to equip students with new skills and employ better pedagogy, but often without giving teachers sufficient training and supportive teaching materials.[i] In such cases, teachers are expected to perform as professionals, but education systems fail to offer them professional development opportunities and create a professional culture for them.[j]

Source: WDR 2018 team.

a. Evans and Yuan (2017).
b. Dolton and Marcenaro-Gutierrez (2011); Hammett (2008); Harris-Van Keuren and Silova (2015).
c. Gamero Burón and Lassibille (2016); Guajardo (2011); Ramachandran, Bhattacharjea, and Sheshagiri (2008).
d. Ávalos and Valenzuela (2016); Gamero Burón and Lassibille (2016); Liu and Onwuegbuzie (2012); Luschei and Chudgar (2017); Osei (2006); Urwick and Kisa (2014).
e. Guajardo (2011); Liu and Onwuegbuzie (2012); Luschei and Chudgar (2017).
f. Alcázar and others (2006); Gamero Burón and Lassibille (2016); Urwick and Kisa (2014).
g. Urwick and Kisa (2014).
h. Gamero Burón and Lassibille (2016).
i. Peng and others (2014); Urwick and Kisa (2014).
j. Mooij (2008).

financial incentives did not improve test scores in several states.[45] However, large financial incentives for teachers did increase student learning in the District of Columbia, United States.[46] In Mexico and Tanzania, teacher financial incentives were effective only in conjunction with another intervention.[47] One interpretation of this scattered evidence is that financial incentives are most likely to be effective when teachers can take straightforward actions to improve learning. In environments with high teacher absenteeism from school or from the classroom while at school, it is likely to be clear to teachers that they can improve learning by simply coming to school and spending more time teaching. Alternatively, in environments like that found in the United States where teacher absenteeism is minimal, the specific actions that teachers should take to improve learning may be less obvious and less easy to implement. Nonfinancial incentives may include providing successful teachers with special recognition. Evidence of the effectiveness of these incentives in education is limited, although there is suggestive evidence in other sectors—for example among health workers in Zambia, where public recognition of worker achievement markedly improved performance.[48]

Financial incentives can also create challenges. In Kenya, responding to a student incentive program, teachers taught specifically to the test, potentially neglecting more holistic learning. In a teacher incentive program in Mexican secondary schools, a significant portion of the identified increase in student learning was attributed to student cheating.[49] In the United States, teacher cheating rose strongly when incentives were increased.[50] And when teacher incentive programs are removed, the results can also be adverse.[51]

With financial incentives, the devil is in the details. Incentives can be based on teacher inputs such as attendance or on outputs such as student learning. They can be based on reaching an absolute level of achievement or on gains. They can be available to all who reach a goal, or they can be competitive across schools. They will vary in size relative to teacher salaries. The evidence on these design elements is still limited, but they merit careful consideration, taking into account local institutions.

Likewise, the precise shape of a system's overall incentive structure will vary by context. In some places, financial incentives may be worth piloting. In others, increased community accountability may be effective. The mixed evidence on these interventions suggests a need to examine carefully the context and to test programs locally. But while details will vary, no education system will be successful unless it provides incentives—whether implicit or explicit—for teacher effort.

* * *

Over time, education systems perform best when their teachers are respected, prepared, selected based on merit, and supported in their work. Countries should work toward these objectives. But in the short run, countries can take actions to strengthen the performance of teachers. They can improve the quality of professional development, shifting resources to the kinds of professional development that will change teacher performance in the classroom. They can support teachers in teaching to the level of the student. They can provide a professional structure so that teachers feel motivated to apply what they know. Teachers are key to learners' education. Making them more effective in both the short and the long run is an excellent investment.

Notes

1. UIS (2017).
2. Bold and others (forthcoming); Tandon and Fukao (2015); World Bank (2016).
3. Bruns and Luque (2015); Mulkeen (2010).
4. Strizek and others (2014).
5. Calderón (2014); World Bank (2014, 2016).
6. Darling-Hammond and others (2009).
7. Hammett (2008); Lauwerier and Akkari (2015).
8. Aaronson, Barrow, and Sander (2007); Buddin and Zamarro (2009); Goldhaber (2007); Rivkin, Hanushek, and Kain (2005).
9. Michaelowa (2001).
10. Popova, Evans, and Arancibia (2016).
11. Walter and Briggs (2012).
12. Darling-Hammond and others (2009); Yoon and others (2007).
13. Kraft, Blazar, and Hogan (2016); Popova, Evans, and Arancibia (2016).
14. Conn (2017).
15. Banerjee and others (2007).
16. Liang, Kidwai, and Zhang (2016).
17. Fryer (2017).
18. Ganimian and Murnane (2016).

19. He, Linden, and MacLeod (2008, 2009); Lucas and others (2014); Spratt, King, and Bulat (2013).
20. Abadzi and Llambiri (2011); Ciaccio (2004); Leder (1987).
21. Zuilkowski, Jukes, and Dubeck (2016).
22. Pritchett and Beatty (2015).
23. Banerjee and others (2016).
24. Banerjee and others (2007, 2016); Duflo, Dupas, and Kremer (2011); Kiessel and Duflo (2014); Muralidharan, Singh, and Ganimian (2016).
25. Cummins (2016); Duflo, Dupas, and Kremer (2011).
26. Banerjee and others (2016).
27. Figlio and Page (2002); Lefgren (2004); Zimmer (2003).
28. Bolyard (2003); Piper and Korda (2010).
29. OECD (2011).
30. Aaronson, Barrow, and Sander (2007); Duflo and others (2014); Muralidharan and Sundararaman (2010).
31. Banerjee and others (2007); Carrillo, Onofa, and Ponce (2010).
32. Muralidharan, Singh, and Ganimian (2016).
33. Sahlberg (2011).
34. Jackson (2012).
35. Estrada (2016).
36. Muralidharan (2016).
37. Hanushek (2011).
38. Buhl-Wiggers and others (2017).
39. Sabarwal, Abu-Jawdeh, and Masood (2017).
40. Gill, Lerner, and Meosky (2016).
41. Lerner and Tetlock (1999).
42. Mizala and Ñopo (2016); OECD (2016a).
43. Muralidharan (2012); Muralidharan and Sundararaman (2011).
44. Duflo, Hanna, and Ryan (2012); Glewwe, Ilias, and Kremer (2010).
45. Fryer (2013); Glazerman, McKie, and Carey (2009); Springer and others (2010).
46. Dee and Wyckoff (2015).
47. Behrman and others (2015); Mbiti, Muralidharan, and Schipper (2016).
48. Ashraf, Bandiera, and Jack (2014).
49. Behrman and others (2015).
50. Jacob and Levitt (2003).
51. Jinnai (2016); Visaria and others (2016).

References

Aaronson, Daniel, Lisa Barrow, and William Sander. 2007. "Teachers and Student Achievement in the Chicago Public High Schools." *Journal of Labor Economics* 25 (1): 95–135.

Abadzi, Helen, and Stavri Llambiri. 2011. "Selective Teacher Attention in Lower-Income Countries: A Phenomenon Linked to Dropout and Illiteracy?" *Prospects* 41 (4): 491–506.

Alcázar, Lorena, F. Halsey Rogers, Nazmul Chaudhury, Jeffrey Hammer, Michael R. Kremer, and Karthik Muralidharan. 2006. "Why Are Teachers Absent? Probing Service Delivery in Peruvian Primary Schools." *International Journal of Educational Research* 45 (3): 117–36.

Ashraf, Nava, Oriana Bandiera, and B. Kelsey Jack. 2014. "No Margin, No Mission? A Field Experiment on Incentives for Public Service Delivery." *Journal of Public Economics* 120: 1–17.

Ávalos, Beatrice, and Juan Pablo Valenzuela. 2016. "Education for All and Attrition/Retention of New Teachers: A Trajectory Study in Chile." *International Journal of Educational Development* 49: 279–90.

Banerjee, Abhijit Vinayak, Rukmini Banerji, James Berry, Esther Duflo, Harini Kannan, Shobhini Mukerji, Marc Shotland, et al. 2016. "Mainstreaming an Effective Intervention: Evidence from Randomized Evaluations of 'Teaching at the Right Level' in India." NBER Working Paper 22746, National Bureau of Economic Research, Cambridge, MA.

Banerjee, Abhijit Vinayak, Shawn Cole, Esther Duflo, and Leigh Linden. 2007. "Remedying Education: Evidence from Two Randomized Experiments in India." *Quarterly Journal of Economics* 122 (3): 1235–64.

Behrman, Jere R., Susan W. Parker, Petra E. Todd, and Kenneth I. Wolpin. 2015. "Aligning Learning Incentives of Students and Teachers: Results from a Social Experiment in Mexican High Schools." *Journal of Political Economy* 123 (2): 325–64.

Bold, Tessa, Deon Filmer, Gayle Martin, Ezequiel Molina, Brian Stacy, Christophe Rockmore, Jakob Svensson, et al. Forthcoming. "Enrollment without Learning: Teacher Effort, Knowledge, and Skill in Primary Schools in Africa." *Journal of Economic Perspectives*.

Bolyard, K. J. 2003. "Linking Continuous Assessment and Teacher Development: Evaluating a Model of Continuous Assessment for Primary Schools in Malawi." EQUIP1 Continuous Assessment, Educational Quality Improvement Program, U.S. Agency for International Development, Washington, DC.

Boyd, Donald J., Pamela L. Grossman, Hamilton Lankford, Susanna Loeb, and James Wyckoff. 2009. "Teacher Preparation and Student Achievement." *Educational Evaluation and Policy Analysis* 31 (4): 416–40.

Bruns, Barbara, and Javier Luque. 2015. *Great Teachers: How to Raise Student Learning in Latin America and the Caribbean*. With Soledad De Gregorio, David K. Evans, Marco Fernández, Martin Moreno, Jessica Rodriguez, Guillermo Toral, and Noah Yarrow. Latin American Development Forum Series. Washington, DC: World Bank.

Buddin, Richard, and Gema Zamarro. 2009. "Teacher Qualifications and Student Achievement in Urban Elementary Schools." *Journal of Urban Economics* 66 (2): 103–15.

Buhl-Wiggers, Julie, Jason T. Kerwin, Jeffrey A. Smith, and Rebecca Thornton. 2017. "The Impact of Teacher Effectiveness on Student Learning in Africa." Paper presented at RISE Annual Conference 2017, Center for Global Development, Washington, DC, June 15–16. http://www.rise programme.org/sites/www.riseprogramme.org/files /Buhl-Wiggers%20The%20Impact%20of%20Teacher%20 Effectiveness%202017-04-30_0.pdf.

Calderón, David. 2014. "Invertir en la Formación Docente." *Animal Político* (blog), November 13. http://www.animal politico.com/blogueros-aprender-es-mi-derecho/2014/11 /13/invertir-en-la-formacion-docente/.

Carrillo, Paul, Mercedes Onofa, and Juan Ponce. 2010. "Information Technology and Student Achievement: Evidence from a Randomized Experiment in Ecuador." IDB

Working Paper IDB-WP-223, Inter-American Development Bank, Washington, DC.

Ciaccio, Joseph. 2004. *Totally Positive Teaching: A Five-Stage Approach to Energizing Students and Teachers*. Alexandria, VA: Association for Supervision and Curriculum Development.

Conn, Katharine M. 2017. "Identifying Effective Education Interventions in Sub-Saharan Africa: A Meta-Analysis of Impact Evaluations." *Review of Educational Research* (May 26). http://journals.sagepub.com/doi/abs/10.3102/0034654317712025.

Cummins, Joseph R. 2016. "Heterogeneous Treatment Effects in the Low Track: Revisiting the Kenyan Primary School Experiment." *Economics of Education Review* 56 (February): 40–51.

Darling-Hammond, Linda, Ruth Chung Wei, Alethea Andree, Nikole Richardson, and Stelios Orphanos. 2009. "Professional Learning in the Learning Profession: A Status Report on Teacher Development in the United States and Abroad." National Staff Development Council, Dallas.

Dee, Thomas S., and James Wyckoff. 2015. "Incentives, Selection, and Teacher Performance: Evidence from Impact." *Journal of Policy Analysis and Management* 34 (2): 267–97.

de Hoyos, Rafael E., Alejandro J. Ganimian, and Peter A. Holland. 2016. "Teaching with the Test: Experimental Evidence on Diagnostic Feedback and Capacity-Building for Schools in Argentina." Working paper, World Bank, Washington, DC.

de Hoyos, Rafael E., Vicente A. Garcia-Moreno, and Harry Anthony Patrinos. 2017. "The Impact of an Accountability Intervention with Diagnostic Feedback: Evidence from Mexico." *Economics of Education Review* 58: 123–40.

de Ree, Joppe, Karthik Muralidharan, Menno Pradhan, and Halsey Rogers. Forthcoming. "Double for Nothing? Experimental Evidence on an Unconditional Teacher Salary Increase in Indonesia." *Quarterly Journal of Economics.*

Dolton, Peter, and Oscar Marcenaro-Gutierrez. 2011. "2013 Global Teacher Status Index." With Vikas Pota, Marc Boxser, and Ash Pajpani. Varkey Gems Foundation, London. https://www.varkeyfoundation.org/sites/default/files/documents/2013GlobalTeacherStatusIndex.pdf.

Duflo, Esther, James Berry, Shobhini Mukerji, and Marc Shotland. 2014. "A Wide Angle View of Learning: Evaluation of the CCE and LEP Programmes in Haryana." 3ie Grantee Final Report, International Initiative for Impact Evaluation, New Delhi.

Duflo, Esther, Pascaline Dupas, and Michael R. Kremer. 2011. "Peer Effects, Teacher Incentives, and the Impact of Tracking: Evidence from a Randomized Evaluation in Kenya." *American Economic Review* 101 (5): 1739–74.

———. 2015. "School Governance, Teacher Incentives, and Pupil-Teacher Ratios: Experimental Evidence from Kenyan Primary Schools." *Journal of Public Economics* 123 (March): 92–110.

Duflo, Esther, Rema Hanna, and Stephen P. Ryan. 2012. "Incentives Work: Getting Teachers to Come to School." *American Economic Review* 102 (4): 1241–78.

Estrada, Ricardo. 2016. "Crony Education: Teacher Hiring and Rent Extraction." Working paper, European University Institute, San Domenico di Fiesole, Italy.

Ethnologue. 2015. Ethnologue: Languages of the World (database). 18th ed., SIL International, Dallas. http://www.ethnologue.com/18/.

Evans, David K., and Fei Yuan. 2017. "The Working Conditions of Teachers in Low- and Middle-Income Countries." WDR 2018 background paper, World Bank, Washington, DC.

Figlio, David N., and Marianne E. Page. 2002. "School Choice and the Distributional Effects of Ability Tracking: Does Separation Increase Inequality?" *Journal of Urban Economics* 51 (3): 497–514.

Fryer, Roland G., Jr. 2013. "Teacher Incentives and Student Achievement: Evidence from New York City Public Schools." *Journal of Labor Economics* 31 (2): 373–407.

———. 2017. "The Production of Human Capital in Developed Countries: Evidence from 196 Randomized Field Experiments." In *Handbook of Field Experiments*, edited by Abhijit Vinayak Banerjee and Esther Duflo, Vol. 2, 95–322. Handbooks in Economics Series. Amsterdam: North-Holland.

Gamero Burón, Carlos, and Gérard Lassibille. 2016. "Job Satisfaction among Primary School Personnel in Madagascar." *Journal of Development Studies* 52 (11): 1628–46.

Ganimian, Alejandro J., and Richard J. Murnane. 2016. "Improving Education in Developing Countries: Lessons from Rigorous Impact Evaluations." *Review of Educational Research* 86 (3): 719–55.

Gill, Brian P., Jennifer S. Lerner, and Paul Meosky. 2016. "Reimagining Accountability in K–12 Education." *Behavioral Science and Policy* 2 (1): 57–70.

Glazerman, Steven, Daniel Mayer, and Paul Decker. 2006. "Alternative Routes to Teaching: The Impacts of Teach for America on Student Achievement and Other Outcomes." *Journal of Policy Analysis and Management* 25 (1): 75–96.

Glazerman, Steven, Allison McKie, and Nancy Carey. 2009. "An Evaluation of the Teacher Advancement Program (TAP) in Chicago: Year One Impact Report, Final Report." Mathematica Policy Research, Princeton, NJ.

Glewwe, Paul W., Nauman Ilias, and Michael R. Kremer. 2010. "Teacher Incentives." *American Economic Journal: Applied Economics* 2 (3): 205–27.

Goldhaber, Dan. 2007. "Everyone's Doing It, but What Does Teacher Testing Tell Us about Teacher Effectiveness?" *Journal of Human Resources* 42 (4): 765–94.

Guajardo, Jarret. 2011. "Teacher Motivation: Theoretical Framework, Situation Analysis of Save the Children Country Offices, and Recommended Strategies." Teacher Motivation Working Group, Save the Children, Fairfield, CT.

Hammett, Daniel. 2008. "Disrespecting Teacher: The Decline in Social Standing of Teachers in Cape Town, South Africa." *International Journal of Educational Development* 28 (3): 340–47.

Hanushek, Eric A. 2011. "Valuing Teachers: How Much Is a Good Teacher Worth?" *Education Next* 11 (3): 40–45.

Harris-Van Keuren, Christine, and Iveta Silova. 2015. "Implementing EFA Strategy No. 9: The Evolution of the Status of the Teaching Profession (2000–2015) and the Impact on the Quality of Education in Developing Countries, Three Case Studies." With Suzanne McAllister. Report ED/EFA/MRT/2015/PI/08, background paper, Education for All Global Monitoring Report, United Nations Educational, Scientific, and Cultural Organization, Paris.

He, Fang, Leigh L. Linden, and Margaret MacLeod. 2008. "How to Teach English in India: Testing the Relative Productivity of Instruction Methods within the Pratham English Language Education Program." Working paper, Columbia University, New York.

——. 2009. "A Better Way to Teach Children to Read? Evidence from a Randomized Controlled Trial." Working paper, Columbia University, New York.

Jackson, C. Kirabo. 2012. "Recruiting, Retaining, and Creating Quality Teachers." Nordic Economic Policy Review 3 (1): 61–104.

Jacob, Brian A., and Steven D. Levitt. 2003. "Rotten Apples: An Investigation of the Prevalence and Predictors of Teacher Cheating." Quarterly Journal of Economics 118 (3): 843–78.

Jinnai, Yusuke. 2016. "To Introduce or Not to Introduce Monetary Bonuses: The Cost of Repealing Teacher Incentives." Economics and Management Series EMS-2016-08, IUJ Research Institute, International University of Japan, Minamiuonuma, Niigata Prefecture. http://www.iuj.ac.jp/research/workingpapers/EMS_2016_08.pdf.

Kiessel, Jessica, and Annie Duflo. 2014. "Cost Effectiveness Report: Teacher Community Assistant Initiative (TCAI)." IPA Brief, Innovation for Poverty Action, New Haven, CT.

Kraft, Matthew A., David Blazar, and Dylan Hogan. 2016. "The Effect of Teacher Coaching on Instruction and Achievement: A Meta-Analysis of the Causal Evidence." Working paper, Brown University, Providence, RI.

Lauwerier, Thibaut, and Abdeljalil Akkari. 2015. "Teachers and the Quality of Basic Education in Sub-Saharan Africa." ERF Working Paper 11, Education Research and Foresight, Paris.

Leder, Gilah C. 1987. "Teacher Student Interaction: A Case Study." Educational Studies in Mathematics 18 (3): 255–71.

Lefgren, Lars. 2004. "Educational Peer Effects and the Chicago Public Schools." Journal of Urban Economics 56 (2): 169–91.

Lerner, Jennifer S., and Philip E. Tetlock. 1999. "Accounting for the Effects of Accountability." Psychological Bulletin 125 (2): 255–75.

Liang, Xiaoyan, Huma Kidwai, and Minxuan Zhang. 2016. How Shanghai Does It: Insights and Lessons from the Highest-Ranking Education System in the World. Directions in Development: Human Development Series. Washington, DC: World Bank.

Liu, Shujie, and Anthony J. Onwuegbuzie. 2012. "Chinese Teachers' Work Stress and Their Turnover Intention." International Journal of Educational Research 53: 160–70.

Lucas, Adrienne M., Patrick J. McEwan, Moses Ngware, and Moses Oketch. 2014. "Improving Early-Grade Literacy in East Africa: Experimental Evidence from Kenya and Uganda." Journal of Policy Analysis and Management 33 (4): 950–76.

Luschei, Thomas F., and Amita Chudgar. 2017. "Supply-Side Explanations for Inequitable Teacher Distribution." In Teacher Distribution in Developing Countries: Teachers of Marginalized Students in India, Mexico, and Tanzania, edited by Thomas F. Luschei and Amita Chudgar, 87–107. New York: Palgrave Macmillan.

Mbiti, Isaac M., Karthik Muralidharan, and Youdi Schipper. 2016. "Inputs, Incentives, and Complementarities in Primary Education: Experimental Evidence from Tanzania." Working paper, University of California at San Diego.

Metila, Romylyn A., Lea Angela S. Pradilla, and Alan B. Williams. 2016. "The Challenge of Implementing Mother Tongue Education in Linguistically Diverse Contexts: The Case of the Philippines." Asia-Pacific Education Researcher 25 (5–6): 781–89.

Michaelowa, Katharina. 2001. "Primary Education Quality in Francophone Sub-Saharan Africa: Determinants of Learning Achievement and Efficiency Considerations." World Development 29 (10): 1699–1716.

Mizala, Alejandra, and Hugo Ñopo. 2016. "Measuring the Relative Pay of School Teachers in Latin America 1997–2007." International Journal of Educational Development 47: 20–32.

Mooij, Jos. 2008. "Primary Education, Teachers' Professionalism and Social Class about Motivation and Demotivation of Government School Teachers in India." International Journal of Educational Development 28 (5): 508–23.

Mulkeen, Aidan G. 2010. Teachers in Anglophone Africa: Issues in Teacher Supply, Training, and Management. Development Practice in Education Series. Washington, DC: World Bank.

Muralidharan, Karthik. 2012. "Long-Term Effects of Teacher Performance Pay: Experimental Evidence from India." Working paper, University of California at San Diego.

——. 2016. "A New Approach to Public Sector Hiring in India for Improved Service Delivery." Working paper, University of California at San Diego.

Muralidharan, Karthik, Abhijeet Singh, and Alejandro J. Ganimian. 2016. "Disrupting Education? Experimental Evidence on Technology-Aided Instruction in India." NBER Working Paper 22923, National Bureau of Economic Research, Cambridge, MA.

Muralidharan, Karthik, and Venkatesh Sundararaman. 2010. "The Impact of Diagnostic Feedback to Teachers on Student Learning: Experimental Evidence from India." Economic Journal 120 (546): F187–F203.

——. 2011. "Teacher Performance Pay: Experimental Evidence from India." Journal of Political Economy 119 (1): 39–77.

Muralidharan, Karthik, and Yendrick Zieleniak. 2013. "Measuring Learning Trajectories in Developing Countries with Longitudinal Data and Item Response Theory." Paper presented at Young Lives Conference, Oxford University, Oxford, U.K., July 8–9.

OECD (Organisation for Economic Co-operation and Development). 2011. Strong Performers and Successful Reformers in Education: Lessons from PISA for the United States. Paris: OECD.

——. 2016a. Education at a Glance 2016: OECD Indicators. Paris: OECD.

——. 2016b. PISA 2015 Results: Excellence and Equity in Education. Vol. 1. Paris: OECD.

Ong'uti, Charles Onchiri, Peter J. O. Aloka, and Pamela Raburu. 2016. "Factors Affecting Teaching and Learning in Mother Tongue in Public Lower Primary Schools in Kenya." *International Journal of Psychology and Behavioral Sciences* 6 (3): 161–66.

Osei, George M. 2006. "Teachers in Ghana: Issues of Training, Remuneration and Effectiveness." *International Journal of Educational Development* 26 (1): 38–51.

Peng, Wen J., Elizabeth McNess, Sally Thomas, Xiang Rong Wu, Chong Zhang, Jian Zhong Li, and Hui Sheng Tian. 2014. "Emerging Perceptions of Teacher Quality and Teacher Development in China." *International Journal of Educational Development* 34: 77–89.

Piper, Benjamin, and Medina Korda. 2010. "EGRA Plus: Liberia, Program Evaluation Report." Research Triangle Institute, Research Triangle Park, NC.

Piper, Benjamin, Stephanie S. Zuilkowski, and Salome Ong'ele. 2016. "Implementing Mother Tongue Instruction in the Real World: Results from a Medium-Scale Randomized Controlled Trial in Kenya." *Comparative Education Review* 60 (4): 776–807.

Popova, Anna, Mary E. Breeding, and David K. Evans. 2017. "Global Landscape of In-Service Teacher Professional Development Programs: The Gap between Evidence and Practice." Background paper, World Bank, Washington, DC.

Popova, Anna, David K. Evans, and Violeta Arancibia. 2016. "Training Teachers on the Job: What Works and How to Measure It." Policy Research Working Paper 7834, World Bank, Washington, DC.

Pritchett, Lant, and Amanda Beatty. 2015. "Slow Down, You're Going Too Fast: Matching Curricula to Student Skill Levels." *International Journal of Educational Development* 40: 276–88.

Ramachandran, Vimala, Suman Bhattacharjea, and K. M. Sheshagiri. 2008. "Primary School Teachers: The Twists and Turns of Everyday Practice." Working paper, Educational Resource Unit, New Delhi.

Rivkin, Steven G., Eric A. Hanushek, and John F. Kain. 2005. "Teachers, Schools, and Academic Achievement." *Econometrica* 73 (2): 417–58.

RTI International. 2016. "Survey of Children's Reading Materials in African Languages in Eleven Countries: Final Report." EdData II: Data for Education Research and Programming in Africa, U.S. Agency for International Development, Washington, DC.

Sabarwal, Shwetlena, Malek Abu-Jawdeh, and Eema Masood. 2017. "Understanding Teacher Effort: Insights from Cross-Country Data on Teacher Perceptions." Background paper, World Bank, Washington, DC.

Sahlberg, Pasi. 2011. *Finnish Lessons: What Can the World Learn from Educational Change in Finland?* New York: Teachers College Press.

Seid, Yared. 2016. "Does Learning in Mother Tongue Matter? Evidence from a Natural Experiment in Ethiopia." *Economics of Education Review* 55: 21–38.

Shin, Jaran, Misty Sailors, Nicola McClung, P. David Pearson, James V. Hoffman, and Margaret Chilimanjira. 2015. "The Case of Chichewa and English in Malawi: The Impact of First Language Reading and Writing on Learning English as a Second Language." *Bilingual Research Journal* 38 (3): 255–74.

Smits, Jeroen, Janine Huisman, and Karine Kruijff. 2008. "Home Language and Education in the Developing World." Report 2009/ED/EFA/MRT/PI/21, background paper, Education for All Global Monitoring Report, United Nations Educational, Scientific, and Cultural Organization, Paris.

Spratt, Jennifer, Simon King, and Jennae Bulat. 2013. "Independent Evaluation of the Effectiveness of Institut pour l'Education Populaire's 'Read-Learn-Lead' (RLL) Program in Mali: Endline Report." Research Triangle Institute, Research Triangle Park, NC.

Springer, Matthew G., Dale Ballou, Laura Hamilton, Vi-Nhuan Le, J. R. Lockwood, Daniel F. McCaffrey, Matthew Pepper, et al. 2010. "Teacher Pay for Performance: Experimental Evidence from the Project on Incentives in Teaching." National Center on Performance Incentives, Vanderbilt University, Nashville, TN.

Strizek, Gregory A., Steve Tourkin, Ebru Erberber, and Patrick Gonzales. 2014. "Teaching and Learning International Survey (TALIS) 2013: U.S. Technical Report." NCES 2015–010, National Center for Education Statistics, Institute of Education Sciences, U.S. Department of Education, Washington, DC.

Tandon, Prateek, and Tsuyoshi Fukao. 2015. *Educating the Next Generation: Improving Teacher Quality in Cambodia.* Directions in Development: Human Development Series. Washington, DC: World Bank.

Taylor, Stephen, and Marisa von Fintel. 2016. "Estimating the Impact of Language of Instruction in South African Primary Schools: A Fixed Effects Approach." *Economics of Education Review* 50: 75–89.

UIS (UNESCO Institute for Statistics). 2017. Education (database). UIS, Montreal. http://data.uis.unesco.org/.

Urwick, James, and Sarah Kisa. 2014. "Science Teacher Shortage and the Moonlighting Culture: The Pathology of the Teacher Labour Market in Uganda." *International Journal of Educational Development* 36: 72–80.

Visaria, Sujata, Rajeev Dehejia, Melody M. Chao, and Anirban Mukhopadhyay. 2016. "Unintended Consequences of Rewards for Student Attendance: Results from a Field Experiment in Indian Classrooms." *Economics of Education Review* 54: 173–84.

Walter, Catherine, and Jessica Briggs. 2012. "What Professional Development Makes the Most Difference to Teachers?" Department of Education, University of Oxford, Oxford, U.K.

Walter, Stephen L., and Diane E. Dekker. 2011. "Mother Tongue Instruction in Lubuagan: A Case Study from the Philippines." *International Review of Education* 57 (5–6): 667–83.

World Bank. 2014. "Teacher Training (% of Total Education Expenditure)." EdStats: Education Statistics (database). World Bank, Washington, DC. http://datatopics.world bank.org/education/.

———. 2016. "Assessing Basic Education Service Delivery in the Philippines: The Philippines Public Education Expenditure Tracking and Quantitative Service Delivery Study." Report AUS6799. Washington, DC: World Bank.

Yoon, Kwang Suk, Teresa Duncan, Silvia Wen-Yu Lee, Beth Scarloss, and Kathy L. Shapley. 2007. "Reviewing the Evidence on How Teacher Professional Development Affects Student Achievement." Issues and Answers Report REL 2007–033, Regional Educational Laboratory Southwest, National Center for Education Statistics, Institute of Education Sciences, U.S. Department of Education, Washington, DC.

Zimmer, Ron. 2003. "A New Twist in the Educational Tracking Debate." *Economics of Education Review* 22 (3): 307–15.

Zuilkowski, Stephanie Simmons, Matthew C. H. Jukes, and Margaret M. Dubeck. 2016. "'I Failed, No Matter How Hard I Tried': A Mixed-Methods Study of the Role of Achievement in Primary School Dropout in Rural Kenya." *International Journal of Educational Development* 50: 100–107.

Everything else should strengthen the teacher-learner interaction

Investments in school inputs, management, and governance often are not guided by how well they improve the teacher-learner relationship. To be effective, they should be.

Learners and teachers have a more productive learning relationship when supported by learning materials and other inputs. Most countries, from the lowest- to the highest-income, are seeking to incorporate technology into their classrooms and education systems. But technology is merely the most discussed of a range of inputs intended to improve the teacher-learner relationship, from pencils and textbooks in the hands of learners to the walls and roofs of school buildings. Good school management also focuses on supporting students learning from teachers. Yet technology—along with other physical inputs—often fails to support the work that teachers and students do, and the potential of school leaders and community members often goes unrealized.

This chapter lays out evidence for the most effective use of these complementary inputs in places where the gap between evidence and practice is largest. In many cases, the failures observed can be illuminated through models of human behavior, which also point the way to solutions (table 7.1). A synthesis of the evidence in these areas reveals three principles that are keys to success in achieving learning through school investments:

- Ensure that other inputs—including new technology—complement teachers, thereby making teaching more effective. Taking this approach, rather than seeking to circumvent teachers, can increase learning.

- Ensure that information and communication technology (ICT) can be implemented in current systems. Otherwise, it will be ineffective.

- Recognize that school management and governance reform, along with community monitoring, can achieve more learning only if they affect interaction between teachers and learners.

Technological interventions increase learning—but only if they enhance the teacher-learner relationship

Technology can strengthen learning.[1] Software can be highly effective if it allows students to learn at their own pace and, in the best cases, adapts dynamically to their knowledge.[2] A game-based computer-assisted learning program in Qinghai, China, intended to improve student language scores not only did that, but also improved students' knowledge of mathematics.[3]

Technology is about much more than giving computers to students. ICT interventions include a wide range of technological monitoring and information systems at all levels of education, from individual students to education systems. Computers and computer-assisted learning software, as well as online platforms such as Google Classroom, Blackboard, and Brazil's Education Connection, enable

Table 7.1 Models of human behavior can guide actions to improve the effectiveness of school inputs and governance: Some examples

Synthesis principle	Where this fails	Models that identify a mechanism behind this failure	Approaches that address the modeled mechanism
Additional inputs should complement rather than substitute for teachers.	Inputs like laptops are sometimes used to circumvent the teacher-learner relationship but fail to deliver learning benefits.	*Information failure:* Policy makers seek to circumvent poorly functioning teacher-learner relationships without evidence on an alternative model of learning.	New books and materials have been ineffective in many places, but in Liberia they increased student learning when combined with teacher training.
Technologies must be implementable in the current education system to achieve more learning.	Education technology investments routinely fail because there is limited capacity to maintain them, or the infrastructure needed for them to work effectively does not exist.	*Behavioral (optimism bias):* Policy makers project unrealistic technological progress.	In India, computer-assisted learning has dramatically improved learning outcomes in dedicated technology centers.
School governance reform and community monitoring improve learning only if they affect the teacher-learner interaction.	School governance reforms and community monitoring often fail to take into account community capacity.	*Information failure:* Community members often do not observe the most important part of the learning process—what happens in the classroom.	In Mexico, community engagement over time, with decentralization of real decision-making power, has been effective.

Source: WDR 2018 team.

learners and parents to communicate with teachers about assignments and materials, and they offer free materials that educators and parents can use in designing age-appropriate development activities.[4] These platforms include interactive whiteboards, text messages to support teachers, and televised programs to improve instructional quality in areas with limited access to trained teachers.[5]

Though ICT offers potentially significant gains for education, the effects of tested interventions have varied greatly. Some programs have been extremely impressive, such as a dynamic computer-assisted learning program for secondary school students in India that increased math and language scores more than most other learning interventions tested there or elsewhere.[6] But others, such as the One Laptop Per Child programs in Peru and Uruguay, have shown no impact on student reading or math ability.[7] Indeed, the vast majority of ICT interventions have had either no impact or—as with certain hardware interventions—a negative impact on student learning (figure 7.1).[8]

Moreover, current evidence likely overestimates the effectiveness of ICT interventions in education because many fail—or stumble badly—before being implemented. In Haiti, a program to use smartphones to monitor teacher attendance had no effect on teacher attendance or student outcomes because implementation proved untenable.[9] Brazil's One

Figure 7.1 Information and communication technology has had a mixed impact on learning

Distribution of the effects of education technology on student learning, by type

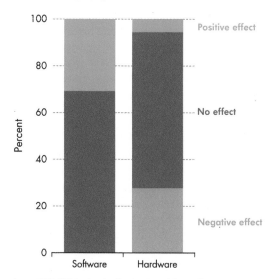

Source: WDR 2018 team, using data from Muralidharan, Singh, and Ganimian (2016, annex 2). Data at http://bit.do/WDR2018-Fig_7-1.

Laptop Per Child initiative faced years of delays in several states. And a year after the laptops made it to classrooms, more than 40 percent of teachers reported never or rarely using them in classroom activities.[10] Rich countries face the same challenges: beyond education, almost a fifth of public sector ICT projects in the United Kingdom have had cost overruns of more than 25 percent, and the typical project takes 24 percent longer to implement than initially expected.[11] It is crucial to focus on technologies that are truly feasible in existing systems. In rural areas, technology may be more attractive because of weak education systems, but at the same time those weak systems—with their limited access to electricity or the internet—have the least capacity to support education technology interventions.

With such varied returns and so many challenges to implementation, why is there so much investment in education technology? Both principal-agent relationships and behavioral biases likely play a role. The principal-agent model is relevant because public officials may derive political returns from flashy technological interventions, independent of their usefulness for better learning. Thus their personal incentives (to make highly visible investments) may diverge from the goals of students (to learn). Cognitive bias may also be a factor, with individuals being unrealistically optimistic. In fact, there is a long history of overestimating the transformative nature of technology in schools, going back to Thomas Edison asserting in 1913 that "books will soon be obsolete in schools. . . . Our school system will be completely changed in the next ten years." Edison predicted that books would be entirely replaced by silent films.[12] Half a century later, as computers gained traction, some scholars wondered if they might replace teachers at some point.[13] Of course, schools in technology-rich environments do look different from those elsewhere: students might do their work on interactive displays rather than on paper. But technology has for the most part not been particularly disruptive in education. The buildings, the processes of the school day, and the interactions between teachers and students are very similar to those of a century ago.[14]

Technologies that complement teachers work better than technologies that substitute for them. Many students have poorly prepared teachers with limited training and motivation, and education systems have been tempted to use technology to circumvent these teachers. Most such attempts have failed. By contrast, using technology to complement teachers offers more promise.[15] Consider a computer-assisted learning program in Gujarat, India, that was implemented in two ways. One approach pulled students out of regular classes to use computer-based math programs—in other words, the program substituted for regular class time. Students under that model performed significantly worse than students left with their regular teachers. In the other approach, where students used the program after school, there were sizable gains, especially for the poorest performers.[16] Another example of technology that complements teachers is a series of prepared videos of high-quality lessons—such as Brazil's Telecurso—which can be used in a classroom.

Technology holds some promise in fragile settings, such as those afflicted by war or epidemic, to maintain a connection to formal education. During the 2014–15 Ebola epidemic in Sierra Leone, schools shut down for eight months, but the government launched an emergency education program with lessons five days a week. A 30-minute lesson over the radio is unlikely to have a deep learning impact, but this kind of program may help children stay connected to learning.[17] Sudan's Can't Wait to Learn program, which provides out-of-school children with computer tablets loaded with learning games, has shown positive learning impacts in mathematics and is now being tested on a large scale in areas receiving Syrian refugees.[18] In places where teachers are unavailable, such approaches may be the best option.

Impacts on literacy and numeracy are not the only measures of success: technology can also promote digital skills. As more jobs require digital literacy, the opportunity to acquire those skills is an end in itself. Students with more access to computers at home have better computer skills.[19] And though Peru's One Laptop Per Child program had no effect on academic achievement or cognitive skills, students did significantly improve their knowledge of how to use laptops.[20] In such cases, clarity of purpose is key. Obviously, youth need computers to learn how to use them. But as tools for teaching reading and numeracy, evidence on their usefulness is mixed.

Other inputs bring learners to school—but promote learning only if they target teaching and learning

Building schools can increase enrollment in places with few schools, especially for girls. In Afghanistan, the provision of community-based schools in just over a dozen communities increased enrollment massively, effectively eliminating the gender gap in enrollment.[21] In Burkina Faso, a program to construct schools with modern amenities increased enrollment by a large margin, with the biggest impacts for girls. Even beyond building entire schools, building latrines—particularly gender-specific ones—significantly increased enrollment of adolescent girls in India.[22] But in places where learners have relatively easy access to schools, additional schools will not be the most cost-effective way to raise access or to improve learning.

Even in places lacking infrastructure, providing it does not necessarily lead to more learning. The Afghanistan and Burkina Faso programs boosted learning, while India's did not. Why? Constructing a school where children previously had no access directly alters the learning process by creating a place to learn that did not exist before. Building latrines makes school a safe space, and so it makes children (especially girls) better able to be at school—but because it does not affect what happens in the classroom, it may not affect learning.

School feeding gets children to school, but it does not always improve learning. The most consistent impact of school-based meal programs has been more children in school, such as in Burkina Faso, Kenya, and Peru.[23] At school age, providing meals contributes less to brain development than earlier in the child's life, but it could still increase learning through improved attention and energy. However, if meals are offered during normal school hours, they reduce time on task. In Kenya and Peru, meals took significant time away from the classroom, and so they had an ambiguous net effect. Impacts on measured learning are mixed, with positive effects in Burkina Faso and Peru.

Similarly, simply increasing the materials available at schools does not improve learning if the materials do not improve teacher-learner interaction. Providing more textbooks in Sierra Leone in 2008 did not result in those books being used in the classroom because administrators put most of the books in storage—potentially to hedge against future textbook shortfalls.[24] Another textbook program, in Kenya, had no impact on learning, most likely because most students did not fully understand the language in which the books were written.[25] Simply providing desktop computers to classrooms in Colombia—where they were not well integrated in the curriculum—likewise had no impact on learning.[26] It seems obvious that resources have to be used to have an impact, but many interventions that provide inputs fail exactly because insufficient thought is given to how resources will be used. Infrastructure and other inputs are essential, but they work only when they serve the relationship between teaching and learning.[27]

School management and governance are crucial, and involving communities can help overcome incentive problems and information failures—but only if communities have capacity

Schools with better management have better test scores.[28] Schools vary significantly in management quality (figure 7.2), and school leadership plays a crucial role in school performance. Effective leadership means having school principals who are actively involved in helping teachers solve problems, including by providing instructional advice.[29] It also means having principals who set goals with teachers to prioritize and achieve high levels of learning. These factors are associated with the highest levels of student learning, and they confirm that effective school leadership improves the quality of teacher-learner interactions. A major school district in the United States improved student learning by training school

Figure 7.2 Schools vary significantly in management quality

Average school management score by country, relative to top-performing country, participating countries

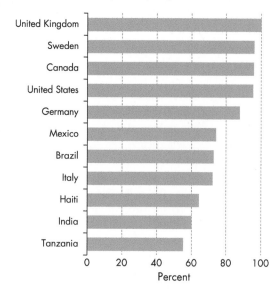

Source: Bloom and others (2015). Data at http://bit.do/WDR2018-Fig_7-2.

Note: The school management score is a combination of 14 basic management practices, each rated from 1 to 5. Schools with higher scores have more structured management practices.

Box 7.1 Training better school principals in Jamaica

Training can improve the quality of school management. In Jamaica, the government invested in a school principal training program with key characteristics that likely led to better management. The program was based on analysis of principals' weaknesses. Principals were trained to provide feedback to teachers on their performance, as well as to use data to evaluate the learning needs of students. The program also provided practical experience: after initial training, principals spent three months implementing the program, with mentoring and coaching from experienced school leaders. The training modules subsequently received high ratings for relevance from participants. Although the program has not been evaluated with a comparison group, both the principals themselves and the teachers in their schools report major gains in management quality. Teachers say they are twice as likely to be observed in their classrooms and to have the principal work with them to develop short-term goals.[a]

Source: WDR 2018 team.

a. Nannyonjo (2017).

principals in three sets of skills: how to give feedback to teachers on lesson plans; how to support teachers in regular learner assessments, as well as to provide feedback on action plans to improve student performance; and how to, through classroom observation, give feedback on teacher performance.[30] In Madagascar, clarifying the management roles of district officers, school principals, and teachers and providing them with coaching and supervision improved student outcomes, at least in schools where the heads had good performance incentives.[31] Likewise, in Jamaica training and mentoring principals improved school management (box 7.1).

Many countries have decentralized some elements of their education systems, often called school-based management. Providing schools and communities with decision-making power and resources can solve two problems. First, by giving local school leaders and parents more direct influence over teachers and other school representatives, it may make teachers more immediately responsive to student needs. Contrast this with supervision by a ministry of education representative based far away, who has little ability to bring shirking teachers to account. Second, schools and communities may have better information about the needs of local schools, which, along with access to discretionary resources, means they can more nimbly meet those needs.

School-based management programs improve learning when the community has the capacity to make and implement smarter decisions.[32] Data on 1 million students from 42 countries suggest that school autonomy is beneficial to student learning in high-income countries but detrimental in developing countries.[33] At the micro level, a school-based management intervention in The Gambia improved test scores only in communities with high literacy rates among parents.[34] A similar result was observed in the impacts of a school grant program in Niger.[35] Several of these programs did not last more than a year or two, in some cases because the programs were pilots and in others because of unstable education policies. Without time for communities to learn how to effectively engage in school management, impacts on learning are unlikely. Because communities are more readily able to monitor school enrollment than learning, school-based management may increase access even in low-capacity communities, as happened in Burkina Faso.[36]

Community monitoring will not help learning if it does not affect what happens in the classroom. A range of interventions seek to increase community monitoring of schools by sharing school information with parents. The structure of these programs varies, from the parents themselves collecting data on teacher attendance or school performance, to the education systems disseminating prepared data to parents, to supplementing information with facilitated meetings in which parents and teachers can discuss grievances and lay out courses of action.[37] But parents are rarely in the classroom, and even when they are, they cannot necessarily identify good classroom practice. This may explain why the growing evidence on these programs reveals mixed results.[38] For example, in Andhra

Pradesh, India, providing community members with report cards on school performance failed to increase either parental engagement or student learning.[39]

Successful community monitoring increases accountability through feedback loops between multiple stakeholders. Low-stakes accountability programs have improved student learning in Mexico, Pakistan, and Uganda.[40] Though some monitoring programs succeed and others fail for multiple reasons, successful programs, such as those in Mexico and Uganda, do not reach out to only one group, but rather share information explicitly with school leaders and teachers, as well as with communities and parents. (The Pakistan experiment is an exception, focusing only on parents.) Parents alone cannot enact accountability, and better information in the hands of school officials helps. To improve learning, parents and communities need to be able to harness increased information to hold teachers and schools more accountable.

School grant programs—in which schools receive regular influxes of resources and more autonomy over budget allocations—are one type of school-based management program. In Haiti, a program that provided schools with grants based on the number of students enrolled significantly increased enrollment.[41] From this perspective, school grants can effectively deliver money to schools, and schools need money to function. But most programs that simply deliver grants to schools do not increase learning. Just distributing grants to schools—as in The Gambia, Indonesia, and Tanzania—had no effect on student learning.[42] In Senegal, observed impacts on learning appeared only for a subset of children, then disappeared by the next year.[43] Some school grant programs increase learning outcomes only when the grants are unanticipated. When parents have known the grants were coming, they have reduced their own investments in education—not a recipe for long-term learning impacts.[44] By themselves, grants act in much the same way as other interventions that simply increase resources in schools. There is no guarantee that they will improve learning.

But grants can be leveraged in the context of broader school-based management programs to improve school outcomes. In Tanzania, grants alone had no impact on student learning, but grants combined with teacher incentives did improve learning. In Niger, grants alone had little impact, but grants with training improved both student learning and parent support for schools.[45] Likewise, grants alone had no impact on learning in Indonesia, but they did improve learning when the program also linked school management committees to village councils, seeking to resolve the principal-agent problem.[46] When grants are included in larger programs to encourage community school councils to engage in school management, the combination can improve learning.[47]

* * *

Whether an education input is a physical item, such as a tablet or textbook, or a process, such as school management and leadership, it will improve learning only if it directly improves the quality of teacher-learner interactions. Without that, more inputs will pile onto an ineffective process and fail to have the desired impact. But used strategically, inputs can work together with prepared learners and knowledgeable, motivated teachers to produce high levels of learning.

Notes

1. McEwan (2015).
2. Banerjee and others (2007); Carrillo, Onofa, and Ponce (2010); Muralidharan, Singh, and Ganimian (2016).
3. Lai and others (2012).
4. Esteves Pereira and Cabral (2016); "Planning Educational Activities for Children (PEACH)," Georgia Department of Early Care and Learning, Atlanta, http://www.peach .decal.ga.gov/app/.
5. Jukes and others (2017); Wolff and others (2002).
6. Muralidharan, Singh, and Ganimian (2016).
7. Cristia and others (2017); de Melo, Machado, and Miranda (2014). For Uruguay, the evaluation covers math and reading impacts in the early years of the program, when its main objective was to provide equipment and connectivity for schools; the program evolved since then to add ICT training for teachers and adaptive educational technology, and new evaluations are expected to be published in late 2017.
8. Bulman and Fairlie (2016); Muralidharan, Singh, and Ganimian (2016).
9. Adelman and others (2015).
10. Lavinas and Veiga (2013).
11. Budzier and Flyvbjerg (2012).
12. Smith (1913, 24).
13. Bellissant (1970); Goodlad (1969).
14. Pritchett (2013).
15. Snilstveit and others (2016).
16. Linden (2008).
17. Powers (2016).
18. War Child Holland (2016).
19. Kuhlemeier and Hemker (2007).
20. Beuermann and others (2015).

21. Burde and Linden (2013).
22. Adukia (2017).
23. Cueto and Chinen (2008); Kazianga, de Walque, and Alderman (2009); Vermeersch and Kremer (2005).
24. Sabarwal, Evans, and Marshak (2014).
25. Glewwe, Kremer, and Moulin (2009).
26. Barrera-Osorio and Linden (2009).
27. Ganimian and Murnane (2016).
28. Bloom and others (2015).
29. Robinson, Lloyd, and Rowe (2008); Waters, Marzano, and McNulty (2003).
30. Fryer (2017).
31. Lassibille (2016).
32. Carr-Hill and others (2015).
33. Hanushek, Link, and Woessmann (2013).
34. Blimpo, Evans, and Lahire (2015).
35. Beasley and Huillery (2017).
36. Sawada and others (2016).
37. Read and Atinc (2016).
38. Cheng and Moses (2016); Read and Atinc (2016).
39. Banerjee and others (2010).
40. Andrabi, Das, and Khwaja (2017); Barr and others (2012); de Hoyos, Garcia-Moreno, and Patrinos (2015).
41. Adelman and Holland (2015).
42. Blimpo, Evans, and Lahire (2015); Mbiti and others (2017); Pradhan and others (2014).
43. Carneiro and others (2015).
44. Das and others (2013).
45. Kozuka (2017); Mbiti and others (2017).
46. Pradhan and others (2014).
47. Gertler, Patrinos, and Rubio-Codina (2012); Santibañez, Abreu-Lastra, and O'Donoghue (2014).

References

Adelman, Melissa, Moussa P. Blimpo, David K. Evans, Atabanam Simbou, and Noah Yarrow. 2015. "Can Information Technology Improve School Effectiveness in Haiti? Evidence from a Field Experiment." Working paper, World Bank, Washington, DC.

Adelman, Melissa A., and Peter Holland. 2015. "Increasing Access by Waiving Tuition: Evidence from Haiti." Policy Research Working Paper 7175, World Bank, Washington, DC.

Adukia, Anjali. 2017. "Sanitation and Education." *American Economic Journal: Applied Economics* 9 (2): 23–59.

Andrabi, Tahir, Jishnu Das, and Asim Ijaz Khwaja. 2017. "Report Cards: The Impact of Providing School and Child Test Scores on Educational Markets." *American Economic Review* 107 (6): 1535–63.

Banerjee, Abhijit Vinayak, Rukmini Banerji, Esther Duflo, Rachel Glennerster, and Stuti Khemani. 2010. "Pitfalls of Participatory Programs: Evidence from a Randomized Evaluation in Education in India." *American Economic Journal: Economic Policy* 2 (1): 1–30.

Banerjee, Abhijit Vinayak, Shawn Cole, Esther Duflo, and Leigh Linden. 2007. "Remedying Education: Evidence from Two Randomized Experiments in India." *Quarterly Journal of Economics* 122 (3): 1235–64.

Barr, Abigail, Frederick Mugisha, Pieter Serneels, and Andrew Zeitlin. 2012. "Information and Collective Action in Community-Based Monitoring of Schools: Field and Lab Experimental Evidence from Uganda." Working paper, Georgetown University, Washington, DC.

Barrera-Osorio, Felipe, and Leigh L. Linden. 2009. "The Use and Misuse of Computers in Education: Evidence from a Randomized Experiment in Colombia." Policy Research Working Paper Series 4836, World Bank, Washington, DC.

Beasley, Elizabeth, and Elise Huillery. 2017. "Willing but Unable? Short-Term Experimental Evidence on Parent Empowerment and School Quality." *World Bank Economic Review* 31 (2): 531–52.

Bellissant, Camille. 1970. "Teaching and Learning Languages." In *IFIP World Conference on Computer Education*, Vol. 3, edited by Bob Scheepmaker and Karl L. Zinn, 145–48. New York: Science Associates International. https://stacks.stanford.edu/file/druid:jd969fg9400/jd969 fg9400.pdf.

Beuermann, Diether W., Julian Cristia, Santiago Cueto, Ofer Malamud, and Yyannu Cruz-Aguayo. 2015. "One Laptop Per Child at Home: Short-Term Impacts from a Randomized Experiment in Peru." *American Economic Journal: Applied Economics* 7 (2): 53–80.

Blimpo, Moussa P., David K. Evans, and Nathalie Lahire. 2015. "Parental Human Capital and Effective School Management." Policy Research Working Paper 7238, World Bank, Washington, DC.

Bloom, Nicholas, Renata Lemos, Raffaella Sadun, and John Van Reenen. 2015. "Does Management Matter in Schools?" *Economic Journal* 125 (584): 647–74.

Budzier, Alexander, and Bent Flyvbjerg. 2012. "Overspend? Late? Failure? What the Data Says about IT Project Risk in the Public Sector." In *Commonwealth Governance Handbook 2012/13: Democracy, Development, and Public Administration*, edited by Andrew Robertson and Rupert Jones-Parry, 145–47. London: Commonwealth Secretariat.

Bulman, George, and Robert W. Fairlie. 2016. "Technology and Education: Computers, Software, and the Internet." In *Handbook of the Economics of Education*, Vol. 5, edited by Eric A. Hanushek, Stephen J. Machin, and Ludger Woessmann, 239–80. Handbooks in Economics Series. Amsterdam: North-Holland.

Burde, Dana, and Leigh L. Linden. 2013. "Bringing Education to Afghan Girls: A Randomized Controlled Trial of Village-Based Schools." *American Economic Journal: Applied Economics* 5 (3): 27–40.

Carneiro, Pedro, Oswald Koussihouèdé, Nathalie Lahire, Costas Meghir, and Corina Mommaerts. 2015. "Decentralizing Education Resources: School Grants in Senegal." NBER Working Paper 21063, National Bureau of Economic Research, Cambridge, MA.

Carr-Hill, Roy, Caine Rolleston, Tejendra Pherali, Rebecca Schendel, Edwina Peart, and Emma Jones. 2015. *The Effects of School-Based Decision Making on Educational Outcomes in Low- and Middle-Income Contexts: A Systematic Review*. 3ie Grantee Final Review. London: International Initiative for Impact Evaluation.

Carrillo, Paul, Mercedes Onofa, and Juan Ponce. 2010. "Information Technology and Student Achievement: Evidence from a Randomized Experiment in Ecuador." IDB Working Paper IDB-WP-223, Inter-American Development Bank, Washington, DC.

Cheng, Xuejiao Joy, and Kurt Moses. 2016. *Promoting Transparency through Information: A Global Review of School Report Cards.* Ethics and Corruption in Education Series. Paris: International Institute for Educational Planning, United Nations Educational, Scientific, and Cultural Organization.

Cristia, Julián, Pablo Ibarrarán, Santiago Cueto, Ana Santiago, and Eugenio Severín. 2017. "Technology and Child Development: Evidence from the One Laptop Per Child Program." *American Economic Journal: Applied Economics* 9 (3): 295–320.

Cueto, Santiago, and Marjorie Chinen. 2008. "Educational Impact of a School Breakfast Programme in Rural Peru." *International Journal of Educational Development* 28 (2): 132–48.

Das, Jishnu, Stefan Dercon, James Habyarimana, Pramila Krishnan, Karthik Muralidharan, and Venkatesh Sundararaman. 2013. "School Inputs, Household Substitution, and Test Scores." *American Economic Journal: Applied Economics* 5 (2): 29–57.

de Hoyos, Rafael E., Vicente A. Garcia-Moreno, and Harry Anthony Patrinos. 2015. "The Impact of an Accountability Intervention with Diagnostic Feedback: Evidence from Mexico." Policy Research Working Paper 7393, World Bank, Washington, DC.

de Melo, Gioia, Alina Machado, and Alfonso Miranda. 2014. "The Impact of a One Laptop Per Child Program on Learning: Evidence from Uruguay." IZA Discussion Paper 8489, Institute for the Study of Labor, Bonn, Germany.

Esteves Pereira, Lucia Helena, and Isabel Cabral. 2016. "Gestão Escolar: A Opinião dos Profissionais de Educação sobre o Sistema de Tecnologia do Estado do Rio de Janeiro." *Regae, Revista de Gestão e Avaliação Educacional* 4 (7): 47–60. https://periodicos.ufsm.br/regae/article/view/14875.

Fryer, Roland G., Jr. 2017. "Management and Student Achievement: Evidence from a Randomized Field Experiment." NBER Working Paper 23437, National Bureau of Economic Research, Cambridge, MA.

Ganimian, Alejandro J., and Richard J. Murnane. 2016. "Improving Education in Developing Countries: Lessons from Rigorous Impact Evaluations." *Review of Educational Research* 86 (3): 719–55.

Gertler, Paul J., Harry Anthony Patrinos, and Marta Rubio-Codina. 2012. "Empowering Parents to Improve Education: Evidence from Rural Mexico." *Journal of Development Economics* 99 (1): 68–79.

Glewwe, Paul W., Michael R. Kremer, and Sylvie Moulin. 2009. "Many Children Left Behind? Textbooks and Test Scores in Kenya." *American Economic Journal: Applied Economics* 1 (1): 112–35.

Goodlad, John I. 1969. "Computers and the Schools in Modern Society." *Proceedings of the National Academy of Sciences of the United States of America* 63 (3): 595–603.

Hanushek, Eric A., Susanne Link, and Ludger Woessmann. 2013. "Does School Autonomy Make Sense Everywhere? Panel Estimates from PISA." *Journal of Development Economics* 104: 212–32.

Jukes, Matthew C. H., Elizabeth L. Turner, Margaret M. Dubeck, Katherine E. Halliday, Hellen N. Inyega, Sharon Wolf, Stephanie Simmons Zuilkowski, et al. 2017. "Improving Literacy Instruction in Kenya through Teacher Professional Development and Text Messages Support: A Cluster Randomized Trial." *Journal of Research on Educational Effectiveness* 10 (3): 449–81.

Kazianga, Harounan, Damien de Walque, and Harold Alderman. 2009. "Educational and Health Impacts of Two School Feeding Schemes: Evidence from a Randomized Trial in Rural Burkina Faso." Policy Research Working Paper 4976, World Bank, Washington, DC.

Kozuka, Eiji. 2017. "Enlightening Communities and Parents for Improving Student Learning: Evidence from Randomized Experiment in Niger." Working Paper, JICA Research Institute, Tokyo.

Kuhlemeier, Hans, and Bas Hemker. 2007. "The Impact of Computer Use at Home on Students' Internet Skills." *Computers and Education* 49 (2): 460–80.

Lai, Fang, Linxiu Zhang, Qinghe Qu, Xiao Hu, Yaojiang Shi, Matthew Boswell, and Scott Rozelle. 2012. "Does Computer-Assisted Learning Improve Learning Outcomes? Evidence from a Randomized Experiment in Public Schools in Rural Minority Areas in Qinghai, China." REAP Working Paper 237, Rural Education Action Program, Freeman Spogli Institute, Stanford University, Stanford, CA.

Lassibille, Gérard. 2016. "Improving the Management Style of School Principals: Results from a Randomized Trial." *Education Economics* 24 (2): 121–41.

Lavinas, Lena, and Alinne Veiga. 2013. "Brazil's One Laptop Per Child Program: Impact Evaluation and Implementation Assessment." *Cadernos de Pesquisa* 43 (149).

Linden, Leigh L. 2008. "Complement or Substitute? The Effect of Technology on Student Achievement in India." Edited by Michael Trucano. InfoDev Working Paper 17, World Bank, Washington, DC.

Mbiti, Isaac M., Karthik Muralidharan, Mauricio Romero, Youdi Schipper, Constantine Manda, and Rakesh Rajani. 2017. "Inputs, Incentives, and Complementarities in Education: Experimental Evidence from Tanzania." Working paper, University of California at San Diego.

McEwan, Patrick J. 2015. "Improving Learning in Primary Schools of Developing Countries: A Meta-Analysis of Randomized Experiments." *Review of Educational Research* 85 (3): 353–94.

Muralidharan, Karthik, Abhijeet Singh, and Alejandro J. Ganimian. 2016. "Disrupting Education? Experimental Evidence on Technology-Aided Instruction in India." NBER Working Paper 22923, National Bureau of Economic Research, Cambridge, MA.

Nannyonjo, Harriet. 2017. "Building Capacity of School Leaders: Strategies That Work, Jamaica's Experience." Working paper, World Bank, Washington, DC.

Powers, Shawn. 2016. "The Impact of Ebola on Education in Sierra Leone." *Education for Global Development* (blog), May 4. http://blogs.worldbank.org/education/impact-ebola-education-sierra-leone.

Pradhan, Menno, Daniel Suryadarma, Amanda Beatty, Maisy Wong, Arya Gaduh, Armida Alisjahbana, and Rima Prama Artha. 2014. "Improving Educational Quality through Enhancing Community Participation: Results from a Randomized Field Experiment in Indonesia." *American Economic Journal: Applied Economics* 6 (2): 105–26.

Pritchett, Lant. 2013. *The Rebirth of Education: Schooling Ain't Learning.* Washington, DC: Center for Global Development; Baltimore: Brookings Institution Press.

Read, Lindsay, and Tamar Manuelyan Atinc. 2016. "Information for Accountability: Transparency and Citizen Engagement for Improved Service Delivery in Education Systems." Global Economy and Development Working Paper 99, Brookings Institution, Washington, DC.

Robinson, Viviane M. J., Claire A. Lloyd, and Kenneth J. Rowe. 2008. "The Impact of Leadership on Student Outcomes: An Analysis of the Differential Effects of Leadership Types." *Educational Administration Quarterly* 44 (5): 635–74.

Sabarwal, Shwetlena, David K. Evans, and Anastasia Marshak. 2014. "The Permanent Input Hypothesis: The Case of Textbooks and (No) Student Learning in Sierra Leone." Policy Research Working Paper 7021, World Bank, Washington, DC.

Santibañez, Lucrecia, Raúl Abreu-Lastra, and Jennifer L. O'Donoghue. 2014. "School Based Management Effects: Resources or Governance Change? Evidence from Mexico." *Economics of Education Review* 39 (April): 97–109.

Sawada, Yasuyuki, Takeshi Aida, Andrew Griffen, Harounan Kazianga, Eiji Kozuka, Haruko Nogushi, and Yasuyuki Todo. 2016. "On the Role of Community Management in Correcting Market Failures of Rural Developing Areas: Evidence from a Randomized Field Experiment of COGES Project in Burkina Faso." Paper presented at annual meeting of Agricultural and Applied Economics Association, Boston, July 31–August 2. http://ageconsearch.umn.edu/bitstream/236323/2/SelectedPaper_9662.pdf.

Smith, Frederick James. 1913. "The Evolution of the Motion Picture, VI: Looking into the Future with Thomas A. Edison." *New York Dramatic Mirror* (July 3).

Snilstveit, Birte, Jennifer Stevenson, Radhika Menon, Daniel Phillips, Emma Gallagher, Maisie Geleen, Hannah Jobse, et al. 2016. "The Impact of Education Programmes on Learning and School Participation in Low- and Middle-Income Countries: A Systematic Review Summary Report." 3ie Systematic Review Summary 7, International Initiative for Impact Evaluation, London. http://www.3ie impact.org/media/filer_public/2016/09/20/srs7-education-report.pdf.

Vermeersch, Christel M. J., and Michael R. Kremer. 2005. "School Meals, Educational Achievement, and School Competition: Evidence from a Randomized Evaluation." Policy Research Working Paper 3523, World Bank, Washington, DC.

War Child Holland. 2016. "Can't Wait to Learn." War Child Holland, Amsterdam. https://www.warchild.nl/sites/default/files/bijlagen/node_13537/27-2016/2016_6_pager_cant_wait_to_learn_english.pdf.

Waters, Tim, Robert J. Marzano, and Brian McNulty. 2003. "Balanced Leadership: What 30 Years of Research Tells Us about the Effect of Leadership on Student Achievement." McRel Working Paper, McRel International, Denver.

Wolff, Laurence, Claudio de Moura Castro, Juan Carlos Navarro, and Norma García. 2002. "Television for Secondary Education: Experience of Mexico and Brazil." In *Technologies for Education: Potentials, Parameters, and Prospects*, edited by Waddi D. Haddad and Alexandria Draxler, 144–52. Washington, DC: Academy for Educational Development; Paris: United Nations Educational, Scientific, and Cultural Organization.

Build on foundations by linking skills training to jobs

After leaving school—whether as dropouts or graduates—many young people land jobs with limited prospects. But training offers a way out. How can successful job skills training programs be replicated? How can they be made available, affordable, and effective for the many young job seekers moving from school to work?

Young people around the world face substantial challenges in their transition from school to work. Many of them, especially youth from disadvantaged backgrounds, leave formal education prematurely, lacking the foundational skills needed to succeed on the job. In other words, the learning crisis manifests itself in the labor market. As a result, many become unemployed or stuck in low-wage, unstable, informal-sector jobs that offer them few opportunities to strengthen their skills. But the same can happen even to secondary school graduates, if they cannot fulfill labor market needs.

When young people leave formal education, they usually take one of three paths to employment. Some join the labor market without any further education or training. For them, workplace training is an important way to build skills. Others enroll in formal technical or vocational training programs that build the skills required for specific fields or occupations of interest.[1] These programs usually result in a formal technical qualification or an industry-recognized certification. Finally, a smaller group postpones looking for work or enrolling in further education and training. Three types of job training programs can help youth improve along these paths:

- Workplace training can benefit both workers and firms, yet it is not widely available to young adults.
- Short-term job training programs often have limited impacts, but careful program design could help improve outcomes.

- Technical and vocational education and training (TVET) offers a viable path, but only when programs are designed and implemented in partnership with employers.

Workplace training can help young people develop skills, yet few benefit from it

Workplace training deepens workers' skills and raises firms' productivity.[2] It can increase workers' output by 10 percent or more, which is similar in magnitude to the payoff from investments in physical capital.[3] In Latin America and the Caribbean, a 1 percent increase in the proportion of trained workers in large firms raised productivity by 0.7 percent.[4] In Mexico, investments in training increased productivity and firm-level wages by 4–7 percent for manufacturing workers.[5] Similarly, returns were 7.7 percent in Malaysia and 4.5 percent in Thailand for workers holding a secondary education qualification or more.[6] In Kenya and Zambia, workplace training was associated with a 20 percent increase in the wages of manufacturing workers.[7]

Despite its potential benefits, young workers rarely receive workplace training. In developing countries, the percentage of working-age adults participating in work-related training ranges from 20 percent in urban Bolivia and Colombia to less than 10 percent in the Lao People's Democratic Republic

Figure 8.1 Few benefit from workplace training, and those who do tend to already have better literacy or education

Workplace training participation in last 12 months, participating countries (2011–14)

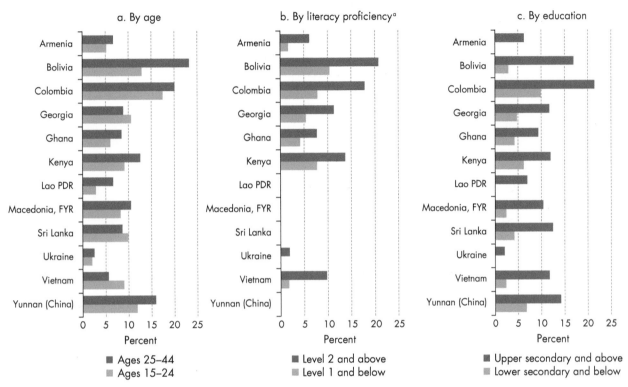

Source: WDR 2018 team, using data from World Bank's STEP Skills Measurement Program (http://microdata.worldbank.org/index.php/catalog/step/about). Data at http://bit.do/WDR2018-Fig_8-1.

Note: Respondents were asked, "In the past 12 months, have you participated in any training courses, such as work-related training or private skills training, that lasted at least 5 days/30 hours (not part of the formal educational system)?" Low proficiency is defined as level 1 and below on the literacy assessments and indicates limited understanding of texts. Medium to high proficiency is defined as level 2 and above and indicates the ability to integrate, evaluate, and interpret information from a variety and complexity of text materials.

a. No literacy proficiency data available for Lao PDR; Macedonia, FYR; Sri Lanka; or Yunnan (China).

and Vietnam.[8] Training participation is even lower for young people with incomplete education, limited skills, or short employment tenure.[9] In Peru, fewer than one in five young workers receive training in their first year on the first job.[10] Employers' decisions to invest in training are affected by potential production improvements, worker turnover, and a firm's overall management practices.[11] Training participation is lower not just for young workers generally (figure 8.1, panel a), but especially for young workers with limited literacy proficiency or education qualifications (figure 8.1, panels b and c). Yet workplace training can be especially beneficial for young adults. A cross-country analysis of 38 workplace training studies finds an average wage increase of 7.2 percent for workers under 35, compared with 4.9 percent for workers over 35.[12]

Informal apprenticeships, which can be thought of as informal workplace traineeships, offer young people a way to upgrade their skills in a workplace setting. In these noncertification-granting arrangements, learning takes place while a young person works alongside an experienced craftsperson over a period of time.[13] Though available in many parts of the world, informal apprenticeships are most common in Sub-Saharan Africa. For example, in Benin, Cameroon, Côte d'Ivoire, and Senegal, informal apprenticeships account for almost 90 percent of the training that prepares workers for crafts jobs, as well as employment in some trades (such as carpentry, welding, hairdressing, plumbing, tailoring, masonry, and weaving).[14] Informal apprentices are more likely to be young people with limited formal education from disadvantaged socioeconomic backgrounds.[15] These apprenticeships vary widely in their institutional setup, training content, working conditions, and financial arrangements. However, most are nested within community customs, norms, and traditions. Experimental evidence on their effectiveness is scant. Evaluations from Senegal have shown positive effects on labor market outcomes, but limited effects on general cognitive skills.[16] But early evidence from an apprenticeship program in Côte d'Ivoire that formalized part of the process shows improvements in the labor market outcomes and psychological well-being of disadvantaged youth.[17]

Unlocking the potential of informal apprenticeships requires up-to-date master trainers and recognition of apprentices' training tenure and performance. Too often, master trainers lack the information, capacity, and incentives to adapt to new workplace practices. This can lead to apprentices learning obsolete workplace practices.[18] Also, because informal apprenticeships are rarely recognized by the formal training system, they offer limited labor market mobility.[19] One way to mitigate this issue is to integrate informal apprenticeships into the formal training system, allowing for skills reengagement with further education and training. In Malawi and Tanzania, for example, competency-based skills certification offers a pathway for young workers who have been apprentices to be acknowledged for their skills.[20]

Short-term job training offers opportunities, but most programs fail to deliver

Many short-term job training programs—which usually last between two weeks and six months—do not meet labor market needs. Meta-analyses of programs from around the world find that less than a third have positive, significant impacts on employment and earnings.[21] Though the estimated effects of short-term programs are somewhat larger in developing countries, they remain small. Skills training that focuses on helping participants accumulate the human capital needed to transition to labor markets can generate positive returns, but, given their short duration and heterogeneous quality, these short-term programs rarely have impacts as large as the returns from completing a formal education.[22] Many programs are poorly designed and implemented, or don't interest the hard-to-reach young people who might need skills upgrading the most.[23] The economic rationale for investing in training is often tenuous: in Liberia, for example, it can cost up to 50 times the resulting monthly income gain, meaning that recovering the investment would take 12 years.[24]

But short-term training interventions do show some positive results when targeting disadvantaged groups, such as low-skilled women. In Uganda, the Empowerment and Livelihoods for Adolescents program targeting young women shows encouraging impacts on graduates' employment prospects.[25] Similarly, Nepal's Adolescent Girls Employment Initiative increases nonfarm employment by 13–19 percentage points for participants.[26] In the Dominican Republic, evaluations of Programa Juventud y Empleo, a skills training program that targets low-income, low-skilled, out-of-school youth with less than a secondary education, increased both employment and earnings.[27] Promising results from interventions in Colombia, the Dominican Republic, Liberia, Nepal, and Peru are identifying effective approaches to improving young women's aspirations, socioemotional skills, and labor market outcomes.[28]

Successful short-term job training programs offer more than skills training. Programs that focus on developing multiple skills and that complement training with wraparound services such as career guidance, mentoring, and job search assistance have better odds of success.[29] For example, comprehensive training schemes that emphasize technical skills, life skills, and internships show positive effects in Kenya, Brazil, and Nepal.[30] In Kenya, the Ninaweza Youth Empowerment program, which integrates information and communication technology (ICT), life skills, internship training, and job placement support for youth, shows positive impacts on labor market outcomes.[31] Similarly, in Brazil the Galpão Aplauso program has improved outcomes through a combination of vocational, academic, and life skills training.[32] In Nepal, the Employment Fund prioritizes comprehensive training programs for youth who are underemployed or unemployed.[33]

TVET can prepare young people for work, but early sorting into TVET can limit career growth

TVET can yield wages on par with equivalent levels of general education. Usually lasting from six months to three years, TVET can be delivered in the dedicated streams of lower secondary, upper secondary, or tertiary schools.[34] In Brazil, workers with upper secondary TVET earn wages about 10 percent higher than those of workers with a general secondary education.[35] In Indonesia, returns to public TVET are positive for all, and greater for women.[36] But despite encouraging results, TVET programs in many developing countries remain an unattractive alternative

Figure 8.2 Most vocational training students enroll during upper secondary school

Gross enrollment rates in general education and technical and vocational education and training (TVET), lower and upper secondary students (circa 2010)

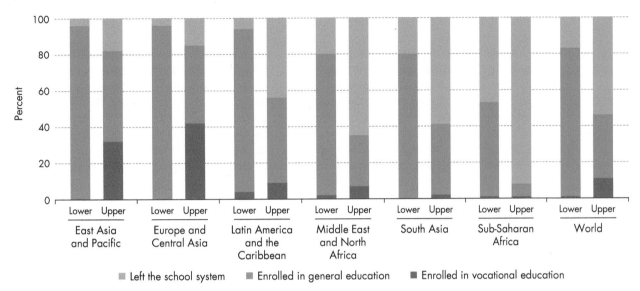

Source: WDR 2018 team, using data from UIS (2016). Data at http://bit.do/WDR2018-Fig_8-2.

for young people, with often poor program quality or labor market relevance.

Putting students on a technical track too early can limit their career opportunities for a lifetime. Young people need to master foundational skills—reading, writing, numeracy, critical thinking, and problem-solving—to participate meaningfully in TVET. They also need to be mature enough to express career preferences that might have long-term consequences. Countries that have delayed streaming into TVET have shown that such changes can lead to improvements. In Poland, delaying vocational education by a year improved students' academic performance.[37] Problems with early tracking are exacerbated in systems that do not allow students to go back and forth between general and technical education, leaving technical graduates with limited opportunities to reengage in further education or training.[38] Despite such concerns, most enrollment in TVET occurs at the start of upper secondary school (figure 8.2). Of equal concern is that, in most regions, more young people are leaving formal education than are continuing in either general education or TVET—a fact that underscores the importance of acquiring robust foundational skills early on as a basis for learning on the job and throughout life.

Developing narrow vocational skills can expedite workers' transitions into the labor force, but broader general skills can help them adapt more easily to technological change. Evidence from advanced economies indicates that narrow technical education conveys early advantages in the labor market, but the advantages dissipate over time. Some workers end up outdated in their occupation-specific skills, making them more vulnerable to job loss.[39] Though the appropriate balance is bound to be country-specific, TVET should not lock participants into narrow occupations that are likely to change in unanticipated ways.

Successful job training programs share several features

Though the evidence available on workplace training and job training interventions—whether short-term or long-term—is limited, some features are consistent across successful programs. To the extent possible, the principles discussed in this section are distilled from experimental evidence. But because of the shortage of rigorous research on interventions in developing countries, this section also integrates relevant findings from different types of studies (nonexperimental, systematic, qualitative).

Establishing partnerships before training is designed

Sectoral training programs[40] partner learners with employers early and sustain their commitment.[41] These programs set up partnerships between intermediary institutions—usually network aggregators

Build on foundations by linking skills training to jobs | 157 or nonprofits with industry-specific expertise—and employers in an industry to anticipate job openings, design program content, and maximize potential placement. Sectoral programs focus on supporting individuals to enter careers rather than jobs. To do so, programs integrate information on career pathways to help participants identify the credentials that are needed for an occupation and that can be pursued to move from an entry-level job to a longer-term career.[42] Success factors include having high-quality intermediaries, along with comprehensive recruitment services, to generate good matches among prospective participants, programs of study, and targeted occupations.[43]

Sectoral training programs can improve labor market outcomes, raise productivity, and reduce employee turnover. Among three U.S. sectoral training programs—Wisconsin Regional Training Partnership (Milwaukee), Jewish Vocational Service (Boston), Per Scholas (New York City)—participants saw 18 percent higher average earnings over a two-year period.[44] Similarly, the Year Up program, which targets vulnerable youth in several U.S. states, has produced high levels of completion, participation in internships, employment, and earnings.[45] Finally, the Generation program—focusing on low-skilled youth in India, Kenya, Mexico, Spain, and the United States—has resulted in high job placement and employer satisfaction.[46] Other potential approaches to engaging employers in training include entering into public-private partnerships with multinational corporations, establishing effective national workforce development initiatives, and fostering workplace training provision through mechanisms such as training funds and tax incentives.[47]

Combining classroom with workplace learning

Formal apprenticeships are a common way to combine classroom with workplace learning; such programs are often referred to as "learning while earning." Formal apprentice programs can last from one to three years and take place at the secondary or postsecondary level or as an alternative to upper secondary education, giving students the opportunity to engage in industry-supervised workplace practices.[48] For programs targeting secondary students, special attention is required to ensure apprentices hone foundational skills, as well as occupation-specific skills, to avoid overly narrow specialization.[49] Formal apprentices are typically paid less than the market wage.[50] Good-practice apprenticeships offer structured training, a professional trainer to oversee apprentices, a written contract that stipulates training

arrangements, and an assessment to verify acquired skills.[51] A strong partnership between the education system and industry is crucial to integrate firm resources, share risk burdens, develop industrywide skill standards, and deliver apprenticeship training at scale.

Studies show positive results for both firms and the individuals who complete formal apprenticeships.[52] In the United States, a study looking at gains from secondary TVET, postsecondary TVET, and apprenticeship programs in the states of Virginia and Washington found positive gains from all three—especially apprenticeships.[53] Studies in Canada, Germany, Switzerland, and the United States find that employers recover initial apprentice costs in the short to medium term.[54] In Brazil, graduates of a large formal apprenticeship program (Lei do Aprendiz) are more likely to find permanent, higher-paying jobs, with larger gains for less educated workers.[55] In Malawi, an innovative formal apprenticeship program targeting young women broadened their opportunities to serve as assistant schoolteachers; graduates gained higher skills and community standing.[56]

Identifying capable teachers

Successful approaches to training depend on capable teachers[57] with industry expertise who can tailor training to meet job requirements.[58] Students' gaps in foundational skills and lack of motivation intensify the complexity of teachers' roles and responsibilities.[59] The global shift toward competency-based standards in training, assessment, and certification amplifies the importance of capable, involved teachers.[60] A study of 10 polytechnics in Ghana highlights the importance of having teachers able to offer constructive feedback as students work through competency modules.[61] However, often teachers lack industry qualifications or up-to-date pedagogical expertise, especially when it comes to teaching using a competency-based skills approach. A study of teaching practices in technical vocational colleges in Malaysia highlights the difficulties that teachers face in moving from assessing a student's knowledge to assessing occupational and task-specific competency.[62]

Yet in many countries, structured professional support is not available to ensure that TVET teachers remain current on curriculums and industry changes.[63] But they could: a review of vocational education systems in 10 countries in the Middle East and North Africa (MENA) finds active experimentation with innovative models to build career structures that reflect common norms, values, and standards to professionalize TVET teaching. Six of the 10 countries have developed occupational standards for technical teachers to recognize career progression, though it is too early to tell whether or how the new standards are influencing student outcomes.[64] Other countries, such as Ethiopia and Lao PDR, are experimenting with introducing standards and expanding the qualifications for technical training instructors. But getting robust information on program effectiveness is difficult because most interventions are not evaluated for impact.[65]

Making student support services and comprehensive information available for decision making

Career information is an important part of training programs, helping students identify opportunities, stay on course, and transition into a career.[66] Career information interventions are usually grouped into *career education programs*, which might include providing direction on coursework selection, and *career planning*, which is usually provided on an individual basis.[67] Career information can be especially useful for students who lack family or social networks that can provide meaningful direction. Since the early 2000s, countries in the European Union have been experimenting with mechanisms to integrate career guidance with national lifelong learning strategies in order to align with the Lisbon Strategy and the strategic framework for European cooperation on education and training.

Still, evidence is limited on how career information initiatives affect students' choices, training trajectories, and outcomes.[68] Career guidance policies are a priority across 28 European countries, yet the scope and depth of programs vary substantially, highlighting the need for a well-articulated vision, cohesive strategy, and robust quality assurance mechanisms linked to funding.[69] Few member countries of the Organisation for Economic Co-operation and Development have program standards to monitor the quality of services, especially for programs delivered by private providers. This results in an overreliance on staff qualifications as indicators of quality.[70]

Successful career guidance programs have clear objectives and outcome measurement to track program performance. They also have different pathways for participants from a diversity of backgrounds, so skilled career guidance staff can tailor skills development trajectories according to need.[71]

* * *

Successful job training programs are typically based on strong ties with employers, with curriculums taught by teachers who have both industry experience and up-to-date pedagogical expertise. These programs also tend to reinforce foundational skills, integrate classroom instruction with workplace learning, and offer certifications that can be further built on. These features keep career paths open for graduates. Though job training programs can yield positive outcomes, a key lesson is that trainees still need strong foundational skills—cognitive and socioemotional—before moving into specialized streams.

Notes

1. Pre-employment job training programs can be grouped into (1) short-term programs of less than six months that focus on vocational subjects and (2) longer-term technical and vocational education and training (TVET) programs of more than six months that are mapped to formal education system levels.
2. Formal workplace training refers to supervised skills development activity that links knowledge gained in the workplace with the needs of business firms (see ILO 2010). A comparison across workplace models is difficult because of the heterogeneity in design, implementation, and effectiveness of training schemes. See Acemoglu and Pischke (1996); Almeida, Behrman, and Robalino (2012); Almeida and Carneiro (2009); Bassanini and others (2005); Blundell and others (1999); Dearden, Reed, and Van Reenen (2006); and Haelermans and Borghans (2012).

3. Dearden, Reed, and Van Reenen (2006); De Grip and Sauermann (2012); Konings and Vanormelingen (2015); Saraf (2017).
4. González-Velosa, Rosas, and Flores (2016).
5. Tan and López-Acevedo (2003).
6. Almeida and de Faria (2014).
7. Rosholm, Nielsen, and Dabalen (2007).
8. Roseth, Valerio, and Gutiérrez (2016).
9. Almeida and Aterido (2010); Cabrales, Dolado, and Mora (2014); Sousounis and Bladen-Hovell (2010).
10. Cavero and Ruiz (2016).
11. Saraf (2017).
12. Haelermans and Borghans (2012).
13. ILO (2012).
14. ILO (2012).
15. Adams and others (2009); Darvas, Farvara, and Arnold (2017); ILO (2012).

16. Aubery, Giles, and Sahn (2017).
17. World Bank (2016).
18. ILO (2012).
19. ILO (2012).
20. Aggarwal, Hofmann, and Phiri (2010); Nübler, Hofmann, and Greiner (2009).
21. Kluve and others (2016); McKenzie (2017).
22. McKenzie (2017).
23. Blattman and Ralston (2015); Kluve and others (2016); LaLonde (2003); McKenzie (2017).
24. Adoho and others (2014); Blattman and Ralston (2015); McKenzie (2017).
25. Bandiera and others (2014).
26. Chakravarty and others (2016).
27. Card and others (2011).
28. Fox and Kaul (2017).
29. Eichhorst and others (2012); Fares and Puerto (2009); Kluve and others (2016).
30. Fox and Kaul (2017).
31. IYF (2013).
32. Calero and others (2014).
33. Chakravarty and others (2016).
34. OECD (2014); Tan and Nam (2012).
35. Almeida and others (2015).
36. Newhouse and Suryadarma (2011).
37. Jakubowski and others (2016).
38. Biavaschi and others (2012).
39. Hampf and Woessmann (2016); Hanushek and others (2017).
40. Sectoral training programs are defined as partnership arrangements between the government, employers, and nonprofit organizations set up to train unemployed or underemployed adults. They usually target young adults who have incomplete upper secondary or tertiary education qualifications whose skills are relatively low, as well as disadvantaged young workers seeking skills upgrading programs to reenter the labor force or move into higher-quality jobs.
41. CED (2015); Conway and Giloth (2014); King (2014); Martinson (2010); NGA (2013).
42. Bragg, Dresser, and Smith (2012).
43. King (2014); Maguire and others (2010).
44. Maguire and others (2010).
45. Roder and Elliott (2011).
46. Mourshed, Farrell, and Barton (2013).
47. Dunbar (2013); Tan and others (2016).
48. Fazio, Fernández-Coto, and Ripani (2016); Mieschbuehler and Hooley (2016); Neumark and Rothstein (2006).
49. OECD (2010).
50. Biavaschi and others (2012); Smith and Kemmis (2013).
51. Cumsille (2016); Fazio, Fernández-Coto, and Ripani (2016); Smith and Kemmis (2013).
52. Dietrich, Pfeifer, and Wenzelmann (2016); Hollenbeck (2008); Lerman (2014); Smith and Kemmis (2013).
53. Hollenbeck (2008).
54. Lerman (2013, 2014).
55. Corseuil, Foguel, and Gonzaga (2014).
56. Safford and others (2013).
57. Here *teachers* is defined broadly to include teachers (secondary education), instructors (postsecondary education), and trainers (workplace training). See Axmann, Rhoades, and Nordstrum (2015) and Stanley, Adubra, and Chakroun (2014).
58. Axmann, Rhoades, and Nordstrum (2015); Biavaschi and others (2012); Grollmann (2008); Maclean and Lai (2011).
59. Hodge (2016).
60. Guthrie and others (2009); ILO (2010). Experimental studies evaluating the impact of different approaches to training and supporting the professional development of vocational teachers are extremely rare.
61. Boahin and Hofman (2014).
62. Azmanirah and others (2014).
63. Axmann, Rhoades, and Nordstrum (2015).
64. OECD (2010, 2014); UNESCO (2014).
65. Gerds (2009); Kingombe (2012); Soysouvanh (2013).
66. OECD and EC (2004); Watts and Sultana (2004).
67. OECD (2010).
68. Hooley (2014); Hooley and Dodd (2015); Kluve and others (2016); OECD (2010); Sultana and Watts (2008).
69. Watts, Sultana, and McCarthy (2010).
70. OECD and EC (2004).
71. OECD and EC (2004).

References

Acemoglu, Daron, and Jorn-Steffen Pischke. 1996. "Why Do Firms Train? Theory and Evidence." NBER Working Paper 5605, National Bureau of Economic Research, Cambridge, MA.

Adams, Arvil V., Harold Coulombe, Quentin Wodon, and Setarah Razmara. 2009. "Education, Skills, and Labor Market Outcomes in Ghana." Working paper, World Bank, Washington, DC.

Adoho, Franck M., Shubha Chakravarty, Dala T. Korkoyah, Jr., Mattias K. A. Lundberg, and Afia Tasneem. 2014. "The Impact of an Adolescent Girls Employment Program: The EPAG Project in Liberia." Policy Research Working Paper 6832, World Bank, Washington, DC.

Aggarwal, Ashwani, Christine Hofmann, and Alexander Phiri. 2010. "A Study on Informal Apprenticeship in Malawi." Employment Report 9, International Labour Office, Geneva.

Almeida, Rita Kullberg, Leandro Anazawa, Naercio Menezes Filho, and Lígia Maria De Vasconcellos. 2015. "Investing in Technical and Vocational Education and Training: Does It Yield Large Economic Returns in Brazil?" Policy Research Working Paper 7246, World Bank, Washington, DC.

Almeida, Rita Kullberg, and Reyes Aterido. 2010. "Investment in Job Training: Why Are SMES Lagging So Much Behind?" Policy Research Working Paper 5358, World Bank, Washington, DC.

Almeida, Rita Kullberg, Jere R. Behrman, and David Robalino, eds. 2012. *The Right Skills for the Job? Rethinking Training Policies for Workers.* Report 70908, Human Development Perspectives Series. Washington, DC: World Bank.

Almeida, Rita Kullberg, and Pedro Manuel Carneiro. 2009. "The Return to Firm Investments in Human Capital." *Labour Economics* 16 (1): 97–106.

Almeida, Rita Kullberg, and Marta Lince de Faria. 2014. "The Wage Returns to on-the-Job Training: Evidence from

Matched Employer-Employee Data." *IZA Journal of Labor and Development* 3 (1): 1–33.

Aubery, Frédéric, John Giles, and David E. Sahn. 2017. "Do Apprenticeships Provide Skills Beyond the Master's Trade? Evidence on Apprenticeships, Skills and the Transition to Work in Senegal." World Bank, Washington, DC.

Axmann, Michael, Amy Rhoades, and Lee Nordstrum. 2015. "Vocational Teachers and Trainers in a Changing World: The Imperative of High-Quality Teacher Training Systems." With contributions from Josée-Anne La Rue and Michelle Byusa. Employment Working Paper 177, International Labour Organization, Geneva.

Azmanirah Ab Rahman, Nurfirdawati Muhamad Hanafi, Marina Ibrahim Mukhtar, and Jamil Ahmad. 2014. "Assessment Practices for Competency Based Education and Training in Vocational College, Malaysia." *Procedia: Social and Behavioral Sciences* 112: 1070–76.

Bandiera, Oriana, Niklas Buehren, Robin Burgess, Markus P. Goldstein, Selim Gulesci, Imran Rasul, and Munshi Sulaiman. 2014. "Women's Empowerment in Action: Evidence from a Randomized Control Trial in Africa." CSAE Working Paper WPS/2014-30, Centre for the Study of African Economies, Department of Economics, University of Oxford, Oxford, U.K..

Bassanini, Andrea, Alison L. Booth, Giorgio Brunello, Maria De Paola, and Edwin Leuven. 2005. "Workplace Training in Europe." IZA Discussion Paper 1640, Institute for the Study of Labor, Bonn, Germany.

Biavaschi, Costanza, Werner Eichhorst, Corrado Giulietti, Michael Jan Kendzia, Alexander Muravyev, Janneke Pieters, Núria Rodríguez-Planas, et al. 2012. "Youth Unemployment and Vocational Training." IZA Discussion Paper 6890, Institute for the Study of Labor, Bonn, Germany.

Blattman, Christopher, and Laura Ralston. 2015. "Generating Employment in Poor and Fragile States: Evidence from Labor Market and Entrepreneurship Programs." Working paper, Columbia University, New York.

Blundell, Richard, Lorraine Dearden, Costas Meghir, and Barbara Sianesi. 1999. "Human Capital Investment: The Returns from Education and Training to the Individual, the Firm and the Economy." *Fiscal Studies* 20 (1): 1–23.

Boahin, Peter, and W. H. Adriaan Hofman. 2014. "Perceived Effects of Competency-Based Training on the Acquisition of Professional Skills." *International Journal of Educational Development* 36 (May): 81–89.

Bragg, Debra D., Laura Dresser, and Whitney Smith. 2012. "Leveraging Workforce Development and Postsecondary Education for Low-Skilled, Low-Income Workers: Lessons from the Shifting Gears Initiative." *New Directions for Community Colleges* 157: 53–66.

Cabrales, Antonio, Juan José Dolado, and Ricardo Mora. 2014. "Dual Labour Markets and (Lack of) on-the-Job Training: PIAAC Evidence from Spain and Other EU Countries." IZA Discussion Paper 8649, Institute for the Study of Labor, Bonn, Germany.

Calero, Carla, Carlos Henrique Corseuil, Veronica Gonzales, Jochen Kluve, and Yuri Soares. 2014. "Can Arts-Based Interventions Enhance Labor Market Outcomes among Youth? Evidence from a Randomized Trial in Rio de Janeiro." IZA Discussion Paper 8210, Institute for the Study of Labor, Bonn, Germany.

Card, David, Pablo Ibarrarán, Ferdinando Regalia, David Rosas-Shady, and Yuri Soares. 2011. "The Labor Market Impacts of Youth Training in the Dominican Republic." *Journal of Labor Economics* 29 (2): 267–300.

Cavero, Denice, and Claudia Ruiz. 2016. "Do Working Conditions in Young People's First Jobs Affect Their Employment Trajectories? The Case of Peru." Work4Youth 33, International Labour Office, Geneva.

CED (Committee for Economic Development of the Conference Board). 2015. "The Role of Business in Promoting Educational Attainment: A National Imperative." CED, Arlington, VA.

Chakravarty, Shubha, Mattias K. A. Lundberg, Plamen Nikolov Danchev, and Juliane Zenker. 2016. "The Role of Training Programs for Youth Employment in Nepal: Impact Evaluation Report on the Employment Fund." Policy Research Working Paper 7656, World Bank, Washington, DC.

Conway, Maureen, and Robert P. Giloth. 2014. *Connecting People to Work: Workforce Intermediaries and Sector Strategies.* New York: Aspen Institute.

Corseuil, Carlos Henrique, Miguel Foguel, and Gustavo Gonzaga. 2014. "Apprenticeship as a Stepping Stone to Better Jobs: Evidence from Brazilian Matched Employer-Employee Data." Texto para Discussão 651, Departamento de Economia, Centro de Ciências Sociais, Pontifícia Universidade Católica do Rio de Janeiro, Rio de Janeiro.

Cumsille, Belén. 2016. "Educación Técnico Vocacional Secundaria: Beneficios y Desafíos para los Sistemas Educativos." Technical Note, Inter-American Dialogue, Washington, DC.

Darvas, Peter, Marta Farvara, and Tamara Arnold. 2017. *Stepping Up Skills in Urban Ghana: Snapshot of the STEP Skills Measurement Survey.* Directions in Development: Human Development Series. Washington, DC: World Bank.

Dearden, Lorraine, Howard Reed, and John Van Reenen. 2006. "The Impact of Training on Productivity and Wages: Evidence from British Panel Data." *Oxford Bulletin of Economics and Statistics* 68 (4): 397–421.

De Grip, Andries, and Jan Sauermann. 2012. "The Effects of Training on Own and Co-worker Productivity: Evidence from a Field Experiment." *Economic Journal* 122 (560): 376–99.

Dietrich, Hans, Harald Pfeifer, and Felix Wenzelmann. 2016. "The More They Spend, the More I Earn? Firms' Training Investments and Post-Training Wages of Apprentices." Economics of Education Working Paper 116, Institute for Strategy and Business Economics, University of Zurich, Switzerland.

Dunbar, Muriel. 2013. "Engaging the Private Sector in Skills Development: Final." Health and Education Advice and Resource Team, Oxford Policy Management, Oxford, U.K.

Eichhorst, Werner, Núria Rodríguez-Planas, Ricarda Schmidl, and Klaus F. Zimmermann. 2012. "A Roadmap to Vocational Education and Training Systems around the World." IZA Discussion Paper 7110, Institute for the Study of Labor, Bonn, Germany.

Fares, Jean, and Olga Susana Puerto. 2009. "Towards Comprehensive Training." Social Protection and Labor Discussion Paper 0924, World Bank, Washington, DC.

Fazio, María Victoria, Raquel Fernández-Coto, and Laura Ripani. 2016. "Apprenticeships for the XXI Century: A Model for Latin America and the Caribbean?" Inter-American Development Bank, Washington, DC.

Fox, Louise M., and U. Kaul. 2017. "What Works for Youth Employment in Low-Income Countries?" USAID, Washington, DC.

Gerds, Peter. 2009. "Standards for Occupation-Directed Professional Development of TVET Personnel in Developing Countries." In International Handbook of Education for the Changing World of Work: Bridging Academic and Vocational Learning, edited by Rupert Maclean and David N. Wilson, Vol. 3, 1407–22. Bonn, Germany: UNESCO-UNEVOC International Center for Education; Dordrecht, the Netherlands: Springer Science+Business.

González-Velosa, Carolina, David Rosas, and Roberto Flores. 2016. "On-the-Job Training in Latin America and the Caribbean: Recent Evidence." In Firm Innovation and Productivity in Latin America and the Caribbean: The Engine of Economic Development, edited by Matteo Grazzi and Carlo Pietrobelli, 137–66. Washington, DC: Inter-American Development Bank; New York: Springer Nature.

Grollmann, Philipp. 2008. "The Quality of Vocational Teachers: Teacher Education, Institutional Roles, and Professional Reality." European Educational Research Journal 7 (4): 535–47.

Guthrie, Hugh, Roger Harris, Michele Simons, and Tom Karmel. 2009. "Teaching for Technical and Vocational Education and Training (TVET)." In International Handbook of Research on Teachers and Teaching, Part 1, edited by Lawrence J. Saha and Anthony Gary Dworkin, 851–63. Springer International Handbooks of Education Series 21. New York: Springer Science+Business.

Haelermans, Carla, and Lex Borghans. 2012. "Wage Effects of On-the-Job Training: A Meta-Analysis." British Journal of Industrial Relations 50 (3): 502–28.

Hampf, Franziska, and Ludger Woessmann. 2016. "Vocational vs. General Education and Employment over the Life-Cycle: New Evidence from PIAAC." IZA Discussion Paper 10298, Institute for the Study of Labor, Bonn, Germany.

Hanushek, Eric A., Guido Schwerdt, Ludger Woessmann, and Lei Zhang. 2017. "General Education, Vocational Education, and Labor-Market Outcomes over the Life-Cycle." Journal of Human Resources 52 (1): 48–87.

Hodge, Steven. 2016. "After Competency-Based Training: Deepening Critique, Imagining Alternatives." International Journal of Training Research 14 (3): 171–79.

Hollenbeck, Kevin. 2008. "State Use of Workforce System Net Impact Estimates and Rates of Return." Paper presented at Association for Public Policy Analysis and Management Conference, "The Next Decade: What Are the Big Policy Challenges?" Los Angeles, November 6–8.

Hooley, Tristram. 2014. "The Evidence Base on Lifelong Guidance: A Guide to Key Findings for Effective Policy and Practice." ELGPN Tools 3, European Lifelong Guidance Policy Network, Finnish Institute for Educational Research, University of Jyväskylä, Jyväskylä, Finland.

Hooley, Tristram, and Vanessa Dodd. 2015. "The Economic Benefits of Career Guidance." Research paper, Careers England, Chorley, Lancashire, U.K.

ILO (International Labour Organization). 2010. "Teachers and Trainers for the Future: Technical and Vocational Education and Training in a Changing World." Report prepared for Global Dialogue Forum on Vocational Education and Training, Geneva, September 29–30.

———. 2012. "Upgrading Informal Apprenticeship: A Resource Guide for Africa." Geneva, International Labour Office.

IYF (International Youth Foundation). 2013. "A Summative Report." Vol. 1, "Testing What Works in Youth Employment: Evaluating Kenya's Ninaweza Program." IYF, Baltimore.

Jakubowski, Maciej, Harry Anthony Patrinos, Emilio Ernesto Porta, and Jerzy Wiśniewski. 2016. "The Effects of Delaying Tracking in Secondary School: Evidence from the 1999 Education Reform in Poland." Education Economics 24 (6): 557–72.

King, Christopher T. 2014. "Sectoral Workforce and Related Strategies: What We Know and What We Need to Know." In Connecting People to Work: Workforce Intermediaries and Sector Strategies, edited by Maureen Conway and Robert P. Giloth, 209–38. New York: Aspen Institute.

Kingombe, Christian. 2012. "Lessons for Developing Countries from Experience with Technical and Vocational Education and Training." In Economic Challenges and Policy Issues in Early Twenty-First-Century Sierra Leone, edited by Omotun E. G. Johnson, 278–365. London: International Growth Centre.

Kluve, Jochen, Olga Susana Puerto, David A. Robalino, Jose Manuel Romero, Friederike Rother, Jonathan Stöterau, Felix Weidenkaff, et al. 2016. "Do Youth Employment Programs Improve Labor Market Outcomes? A Systematic Review." IZA Discussion Paper 10263, Institute for the Study of Labor, Bonn, Germany.

Konings, Jozef, and Stijn Vanormelingen. 2015. "The Impact of Training on Productivity and Wages: Firm-Level Evidence." Review of Economics and Statistics 97 (2): 485–97.

LaLonde, Robert J. 2003. "Employment and Training Programs." In Means-Tested Transfer Programs in the United States, edited by Robert A. Moffitt, 517–86. Chicago: University of Chicago Press.

Lerman, Robert I. 2013. "Skill Development in Middle Level Occupations: The Role of Apprenticeship Training." IZA Policy Paper 61, Institute for the Study of Labor, Bonn, Germany.

———. 2014. "Do Firms Benefit from Apprenticeship Investments? Why Spending on Occupational Skills Can Yield Economic Returns to Employers." IZA World of Labor, Institute for the Study of Labor, Bonn, Germany.

Maclean, Rupert, and Ada Lai. 2011. "Editorial: The Future of Technical and Vocational Education and Training: Global Challenges and Possibilities." International Journal of Training Research 9 (1–2): 2–15.

Maguire, Sheila, Joshua Freely, Carol Clymer, Maureen Conway, and Deena Schwartz. 2010. "Tuning In to Local Labor Markets: Findings from the Sectoral Employment Impact Study." Public/Private Ventures, Philadelphia.

Martinson, Karin. 2010. "Partnering with Employers to Promote Job Advancement for Low-Skill Individuals." National Institute for Literacy, Washington, DC.

McKenzie, David J. 2017. "How Effective Are Active Labor Market Policies in Developing Countries? A Critical Review of Recent Evidence." Policy Research Working Paper 8011, World Bank, Washington, DC.

Mieschbuehler, Ruth, and Tristram Hooley. 2016. "World-Class Apprenticeship Standards: Report and Recommendations." International Centre for Guidance Studies, College of Education, University of Derby, Derby, U.K.

Mourshed, Mona, Diana Farrell, and Dominic Barton. 2013. "Education to Employment: Designing a System That Works." McKinsey Center for Government, Copenhagen.

Neumark, David, and Donna Rothstein. 2006. "School-to-Career Programs and Transitions to Employment and Higher Education." Economics of Education Review 25 (4): 374–93.

Newhouse, David, and Daniel Suryadarma. 2011. "The Value of Vocational Education: High School Type and Labor Market Outcomes in Indonesia." World Bank Economic Review 25 (2): 296–322.

NGA (National Governors Association). 2013. "State Sector Strategies Coming of Age: Implications for State Workforce Policymakers." NGA Center for Best Practices, NGA, Washington, DC. https://www.nga.org/files/live /sites/NGA/files/pdf/2013/1301NGASSSReport.pdf.

Nübler, Irmgard, Christine Hofmann, and Clemens Greiner. 2009. "Understanding Informal Apprenticeship: Findings from Empirical Research in Tanzania." Employment Working Paper 32, International Labour Organization, Geneva.

OECD (Organisation for Economic Co-operation and Development). 2010. Learning for Jobs: Synthesis Report. OECD Reviews of Vocational Education and Training Series. Paris: OECD.

———. 2014. Skills beyond School: Synthesis Report. OECD Reviews of Vocational Education and Training Series. Paris: OECD.

OECD (Organisation for Economic Co-operation and Development) and EC (European Commission). 2004. "Career Guidance: A Handbook for Policy Makers." OECD, Paris.

Roder, Anne, and Mark Elliott. 2011. "A Promising Start: Year Up's Initial Impacts on Low-Income Young Adults' Careers." Economic Mobility Corporation, New York.

Roseth, Viviana V., Alexandria Valerio, and Marcela Gutiérrez. 2016. Education, Skills, and Labor Market Outcomes: Results from Large-Scale Adult Skills Surveys in Urban Areas in 12 Countries. STEP Skills Measurement Series. Washington, DC: World Bank.

Rosholm, Michael, Helena Skyt Nielsen, and Andrew Dabalen. 2007. "Evaluation of Training in African Enterprises." Journal of Development Economics 84 (1): 310–29.

Safford, Kimberly, Deborah Cooper, Freda Wolfenden, and Joyce Chitsulo. 2013. "'Give Courage to the Ladies': Expansive Apprenticeship for Women in Rural Malawi." Journal of Vocational Education and Training 65 (2): 193–207.

Saraf, Priyam. 2017. "Returns, Barriers, and Policy Outcomes to On-the-Job Training: Creating Gains for Workers, Firms, and Society." Background paper, World Bank, Washington, DC.

Smith, Erica, and Ros Brennan Kemmis. 2013. "Towards a Model Apprenticeship Framework: A Comparative Analysis of National Apprenticeship Systems." World Bank and International Labour Office, New Delhi.

Sousounis, Panos, and Robin Bladen-Hovell. 2010. "Persistence in the Determination of Work-Related Training Participation: Evidence from the BHPS, 1991–1997." Economics of Education Review 29 (6): 1005–15.

Soysouvanh, Boualinh. 2013. "Development of Standards for Vocational Teachers at Bachelor Level in Lao PDR." Research and Development Series 2, Regional Cooperation Platform for Vocational Teacher Education in Asia, Shanghai.

Stanley, Julian, Edem Adubra, and Borhene Chakroun. 2014. Technical and Vocational Teachers and Trainers in the Arab Region: A Review of Policies and Practices on Continuous Professional Development. Paris: United Nations Educational, Scientific, and Cultural Organization.

Sultana, Ronald G., and Anthony Gordon Watts. 2008. "Career Guidance in the Middle East and North Africa." International Journal for Educational and Vocational Guidance 8 (1): 19–34.

Tan, Hong, and Gladys López-Acevedo. 2003. "Mexico: In-Firm Training for the Knowledge Economy." Policy Research Working Paper 2957, World Bank, Washington, DC.

Tan, Jee-Peng, Kiong Hock Lee, Ryan Flynn, Viviana V. Roseth, and Yoo-Jeung Joy Nam. 2016. Workforce Development in Emerging Economies: Comparative Perspectives on Institutions, Praxis, and Policies. Directions in Development: Human Development Series. Washington, DC: World Bank.

Tan, Jee-Peng, and Yoo-Jeung Joy Nam. 2012. "Pre-Employment Technical and Vocational Education and Training: Fostering Relevance, Effectiveness, and Efficiency." In The Right Skills for the Job? Rethinking Training Policies for Workers, edited by Rita Kullberg Almeida, Jere R. Behrman, and David Robalino, 67–103. Report 70908, Human Development Perspectives Series. Washington, DC: World Bank.

UIS (UNESCO Institute for Statistics). 2016. "Education." Montreal. http://uis.unesco.org.

UNESCO (United Nations Educational, Scientific, and Cultural Organization). 2014. "Technical and Vocational Teachers and Trainers in the Arab Region: A Review of Policies and Practices on Continuous Professional Development." UNESCO, Paris.

Watts, Anthony Gordon, and Ronald G. Sultana. 2004. "Career Guidance Policies in 37 Countries: Contrasts and Common Themes." International Journal for Educational and Vocational Guidance 4 (2–3): 105–22.

Watts, Anthony Gordon, Ronald G. Sultana, and John McCarthy. 2010. "The Involvement of the European Union in Career Guidance Policy: A Brief History." International Journal for Educational and Vocational Guidance 10 (2): 89–107.

World Bank. 2016. "Projet Emploi Jeune et Développement des Compétences (PEJEDEC); Evaluation d'impact du programme de Travaux à Haute Intensité de Main d'œuvre (THIMO): Résultats intermédiaires à court terme." World Bank, Washington, DC.

Technology is changing the world of work: What does that mean for learning?

The nature of work is changing. Within countries, jobs have been shifting across sectors—sometimes on a massive scale. Some shifts have been out of agriculture. In what are now high-income countries, people have shifted out of agriculture dramatically over the last half-century. In the Republic of Korea, the share of workers in farm jobs fell from 80 percent in 1950 to less than 7 percent in 2009. In Chile, the share of farm workers fell from 30 percent to under 15 percent in the same period. Other shifts have been out of industrial production. In the United States, the share of workers in manufacturing halved between 1950 and 2009.[1] In low- and middle-income countries, the shift is ongoing. Across Sub-Saharan Africa, employment in agriculture is expected to drop nearly 10 percent this decade, with a large rise in the numbers of people running small household businesses.[2]

Technology—including digital technology—is central to these changes. Eighty-five percent of the population worldwide now has access to electricity. Digital technologies penetrate most corners of the world, with one mobile phone subscription per person globally, and 4 in 10 persons connected to the internet.[3] As the *World Development Report 2016* points out, "With rising computing power, combined with the connectivity and informational value of the internet, digital technologies are taking on more tasks."[4] This is particularly true for routine tasks that are easy to automate such as a cashier's job. But other jobs—such as a teacher's—are not easy to automate. Technology ultimately substitutes for some workers. For workers whose jobs are not replaced, such as hairdressers or surgeons, technology has varied effects. While it may leave the hairdresser relatively untouched, it can make the surgeon dramatically more productive—with

digital imaging, for example. And, of course, technology creates new jobs as well. So technology eliminates some jobs, creates others, and increases the returns to yet others.[5]

The impact of technology on jobs varies dramatically across countries. For rich countries, predictions range from dire (in which "robot overlords" take over most jobs) to the much more modest estimate that 9 percent of jobs in rich countries could currently be automated.[6] For low-income countries, where technological penetration is much lower, the impact of technology on work will likely be more incremental (figure S5.1). Small-scale agriculture and household enterprises will not be automated in the near future, especially in countries such as Nicaragua, where less than 20 percent of households have access to the internet, or Liberia, where less than 10 percent of the population has access to electricity.[7] Those numbers will surely grow; greater access to technology will enable more poor nations and individuals to access those sectors that see high returns to technological growth. But in the short run, technology will change the demand for skills much more in countries that have the infrastructure to support automation.

Individuals who enter the workforce with better technological skills will see benefits. Because technology affects different workers in different ways, those who emerge from the education system with technological skills are more likely to be able to enter those professions (high-skilled, high-paying) that are gaining from technology.[8] Around the world, the rise of information technology is increasing the demand for high-skilled graduates who can use that technology effectively.[9] That rising demand translates into higher wages.[10] Because this dynamic can widen

Figure S5.1 **Technology use has increased dramatically over the past decade—but remains low in many countries**

Percentage of population who have access to electricity (2005–14) and who use the internet (2005–15), by country income group

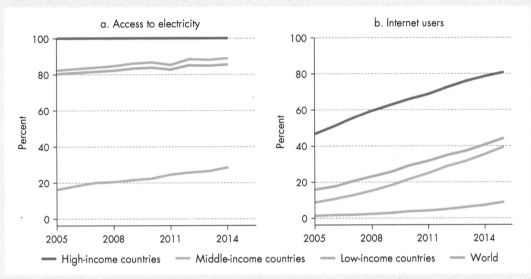

Source: WDR 2018 team, using data from World Bank (2017a) for electricity access and ITU (2016a) for internet users. Data at http://bit.do/WDR2018-Fig_S5-1.

inequality, ensuring that much of the population has access to these skills is essential. Globally, 85 percent of countries include computer skills in their curriculums for upper secondary school. But some regions lag, with Sub-Saharan Africa at only 50 percent, and much lower at lower levels of schooling.[11] Beyond the benefits to individuals, a population with strong technical skills is more likely to attract international industries that require those skills, such as modern manufacturing.

In environments with extremely limited access to computing technology, simple exposure can make a difference, but the skills that students gain are not the skills they need. Replacing traditional textbooks with laptops equipped with electronic textbooks neither helped nor harmed reading ability in Honduras, but in an environment where only 7 percent of students normally use the internet at school, the laptops allowed many more of them to develop the ability to search for content online and do basic word processing.[12] In Romania, vouchers to purchase standard home computers improved very basic general computing skills.[13] But such skills that are gained from mere exposure may not be the skills needed to succeed in the marketplace. Distributing simple laptops for home use in Peru made learners more competent on those laptops, but that did not translate to better skills on other, general-use operating systems (such as Microsoft Windows).[14] Among high school students in

Chile, more than 90 percent used computers at school and two-thirds had access to computers at home. Although two-thirds of them were able to search for information online, only half could organize information (such as arranging folders on the computer). Less than one-third could produce information (such as writing an email with adequate content).[15] Individuals need structured training in computing skills if they are to reap the returns of the technological revolution.

Students entering the workforce need better critical thinking and socioemotional skills. The ability to use technology is one way for them to take advantage of technological advancement. But another is to excel at those skills that technology carries out less well. Those include higher-order cognitive skills and interpersonal, socioemotional skills.[16] In the United States, jobs that require high socioemotional skills (such as nurses or social workers) are growing and jobs that require high socioemotional skills along with high cognitive ability (such as financial managers) are growing the fastest.[17] Education systems are beginning to learn how to cultivate socioemotional skills in learners: Recent efforts in Peru and Turkey have resulted not only in better socioemotional ability but also in better academic performance.[18] It is not enough to train learners to use computers: to navigate a rapidly changing world, they have to interact effectively with others, think creatively, and solve problems.

All of those skills that help individuals succeed in rapidly changing economies are built on the same foundations of literacy and numeracy. It may be tempting to divert resources from the development of foundational skills into the technological skills, higher-order cognitive skills, and socioemotional skills needed in the 21st century, which seem more novel and exciting. But these are complements to foundational skills, not substitutes for them—they can only be built on a solid foundation. Workers can search effectively for digital information or create digital content only if they have strong literacy skills. They can program new online applications only if they have confident numeracy skills. Socioemotional skills like grit, which are most malleable in childhood, can be practiced and strengthened in the service of gaining strong foundational skills. Higher-order cognitive skills involve consuming information using literacy and numeracy skills and combining it in new ways. Innovations in developing 21st-century skills are much needed, but these skills work best in conjunction with strong foundational abilities.

Notes

1. Handel (2012).
2. Fox and others (2013).
3. ITU (2016b); World Bank (2017a).
4. World Bank (2016, 120).
5. World Bank (2016).
6. Arntz, Gregory, and Zierahn (2016); Drum (2013).
7. ITU (2016b); World Bank (2017a).
8. World Bank (2016).
9. Autor, Katz, and Krueger (1998); Michaels, Natraj, and Van Reenen (2014).
10. Falck, Heimisch, and Wiederhold (2016).
11. UIS (2017).
12. Bando and others (2017).
13. Malamud and Pop-Eleches (2011).
14. Beuermann and others (2015).
15. Claro and others (2012).
16. World Bank (2016).
17. Deming (forthcoming).
18. Alan, Boneva, and Ertac (2015); World Bank (2017b).

References

Alan, Sule, Teodora Boneva, and Seda Ertac. 2015. "Ever Failed, Try Again, Succeed Better: Results from a Randomized Educational Intervention on Grit." HCEO Working Paper 2015-009, Human Capital and Economic Opportunity Global Working Group, Economics Research Center, University of Chicago.

Arntz, Melanie, Terry Gregory, and Ulrich Zierahn. 2016. "The Risk of Automation for Jobs in OECD Countries: A Comparative Analysis." OECD Social, Employment, and Migration Working Papers 189, Organisation for Economic Co-operation and Development, Paris.

Autor, David H., Lawrence F. Katz, and Alan B. Krueger. 1998. "Computing Inequality: Have Computers Changed the Labor Market?" Quarterly Journal of Economics 113 (4): 1169–1213.

Bando, Rosangela, Francisco Gallego, Paul Gertler, and Dario Romero Fonseca. 2017. "Books or Laptops? The Effect of Shifting from Printed to Digital Delivery of Educational Content on Learning." Economics of Education Review. In press.

Beuermann, Diether W., Julian Cristia, Santiago Cueto, Ofer Malamud, and Yyannu Cruz-Aguayo. 2015. "One Laptop Per Child at Home: Short-Term Impacts from a Randomized Experiment in Peru." American Economic Journal: Applied Economics 7 (2): 53–80.

Claro, Magdalena, David D. Preiss, Ernesto San Martín, Ignacio Jara, J. Enrique Hinostroza, Susana Valenzuela, Flavio Cortes, et al. 2012. "Assessment of 21st Century ICT Skills in Chile: Test Design and Results from High School Level Students." Computers and Education 59 (3): 1042–53.

Deming, David J. Forthcoming. "The Growing Importance of Social Skills in the Labor Market." Quarterly Journal of Economics.

Drum, Kevin. 2013. "Welcome, Robot Overloads; Please Don't Fire Us? Smart Machines Probably Won't Kill Us All, but They'll Definitely Take Our Jobs and Sooner Than You Think." Mother Jones (May/June). http://www.motherjones.com/media/2013/05/robots-artificial-intelligence-jobs-automation.

Falck, Oliver, Alexandra Heimisch, and Simon Wiederhold. 2016. "Returns to ICT Skills." OECD Education Working Paper 134, Organisation for Economic Co-operation and Development, Paris.

Fox, Louise M., Cleary Haines, Jorge Huerta Muñoz, and Alun H. Thomas. 2013. "Africa's Got Work to Do: Employment Prospects in the New Century." IMF Working Paper WP/13/201, International Monetary Fund, Washington, DC.

Handel, Michael J. 2012. "Trends in Job Skill Demands in OECD Countries." OECD Social, Employment, and Migration Working Paper 143, Organisation for Economic Co-operation and Development, Paris.

ITU (International Telecommunication Union). 2016a. World Telecommunication/ICT Indicators Database. ITU, Geneva. http://www.itu.int/en/ITU-D/Statistics/Pages/publications/wtid.aspx.

———. 2016b. Measuring the Information Society Report 2016. Geneva: ITU. http://www.itu.int/en/ITU-D/Statistics/Documents/publications/misr2016/MISR2016-w4.pdf.

Malamud, Ofer, and Cristian Pop-Eleches. 2011. "Home Computer Use and the Development of Human Capital." Quarterly Journal of Economics 126 (2): 987–1027.

Michaels, Guy, Ashwini Natraj, and John Van Reenen. 2014. "Has ICT Polarized Skill Demand? Evidence from Eleven Countries over Twenty-Five Years." *Review of Economics and Statistics* 96 (1): 60–77.

UIS (UNESCO Institute for Statistics). 2017. "Curriculum and ICT in Education." UIS, Montreal. http://data.uis.unesco.org.

World Bank. 2016. *World Development Report 2016: Digital Dividends.* Washington, DC: World Bank.

———. 2017a. World Development Indicators (database). World Bank, Washington, DC. http://data.worldbank.org/data-catalog/world-development-indicators.

———. 2017b. "Peru: If You Think You Can Get Smarter, You Will." *What We Do: Projects and Operations* (April 25), World Bank, Washington, DC. http://www.worldbank.org/en/results/2017/04/25/peru-if-you-think-you-can-get-smarter-you-will?CID=POV_TT_Poverty_EN_EXT.

PART IV

Making the system work for learning at scale

Education systems are misaligned with learning

Education systems are often poorly aligned with learning goals. These misalignments are driven in part by technical complexities: education systems simultaneously pursue many (often conflicting) goals, with the many system actors continually interacting in complex ways. Compounding these technical challenges is the limited policy implementation capacity of the many government agencies responsible for learning.

Kenya's government discovered just how difficult it is to turn successful small-scale interventions into systemwide improvements in learning. In the late 2000s, even though access to primary schooling was high, many children failed to acquire even basic skills. The government argued that large classes, with their overburdened teachers, lay behind these disappointing results. But a constrained education budget meant that hiring more civil service teachers to address these problems was not an option. Instead, in 2009 the government hired 18,000 temporary contract teachers. The new program shared many of the same features of an earlier pilot experiment by a nongovernmental organization that provided government schools with contract teachers.[1] The pilot reduced class sizes, leading to improved learning outcomes for students taught by the new contract teachers. Moreover, these gains were achieved at a cost well below the cost of the alternative of hiring more civil service teachers.

But unlike the pilot intervention, the government program failed to deliver any improvements in learning.[2] A combination of union resistance and lack of Ministry of Education capacity to manage contract teachers underpinned the program's lack of impact. The Kenyan teachers' union successfully challenged the program in the courts, arguing that hiring

teachers on a contract basis violated constitutional rights to equal pay for equal work. The ruling led to guarantees from the government to gradually absorb all contract teachers into the civil service and provide them with the same employment protections. These developments significantly changed the employment prospects of contract teachers. In particular, they weakened the link between performance and the chances of contract renewal—the main channel through which the original trial had improved student learning. At the same time, the ministry also struggled to implement the program. Government-employed contract teachers were paid on average three months late, hurting student learning.

This example illustrates a more common finding that working at scale is not the same as "scaling up."[3] Similar difficulties in changing teacher employment conditions in government schools have occurred in many other countries, despite evidence from pilot programs showing their potential to improve learning.[4] These examples show that implementing interventions at scale can also induce responses from other actors or parts of an education system that can alter the potential impacts on learning.

In many countries, education systems suffer from two related weaknesses. First, systems are not well aligned with the overall goal of learning; other goals can detract from, and in some cases compete with, efforts to improve learning outcomes. Second, the elements of an education system are often incompatible or incoherent. For example, government funding allocations sometimes fail to provide the resources schools need to improve learning. Even when school funding is available, the rules governing its use often leave little flexibility for schools to use it in ways tailored to the specific needs of students.

Technical and political factors underlie these system weaknesses. Getting all parts of an education system to work together is difficult, and the agencies responsible for designing, implementing, and evaluating education policies often lack the capacity to take on this role. For example, timely information on student learning outcomes is not available in many low-income countries, making it harder to design appropriate interventions and to monitor their effectiveness. The interests of system actors can also contribute to misalignments. For example, calls to devolve control over resources to schools are sometimes resisted because private textbook providers fear losing out on lucrative centralized contracts.[5]

Failure to tackle these technical and political constraints can trap countries in a low-learning, low-accountability, high-inequality equilibrium. When different parts of a system fail to work together, education outcomes will fall far short of what is possible. When actors in the system interact to pursue many goals, the mechanisms that hold them accountable for learning are weakened. And where powerful groups can divert resources to align with their own interests, education systems can exacerbate inequalities. Together, these factors can pull an education system out of alignment with the overall goal of learning (figure 9.1).

Misalignments and incoherence impede learning

Taking a systems approach can help to identify the elements that are incoherent with each other or misaligned with learning (box 9.1). Though every education system faces its own challenges, incoherence and misalignments tend to occur across four elements:

- *Learning objectives and responsibilities.* Clearly articulated learning goals are often missing. But even when they exist, the roles and responsibilities of different system actors in achieving them are unclear, resulting in limited accountability.

Figure 9.1 Technical and political barriers pull education systems away from the goal of learning

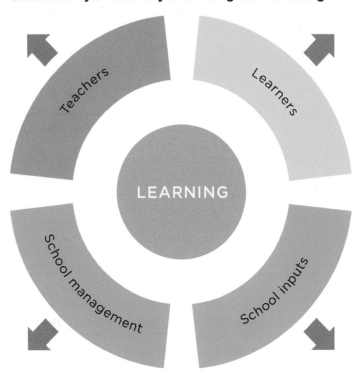

Source: WDR 2018 team.

- *Information and metrics.* Accurate, credible information on learning is often unavailable. This can divert attention from learning and hinder monitoring and evaluation of interventions aimed at improving outcomes.
- *Finance.* Education funding is sometimes inadequate and often allocated in ways inconsistent with a goal of providing equitable opportunities for effective learning.
- *Incentives.* The motivation and incentives of system actors are often only weakly linked to student learning.

Learning objectives and responsibilities

Though most education systems recognize learning as a central goal, it often receives less prominence than other objectives. Looking beyond high-level policy documents often reveals the objectives that matter most in the day-to-day affairs of education agencies. Bangladesh has made progress in linking education sector objectives explicitly to government budgets—for example, budget documents link allocations to specific activities aimed at improving education outcomes. However, the government's key

Box 9.1 It's all about (education) systems

What's an education system?

An education system is a collection of "institutions, actions and processes that affect the 'educational status' of citizens in the short and long run."[a] Education systems are made up of a large number of actors (teachers, parents, politicians, bureaucrats, civil society organizations) interacting with each other in different institutions (schools, ministry departments) for different reasons (developing curriculums, monitoring school performance, managing teachers). All these interactions are governed by rules, beliefs, and behavioral norms that affect how actors react and adapt to changes in the system.[b]

Why is it useful to take a systems approach?

A systems approach takes into account the interactions between the parts of an education system. In doing so, it seeks to understand how they work together to drive system outcomes, instead of focusing on specific elements in isolation.[c] It can help assess whether different actors and subsystems align with education goals and shed light on the underlying drivers of system performance. For example, limited teacher capacity is often highlighted as a major cause of poor performance. But trials introducing contract teachers into schools have shown that they can deliver the same or better learning outcomes than government teachers despite lower levels of education, training, and pay.[d] This finding suggests that some poor performance is driven not so much by a teacher's individual capacity but by the organizational setting—incentives, accountability mechanisms, power relations—in which government teachers operate. A systems approach aims to identify these underlying factors so that policy design can tackle the deeper causes of poor performance.

A systems approach can also highlight where system elements are incoherent. For example, curriculum improvements may lead to few improvements in student learning if other parts of the system (such as assessment or teacher development) fail to adapt. A systems view can reveal how changes in one part of the system affect other subsystems and support better alignment and ultimately better outcomes.[e]

A systems approach is also better suited to working with the complexity of education systems. The many objectives that education systems tend to pursue at the same time, coupled with the many different actors involved in pursuing these objectives, make it difficult to predict how different interventions will affect learning. A systems approach shifts the focus away from interventions designed to address specific problems, toward the broader changes required to improve learning sustainably.

Source: WDR 2018 team.

a. Moore (2015, 1).
b. World Bank (2003).
c. Bowman and others (2015).
d. Bruns, Filmer, and Patrinos (2011).
e. Newman, King, and Abdul-Hamid (2016).

performance indicators mostly deal with access and completion; only 1 of the 12 indicators targets learning. Moreover, that indicator tracks literacy rates in the population over age 15, which is insensitive to changes in school performance over the medium term.[6]

Even where learning is a clear goal, the way education systems are organized sometimes hampers performance. Because tasks are often fragmented across education departments and government agencies, it can be hard to identify who is accountable for outcomes. In Romania, responsibilities for textbook provision were split among four different agencies, yet none of them was solely responsible for ensuring that schools received the right books.[7] Delivering early childhood development services typically requires coordination among several government agencies, including health and education ministries. Managing these many agencies is challenging. In the early 1990s, constant shifts in responsibility for early childhood development in Ghana resulted in inadequate stewardship of these services.[8]

Information and metrics

Systems often lack the information needed to support the design and implementation of reform. Education management information systems cover a wide range of indicators on service delivery, but in many countries they do not routinely include data on learning. India's District Information System for Education (DISE) is designed to provide report cards for districts, but of the 980 data points reported, none covers student learning.[9] That omission can make it difficult for systems to track interventions to improve learning, for parents to demand better services from politicians or directly from schools, and for agencies to design effective policies to improve learning.

Finance

Public spending does not correlate strongly with learning. The link between spending and learning differs enormously, even among countries at similar levels of economic development. In 2015 Peru spent 28 percent less per student than the Dominican Republic, but it had Programme for International Student Assessment (PISA) mathematics scores that were more than half a standard deviation higher.[10] More generally, cross-country correlations between public spending and learning levels are weak and statistically insignificant after controlling for income per capita. Moreover, for any given level of spending there is a wide range of outcomes. Even changes in public education spending over time sometimes result in unexpected outcomes. For example, Bulgaria's PISA mathematics scores increased between 2009 and 2015, despite reductions in spending per student

(figure 9.2). Public expenditure reviews and other studies reveal similar patterns across subnational administrations and even across schools (spotlight 6).

The weak link between spending and learning is a feature of the different environments in which education systems operate. Systems with higher corruption or lower bureaucratic quality are less likely to use resources effectively to raise learning.[11]

These simple correlations also suggest that many education systems are delivering learning outcomes well below what is possible given current levels of funding. In India, excess teacher absenteeism in the public sector is estimated to cost US$1.5 billion a year. If teacher accountability systems were more strongly aligned with learning, teacher attendance would improve, allowing the system to achieve higher levels of learning at the same cost.[12]

Improvements in learning are unlikely when additional resources are allocated like past funding. The composition of education spending in many countries is suboptimal. Funding for teacher salaries often absorbs more than 80 percent of education budgets in low-income countries, leaving little room for spending in other areas. Using additional funding to shift spending patterns to ensure that teachers have the complementary inputs needed—such as textbooks and in-service training—would improve alignment and significantly aid learning.[13]

Figure 9.2 Simple associations between education spending and learning are weak

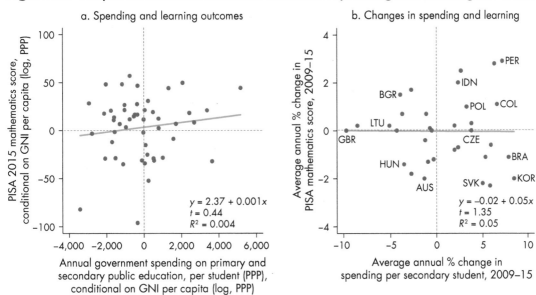

a. Spending and learning outcomes

b. Changes in spending and learning

Sources: WDR 2018 team, using data from OECD (2016); UIS (2017); World Bank (2017a). Data at http://bit.do/WDR2018-Fig_9-2.

Note: AUS = Australia; BGR = Bulgaria; BRA = Brazil; COL = Colombia; CZE = Czech Republic; GBR = United Kingdom; HUN = Hungary; IDN = Indonesia; KOR = Republic of Korea; LTU = Lithuania; PER = Peru; POL = Poland; SVK = Slovak Republic. GNI = gross national income; PISA = Programme for International Student Assessment; PPP = purchasing power parity U.S. dollars.

Incentives

Education system actors face many incentives, but only some of these incentives are aligned with learning. System actors are motivated by a range of factors that affect how they carry out their duties.[14] Professional rewards—the social status afforded to their occupation, the ability to develop new competencies, intrinsic motivation—are all important factors driving behavior. Financial rewards and accountability mechanisms, such as feedback from parents or from managers, can also affect how system actors perform. Though some of these factors that motivate system actors are aligned with learning, some are not. For example, salaries and career progression are often determined largely by a combination of qualifications and experience, despite these characteristics having only a weak relationship with learning.[15] Even where countries have invested in mechanisms to evaluate teacher performance, those mechanisms are often disconnected from decisions on professional development. Edo State in Nigeria conducts annual performance evaluations, but these evaluations do not affect decisions on teacher promotions, nor do they lead to sanctions or rewards for teachers based on their performance.[16]

Coherence matters: Getting all parts of the system working together

Ensuring that the parts of an education system work together is as important as ensuring alignment toward learning. Even if a country has prioritized student learning, established reasonable learning metrics, and aligned funding with incentives, it still needs to ensure that system elements are coherent (box 9.2). If a country adopts a new curriculum that places greater emphasis on active learning and creative

---

Box 9.2 Aligning all the ingredients for effective teaching in Shanghai

When 15-year-old students in Shanghai, China, outscored their peers in every other education system in the 2012 Programme for International Student Assessment (PISA), they sparked global interest in figuring out how Shanghai did it. One lesson is that coherence among key system elements, all aligned toward learning, has made Shanghai's teacher workforce particularly effective:

1. *Learning objectives and responsibilities*. Learning standards lay out clearly the competencies that students are expected to master in each grade. Teachers are expected to translate these standards into detailed lesson plans, so that students can learn the curriculum effectively.
2. *Information and metrics*. Based on the learning standards, schools routinely assess student progress. The results of these assessments are fed directly into the classroom, where teachers use them to adjust lesson plans and schedule additional time for areas in which students are weak. Student assessments are also an important input to a comprehensive system to monitor, evaluate, and support teachers.
3. *Finance*. The salary and benefits package for teachers in Shanghai is generous compared with those in other parts of China. In fact, it is comparable with those of other professional occupations. Moreover, the salary

scale allows high-performing and long-serving teachers to earn significantly more than new teachers. Adequate financing keeps teaching workloads relatively low, giving teachers the time to develop and prepare lesson plans.

4. *Incentives*. Because of this attractive compensation package and the high societal respect for teachers, Shanghai can attract skilled, able candidates to teaching. Incentives—both monetary and nonmonetary—encourage teachers to maintain high standards and continue improving their teaching skills. For example, high-performing teachers are recognized through the title of "model teacher," and a (small) share of a teacher's overall pay is based on performance. Teachers also have opportunities to act on these incentives, thanks to a well-established professional development system aligned with their needs. For example, school leaders draw on their close monitoring of teachers to develop targeted training plans for individual teachers.

No two education systems are alike, and attempting to exactly replicate Shanghai's system of teacher management in other countries is unlikely to work. Still, the core principle likely applies anywhere: aligning the various parts of the system coherently toward learning pays off.

Source: WDR 2018 team, based on Liang, Kidwai, and Zhang (2016).

---

thinking, the curriculum alone will not change much. Teachers need training so that they use more active learning methods, and they need to care enough to make the change—given that teaching to the new curriculum could be much more demanding than old methods that favor rote learning. Even if teachers are on board with curriculum reform, students and their families could weaken its effects if an unreformed examinations system creates misaligned incentives. In the Republic of Korea, efforts to introduce a more student-centered curriculum—one that encourages greater creativity—have sometimes conflicted with pressure on students to succeed on the all-important university entrance examinations.[17]

The need for coherence between different parts of an education system makes it risky to borrow from other countries. Education policy makers often scrutinize higher-performing systems to identify what they could borrow to improve learning outcomes in their own systems. Indeed, the search for the secret ingredient behind Finland's record of learning led in the 2000s to a swarm of visiting delegations in what has been dubbed "PISA tourism." Finland's system gives its well-educated teachers considerable autonomy, so they are able to tailor their teaching to the needs of their students. But lower-performing systems that simply import Finland's teacher autonomy into their own contexts—contrary to the advice of Finnish educators who emphasize coherence—are likely to be disappointed. If teachers are poorly prepared, unmotivated, and loosely managed, then giving them greater autonomy will likely compound the problem. South Africa discovered this in the 1990s and 2000s, when it adopted a curriculum approach that set objectives centrally but left implementation up to teachers. The approach failed in many schools, in part because it proved to be a poor fit for the capacity of teachers and the resources they had at their disposal.[18] This example illustrates why coherence between different system elements and the development of home-grown solutions are so important.

Technical complexities make it hard to align education systems with learning

Every day 23 million children—a fifth of the population—attend one of the 47,000 public elementary and high schools in the Philippines.[19] When their parents are included, about two-thirds of Filipinos interact with the school system on a regular basis.

The national government in Manila manages the system through a network of more than 200 division and 2,500 district education offices. These offices oversee over 600,000 public school teachers, or more than 40 percent of the public sector workforce. Even routine tasks involve coordination between many parts of the system. For example, management of public school operational funds relies on student data from the central office. Once schools have their allocations, they issue about 500,000 checks and generate as many spending reports, each detailing individual spending items. The monitoring of these financial flows alone puts a significant strain on the system, even though they account for less than 5 percent of government education spending.[20]

Three characteristics of complex education systems magnify the technical challenges of managing them. First, systems are opaque. Many of the goals pursued by these actors are hard to observe, as are many of the interactions among the actors, whether they take place in the classroom or in the bureaucracy. Second, systems are "sticky": reforms to improve learning are hard to launch, and they take time to bear fruit. Third, implementing reforms successfully requires capacity that many bureaucracies lack.

Many goals and actors make education systems opaque

Education systems typically have a range of goals, including equipping students with the skills needed for the labor market, advancing social equity, and teaching children the norms, beliefs, and histories of their community. But education systems can have other goals that can hamper efforts to improve learning. For example, politicians sometimes view education systems as a tool for rewarding their supporters with civil service jobs, or for impressing voters with school construction programs that are visible but not strategically planned. These goals can be misaligned with learning, leaving schools with buildings they cannot use and teachers who are not proficient.[21] Where these goals compete with other goals, the result is that the overall education system and its actors are not aligned toward learning.

Managing the system to improve learning is difficult. Promoting learning in the classroom involves significant discretion for teachers, who must use their professional assessment to tailor their teaching to the needs of their students. Teaching also involves regular, repeated interactions between students and teachers over a relatively long period. These characteristics—coupled with a dearth of information and metrics on student outcomes at the school level—make it hard to manage and monitor learning. These challenges may be exacerbated if private schools are a major player, because those schools typically operate outside the direct control of the public system (box 9.3).

Some things are easier to monitor.[22] School building and cash transfer programs are highly visible and easily monitored investments aimed at expanding access. By contrast, investments to raise teacher competence or improve the curriculum are less visible, and monitoring their impact on student learning is more difficult. Such challenges can sometimes prompt education systems to emphasize improvements in access over improvements in quality.[23] Even when systems

Box 9.3 Can private schooling be aligned to learning for all?

Private schools play a major role in education, even for the poor. Globally, roughly one in eight primary school students attends a private school. At the secondary level, the number rises to one in four among middle-income countries (table B9.3.1).[a] The numbers are similar for low-income countries, where they may be underestimates if informal schools are undercounted.[b] In some places, the share of students attending private schools is much higher than these global figures. In one Nigerian state, 57 percent of all basic education learners attend private schools.[c] These enrollments are not limited to high-income households. In slum communities in Nairobi, Kenya, 43 percent of the poorest quintile of families send their children to private schools. This is higher than the proportion among the richest quintile of families in nonslum communities who send their children to private schools (35 percent).[d] In Jamaica, 10 percent of learners from the poorest economic groups enroll in private schools.[e]

Low-income households are willing to make this sacrifice because they perceive that private schools deliver better education at comparable cost. In many countries, parents say that teacher absenteeism is lower in private schools and that learning outcomes are better.[f] In Jamaica and South Africa, parents suggest that private schools are safer than public schools.[g] Furthermore, although public primary education is formally free in the vast majority of countries, many informal fees remain, reducing the cost difference between public and private schools.

But there is no consistent evidence that private schools deliver better learning outcomes than public schools, or the opposite. In Colombia, India, and the United States, experimental evaluations of the consequences of enrolling in a private versus a public school show mixed results.[h] In some contexts, private schools may deliver comparable learning levels at lower cost than public systems, often by paying lower teacher salaries.[i] Even so, lower teacher salaries may reduce the supply of qualified teachers over time.

Much of the evidence cited in this debate is nonexperimental, so it may conflate the effects of private schools themselves with the effects of the type of students who enroll in private schools. Comparisons across 40 countries that seek to adjust for these differences in student characteristics find no private school advantage in the vast majority of countries.[j] Moreover, little rigorous research has assessed the effects of private schooling on students' values or on the long-term health of the public school system.

From a public policy perspective, how should governments view the growth in private schooling? Should

Table B9.3.1 Private providers account for a significant share of school enrollment

Percentage of learners enrolled in private education, by country income group (2014)

Country income group	Preprimary	Primary	Secondary
Low-income	57	14	20
Middle-income	42	13	25
High-income	42	12	20

Source: World Bank (2017a).

(Box continues next page)

Box 9.3 Can private schooling be aligned to learning for all? *(continued)*

governments encourage its growth, whether by removing restrictions on new schools or even by providing public subsidies that allow more students to enroll in private schools? Is there a trade-off between the short-term growth of private schools and the long-term health of the education system?

Private schools offer a variety of potential benefits. A straightforward one is proximity: new private schools can fill a gap when the nearest public schools are far away, or when there is demand to expand faster than public infrastructure can be built.[k] As for cost, in China, Ghana, and Kenya some private schools are comparable in cost to the public alternative.[l] Private schools can also innovate in ways that public schools cannot because they operate under fewer constraints. Moreover, private schools can fulfill niches for families with preferences different from the government's—for example, if parents value single-sex or religious education. Private schools may also have lower rates of teacher absence, such as in four countries in Sub-Saharan Africa.[m] In those schools, nonperforming teachers can be let go more easily than in public schools, increasing their accountability. Finally, competition from private schools could improve the performance of nearby public schools.[n]

But these benefits come with many risks. Private schools may skim off the higher-income students who are easiest and most profitable to teach, leaving only the more disadvantaged students in the public system.[o] Private schooling may also deepen social cleavages along dimensions other than income if it causes students to be sorted by language, ethnicity, or religion. Because families are not necessarily knowledgeable about pedagogy, private schools can induce them to make choices that slow student learning—for example by discouraging mother tongue instruction. And because families cannot evaluate quality or learning perfectly, private providers may try to take advantage of them to increase profits or achieve their other goals. Finally, even if the expansion of private schooling brings short-term benefits, it can undermine the political constituency for effective public schooling in the longer term. It is impossible to make any global statement about whether the benefits or risks dominate.

Experience with public-private partnerships is growing. As governments face their own limited capacity to cope with the learning crisis, some have turned to public-private partnerships in which they provide private schools with resources. In Pernambuco, Brazil, the state government is seeking to place half of the state's students in government-funded private schools.[p] In Uganda, the government provided hundreds of private schools with the resources needed to meet the growing demand for secondary education.[q] In some cases, this means private providers essentially mirror public schools in terms of education policy, such as in the government-"aided" schools in India.[r] But in other cases, such as in voucher schools in the United States or Liberia's Partnership Schools pilot, publicly funded private schools have significant leeway in how they run their schools, letting student learning results be the measure of quality.[s] In Uganda, public resources increased the quality of private schools, and public-private partnerships are likely a useful strategy if countries seek to expand enrollments dramatically in a short time.[t]

But overseeing private schools may be no easier than providing quality schooling. The key challenge for policy makers is to develop a policy and regulatory framework that ensures access for all children, protects families from exploitation, and establishes an environment that encourages education innovation. Managing a regulatory framework to achieve this is difficult: the same technical and political barriers that education systems face more generally come into play. From a technical perspective, developing a framework to accommodate the diverse nature of nonstate provision is complicated. In Bangladesh, for example, there are 11 separate categories for the nonstate provision of presecondary education (figure B9.3.1). Unlike government schools that are relatively homogeneous, nonstate provision reflects many different philosophies or approaches to education. The capacity of education agencies to effectively align incentives and monitor services is often limited, and assessing quality in contexts where education is provided in very different ways requires added skills. Though neither is easy, governments may deem it more straightforward to provide quality education than to regulate a disparate collection of providers that may not have the same objectives.

The bottom line is that countries need to ensure that private schooling does not undermine learning for all. Different countries make different choices on private

(Box continues next page)

Box 9.3 Can private schooling be aligned to learning for all? *(continued)*

delivery, acting on a variety of motivations. But if they do allow or even encourage private schooling, they need to remain alert to all the risks just outlined. The problems outlined in this Report do not disappear simply because of a change in a delivery mechanism. Governments may choose to contract out some service delivery, but they should never contract out the responsibility for ensuring that all children and youth have the opportunity to learn.

Figure B9.3.1 In Bangladesh, there are 11 different kinds of nonstate providers of presecondary education

Number of institutions under each nongovernment provider of presecondary education (2016)

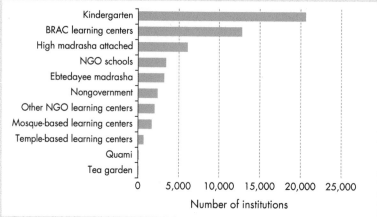

Source: WDR 2018 team, using data from Directorate of Primary Education, Bangladesh (2016). Data at http://bit.do/WDR2018-Fig_B9-3-1.

Note: NGO = nongovernmental organization.

Source: WDR 2018 team.

a. World Bank (2017a).
b. D. Capital Partners (2016).
c. Härmä (2013).
d. Oketch and others (2010).
e. Heyneman and Stern (2014).
f. Day Ashley and others (2014); Heyneman and Stern (2014).
g. Heyneman and Stern (2014).
h. Kingdon (2017); Urquiola (2016).
i. Andrabi, Das, and Khwaja (2008); Day Ashley and others (2014); Muralidharan and Sundararaman (2015).
j. Sakellariou (2017).
k. Oketch and others (2010); Tooley (2005).
l. Heyneman and Stern (2014).
m. Bold and others (2017).
n. de la Croix and Doepke (2009); Kosec (2014); Sandström and Bergström (2005).
o. Akaguri (2014); Härmä (2011).
p. "Educação Integral," Secretaria de Educação, State of Pernambuco, Várzea, Recife, Brazil, http://www.educacao.pe.gov.br/portal/?pag=1&men=70.
q. Barrera-Osorio and others (2016).
r. Kingdon (2017).
s. *Economist* (2017).
t. Barrera-Osorio and others (2016).

to monitor student learning are effective, they can sometimes lead to biases toward better-performing students, short-term test preparation, or a narrow focus on subjects that are explicitly tested.

The multiplicity of actors and institutions in an education system makes the outcomes of efforts to improve learning unpredictable.[24] Learning is a complex process that is difficult to break down into simple linear relationships from cause to effect. The multiple interactions that characterize teaching and learning and the almost continuous feedback that they provide can result in teachers, parents, and students adapting their behavior in unpredictable ways. For example, the introduction of school grants in Andhra Pradesh, India, and in Zambia failed to improve student learning in the long term because parents reduced their financial support in anticipation of the increase in government funding.[25] Reducing the financial burden on parents may be a desirable effect of these grants, but it was not their primary intent. More generally, many factors outside the classroom and the school system, including health and economic shocks, can alter the impact of interventions aimed at improving learning. Failure to learn and adjust policies in response to such changes often means that interventions do not work as planned.

Education systems are "sticky"

Education systems are slow to change. Some of the best-known successes in reforming systems, such as in Chile or Finland, took decades from initiation to fruition. Even at the micro level, such as in schools in the United States that enacted comprehensive school reform, it took 8–14 years for the full effects to be felt.[26] These long time frames present two further challenges to better aligning education systems with learning. First, to improve learning, policies usually have to remain relatively consistent. This is difficult under normal circumstances: changes in government, volatile funding, and shifts in the overall economic context all threaten the sustainability of policies.[27] But staying the course is even more challenging when the reforms fail to show any benefits in the short run. Second, the long lags make program evaluation more difficult, because attributing improvements to specific interventions is especially challenging when their impacts emerge only in the long run.

Implementation capacity to improve learning at scale is often lacking

Opacity and stickiness make technical alignment hard enough to achieve; weaknesses in implementation capacity make the task even more daunting. Successful implementation depends on effective leadership, coordination between education agencies, and implementation teams that are motivated, use resources efficiently, and can troubleshoot in real time—all of which are in short supply in many systems. Moreover, behavioral economics highlights many cognitive pitfalls that policy makers commonly face in complex operating environments. These include difficulty in evaluating policy effectiveness when faced with too many options; loss aversion, or the tendency to feel failures more intensely than successes, which makes policy makers wary of experimentation; biases that lead to selective use of information to reinforce existing views; and relational bias, which makes it harder for officials with elite educational backgrounds to grasp the challenges of mass education.[28]

Education agencies often lack the capabilities needed to deal with these complexities.[29] A recent assessment shows how multitasking and fragmentation within education agencies can blur lines of accountability for learning. In Cyprus, because of the absence of a department for human resources and general administration, pedagogical departments had to manage these responsibilities, diverting time from developing programs and policies.[30] Public expenditure and financial accountability assessments also highlight the low capacity in many developing countries in key areas. For example, only about half of the 72 low- and middle-income countries assessed since 2010 had any system in place to ensure that resources intended for schools, health clinics, and other service delivery units reached the front lines.[31]

* * *

Technical challenges and lack of implementation capacity result in misaligned education systems. When countries are unable to overcome these challenges, their education systems deliver levels of learning far below what is possible. But tackling the technical barriers to better learning is only part of the battle. To break out of low-learning equilibriums, countries must also address the political constraints that are often at the heart of these technical misalignments.

Notes

1. Duflo, Dupas, and Kremer (2015).
2. Bold and others (2013).
3. Acemoglu (2010).
4. Béteille and Ramachandran (2016); Bruns, Filmer, and Patrinos (2011); Duthilleul (2005).
5. Hallak and Poisson (2007); Transparency International (2009).
6. Ministry of Finance, Bangladesh (2017).
7. World Bank (2010).
8. World Bank (2015b).
9. See DISE website, http://udise.in/.
10. OECD (2016); UIS (2017).
11. Rajkumar and Swaroop (2008); Suryadarma (2012).
12. Muralidharan and others (2017).
13. Pritchett and Filmer (1999).
14. Bruns and Luque (2015); Finan, Olken, and Pande (2015).
15. Glewwe and others (2011); OECD (2009).
16. World Bank (2015a); Reboot (2013).

17. King and Rogers (2014); Park (2016).
18. Chisholm and Leyendecker (2008); Todd and Mason (2005).
19. See Uy (2017) for number of children; Department of Education, Philippines (2015) for number of schools.
20. World Bank (2016).
21. Harding and Stasavage (2014); Pierskalla and Sacks (2015); Wales, Magee, and Nicolai (2016).
22. Holmstrom and Milgrom (1991).
23. Harding and Stasavage (2014).
24. Burns and Köster (2016); Snyder (2013).
25. Das and others (2013).
26. Although these comprehensive school reforms differed across schools, they all targeted reorganizing entire schools in a coordinated way rather than implementing single or specialized interventions. See Borman and others (2003).
27. World Bank (2017b).
28. Thaler and Sunstein (2008); World Bank (2015c).
29. Pritchett and Woolcock (2004).
30. World Bank (2014).
31. PEFA (2017).

References[a]

Acemoglu, Daron. 2010. "Theory, General Equilibrium, and Political Economy in Development Economics." *Journal of Economic Perspectives* 24 (3): 17–32.

Akaguri, Luke. 2014. "Fee-Free Public or Low-Fee Private Basic Education in Rural Ghana: How Does the Cost Influence the Choice of the Poor?" *Compare: A Journal of Comparative and International Education* 44 (2): 140–61.

Andrabi, Tahir, Jishnu Das, and Asim Ijaz Khwaja. 2008. "A Dime a Day: The Possibilities and Limits of Private Schooling in Pakistan." *Comparative Education Review* 52 (3): 329–55.

Barrera-Osorio, Felipe, Pierre Gaspard de Galbert, James P. Habyarimana, and Shwetlena Sabarwal. 2016. "Impact of Public-Private Partnerships on Private School Performance: Evidence from a Randomized Controlled Trial in Uganda." Policy Research Working Paper 7905, World Bank, Washington, DC.

Béteille, Tara, and Vimala Ramachandran. 2016. "Contract Teachers in India." *Economic and Political Weekly* 51 (25): 40–47.

Bold, Tessa, Deon Filmer, Gayle Martin, Ezequiel Molina, Brian Stacy, Christophe Rockmore, Jakob Svensson, et al. 2017. "What Do Teachers Know and Do? Does It Matter? Evidence from Primary Schools in Africa." Policy Research Working Paper 7956, World Bank, Washington, DC.

Bold, Tessa, Mwangi S. Kimenyi, Germano Mwabu, Alice Ng'ang'a, and Justin Sandefur. 2013. "Scaling Up What Works: Experimental Evidence on External Validity in Kenyan Education." CSAE Working Paper WPS/2013-04, Centre for the Study of African Economies, University of Oxford, Oxford, U.K.

Borman, Geoffrey D., Gina M. Hewes, Laura T. Overman, and Shelly Brown. 2003. "Comprehensive School Reform and Achievement: A Meta-Analysis." *Review of Educational Research* 73 (2): 125–230.

Bowman, Kimberly, John Chettleborough, Helen Jeans, Jo Rowlands, and James Whitehead. 2015. "Systems Thinking: An Introduction for Oxfam Programme Staff." Oxfam, Oxford, U.K.

Bruns, Barbara, Deon Filmer, and Harry Anthony Patrinos. 2011. *Making Schools Work: New Evidence on Accountability Reforms.* Human Development Perspectives Series. Washington, DC: World Bank.

Bruns, Barbara, and Javier Luque. 2015. *Great Teachers: How to Raise Student Learning in Latin America and the Caribbean.* With Soledad De Gregorio, David K. Evans, Marco Fernández, Martin Moreno, Jessica Rodriguez, Guillermo Toral, and Noah Yarrow. Latin American Development Forum Series. Washington, DC: World Bank.

Burns, Tracey, and Florian Köster, eds. 2016. *Educational Research and Innovation: Governing Education in a Complex World.* Paris: Organisation for Economic Co-operation and Development.

Chisholm, Linda, and Ramon Leyendecker. 2008. "Curriculum Reform in Post-1990s Sub-Saharan Africa." *International Journal of Educational Development* 28 (2): 195–205.

D. Capital Partners. 2016. "The Impact of Private Investment in Education in Sub-Saharan Africa: How Can Private Capital Shape Education across the Continent?" D. Capital Partners, Dalberg Global Development Advisors, London. http://www.dalberg.com/wp-content /uploads/2016/05/Private-investments-in-SSA-Education .pdf.

Das, Jishnu, Stefan Dercon, James Habyarimana, Pramila Krishnan, Karthik Muralidharan, and Venkatesh Sundararaman. 2013. "School Inputs, Household Substitution, and Test Scores." *American Economic Journal: Applied Economics* 5 (2): 29–57.

Day Ashley, Laura, Claire Mcloughlin, Monazza Aslam, Jakob Engel, Joseph Wales, Shenila Rawal, Richard Batley, et al. 2014. "The Role and Impact of Private Schools in Developing Countries." Education Rigorous Literature Review, U.K. Department for International Development, London. https://www.gov.uk/government /uploads/system/uploads/attachment_data/file/439702 /private-schools-full-report.pdf.

de la Croix, David, and Matthias Doepke. 2009. "To Segregate or to Integrate: Education Politics and Democracy." *Review of Economic Studies* 76 (2): 597–628.

Department of Education, Philippines. 2015. "Fact Sheet— Basic Education Statistics." Manila.

Directorate of Primary Education, Bangladesh. 2016. *Annual Primary School Census.* Dhaka, Bangladesh: Information Management Division and Monitoring and Evaluation Division, DPE, Ministry of Primary and Mass Education.

Duflo, Esther, Pascaline Dupas, and Michael R. Kremer. 2015. "School Governance, Teacher Incentives, and Pupil-Teacher Ratios: Experimental Evidence from Kenyan Primary Schools." *Journal of Public Economics* 123 (March): 92–110.

Duthilleul, Yael. 2005. "Lessons Learnt in the Use of 'Contract' Teachers: Synthesis Report." International

a. References to titles of publications that include South Korea refer to the Republic of Korea.

Institute for Educational Planning, United Nations Educational, Scientific, and Cultural Organization, Paris.

Economist. 2017. "Ashes to Classes: Liberia's Bold Experiment in School Reform." February 23. http://www.economist.com/news/middle-east-and-africa/21717379-war-scorched-state-where-almost-nothing-works-tries-charter-schools-liberias.

Finan, Frederico S., Benjamin A. Olken, and Rohini Pande. 2015. "The Personnel Economics of the State." NBER Working Paper 21825, National Bureau of Economic Research, Cambridge, MA.

Glewwe, Paul W., Eric A. Hanushek, Sarah D. Humpage, and Renato Ravina. 2011. "School Resources and Educational Outcomes in Developing Countries: A Review of the Literature from 1990 to 2010." NBER Working Paper 17554, National Bureau of Economic Research, Cambridge, MA.

Hallak, Jacques, and Muriel Poisson. 2007. Corrupt Schools, Corrupt Universities: What Can Be Done? Paris: International Institute for Educational Planning, United Nations Educational, Scientific, and Cultural Organization.

Harding, Robin, and David Stasavage. 2014. "What Democracy Does (and Doesn't Do) for Basic Services: School Fees, School Inputs, and African Elections." Journal of Politics 76 (1): 229–45.

Härmä, Joanna. 2011. "Low Cost Private Schooling in India: Is It Pro Poor and Equitable?" International Journal of Educational Development 31 (4): 350–56.

———. 2013. "Access or Quality? Why Do Families Living in Slums Choose Low-Cost Private Schools in Lagos, Nigeria?" Oxford Review of Education 39 (4): 548–66. http://www.tandfonline.com/doi/full/10.1080/03054985.2013.825984.

Heyneman, Stephen P., and Jonathan M. B. Stern. 2014. "Low Cost Private Schools for the Poor: What Public Policy Is Appropriate?" International Journal of Educational Development 35 (March): 3–15.

Holmstrom, Bengt, and Paul Milgrom. 1991. "Multitask Principal-Agent Analyses: Incentive Contracts, Asset Ownership, and Job Design." Journal of Law, Economics, and Organization 7 (January): 24–52.

King, Elizabeth, and F. Halsey Rogers. 2014. "Intelligence, Personality, and Creativity: Unleashing the Power of Intelligence and Personality Traits to Build a Creative and Innovative Economy." Paper presented at Republic of Korea–World Bank symposium, "Achieving HOPE (Happiness of People through Education): Innovation in Korean Education for a Creative Economy," Seoul, November 4.

Kingdon, Geeta Gandhi. 2017. "The Private Schooling Phenomenon in India: A Review." IZA Discussion Paper 10612, Institute for the Study of Labor, Bonn, Germany.

Kosec, Katrina. 2014. "Relying on the Private Sector: The Income Distribution and Public Investments in the Poor." Journal of Development Economics 107 (March): 320–42.

Liang, Xiaoyan, Huma Kidwai, and Minxuan Zhang. 2016. How Shanghai Does It: Insights and Lessons from the Highest-Ranking Education System in the World. Directions in Development: Human Development Series. Washington, DC: World Bank.

Ministry of Finance, Bangladesh. 2017. "Medium-Term Budgetary Framework (MTBF) 2017–18 to 2019–20." Financial System Management Unit, Finance Division, Ministry of Finance, Dhaka, Bangladesh. https://mof.gov.bd/en/index.php?option=com_content&view=article&id=397&Itemid=1.

Moore, Mark. 2015. "Creating Efficient, Effective, and Just Educational Systems through Multi-Sector Strategies of Reform." RISE Working Paper 15/004, Research on Improving Systems of Education, Blavatnik School of Government, Oxford University, Oxford, U.K.

Muralidharan, Karthik, Jishnu Das, Alaka Holla, and Aakash Mohpal. 2017. "The Fiscal Cost of Weak Governance: Evidence from Teacher Absence in India." Journal of Public Economics 145: 116–35.

Muralidharan, Karthik, and Venkatesh Sundararaman. 2015. "The Aggregate Effect of School Choice: Evidence from a Two-Stage Experiment in India." Quarterly Journal of Economics 130 (3): 1011–66.

Newman, John L., Elizabeth M. King, and Husein Abdul-Hamid. 2016. "The Quality of Education Systems and Education Outcomes." Background Paper: The Learning Generation, International Commission on Financing Global Education Opportunity, New York.

OECD (Organisation for Economic Co-operation and Development). 2009. Evaluating and Rewarding the Quality of Teachers: International Practices. Paris: OECD.

———. 2016. PISA 2015 Results: Excellence and Equity in Education. Vol. 1. Paris: OECD.

Oketch, Moses, Maurice Mutisya, Moses Ngware, and Alex C. Ezeh. 2010. "Why Are There Proportionately More Poor Pupils Enrolled in Non-state Schools in Urban Kenya in Spite of FPE Policy?" International Journal of Educational Development 30 (1): 23–32.

Park, Rufina Kyung Eun. 2016. "Preparing Students for South Korea's Creative Economy: The Successes and Challenges of Educational Reform" [refers to Republic of Korea]. Research report, Asia Pacific Foundation of Canada, Vancouver.

PEFA. 2017. "Assessment Pipeline." PEFA, World Bank, Washington, DC. https://pefa.org/assessments/listing.

Pierskalla, Jan, and Audrey Sacks. 2015. "Personnel Politics: Elections, Clientelistic Competition, and Teacher Hiring in Indonesia." Working paper, World Bank, Jakarta, Indonesia.

Pritchett, Lant, and Deon Filmer. 1999. "What Education Production Functions Really Show: A Positive Theory of Education Expenditures." Economics of Education Review 18 (2): 223–39.

Pritchett, Lant, and Michael Woolcock. 2004. "Solutions When the Solution Is the Problem: Arraying the Disarray in Development." World Development 32 (2): 191–212.

Rajkumar, Andrew Sunil, and Vinaya Swaroop. 2008. "Public Spending and Outcomes: Does Governance Matter?" Journal of Development Economics 86 (1): 96–111.

Reboot. 2013. "Addressing Teacher Absenteeism in Edo State: Summary of Findings." Reboot, Abuja, Nigeria.

Sakellariou, Chris. 2017. "Private or Public School Advantage? Evidence from 40 Countries Using PISA 2012-Mathematics." Applied Economics 49 (29): 2875–92.

Sandström, F. Mikael, and Fredrik Bergström. 2005. "School Vouchers in Practice: Competition Will Not Hurt You." *Journal of Public Economics* 89 (2–3): 351–80.

Snyder, Sean. 2013. "The Simple, the Complicated, and the Complex: Educational Reform through the Lens of Complexity Theory." OECD Education Working Paper 96, Organisation for Economic Co-operation and Development, Paris.

Suryadarma, Daniel. 2012. "How Corruption Diminishes the Effectiveness of Public Spending on Education in Indonesia." *Bulletin of Indonesian Economic Studies* 48 (1): 85–100.

Thaler, Richard H., and Cass R. Sunstein. 2008. *Nudge: Improving Decisions about Health, Wealth, and Happiness.* New Haven, CT: Yale University Press.

Todd, Alexa, and Mark Mason. 2005. "Enhancing Learning in South African Schools: Strategies beyond Outcomes-Based Education." *International Journal of Educational Development* 25 (3): 221–35.

Tooley, James. 2005. "Private Schools for the Poor: Education Where No One Expects It." *Education Next* 5 (4): 11.

Transparency International. 2009. "Corruption in the Education Sector." Working Paper 04, Transparency International, Berlin.

UIS (UNESCO Institute for Statistics). 2017. Education (database). UIS, Montreal. http://data.uis.unesco.org/.

Urquiola, Miguel. 2016. "Competition among Schools: Traditional Public and Private Schools." In *Handbook of the Economics of Education*, Vol. 5, edited by Eric A. Hanushek, Stephen J. Machin, and Ludger Woessmann, 209–37. Handbooks in Economics Series. Amsterdam: North-Holland.

Uy, Jocelyn R. 2017. "DepEd Braces for 22m Students." *Newsinfo.* June 2. http://newsinfo.inquirer.net/901949/deped-braces-for-22m-students.

Wales, Joseph, Arran Magee, and Susan Nicolai. 2016. "How Does Political Context Shape Education Reforms and Their Success? Lessons from the Development Progress Project." ODI Dimension Paper 06, Overseas Development Institute, London.

World Bank. 2003. *World Development Report 2004: Making Services Work for Poor People.* Washington, DC: World Bank; New York: Oxford University Press.

——. 2010. "Romania Functional Review: Pre-University Education Sector, Final Report." Report 74287, World Bank, Washington, DC.

——. 2014. "Analysis of the Function and Structure of the Ministry of Education and Culture of the Republic of Cyprus." World Bank, Washington, DC.

——. 2015a. "Governance and Finance Analysis of the Basic Education Sector in Nigeria." Report ACS14245, World Bank, Washington, DC.

——. 2015b. *World Bank Support to Early Childhood Development: An Independent Evaluation.* Washington, DC: World Bank.

——. 2015c. *World Development Report 2015: Mind, Society, and Behavior.* Washington, DC: World Bank.

——. 2016. *Assessing Basic Education Service Delivery in the Philippines: The Philippines Public Education Expenditure Tracking and Quantitative Service Delivery Study.* Report AUS6799. Washington, DC: World Bank.

——. 2017a. World Development Indicators (database). World Bank, Washington, DC. http://data.worldbank.org/products/wdi.

——. 2017b. *World Development Report 2017: Governance and the Law.* Washington, DC: World Bank.

Spending more or spending better—or both?

Good teachers, conducive learning environments, reliable assessment systems, and innovative learning technologies all cost money. And as more students progress further in school, financing needs will rise. Yet more funding leads to better learning only if it is used well, with an intentional focus on learning outcomes.

Patterns of public education spending

Decisions over how to allocate public spending inevitably require difficult trade-offs. When deciding how to spend scarce resources, governments have to weigh the costs and benefits of different spending decisions, both of which are typically estimated with large margins of error. Governments also have to weigh the short- and long-term benefits of different spending choices. Should they spend more on urban infrastructure improvements to reduce air pollution in the future, or should they invest today in better primary health care services to treat respiratory infections?

Spending on education is subject to this same calculus. Education's many potential benefits for both individuals and societies (see chapter 1) make it a strong candidate for public support. In fact, the obligation to provide equitable education is often enshrined in law. Although the high returns to education mean that many students are willing to bear the costs themselves, there are strong rationales for public financing of at least some parts of the education system. First, a concern for fairness induces countries to subsidize education for children and youth from the poorest households, because their families may be unable or unwilling to finance their education. Second, because education has positive spillovers for others—such as when it reduces the propensity to commit crime—individuals may underinvest in their own education, from society's perspective. Third, governments want

to use education to create shared values; delivering education directly, or at least financing it, gives them leverage to ensure this happens. But in all these cases, governments must weigh benefits against the costs of investing in education rather than in some other area—and they must decide how to spend within the education sector.

As their spending patterns show, countries are increasingly willing to invest in education. Whether because of the public economics calculations just discussed or for other political reasons, countries have devoted a rising share of their national income to education (figure S6.1). In 2012 about two-thirds of countries that reported information on spending devoted over 4 percent of national income to public spending on education. Education also typically absorbs the largest single share of a government's budget, averaging about 15 percent of the budget across low- and middle-income countries. In some countries, the investment in education is still low, indicating scope for further prioritization, but the aggregate trends suggest that governments recognize the importance of education.

Does more spending improve learning outcomes?

While there is a strong rationale for public investment in education, the relationship between spending and learning outcomes is often weak. In global learning assessments, for example, although higher per-student spending initially appears to lead to more

Figure S6.1 Governments devote a large share of their budgets to education

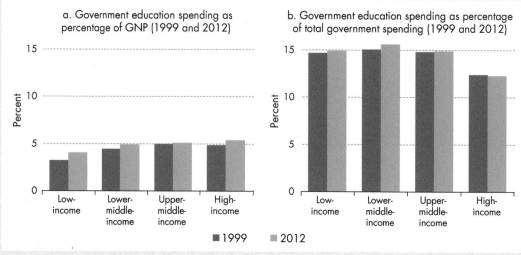

a. Government education spending as percentage of GNP (1999 and 2012)

b. Government education spending as percentage of total government spending (1999 and 2012)

■ 1999   ■ 2012

Source: UNESCO (2015). Data at http://bit.do/WDR2018-Fig_S6-1.

Note: Median values are shown. GNP = gross national product.

learning at the poorer end of the global income scale, the correlation largely disappears once controlling for countries' per capita income. This finding suggests that the correlation is driven more by economic development than by the level of public spending.[1]

Regional learning assessments—which include many more low- and lower-middle-income countries—also show how inconsistent the association between spending and learning can be. For example, public spending per primary school student increased over the 2000s in both Kenya and Lesotho; yet student learning outcomes improved in Lesotho but declined in Kenya (figure S6.2, panels a and b). Guatemala improved student learning significantly between 2006 and 2013, even though per-student spending declined over the same period (figure S6.2, panels c and d). Comparing across regions within a country often reveals similar patterns. In Indonesia during the 2000s, the link between changes in district education spending and secondary school examination results was very weak.[2] These findings indicate that education systems, and even schools within the same system, vary in their ability to translate increased spending into better learning outcomes.

Providing more resources directly to schools has also had mixed effects on learning in different environments. A review of two decades of research reveals that the association between many school-level resources (such as textbooks) and student outcomes is variable.[3] School grants have become

a commonly used mechanism in many countries to provide schools with the resources needed to support school improvement. Although grants have often increased student enrollment and retention, they have had relatively limited effects on learning. For example, recent evaluations in Indonesia and Tanzania found that school grants alone did not increase student learning.[4]

Weak links in the spending-learning chain

There are five main reasons why spending does not always lead to better and more equal student learning outcomes:[5]

- Spending is not allocated equitably.
- Funds do not reach schools or are not used for their intended purposes.
- Public spending can substitute for private spending.
- Decisions on the use of public funding are not coherently aligned with learning.
- Government agencies lack the capacity to use funding effectively.

Public spending is often allocated in ways that exclude poor and marginalized children, reducing its overall impact on learning. Overall, public education expenditure tends to favor wealthier, more powerful groups (table S6.1). Poorer households do tend to

Figure S6.2 The relationship between changes in public education spending and student learning is often weak

Changes in public education spending and in sixth-grade mathematics learning outcomes, selected countries

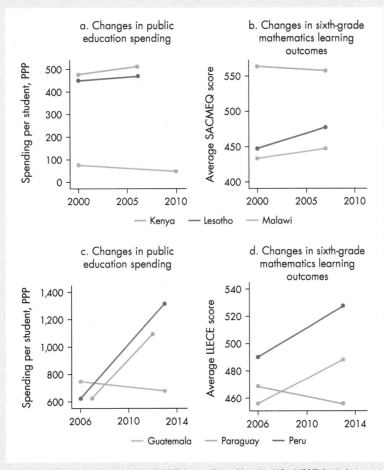

Sources: WDR 2018 team, using data from UIS (2016) for spending and from World Bank (2017) for student learning. Data at http://bit.do/WDR2018-Fig_S6-2.

Note: Per student spending is reported in purchasing power parity (PPP) U.S. dollars. Student learning data are derived from data collected by the Southern and Eastern Africa Consortium for Monitoring Educational Quality (SACMEQ) and the Latin American Laboratory for Assessment of the Quality of Education (LLECE). For each country, the two plotted data points reflect the years for which data are available.

receive a greater share of public spending on primary education because they tend to have more children than wealthier households. But public spending on secondary and tertiary education overwhelmingly favors wealthier groups, because by the time students reach those levels, many of the poor have already left school. In Zambia, 39 percent of secondary education spending was allocated to the richest fifth of households, compared with only 8 percent for the poorest. The gap is even wider at the tertiary level, where 86 percent of all public spending is captured by the richest households. These estimates likely understate the

differences across socioeconomic groups, since they typically do not account for the fact that students from poorer families tend to receive lower-quality schooling than those from wealthier families. Allocating resources more equitably could therefore raise average learning levels.

Public funds sometimes fail to reach schools or are not used as intended. In 2013–14, almost a third of school capitation grants failed to reach Zambian primary schools.[6] In the Philippines, in 2013 about a quarter of similar funds did not reach primary and lower secondary schools.[7] In Zambia, funds were diverted

Table S6.1 Inequalities in public education spending are common

Incidence of public education spending by household income quintile, selected countries and years

Percent

Country	Year(s)	Primary		Secondary		Tertiary		Total	
		Poorest	Richest	Poorest	Richest	Poorest	Richest	Poorest	Richest
Bangladesh	2010	27	13	13	23	2	55	20	20
Burundi	2006	23	13	12	27	4	59	15	29
Congo, Rep.	2011	21	16	18	18	1	62	—	—
Ghana	2007	19	13	13	20	4	65	12	34
Honduras	2004	31	6	5	20	1	67	—	—
Indonesia	2007	26	11	15	19	4	57	20	23
Pakistan	2007–08	25	11	16	23	9	55	17	28
Thailand	2011	25	14	—	—	1	73	20	26
Uganda	2009–10	19	15	6	38	1	68	—	—
Zambia	2010	22	14	8	39	0	86	15	31

Sources: Bangladesh: World Bank (2013a); Burundi: Tsimpo and Wodon (2014); the Republic of Congo: World Bank (2014); Ghana: Wodon (2012); Honduras: Gillingham, Newhouse, and Yackovlev (2008); Indonesia: Wika and Widodo (2012); Pakistan: Asghar and Zahra (2012); Thailand: Buracom (2016); Uganda: Guloba (2011); Zambia: World Bank (2016b).

Note: Poorest (richest) refers to the poorest (richest) 20 percent of households. Estimates for secondary in Ghana and the Republic of Congo are for lower secondary. Primary estimates for Thailand also include secondary. — = data not available.

for other uses, including to fund district-level operating costs. In the Philippines, while district education offices reported using some of the funds to pay school expenses, this use was not recorded and schools had no way of monitoring the spending. Schools in the Philippines that served poorer students also received a smaller share of their intended allocation than schools serving wealthier students.[8] Even when resources are delivered to schools, they are sometimes not used. In Sierra Leone, a 2008 program successfully increased the delivery of textbooks to schools, but the textbooks had no impact on learning because they were stored as a hedge against future shortfalls rather than distributed to students.[9]

Household spending can also affect the link between public spending and outcomes. Taking account of household spending on education can alter the picture of overall spending across countries. Government expenditure as a proportion of gross domestic product (GDP) in Nepal is much lower than in Vietnam. However, when all public and private spending on education is taken into account, spending in Nepal is much higher.[10] Households can also react to increases in public education spending by lowering their own contributions. For example, the introduction of school grants in India and Zambia had no effect on learning because parents reduced their own financial support in anticipation of increased government funding.[11]

Decisions on how to use public resources often lack coherent alignment with learning. The evidence on ways to improve learning is growing, suggesting ways to use funding more effectively. Also important is ensuring that the mix of inputs and interventions that are funded work together well. Many education systems find this difficult. For example, more classrooms may be built, but there are insufficient funds to hire the teachers needed to use them. Teachers are present in classrooms, but they lack the learning materials needed to teach effectively. Improving coherence is not just about the mix of inputs, but also about the systems that manage these inputs. In Tanzania, grants given to schools were ineffective on their own, but combining grants with teacher incentives ensured the grants were used effectively to improve student learning.[12] In Indonesia, school grants improved learning only when they were combined with measures to link school committees with village authorities.[13]

The government agencies responsible for managing education often lack the capacity to use resources effectively. The Philippines recently embarked on an ambitious education reform backed up with significant increases in public investment. A central element of the program is the introduction of two additional years of secondary education, which in turn requires the rehabilitation and expansion of school infrastructure to provide the places needed for senior high school. Despite a 19-fold increase in the infrastructure budget between 2005 and 2015, lack of government capacity to manage such a massive school building program has meant that a large share of the resources remained unspent. In 2014 only 64 percent of the infrastructure budget was committed. And even where classrooms were built, school principals have been largely unsatisfied with their quality.[14]

Spending to improve learning

Achieving education goals, whether national or global, will certainly require more spending in the coming decades. The Education Commission estimates that low- and middle-income countries will have to increase spending by 117 percent between 2015 and 2030 to enable most children to complete primary and secondary education with minimum levels of learning, as the Sustainable Development Goals call for.[15] Reliably estimating such global costs is difficult because doing so requires accurate information on many aspects of country systems that is often unavailable. It also requires making assumptions—for example, about optimal class size—that, while valid for some countries, may not apply to others. Notwithstanding these difficulties, exercises of this kind offer useful information on what school expansion of reasonable quality might cost. That information indicates that, even with greater efficiencies, it will be impossible to extend schooling for hundreds of millions of students without investing more in education.

The key will be to use those additional resources in ways that improve learning, especially for disadvantaged children. Costing exercises are sometimes misinterpreted as implying that more spending is all that is needed. But because there is no certainty that spending will lead to better outcomes, spending better will also be essential—as the Education Commission emphasizes. When education is funded using resources diverted from other pressing public needs such as health or infrastructure, or funded through debt to be repaid by the next generation, it is crucial that spending be oriented toward what will improve learning for all. How to achieve this is the focus of this *World Development Report*.

Spending more can be an important first step to spending better, but, again, increasing spending alone is not sufficient to improve learning. The politics of education reform sometimes requires compensating stakeholders who might lose out, or spending more to lay the foundations for future reform. For example, addressing the low pay of teachers in Peru was an important prerequisite for introducing the reforms (such as linking teacher career paths to performance) that underpinned improvements in learning outcomes.[16] However, in other cases strategies of this kind have worked less well. A 2006 education finance law in Argentina aimed at reversing declines in quality led to a near-doubling of education spending as a share of GDP (from 3.5 to 6 percent) between 2005 and 2013. The new resources were used to increase teacher hiring, raise teacher pay, and improve school infrastructure. Yet despite these improvements in inputs, learning outcomes have improved only marginally in recent years and are still below 2003 levels.[17] These experiences highlight the need to strengthen the links in the spending-learning chain, if more spending is to lead to better learning outcomes.

Notes

1. See chapter 9 and Altinok (2010).
2. World Bank (2013b).
3. Glewwe and others (2011).
4. Mbiti, Muralidharan, and Schipper (2016); Pradhan and others (2014).
5. See Filmer, Hammer, and Pritchett (2000) for a similar analysis of health spending.
6. World Bank (2016c).
7. World Bank (2016a).
8. See Policy Note 5, figure 8 in World Bank (2016a).
9. Sabarwal, Evans, and Marshak (2014).
10. UIS (2016).
11. Das and others (2013). This may be beneficial if it reduces financial burdens on parents, but that was not the primary purpose of these grants.
12. Mbiti, Muralidharan, and Schipper (2016).
13. Pradhan and others (2014).
14. World Bank (2016a).
15. This includes only projected costs of primary and secondary education. See Education Commission (2016, table 3).
16. Bruns and Schneider (2016).
17. de Hoyos, Holland, and Troiano (2015).

References

Altinok, Nadir. 2010. "Do School Resources Increase School Quality?" *Brussels Economic Review* 51 (4): 435–58.

Asghar, Zahid, and Mudassar Zahra. 2012. "A Benefit Incidence Analysis of Public Spending on Education in Pakistan Using PSLM Data." *Lahore Journal of Economics* 17 (2): 111–36.

Bruns, Barbara, and Ben Ross Schneider. 2016. "Managing the Politics of Quality Reforms in Education: Policy Lessons from Global Experience." Background Paper: The Learning Generation, International Commission on Financing Global Education Opportunity, New York.

Buracom, Ponlapat. 2016. "The Distributional Effects of Social Spending in Thailand: Evidence from a New Database." *Asian Politics and Policy* 8 (2): 263–79.

Das, Jishnu, Stefan Dercon, James Habyarimana, Pramila Krishnan, Karthik Muralidharan, and Venkatesh Sundararaman. 2013. "School Inputs, Household Substitution, and Test Scores." *American Economic Journal: Applied Economics* 5 (2): 29–57.

de Hoyos, Rafael E., Peter A. Holland, and Sara Troiano. 2015. "Understanding the Trends in Learning Outcomes in Argentina, 2000 to 2012." Policy Research Working Paper 7518, World Bank, Washington, DC.

Education Commission. 2016. *The Learning Generation: Investing in Education for a Changing World.* New York: International Commission on Financing Global Education Opportunity.

Filmer, Deon, Jeffrey S. Hammer, and Lant H. Pritchett. 2000. "Weak Links in the Chain: A Diagnosis of Health Policy in Poor Countries." *World Bank Research Observer* 15 (2): 199–224.

Gillingham, Robert, David Newhouse, and Irene Yackovlev. 2008. "The Distributional Impact of Fiscal Policy in Honduras." IMF Working Paper WP/08/168, International Monetary Fund, Washington, DC.

Glewwe, Paul W., Eric A. Hanushek, Sarah D. Humpage, and Renato Ravina. 2011. "School Resources and Educational Outcomes in Developing Countries: A Review of the Literature from 1990 to 2010." NBER Working Paper 17554, National Bureau of Economic Research, Cambridge, MA.

Guloba, Madina. 2011. "Public Expenditure in the Education Sector in Uganda: A Benefit Incidence Analysis (Phase 2)." Research Series 110, Economic Policy Research Centre, Kampala, Uganda.

Mbiti, Isaac M., Karthik Muralidharan, and Youdi Schipper. 2016. "Inputs, Incentives, and Complementarities in Primary Education: Experimental Evidence from Tanzania." Working paper, University of California at San Diego.

Pradhan, Menno, Daniel Suryadarma, Amanda Beatty, Maisy Wong, Arya Gaduh, Armida Alisjahbana, and Rima Prama Artha. 2014. "Improving Educational Quality through Enhancing Community Participation: Results from a Randomized Field Experiment in Indonesia." *American Economic Journal: Applied Economics* 6 (2): 105–26.

Sabarwal, Shwetlena, David K. Evans, and Anastasia Marshak. 2014. "The Permanent Input Hypothesis: The Case of Textbooks and (No) Student Learning in Sierra Leone." Policy Research Working Paper 7021, World Bank, Washington, DC.

Tsimpo, Clarence, and Quentin Wodon. 2014. "Measuring the Benefit Incidence of Public Spending for Education in Burundi." Global Partnership for Education, World Bank, Washington, DC.

UIS (UNESCO Institute for Statistics). 2016. "Who Pays for What in Education? The Real Costs Revealed through National Education Accounts." UIS, Montreal.

UNESCO (United Nations Educational, Scientific, and Cultural Organization). 2015. "Global Monitoring Report 2015: Education for All 2000–2015: Achievements and Challenges." UNESCO, Paris.

Wika, Gek Sintha Mas Jasmin, and Tri Widodo. 2012. "Distribution of Government Spending on Education in Indonesia." MPRA Paper 79501, Munich Personal RePEc Archive, University Library of Munich.

Wodon, Quentin, ed. 2012. *Improving the Targeting of Social Programs in Ghana.* World Bank Study Series. Washington, DC: World Bank.

World Bank. 2013a. "Bangladesh Education Sector Review—Seeding Fertile Ground: Education That Works for Bangladesh." Report 86237, World Bank, Dhaka, Bangladesh.

———. 2013b. "Spending More or Spending Better: Improving Education Financing in Indonesia." Report 73050-ID, World Bank, Jakarta, Indonesia.

———. 2014. *Republic of Congo: Enhancing Efficiency in Education and Health Public Spending for Improved Quality Service Delivery for All.* Report AUS5649. Washington, DC: World Bank.

———. 2016a. *Assessing Basic Education Service Delivery in the Philippines: The Philippines Public Education Expenditure Tracking and Quantitative Service Delivery Study.* Report AUS6799. Washington, DC: World Bank.

———. 2016b. "Education Public Expenditure Review in Zambia." Education Global Practice Series, World Bank, Washington, DC.

———. 2016c. "Education Sector Public Expenditure Tracking and Service Delivery Survey in Zambia." Education Global Practice Series, World Bank, Washington, DC.

———. 2017. EdStats: Education Statistics (database). Washington, DC. datatopics.worldbank.org/education/.

Unhealthy politics
drives misalignments

Politics can intensify misalignments in education systems, when the vested interests of stakeholders divert systems away from learning. This can happen at various stages, from setting policy goals to designing, implementing, evaluating, and sustaining reforms. Even when many individual actors are committed to learning, a system can remain stuck in a low-learning trap.

Education systems are complex. Aligning an education system's goals, financing, and incentives with student learning is difficult for technical reasons. But there are also political reasons systems do not prioritize student learning. Political impetus to fix misalignments can help achieve important educational objectives—as it has in Chile, England, and India (see chapter 11)—but unhealthy politics can make things worse. Too often, education interventions, whether big reforms or day-to-day implementation steps, are compromised because powerful individuals or groups can make others act in ways that serve private interests rather than the collective good.[1] Powerful actors frequently benefit from the status quo and devise mechanisms to preserve it, regardless of the impact on system performance. These mechanisms result in actors being trapped in low-learning equilibriums.

Unhealthy politics can intensify misalignments in education systems

Many education systems encounter political impediments and rent-seeking, making alignment much harder to achieve. Consider these examples:

- Using computers to educate students requires difficult technical decisions on program design. But

even when there is consensus on technical design, students may not benefit. For example, in 1996–97 the superintendent of New York City's District 29 rigged a $6 million contract, awarding it to a computer company affiliated with a politically connected property developer. In return, the company gave the superintendent expensive gifts, while delivering archaic or nonfunctioning computers to students. Teachers had been counting on decent computers to help their students in math; without the computers, the students lost out.[2]

- In 2009 Mexico's federal government introduced a plan for competitive recruitment of teachers, whereby all candidates were required to take a test covering content knowledge, pedagogical mastery, and ethics. Designing the tests was technically difficult. But the technical challenges paled next to the political impediments created by local affiliates of Mexico's teachers' union, the Sindicato Nacional de Trabajadores de la Educación (SNTE), which has 1.4 million members. The policy change meant that the opportunity for patronage-driven hiring would vanish. Because of strong opposition from the SNTE, the reform was diluted, making it applicable only to a small pool of vacancies. Estimates suggest that up to 85 percent of hiring in 2010 was discretionary rather than competitive. Recent evidence indicates that the teachers hired through discretionary methods were much less effective at improving student learning than those hired competitively.[3]

- Vyapam (http://www.vyapam.nic.in) is the government-run professional examination board in Madhya Pradesh, India. It conducts large-scale entrance tests for admission into courses such as medicine and for recruitment into state government jobs such as the police. Designing entrance tests and ranking candidates are technically challenging when there can be more than 100,000 candidates. But political economy factors intrude as well: recently, rent-seeking is alleged to have undermined the goal of fair, transparent admissions. In 2013 an independent probe exposed a potential multibillion-dollar scheme in which senior politicians and government officials had allegedly set up a system allowing unqualified candidates to pay bribes, often to middlemen, to receive high rankings in entrance tests.[4] In 2015, the Supreme Court of India transferred the case from the state government to the country's premier investigative agency, the Central Bureau of Investigation, which is currently pursuing the investigation.

Education systems involve many stakeholders with multiple, often contradictory, interests.[5] These systems are not just about students, teachers, or principals. They also involve politicians, bureaucrats, the judiciary, private players, and more. Participants linked to these institutions have a vested interest in how the system works, including its structure and funding. A textbook supplier may want to provide a quality product, but it also cares about profits. A politician may want to make teachers accountable for student learning, but also realizes the electoral risks of teacher opposition. A bureaucrat may support meritocratic admissions, but also accepts a "token of appreciation" for ensuring the admission of an acquaintance's child to a desirable school. A parent may want to complain about a teacher, but worries that her child could suffer retaliation.

Vested interests are not confined to private or rent-seeking interests. Actors in education systems are often driven by their values or ideology, especially when the consequences of education policies are not readily apparent. Examples include a commitment to public schools versus public-private choice, secular education versus religious, and accountability for test scores versus a focus on teacher qualifications. In addition, education systems can be used by dominant ethnic groups—especially in multilingual or multireligious societies—to promote their positions while suppressing minorities.

Multiple interests jeopardize learning goals. Balancing multiple interests is difficult. When education interventions threaten interests, whether they be a person's financial, ideological, or status-related interests, resistance from different parts of the system can be expected. The net effect: the system is pulled away from a focus on learning (figure 10.1).

Education systems are vulnerable to political interference because they are opaque and because teachers constitute a large base of government employees. The opacity of education systems, coupled with uncertainty about how a specific education policy will affect learning, is fertile ground for contestation of reforms. Teachers—the most important factor in learning—have traditionally been important grassroots political actors, because of their geographic spread and regular interaction with parents. Two characteristics make teachers especially attractive as patronage appointees. First, entry costs to the profession are often low. Second, the impact of incompetent patronage appointees on learning is not immediately visible, so it has few reputational consequences for politicians, especially if they are already operating on a short time horizon.[6]

Because of the size of the teaching force, teachers' unions can be politically important. The political power of a union depends on how effectively its leadership can mobilize teachers, which varies widely within and across countries. In many countries, not all teachers are union members or engaged in union activity.[7] Whether union activity helps or hinders education reform ultimately depends on several factors (box 10.1).

Multiple actors and interests: Pulling the system out of alignment at each step of the policy cycle

Personal interests influence reform at every step. Vested interests—of teachers, principals, bureaucrats, politicians, parents, students, the judiciary, civil society organizations, the private sector—are influential at every step of the education policy cycle. Broadly, these steps are setting policy goals, designing policies, implementing policies, evaluating policies, and sustaining policy reforms. The forces that detract from alignment tend to be magnified in conflict settings (box 10.2).

Setting policy goals

In many cases, policies are not chosen for their effectiveness in improving learning. Often, they are guided instead by the vested interests of powerful actors. Policies to hire teachers tend to be popular with politicians, teachers, and parents because they

Figure 10.1 Contradictory interests detract from learning objectives

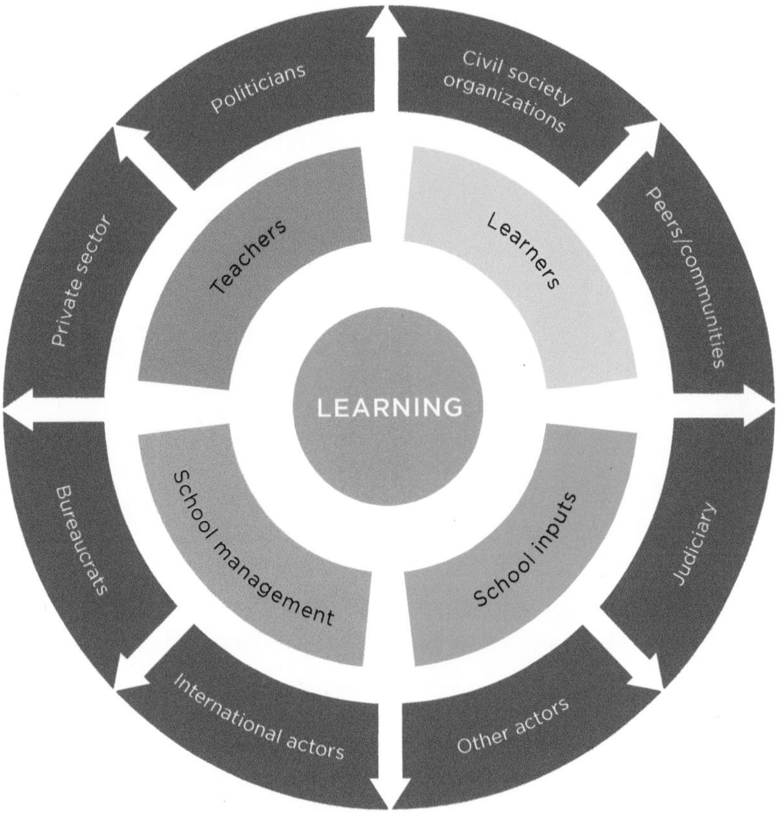

Source: WDR 2018 team.

Box 10.1 How do teachers' unions affect learning?

Teachers' unions are important institutions for protecting the rights of teachers, but do they matter for student learning? The quantitative literature identifies situations in which unions may have undermined high-quality teaching and learning. By fighting for higher salaries while protecting incumbent teachers from outside competition, unions sometimes stifle the formation of an effective teaching cadre.[a] A study in India finds that union membership is negatively correlated with student achievement.[b] However, hidden behind large-scale correlations is evidence of union behavior that has been beneficial for education reform efforts, including efforts by the Zambia National Education Coalition, the Uganda National Teachers' Union, and the Confederación Nacional de Maestros de Educación Rural de Bolivia.

It is impossible to say that unions always help or harm student learning; it depends on their characteristics and behaviors, as well as the context in which they operate. All countries have unions, but they vary in membership and number. Figure B10.1.1 shows the wide variation in teacher unionization across countries. Some countries, such as Finland and Mexico, have one dominant teachers' union, whereas others, such as India and South Africa, have several.

There are also institutional variations in teachers' unions, such as differences in internal organization, stability, and party affiliation. In the United States, some have argued that teachers' unions resist education reforms because union leaders represent the median teacher, and if leaders supported these reforms, they would be voted out.[c] On the

(Box continues next page)

Box 10.1 How do teachers' unions affect learning? *(continued)*

Figure B10.1.1 Teacher unionization varies across countries

Union membership as a percentage of total teachers, selected countries (2012–15)

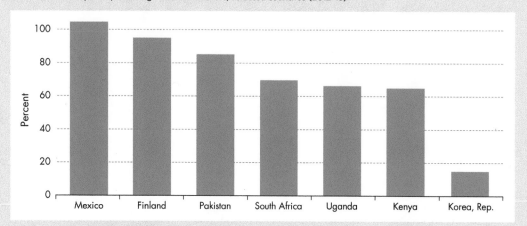

Source: Shrestha (2017). Data at http://bit.do/WDR2018-Fig_B10-1-1.

Note: Bars represent the ratio of union members to teachers. In Mexico, because the union includes a sufficient number of retirees and nonteaching staff, the ratio exceeds 100 percent.

other hand, evidence from Argentina and Mexico suggests that union behavior (and ability to resist reform) depends on the influence of partisan identities, organizational fragmentation, and the competition for union leadership.[d]

In summary, the outcome of union behavior will depend on how the proposed reform aligns with the interplay of a union's goals, quantitative strength, stability, and strategic alliances.

Sources: WDR 2018 team, based on: Carnoy (2007); Eberts and Stone (1987); Hoxby (1996); Kingdon and Teal (2010); Moe (2001, 2011); Murillo (1999, 2012); Shrestha (2017).

a. Hoxby (1996).
b. Kingdon and Teal (2010).
c. Moe (2011).
d. Murillo (1999).

bring visible, immediate benefits. Likewise, large-scale school construction programs tend to attract considerable support. In a diverse range of countries (Cambodia, Colombia, Mozambique), policy makers have invested in building preschools instead of in less visible but more effective process-oriented early childhood initiatives, such as programs to improve parent-child interactions. In Bangladesh, until recently it was much easier to unite elites around the need for mass education than around raising educational standards in schools.[8]

It is also difficult to adopt a policy goal that threatens or reconfigures jobs, as is true for most quality-enhancing education policies. For example, an alternative to the politically popular policy of reducing class size would be to introduce serious teacher performance appraisal, accompanied by tools to help teachers improve. Yet, because such reforms could expose poorly performing teachers, the reforms rarely reach the policy arena. Other policies that threaten teaching jobs include school consolidation or closing. Such policies have been difficult to implement, because parental support for local schools makes it politically infeasible to close small, high-cost rural schools.[9] In Bulgaria, school principals have been reluctant to let teachers go, despite declining school-age populations. In several countries, strong teachers' unions have prevented large-scale teacher redundancies.[10]

Designing policies

Even when the goal of a policy is to improve student learning, its final design often reflects what

Box 10.2 How politics can derail learning in conflict-affected states

Conflict-affected regions face important political economy constraints in developing their education systems. Violent conflict hampers learning in an immediate sense when schools, students, and teachers are targeted, and also over the long term when security issues divert attention and resources from schools. The "security first" approach often hides the vested interests in the security sector—powerful military and political actors, as well as external political interests—which have agendas that overshadow development.

Policy in politically weak or fragile conflict-affected states can be influenced by both external and internal power relations. External aid agencies are often handicapped by the difficulty of delivering aid in violent or insecure contexts. This difficulty usually leads to an emphasis on generalized educational frameworks rather than context-specific ones because

of the security challenge of examining and addressing local differences during a violent conflict. Domestic considerations create challenges as well, as in decisions about the medium of instruction in schools. For example, approaches that guarantee the right of all children to be educated in their "own" language can be used by vested groups to segregate communities, as happened in Bosnia and Herzegovina in the 1990s. Political economy challenges can also occur within healthy democracies that have conflict regions. Insurgency-affected parts of Chhattisgarh, India, have found it difficult to implement education reforms aimed at improving teacher accountability and student learning. A key concern has been an overall lack of funding, payment delays, and interruption of teachers' pay. Reduced funding may steer systems toward employing patronage hires, allowing less qualified and often uncertified teachers to replace trained teachers.

Sources: WDR 2018 team, based on: Bensalah (2002); De Herdt, Titeca, and Wagemakers (2010); Magill (2010); Mosselson, Wheaton, and Frisoli (2009); Novelli and others (2014); Rose and Greeley (2006); Shields and Rappleye (2008).

powerful interests want, which can undermine the goal. Decentralization policies aim to increase policy responsiveness and accountability, but many times they delegate accountability for results without the authority or resources to achieve them. In Indonesia, Pakistan, and some Latin American countries, major decentralization efforts have struggled (at least initially) to find the right balance between central and local funding, or between central and local authority.[11] Central authorities often attempt to limit the power of lower units of government because local governments—being closer to the people—can threaten the political power of more distant governments. At the same time, local governments may be unwilling to assume greater responsibility or adopt national norms—for example, on the inclusion of marginalized groups.

Implementing policies

Policy makers may face little resistance when signing off on a policy, but implementation can be compromised if the policy threatens powerful interests. Policies designed to measure teacher performance have been particularly difficult to implement. In 2000 South Africa's (then) Department of Education introduced the National Policy on Whole-School

Evaluation to establish standardized procedures for monitoring school performance and establishing the support needs of schools.[12] Though the policy was meant to be supportive, premised on building collaborations and mentorship, the South African Democratic Teachers' Union—the country's largest—remained opposed to it. Many of the union's chapters blocked the adoption of the policy in schools in their areas. A similar situation occurred in Mexico in 2012.[13]

Well-intentioned reforms may threaten the legal entitlements of individuals—and when, understandably, they turn to the courts for redress, reforms risk being stalled. In Peru, unions resisted a new law on teacher evaluations by challenging its constitutionality.[14] The ensuing court process then delayed implementation of the first round of evaluations. Though the court eventually upheld the law, for political reasons the union was given a major concession: the law applied only to newly hired teachers. Similarly, in 2002 teachers in Andhra Pradesh, India, stalled implementation of a policy on teacher transfers by filing a court case.[15]

Parents can also make it difficult to implement learning-focused policies. A common example is parents helping children to cheat on examinations, which makes it hard to measure student learning. In 2015 the global media broadcast images of family members in Bihar, India, handing cheat sheets to children inside a building taking exams.[16] Perhaps parents are aware that their children have not learned much in school, leaving them uncompetitive against better-prepared or more affluent children.

Evaluating policies

Indicators of the effectiveness of policies are often chosen in a way that lets powerful groups off the hook. When a policy fails, frontline bureaucrats or principals may face repercussions regardless of whether failure was in their control. As a result, decisions on what to measure and track are less a reflection of what the education system values than of who is willing to be held accountable for what. For example, India's landmark Right to Education Act (Act No. 35, 2009) did not originally contain any measure of teacher effectiveness or of student learning (although subsequent rules and amendments have sought to introduce the quality dimension). Similarly, accreditation systems in higher education tend to focus on inputs—such as number of classrooms, amount of equipment, or faculty-student ratios—instead of what students have learned or whether they become employed.[17] Such an approach limits liability, but jeopardizes learning goals.

Data can be manipulated. Even when indicators track meaningful variables, data quality may be compromised. Data on outcomes can be gamed; decisions on who collects data and how often are made using subjective criteria. Gaming might take the form of candidates hiring test takers, parents facilitating cheating, teachers misreporting student test scores, or government officials encouraging teachers to modify test scores.[18] In several countries, comparisons of national enrollment data with household survey data find systematic discrepancies, with official statistics sometimes exaggerating progress.[19]

A subtler barrier to effective monitoring and evaluation is when governments collect mountains of data but not in a format that facilitates decision making. In some countries, the many efforts to collect data on indicators create the illusion that policy makers are actively engaged in data-driven decision making to improve school quality. But by the time data entry is completed, it is time for the next round of data collection. No serious analysis is conducted, feedback is not provided to schools, or the data are too broad to be useful.[20] Such instances devalue data in decision making.

Sustaining policy reforms

Even when difficult reforms are implemented, they can be undone. Reversal can be incremental, with policy makers softening elements to appease specific groups. In the late 1990s, the government of Madhya Pradesh, India, began hiring teachers from the newly created *shiksha karmi* cadre, under which all new teachers were to be locally recruited and put on 10-month contracts. In response, teacher applicants filed court cases arguing that the policy violated their constitutional rights, which emphasize that no citizen can be ineligible for office based on criteria such as place of birth. Burdened with litigation and pressure, the government redesigned the policy, making concessions on local recruitment and qualifications.[21] Similarly, in São Paulo, Brazil, reforms of teacher career tracks introduced in 2009 were gradually undone by 2011 under a new education minister.[22]

Reversal can be sudden. In Ghana, an early childhood care and development body was set up under the office of the president, with high-level support. But a change in administration put the office under the Ministry of Gender, Children, and Social Protection, lowering the priority and visibility given to early childhood issues.[23] In República Bolivariana de Venezuela, decades of reforms that had created a strong higher education system were reversed when a new populist government set the goal of universalizing higher education. That effort, without prepared students, adequate faculty, or the appropriate infrastructure, has weakened the country's education system.[24]

These cases raise two important issues. First, why do parents and students have such a limited voice in influencing the vested interests that jeopardize quality-enhancing reforms? It could be that those most likely to benefit from reforms—especially parents and students—are often poorly organized. Moreover, the immediate gains of any proposed policy tend to be uncertain, making it harder to mobilize support for the reform. Parents may also find that the potential ramifications of opposing a teacher or politician could be formidable for their children. By contrast, those who stand to lose from reforms tend to be better aware of their losses and, in many cases, are better organized for collective action.[25]

Second, more generally, why do these low-learning equilibriums persist? For every teacher, bureaucrat, politician, judge, or businessperson who jeopardizes learning, there are several who feel deeply accountable for student learning and act to strengthen education systems. Yet individual actors find it hard to escape these traps. Why?

Trapped in low-accountability, low-learning equilibriums

The formal rules of the game—that is, the laws and policies governing education systems—already reflect power asymmetries.[26] When specific policy goals are chosen, when finance is allocated to certain tasks, when teachers' unions bargain for concessions, preexisting power asymmetries and struggles are expressed through policy.

But such decisions also reveal the informal contracts that determine which formal rules are chosen or followed. Unwritten codes of conduct derive from the values, expectations, and cultural norms in a social setting, and they are important in determining the extent, nature, and strength of politics in that setting.[27] In Indonesia, where older colleagues are treated with considerable courtesy, school mergers have often been delayed informally until principals who stood to lose their jobs retired.[28] In rural Rajasthan, India, field research finds that teachers often have to pay bribes to get needed services, such as a transfer. Interestingly, the norm differs by gender: male teachers make the payments directly, while female teachers typically go through a male relative.[29]

The widespread operation of informal networks reveals a lack of generalized trust within systems. Unwritten codes of conduct between individuals can thrive only if there is sufficient trust between them. Each must trust that the other will behave as expected. Yet as individuals cultivate personalized trust-based relationships—often undermining learning or equity goals in the process—overall trust in the system suffers.[30]

As systems grow more complex and the number of actors and interactions increases, uncertainty multiplies. Trusting others becomes increasingly difficult. Creating reciprocal obligations helps manage the uncertainty.[31] These obligations do not need to be spelled out; the social setting ensures they are understood. During the Suharto era in Indonesia, teachers were required to display "mono-loyalty" to the state and teach compulsory courses in the state ideology, Pancasila.[32] If they did not, they knew they risked demotion or transfer to schools in undesirable areas. In SNTE-dominant parts of Mexico, teachers knew that if they did not support the SNTE, they risked unfavorable transfers or being sidelined.

Reciprocal obligations complicate accountability. Power relations between entities and groups depend on context. One group may be more dependent on another—and therefore less powerful—in one context.

Figure 10.2 Interdependencies characterize the relationship between teachers and politicians

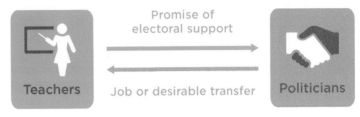

Source: WDR 2018 team, based on Béteille (2009).

But in another context, dependence patterns could reverse. In 2007, when teachers in Rajasthan threatened the ruling party with electoral sabotage, they were the ones who wielded power, with the ruling party dependent on them for victory. But in another context at the same time, the ruling party controlled individual teachers through patronage-based appointments and transfers (figure 10.2). Because these opposing relations occurred simultaneously, the distinctions between who was more dependent and who was accountable to whom became blurred.[33] Such interdependencies govern relationships between various participants in education systems, such as parent-teacher or bureaucrat-middleman interactions.

Interdependencies can become coercive and entrenched. This happens when actors are unable to break out of informal contracts. In the Vyapam case in Madhya Pradesh, India, several bureaucrats, fearing adverse career repercussions, allegedly joined the scam, making it much worse than otherwise possible. Then others joined—with middlemen purportedly profiting off the connections made between the various players. What started out as a small-time operation allegedly became institutionalized (albeit informally) as people began to believe they would lose out if they questioned the status quo.[34] Likewise, in New York City the unwritten power of school board members forced superintendents and principals to routinely allow wasteful practices.[35] This pattern repeats itself across cases, countries, and time.

As participants get trapped in unhealthy interdependencies, they devise mechanisms to protect themselves from undue blame and punishment—and avoid taking risks. Fearing repercussions for uncooperative behavior, actors make choices that provide the appearance of change—for example, when a politician presides over school openings but does not address teacher absenteeism, a judge delays case hearings endlessly, or a parent sits on a dormant school committee. These actors become averse to taking risks or innovating. Such behavior coexists with a perverse form of information management. For fear of being wrongly implicated in illegal behavior, officials sometimes generate mountains of paper, files, and data, paralyzing the system instead of providing relevant information.[36] The opacity, stickiness, and low capacity of education systems make it easier to exaggerate accomplishments and cover up performance problems.

Abdicating responsibility and avoiding blame erode an education system's ability to function, thereby perpetuating a low-accountability, low-learning equilibrium. Teachers, bureaucrats, judges, or politicians who fail to cooperate with the status quo are likely to put themselves at considerable professional risk. The system leaves them little choice but to conform. The problem is not limited to specific individuals, but arises from the multiple interests of actors and the underlying incentives in education systems. The accountability needed to ensure student learning becomes secondary.

* * *

This is the story of unhealthy politics.[37] Healthy politics can generate the momentum for reform and deliver results for education outcomes, as chapter 11 shows.

Notes

1. World Bank (2017).
2. Segal (2005).
3. Bruns and Luque (2015); Estrada (2016).
4. *Hindustan Times* (2015); Sethi (2015).
5. Grindle (2004); Moe and Wiborg (2017).
6. Bruns and Schneider (2017).
7. Moe and Wiborg (2017); Murillo (1999).
8. Hossain and others (2017).
9. Forgy (2009).
10. Forgy (2009); Pepinsky, Pierskalla, and Sacks (2017).
11. Indonesia: Rosser and Fahmi (2016); World Bank (2007); Pakistan: Dundar and others (2014); Ghaus-Pasha (2011); Latin America: Willis, da CB Garman, and Haggard (1999).
12. Taylor, Muller, and Vinjevold (2003).
13. Bruns and Luque (2015).
14. Bruns and Luque (2015).
15. Sharma and Ramachandran (2009).
16. CNN.com (2015).
17. Stevens and Kirst (2015).
18. Jhingran (2016); Levitt and Dubner (2010).
19. Sandefur and Glassman (2015).
20. Bill and Melinda Gates Foundation (2015); Jhingran (2016).
21. Sharma (1999).
22. Bruns and Luque (2015).
23. IEG (2015).
24. Albornoz (2007).
25. Grindle (2004).
26. World Bank (2017).
27. Bailey (1969); Easton (1979); Greif (2006); North (1991).
28. Rosser and Fahmi (2016).
29. Béteille (2015).
30. Burns, Köster, and Fuster (2016); Gambetta (1988).
31. Gouldner (1960).
32. Bjork (2006).
33. Béteille (2009).
34. Sethi (2015).
35. Segal (2005).
36. Mathur (2010).
37. World Bank (2016).

References

Albornoz, Orlando. 2007. "Recent Changes in Venezuelan Higher Education." *International Higher Education* 48 (Summer): 18–19.

Bailey, Frederick George. 1969. *Strategems and Spoils: A Social Anthropology of Politics.* Pavilion Series: Social Anthropology. New York: Schocken Books.

Bensalah, Kacem, ed. 2002. "Guidelines for Education in Situations of Emergency and Crisis: EFA Strategic Planning." Division of Policies and Strategies of Education, United Nations Educational, Scientific, and Cultural Organization, Paris.

Béteille, Tara. 2009. "Absenteeism, Transfers and Patronage: The Political Economy of Teacher Labor Markets in India." PhD dissertation, Stanford Graduate School of Education, Stanford University, Stanford, CA.

————. 2015. "Fixers in India's Teacher Labor Markets." *Asian Survey* 55 (5): 942–68.

Bill and Melinda Gates Foundation. 2015. "Teachers Know Best: Making Data Work for Teachers and Students." https://s3.amazonaws.com/edtech-production/reports /Gates-TeachersKnowBest-MakingDataWork.pdf.

Bjork, Christopher. 2006. "Decentralisation in Education, Institutional Culture, and Teacher Autonomy in Indonesia." In *Decentralisation and Privatisation in Education: The Role of the State,* edited by Joseph Zajda, 133–50. Dordrecht, the Netherlands: Springer.

Bruns, Barbara, and Javier Luque. 2015. *Great Teachers: How to Raise Student Learning in Latin America and the Caribbean.* With Soledad De Gregorio, David K. Evans, Marco Fernández, Martin Moreno, Jessica Rodriguez, Guillermo Toral, and Noah Yarrow. Latin American Development Forum Series. Washington, DC: World Bank.

Bruns, Barbara, and Ben Ross Schneider. 2017. "Reforming Education Quality: Difficult Reforms Facing Disruptive Opponents." Paper presented at the Workshop on the Political Economy of Education Reform, Mexico City, February 3–4.

Burns, Tracey, Florian Köster, and Marc Fuster. 2016. *Education Governance in Action: Lessons from Case Studies.* Educational Research and Innovation Series. Paris: Centre for

Educational Research and Innovation, Organisation for Economic Co-operation and Development.

Carnoy, Martin. 2007. *Cuba's Academic Advantage: Why Students in Cuba Do Better in School.* With Amber K. Gove and Jeffery H. Marshall. Stanford, CA: Stanford University Press.

CNN.com. 2015. "Bihar Cheating Scandal: What Parents in India Will Do for Good Grades." March 20. http://www.cnn.com/2015/03/20/asia/india-cheating-parents-school-tests/.

De Herdt, Tom, Kristof Titeca, and Inge Wagemakers. 2010. "Making Investment in Education Part of the Peace Dividend in the DRC." Paper presented at Chronic Poverty Research Centre conference, "Ten Years of War against Poverty," Manchester, U.K., September 8–10.

Dundar, Halil, Benoît Millot, Yevgeniya Savchenko, Harsha Aturupane, and Tilkaratne A. Piyasiri. 2014. *Building the Skills for Economic Growth and Competitiveness in Sri Lanka.* Directions in Development: Human Development Series. Washington, DC: World Bank.

Easton, David. 1979. *A Framework for Political Analysis.* Chicago: University of Chicago Press.

Eberts, Randall W., and Joe A. Stone. 1987. "Teacher Unions and the Productivity of Public Schools." *Industrial and Labor Relations Review* 40 (3): 354–63.

Estrada, Ricardo. 2016. "Crony Education: Teacher Hiring and Rent Extraction." Working paper, European University Institute, San Domenico di Fiesole, Italy.

Forgy, Larry. 2009. "Per Student Financing in ECA School Systems." Europe and Central Asia Knowledge Brief 6, World Bank, Washington, DC.

Gambetta, Diego. 1988. *Trust: Making and Breaking Cooperative Relations.* Oxford, U.K.: Blackwell Publishers.

Ghaus-Pasha, Aisha. 2011. "Fiscal Implications of the 18th Amendment: The Outlook for Provincial Finances." Policy Notes Series on Pakistan No. 1, World Bank, Washington, DC.

Gouldner, Alvin Ward. 1960. "The Norm of Reciprocity: A Preliminary Statement." *American Sociological Review* 25 (2): 161–78.

Greif, Avner. 2006. *Institutions and the Path to the Modern Economy: Lessons from Medieval Trade.* Political Economy of Institutions and Decisions Series. Cambridge, U.K.: Cambridge University Press.

Grindle, Merilee Serrill. 2004. *Despite the Odds: The Contentious Politics of Education Reform.* Princeton, NJ: Princeton University Press.

Hindustan Times. 2015. "25 Mystery Deaths and 2,000 Arrests: All about MP's Vyapam Scam." June 29. http://www.hindustantimes.com/bhopal/25-mystery-deaths-and-2-000-arrests-all-about-mp-s-vyapam-scam/story-Y3dLEQdkEsVyCwuPQXxaXI.html.

Hossain, Naomi, Mirza Hassan, Md Ashikur Rahman, Khondokar Shakhawat Ali, and M. Sajidul Islam. 2017. "The Problem with Teachers: The Political Settlement and Education Quality Reforms in Bangladesh." ESID Working Paper 86, Effective States and Inclusive Development Research Centre, Global Development Institute, School of Environment, Education, and Development, University of Manchester, Manchester, U.K.

Hoxby, Caroline Minter. 1996. "How Teachers' Unions Affect Education Production." *Quarterly Journal of Economics* 111 (3): 671–718.

IEG (Independent Evaluation Group). 2015. *World Bank Support to Early Childhood Development: An Independent Evaluation.* What Works Series. Washington, DC: World Bank.

Jhingran, Dhir. 2016. "Data Collection Alone Cannot Improve Learning Outcomes in State-Run Schools." *Hindustan Times,* November 25. http://www.hindustantimes.com/analysis/data-collection-alone-cannot-improve-learning-outcomes-in-state-run-schools/story-xGSCZ8yXxMtElQ3qa8Cn4L.html.

Kingdon, Geeta, and Francis Teal. 2010. "Teacher Unions, Teacher Pay, and Student Performance in India: A Pupil Fixed Effects Approach." *Journal of Development Economics* 91 (2): 278–88.

Levitt, Steven D., and Stephen J. Dubner. 2010. *Freakonomics: Il Calcolo dell'Incalcolabile.* Milan: Sperling and Kupfer.

Magill, Clare. 2010. "Education and Fragility in Bosnia and Herzegovina." Research Paper IIEP, Education in Emergencies and Reconstruction Series, International Institute for Educational Planning, United Nations Educational, Scientific, and Cultural Organization, Paris.

Mathur, Nayanika. 2010. "Paper Tiger? The Everyday Life of the State in the Indian Himalaya." PhD dissertation, University of Cambridge, Cambridge, U.K.

Moe, Terry M. 2001. "Teachers Unions and the Public Schools." In *A Primer on America's Schools,* edited by Terry M. Moe, 151–83. Stanford, CA: Hoover Institution Press.

———. 2011. *Special Interest: Teachers Unions and America's Public Schools.* Washington, DC: Brookings Institution Press.

Moe, Terry M., and Susanne Wiborg. 2017. *The Comparative Politics of Education: Teachers Unions and Education Systems around the World.* Cambridge, U.K.: Cambridge University Press.

Mosselson, Jacqueline, Wendy Wheaton, and Paul St. John Frisoli. 2009. "Education and Fragility: A Synthesis of the Literature." *Journal of Education for International Development* 4 (1): 1–17.

Murillo, Maria Victoria. 1999. "Recovering Political Dynamics: Teachers' Unions and the Decentralization of Education in Argentina and Mexico." *Latin American Politics and Society* 41 (1): 31–57.

———. 2012. "Teachers Unions and Public Education." *Perspectives on Politics* 10 (1): 134–36.

North, Douglass C. 1991. "Institutions." *Journal of Economic Perspectives* 5 (1): 97–112.

Novelli, Mario, Sean Higgins, Mehmet Ugur, and Oscar Valiente. 2014. "The Political Economy of Education Systems in Conflict-Affected Contexts: A Rigorous Literature Review." U.K. Department for International Development, London.

Pepinsky, Thomas B., Jan H. Pierskalla, and Audrey Sacks. 2017. "Bureaucracy and Service Delivery." *Annual Review of Political Science* 20 (1): 249–68.

Rose, Pauline, and Martin Greeley. 2006. "Education in Fragile States: Capturing Lessons and Identifying Good Practice." DAC Fragile States Group, Development Assistance

Committee, Organisation for Economic Co-operation and Development, Paris.

Rosser, Andrew J., and Mohamad Fahmi. 2016. "The Political Economy of Teacher Management in Decentralized Indonesia." Policy Research Working Paper 7913, World Bank, Washington, DC.

Sandefur, Justin, and Amanda Glassman. 2015. "The Political Economy of Bad Data: Evidence from African Survey and Administrative Statistics." *Journal of Development Studies* 51 (2): 116–32.

Segal, Lydia G. 2005. *Battling Corruption in America's Public Schools.* Cambridge, MA: Harvard University Press.

Sethi, Aman. 2015. "The Mystery of India's Deadly Exam Scam." *Guardian*, December 17. https://www.theguardian.com/world/2015/dec/17/the-mystery-of-indias-deadly-exam-scam.

Sharma, Rashmi. 1999. "What Manner of Teacher: Some Lessons from Madhya Pradesh." *Economic and Political Weekly* 34 (25): 1597–1607.

Sharma, Rashmi, and Vimala Ramachandran, eds. 2009. *The Elementary Education System in India: Exploring Institutional Structures, Processes, and Dynamics.* New Delhi: Routledge.

Shields, Robin, and Jeremy Rappleye. 2008. "Differentiation, Development, (Dis)Integration: Education in Nepal's 'People's War.'" *Research in Comparative and International Education* 3 (1): 91–102.

Shrestha, Unika. 2017. "Beyond Politics: The Role of Teachers' Unions in Promoting Quality Education." Background note, World Bank, Washington, DC.

Stevens, Mitchell, and Michael Kirst. 2015. *Remaking College: The Changing Ecology of Higher Education.* Stanford, CA: Stanford University Press.

Taylor, Nick, Johan Muller, and Penny Vinjevold. 2003. *Getting Schools Working: Research and Systemic School Reform in South Africa.* Cape Town: Pearson Education South Africa.

Wiborg, Susanne. 2017. "Teachers Unions in the Nordic Countries: Solidarity and the Politics of Self-Interest." *The Comparative Politics of Education: Teachers Unions and Education Systems around the World*, edited by Terry M. Moe and Susanne Wiborg, 144–91. Cambridge, U.K.: Cambridge University Press.

Willis, Eliza, Christopher da CB Garman, and Stephan Haggard. 1999. "The Politics of Decentralization in Latin America." *Latin American Research Review* 34 (1): 7–56.

World Bank. 2007. "Spending for Development: Making the Most of Indonesia's New Opportunities; Indonesia Public Expenditure Review 2007." World Bank, Washington, DC.

———. 2016. *Making Politics Work for Development: Harnessing Transparency and Citizen Engagement.* Policy Research Report Series. Washington, DC: World Bank.

———. 2017. *World Development Report 2017: Governance and the Law.* Washington, DC: World Bank.

How to escape low-learning traps

Tackling the technical and political constraints that misalign education systems requires action on three fronts: investing in better information on learning; mobilizing coalitions for learning; and adopting a more iterative, adaptive approach to change.

Since 1995, England has substantially improved the literacy and numeracy skills of primary schoolchildren using good political strategy and sound technical solutions.[1] As a result, the proportion of students in grade 4 reaching the intermediate benchmark in the Trends in International Mathematics and Science Study (TIMSS) assessment of mathematics shot up from 54 percent in 1995 to 80 percent in 2015 (figure 11.1)—an achievement matched by few other countries.[2] Poor education outcomes had become an important issue in the 1997 national elections, and the new government responded with a national strategy at the start of its term in 1998.[3]

At the heart of the reforms was a redesign of how teachers taught. The new strategy set clear targets for the country, as well as for individual schools, based on regular, publicly available data on student achievement. The targets provided incentives for local education authorities, teachers, and principals. The government adjusted school inspections to reflect the new curriculum; it also strengthened the links between teacher performance and pay. A revamped professional development program, supported by local literacy consultants, helped teachers implement the new strategy. Local governments received substantial new funding for implementation. Literacy and numeracy "hours," introduced as part of the new strategy, significantly improved early learning outcomes.[4] The program has continued to evolve, with more support focused on disadvantaged learners.

Reforms that improve learning rely on good strategies—both political and technical. This chapter draws lessons from various experiences to identify how opportunities for reform emerge and how politicians, bureaucrats, parents, and students can seize them. It focuses on three entry points for addressing systemic political and technical challenges: improving information, building coalitions and strengthening incentives, and encouraging innovation and agility. Most countries need all three.

Improving information

Addressing weaknesses in education systems is difficult when accurate, usable information on learning is lacking. Without it, stakeholders cannot hold politicians and bureaucrats accountable, assess system performance, or design effective policies to improve learning. Though it might not be enough on its own, better information on learning can provide the substance needed for better political strategies and the evidence base needed for effective policies.

Information can increase political incentives to improve learning

The absence of information on learning can weaken the political incentives to provide good public services. Targeted programs or even direct vote buying are sometimes exchanged for political support,

Figure 11.1 Primary school numeracy has increased dramatically in England

TIMSS mathematics scores for grade 4 students, and share of students reaching the intermediate benchmark in TIMSS mathematics assessment

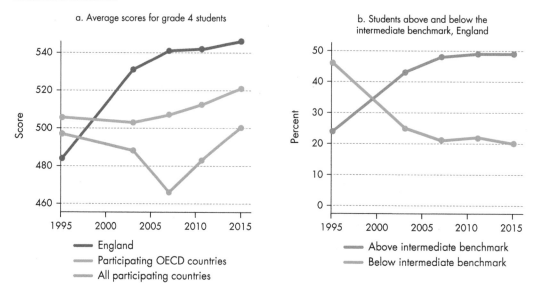

a. Average scores for grade 4 students

b. Students above and below the intermediate benchmark, England

England
Participating OECD countries
All participating countries

Above intermediate benchmark
Below intermediate benchmark

Source: WDR 2018 team, using data from Trends in International Mathematics and Science Study (TIMSS), 1995–2015 (https://timssandpirls.bc.edu/). Data at http://bit.do/WDR2018-Fig_11-1.

Note: Students at the intermediate level are able to apply basic mathematical knowledge in straightforward situations; demonstrate an understanding of whole numbers and some understanding of fractions; visualize three-dimensional shapes from two-dimensional representations; and interpret bar graphs, pictographs, and tables to solve simple problems.

resulting in poor service delivery.[5] Better information can encourage voters to elect politicians who deliver results.[6] For example, using a metric that combines student passing rates with test scores, the federal government in Brazil sets credible education targets that are widely scrutinized (box 11.1). Meeting these targets increases the chances of an incumbent politician being reelected and of bureaucrats keeping their jobs.[7] This example also highlights the value of providing information on learning for areas that correspond with political jurisdictions; because of the overlap, citizens can hold politicians accountable for progress on education targets. But whether information can shift incentives toward a greater focus on learning depends on the broader context. For example, better information in just one sector is unlikely to disrupt patronage networks in countries where clientelism is entrenched across the political system.

Information can also improve incentives in schools

Information on school performance can make local education systems work better. In many developing countries, parents have limited information on the quality of their local schools. In Pakistan, providing parents with information on learning outcomes

increased competition between schools. As a result, learning outcomes improved in both public and private schools, and private school fees were cut.[8] Parents can also use information to pressure schools to raise standards.[9] For example, the provision of report cards has strengthened accountability in some countries.[10] Interventions of this kind work best where power relations between actors in an education system are not highly unequal or organized to support patronage networks, and where frontline service providers have autonomy to respond to community demands.[11] When these factors prevent parents' voices from being heard, it can encourage some, especially middle-class parents, to opt out of the public education system, weakening pressure on governments to improve learning across the system.[12]

Information can also help ensure that resources go where they are intended. In the mid-1990s, schools in Uganda received only around a quarter of their intended per student grant allocations. The government began to publish information on the timing and amount of transfers made to districts for school capitation grants so that schools could monitor local administrators. This move increased the share of grant funding reaching schools by reducing capture of funding by district offices. Consistent with the feedback

Box 11.1 Using information to align incentives with learning in Brazil

From 2000 to 2012, Brazil's learning outcomes on the Programme for International Student Assessment (PISA) showed steady improvement, with gains in some subjects concentrated among poorer-performing students. Underlying this progress were reforms that strengthened accountability for system performance, reduced funding inequalities across Brazil's diverse regions, and provided cash transfers to the neediest families. Improvements in information underpinned these reforms.

Better information made it much easier to hold education agencies accountable for learning. A state-level learning assessment introduced in 1995 was extended 10 years later to cover all fourth- and eighth-grade students. The central government combined assessment results with student promotion rates to create an index of basic education quality (Índice de Desenvolvimento da Educação Básica, IDEB) for every school, municipality, state, and

region in Brazil. Targets based on this index are used by system administrators at every level, as well as by parents, to hold schools and local administrations accountable for learning.

Better information also raised the incentives for politicians to improve performance. Public awareness of the index is high, with the biannual release of IDEB scores generating extensive media coverage and debate. This not only places education quality high on the political agenda, but also makes it an important factor when citizens choose their local representatives.

Crucially, the government also uses the index to target low-performing schools for additional support and introduce programs to motivate system actors. For example, schools receive bonuses based on annual improvements in IDEB scores, and evidence suggests this move has contributed to better learning.

Sources: WDR 2018 team, based on Bruns, Evans, and Luque (2011); Ferraz and Bruns (2012); OECD (2016); Toral (2016).

loop described in the next section, schools in areas with better access to newspapers benefited the most.[13]

Good information is also vital for monitoring, evaluating, and guiding systems

System managers need information to monitor and analyze system performance. School supervisors need information on student learning outcomes to identify and address poorly performing schools. Good research and evaluation on programs and policies aimed at improving learning can support better implementation by enabling feedback loops. In the early 2000s, Cambodia's scholarship program sought to improve learning outcomes for disadvantaged students. An early evaluation of the program found that it improved attainment and narrowed gender gaps in enrollment, but it failed to reach the poorest children or improve learning.[14] In 2006, as a result of these findings, the government improved the targeting of poorer children. It then experimented with using the scholarships to encourage learning. Introducing merit-based criteria into student selection increased enrollment and improved learning, raising mathematics test scores by about 0.17 standard deviations.[15]

Research and evaluation can also build support for effective programs across political cycles.

Oportunidades, Mexico's conditional cash transfer program, has endured since 1997 despite political and economic changes. Because they provided solid evidence of how the program improved the lives of children, impact evaluations were key to the decision to continue the program after a new government was elected in 2000.[16]

But many information and knowledge systems are not serving these purposes

Information needed to improve learning is lacking in many countries. An assessment of capacity to monitor progress toward the Sustainable Development Goals found that, of 121 countries, a third lacked data on learning outcomes at the end of primary school, and half had insufficient information on learning at the end of lower secondary school.[17] Even fewer have the data to track these learning outcomes over time. Information systems in the education sector, which are often weak, are rarely used for decision making, planning, or implementation.

There are many barriers to using information to improve learning outcomes. In Tanzania, widely publicized results from citizen-led learning assessments influenced public perceptions of education and shifted the government's focus toward learning (box 11.2). Yet such direct links between evidence and

Box 11.2 Citizen-led assessments have raised awareness of the learning crisis in South Asia and Sub-Saharan Africa

Citizen-led learning assessments are locally designed measurements of basic reading and mathematics competencies. Typically conducted by networks of civil society organizations, these assessments test children whether they are in or out of school—something that conventional testing cannot do. Their goal is to increase awareness of learning outcomes and to encourage stakeholders to take action to improve learning. Citizen-led assessments have been conducted mainly in South Asia and Sub-Saharan Africa. For example, the Campaign for Popular Education (CAMPE)—a network of over 1,000 nongovernmental organizations (NGOs), researchers, and educators in Bangladesh—began carrying out assessments of this kind in 1999.

Evaluations of these initiatives concluded that:

- The public finds these assessments more salient than larger-scale, more complex national assessments, because the citizen-led assessments focus on a narrower set of basic competencies, starting with recognizing letters and numbers.

- The initiatives successfully disseminated their results and raised awareness about the learning crisis. They also increased the focus on learning in government planning documents.
- In India, partnerships between some state governments and Pratham, an NGO that seeks to improve education quality, have designed interventions to address the problems identified by the Annual Status of Education Report (ASER) assessment. Moreover, the government of India now holds its National Achievement Survey annually (rather than once every three years) to track learning more frequently.

While the assessment results have led to action in some cases, the link to improved learning is not automatic. Over the short period that the ASER in India and Uwezo[a] in Tanzania have been operating, their assessment results do not show any clear overall pattern of increases in learning—although some Indian states showed significant improvements between 2010 and 2016.

Sources: WDR 2018 team, based on Chowdhury, Choudhury, and Nath (1999); Rath and others (2015); R4D (2015).

a. *Uwezo* means "capability" in Kiswahili.

policy making are often missing.[18] Some evaluations take too long to inform decision making; others fail to track key drivers of low system performance. Even where usable information exists, government agencies may lack the incentives or capacity to use it well.[19] Independence also matters: reliable, salient information can provide incentives for better performance, but biased media may protect the interests of particular groups at the expense of better public services. In Argentina between 1998 and 2007, newspapers that received government funding published fewer reports on corruption than did others.[20]

What are the characteristics of an information system that promotes learning (table 11.1)? First, information needs to be credible, politically salient, and publicly available. Second, clear targets for progress

Table 11.1 Principles for making the most of information and the roles that actors can play

Principles for making the best use of information	Roles that different actors can play
• Provide regular, credible, politically salient, and publicly available information on learning. • Set clear targets or expectations for learning, so there is a benchmark for judging performance. • Align information with the political and administrative jurisdictions that have authority to act. • Build information systems that are responsive to the policy cycle and facilitate decision making.	• *Government institutions:* Produce and disseminate national assessment results; conduct in-house evaluations; support education research and evaluation in external research institutes. • *Civil society and private sector:* Produce and disseminate citizen-led learning assessments; use assessments and research to support interventions that improve learning.

Source: WDR 2018 team.

on learning can strengthen incentives by providing measures of system performance. Third, meaningful information on learning needs to be aligned with political or decision-making power, so that the public can hold education decision makers more accountable. Finally, information needs to be usable by policy makers, administrators, and other system actors—that is, it must be timely, accurate, policy relevant, and sensitive to the policy cycle.

Building coalitions and strengthening incentives

Education systems are made up of many actors who pursue interests that do not always align with learning. Addressing this requires action on two fronts. First, coalitions of interest groups are needed to build a consensus around the actions that will strengthen accountability for better learning. This often requires mobilizing support from groups that are not actively involved in agenda-setting or that do not engage with others. Second, the incentives of bureaucrats and other system actors need to align more closely with learning (table 11.2).

Mobilizing support and building coalitions to improve learning

System actors have a better chance of enacting reforms when they act collectively. Some actors have more power to shift policy toward learning, in part because they are better organized.[21] For example, in many countries teachers' unions have a powerful voice in debates on reform, whereas the collective voice of parents and students is often muted.

Mobilizing support and building coalitions of a range of system actors have helped to improve learning. Many countries have built support for proposed policy changes through wide-ranging consultations that try to bring together key interest groups.[22] Peru's Business Association for Education organized an information campaign that helped shift public opinion to support reforms that began in 2006. Government reformers used information on the poor learning outcomes of the education system to mobilize public support for efforts to strengthen teacher accountability, which led to sustained improvements in learning.[23] Alliances between education stakeholders have also formed in some countries to realize the right to education through the legal system (box 11.3).

Though mobilization efforts can be successful at rebalancing interests, they may be less successful at shifting the interests of those opposed to reforms. Education reform is a long process, and well-organized opposition can derail it, particularly during implementation. In Peru, the government successfully mobilized public support to get reforms approved, but it was less successful at getting buy-in from teachers, which led to continued resistance from teachers' unions during implementation. While the broad reform direction remained intact and learning improved, this experience highlights a potential trade-off between managing the politics of reform and getting implementation right. When reformers have to devote effort to managing opposition, that effort can divert attention from implementing reforms well. Lack of buy-in from important groups deters them from contributing to policy design or implementation, thereby undermining the sustainability of the reform.[24]

Building broad-based coalitions of stakeholders is important at all stages of the policy cycle. Malaysia created a performance delivery unit to spearhead comprehensive reforms in many sectors, including education. The unit uses "labs" that build coalitions of stakeholders and involve them in all stages of reform,

Table 11.2 Principles for building effective coalitions and the roles that actors can play

Principles for building effective coalitions	Roles that different actors can play
• Mobilize support for reforms through clear articulation of the problems of low learning. • Develop a political strategy to mobilize support and build long-term coalitions for learning. • Avoid direct confrontation in favor of negotiation and compensation where possible. • Encourage strong partnerships between schools and communities. • Strengthen the capabilities of organizations responsible for education services.	• *Government institutions:* Develop open, inclusive spaces to discuss reform and identify technically and politically feasible solutions; build the appropriate institutional capacity. • *Civil society and business organizations:* Advocate for better education systems; support community and parent action at all levels to improve outcomes. • *Teachers and unions:* Advocate for system improvements; use system knowledge to engage in debates on reform.

Source: WDR 2018 team.

Box 11.3 Using the legal system to press for change

With more than 80 percent of national constitutions recognizing the right to education, courts have become an increasingly important arena for holding governments accountable for education policies and practices.

In recent years, India and Indonesia have seen a significant increase in education rights litigation. In India, this trend has been driven by the adoption in 2009 of the landmark Right of Children to Free and Compulsory Education Act. Cases have included demands to ensure equal access to education, the fulfillment of minimum service standards, and assurance that governments will fulfill their spending obligations. Many of these cases have been successful. The Indian Supreme Court has consistently ruled in favor of upholding quotas for poor children in private schools. The High Court in Uttarakhand required the state government to adopt minimum qualification standards for teachers. And in Indonesia, parents succeeded in enforcing constitutional provisions that obligated the government to spend 20 percent of its budget on education.

These cases have often been brought by individuals or small groups, with nongovernmental organization (NGO) activists and teachers' unions providing technical and financial support. An assessment of the impact of litigation of this kind in India and Indonesia found the following:

- The extent to which the legal system has been used to press for policy changes depends significantly on the nature of the court system, the presence of support structures for legal mobilization, and the ideology of the courts.
- Using education rights litigation effectively is conditional on judges who are open to such cases; civil society groups that can help citizens press their claims; and broader political mobilization.
- Policy-oriented litigation has mainly served the interests of poor or marginalized groups, even though sections of the middle class have been centrally involved in much of the litigation. Gains have largely come through better access to education, although successes have often been at the expense of quality education for the middle class.
- Litigation as a strategy for improving learning outcomes has its limitations. Often, judgments need to be enforced by the same public officials who were the target of the initial lawsuit. Even when judgments are implemented, they are more often about ensuring access than improving learning. Courts typically lack the necessary expertise on learning, especially where information on learning outcomes is scarce.

Source: WDR 2018 team, based on Rosser and Joshi (2017).

from design to implementation.[25] Stakeholders typically come together in the labs for six to nine weeks at the start of reforms to discuss priorities, agree on performance indicators, and produce implementation plans. During implementation, minilabs bring stakeholders together to adjust plans. Programs introduced under the process are credited with increasing grade 3 literacy rates in Malaysia from 89 percent in 2009 to close to 100 percent in 2012. The approach has been exported to other countries, including India, South Africa, and Tanzania (box 11.4).

Without efforts to build coalitions for learning, reforms are less likely to endure. Even if evidence shows that the reforms improve learning, their sustainability is at risk when they are misunderstood or unpopular among system actors. In Poland, large-scale changes in the structure of the education system were introduced in 1999 as part of broader decentralization reforms. These reforms have been credited with improving student learning outcomes significantly.[26]

At the outset, efforts to build a supporting coalition were only half-hearted, and despite the learning gains, the reforms have remained unpopular. The election of a new government in 2015 led to heated debate on whether to scrap key elements of the original reforms.[27] Building a coalition may require better communication strategies—or it may require changing the reform design, to one that is second-best technically but easier to implement and sell to stakeholders.

A gradual, negotiated approach to reform may work better than confrontation. Where coalitions of system actors foster collaboration around shared goals, reforms are more likely to succeed. The history of reforms to improve teaching in Chile demonstrates how gradual, negotiated reforms can build strong coalitions for change (box 11.5). Since Chile's return to democracy, successive governments have adjusted the working conditions of teachers to improve their welfare, while also linking pay and career development more closely to performance. These changes

Box 11.4 Using "labs" to build coalitions for learning

Rapidly deteriorating results on school-leaving examinations, together with other newly available information on poor system performance, motivated policy makers in Tanzania to launch the ambitious Big Results Now in Education (BRN) program in 2013. The BRN adopted a "service delivery" approach that was first introduced in the United Kingdom in the early 1990s and then adapted successfully in Malaysia in 2009.

At the heart of the approach was a six-week-long "lab" to identify priority reform areas and develop mutually agreed-on delivery plans. The lab brought together all the key system actors—government officials, academics, teachers' unions, development partners, civil society organizations—at a level senior enough to ensure follow-through. Together, the lab participants drafted nine key initiatives, developed step-by-step implementation plans, and assigned responsibilities for those steps.

The lab process made it possible to introduce a complex package of politically sensitive reforms. For example, the government introduced monetary and nonmonetary incentives to reward the most improved schools, along with accountability measures that used public examination results to rank schools. The BRN also introduced, for the first time, a national sample-based assessment to measure early grade literacy and numeracy. Communication campaigns succeeded in generating very high levels of public awareness of the BRN's objectives nationwide.

Although the program has been running for only four years, there are signs that it has begun to improve learning outcomes. However, the program has not been without its difficulties; for example, a recent review highlighted the difficulties in coordination between the government agencies responsible for education. But over the past few years, examination results have slowly improved, and primary school students have made gains in early grade reading.

Sources: WDR 2018 team, based on Sabarwal, Joshi, and Blackmon (2017); Todd and Attfield (2017); World Bank (2017b).

Box 11.5 Reformers in Chile negotiated changes gradually

In the early 2000s Chile's education system registered significant, sustained improvements in learning levels. The proportion of 15-year-olds who achieved reading scores at or above a Programme for International Student Assessment (PISA) level of proficiency increased from 52 percent to 69 percent between 2000 and 2015 (figure B11.5.1).

Much of the improvement was attributable to the Sistema Nacional de Evaluación de Desempeño (National Performance Evaluation System; SNED) program implemented in 1996. This program began by awarding teacher bonuses based on school-level indicators of performance. In 2004 individual teacher incentives were introduced, based on mandatory performance evaluations of public school teachers. By the end of the 2000s, these incentives accounted for 15–25 percent of the average teacher salary. Rigorous evaluations of the group-based program revealed that the incentives significantly improved student learning.

The gradual shift from school to individual incentive payments was a pragmatic attempt to address the potential

Figure B11.5.1 Reading scores have improved in Chile

PISA reading scores

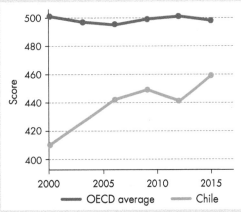

Source: WDR 2018 team, using data from the Programme for International Student Assessment (PISA) (www.oecd.org/pisa). Data at http://bit.do /WDR2018-Fig_B11-5-1.

(Box continues next page)

Box 11.5 Reformers in Chile negotiated changes gradually (continued)

opposition of teachers' unions to performance-related pay. Before implementing a mandatory program for all teachers, the administration introduced a voluntary individual assessment and incentive system that set a precedent for teacher evaluation. Because these steps allowed time to adjust and gain support for the new system, they were key to its success.

Establishing credibility with the teachers' union early on was another key strategy. The Teacher Statute passed in 1991 conferred civil service status on teachers, guaranteeing associated job benefits, protection, and an opportunity for centralized wage negotiations. This move sent a positive signal to teachers. Trust between the union and the government increased further through regular discussions on the implementation of reforms. As part of these efforts, union members codesigned the performance evaluations used for the incentive program.

A final factor in the successful adoption of these reforms was their inclusion in a broader set of reforms that increased resources for education and raised teachers' salaries. SNED became part of the teacher professionalism pillar of the Full School Day reform package. More teachers were covered by the reforms, and the incentive amount was increased. Salary increases before the start of the program may have helped to lessen opposition to the mandatory individual pay incentive.

As a consequence, the Chilean programs remain one of the few long-running "pay for performance"–type reforms that have been successfully scaled to the national level. In other contexts, such reforms have often been unpopular, but in Chile the reforms continue: in 2016 new legislation passed to widen the coverage of the incentive program, while strengthening teacher professional development.

Sources: WDR 2018 team, based on Avalos and Assael (2006); Contreras and Rau (2012); Delannoy (2000); Mizala and Schneider (2014); OECD (2016); World Bank (2017a).

have contributed to Chile's steady improvement in international learning assessments.

Negotiations can also include strategies to compensate actors disadvantaged by reform. One such strategy is to provide targeted assistance to students harmed by reforms to improve system efficiency. Additional services for children affected by school closures, for example, can ease school consolidations.[28] Another strategy is to use "dual-track" reforms to protect some incumbents from the negative impacts of reforms. For example, pay-for-performance programs in Peru and in the District of Columbia in the United States were initially introduced voluntarily.

Compensating perceived losers can help get reforms approved, but that approach comes with risks. In 2005 the Indonesian government introduced a comprehensive reform program aimed at raising the competencies of teachers. Teacher certification was the centerpiece of the reforms, with teachers required to pass a competency test to continue teaching.[29] In exchange for these new obligations, the negotiated agreement provided certified teachers with an additional monthly allowance as large as their base salary. But early in implementation, the requirements for certification were diluted because of political pressures, so that teachers were no longer required to pass a competency test. In the end, the reforms had little impact on teacher competencies or student learning,

but they had a major impact on public spending.[30] By 2011, with less than a third of teachers certified, 9 percent of the education budget already went to certification allowances.[31]

Building partnerships between schools and communities

Sustained reform requires strong partnerships between schools and communities. Where incentives for systemwide reform are weak, local action can substitute. In South Africa, the political and economic context has constrained efforts to improve education performance in some provinces, but local progress has been made possible in some schools through strong partnerships between parents and schools.[32] Local partnerships are particularly important in fragile and conflict-affected areas.[33] For example, a program that built community-based schools in Afghanistan reduced the distance to school, increased enrollment, and improved learning outcomes, particularly for girls.[34] Yet these local partnerships tend to work best when supported by responsive higher-level institutions, which are sorely lacking in fragile environments.

Aligning the incentives and capacity of system actors with learning

The success of reforms depends on the ability, incentives, and motivations of public officials. Managing education systems effectively requires competent public service–oriented personnel, which in turn means commensurate pay and working conditions.[35] But if the political economy of education is misaligned with public goals, candidates with less desirable attributes may be attracted to public service. In Mexico, teachers were often hired based on political patronage rather than merit, which resulted in lower-quality hires compared with those in test-based systems.[36]

Efforts to build the capacity of bureaucracies have been disappointing.[37] Even where individual capacity is built successfully, the incentives to use this capacity to develop and implement effective policies are often absent.[38] Put another way, building organizational capability to improve education outcomes tends to work best when incentives in education systems are aligned with the same goals. For example, where politicians face stronger incentives to provide public goods, this has inspired efforts to build professional bureaucracies that can deliver better public services.[39]

Encouraging innovation and agility

Political and technical complexities make it challenging to design and implement policies to improve learning. Some parts of the solution to low learning are relatively straightforward. Inadequate infrastructure and learning materials, while logistically challenging, can be addressed directly: the technologies needed are well known, and most education systems have enough experience solving these issues. But improving what happens in the classroom is much harder. It involves changing student and teacher behavior, as well as supporting teachers in efforts to tailor their teaching to the needs of their students. The traditional approaches to reform—in which predefined interventions are introduced with little room to adapt during implementation—are rarely effective.

Learning reforms need a more agile approach, with room for adaptation.[40] This is not the same as experimenting with different interventions in pilot projects. Rather, it means testing approaches at scale in their political and economic contexts and using the existing capabilities of implementing agencies. A recent review of complex public management reforms, including in education, highlighted the key elements of successful reforms.[41] Those reforms started out with a clear articulation of the problem, together with an initial set of potential solutions, and then adopted solutions that emerged from experimentation during implementation (figure 11.2). Final interventions tended to be hybrids, drawing on local and global evidence.

Figure 11.2 Problem-driven iterative adaptation drives successful reforms

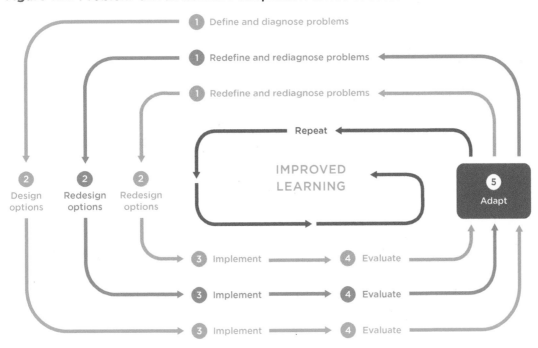

Source: Adapted from Andrews, Pritchett, and Woolcock (2017).

Searching for solutions to local problems

All systems have some parts that work well; these parts can be used to identify technically and politically feasible approaches to improving learning. In Misiones Province, Argentina, student dropout rates were high. But some schools bucked the trend: teachers agreed on informal learning contracts with parents instead of blaming them for poor student performance. Schools that adopted more constructive approaches to parent-teacher relations saw dropout fall significantly.[42] Schools approach challenges in different ways, so analysis of positive outliers could be useful for policy making (box 11.6).

Local innovations, however, may not be enough to close the learning gap between countries. Employing principles from the growing global knowledge can provide useful ideas for improving learning in specific contexts. A more iterative approach to system change can be a way to adapt interventions inspired by global experiences to local contexts.

Integrating an iterative and adaptive approach to policy making and implementation

Recent examples show how an iterative, adaptive approach can strengthen education systems and improve learning. In India, an experiment showed that grouping children by ability and using level-appropriate teaching along with continual assessment improved students' reading abilities. Recognizing that a small-scale experiment was no guarantee of success in the government system, Pratham—the NGO responsible for the original evaluation—experimented with different approaches to level-appropriate teaching in government schools. This experimentation tested the assumptions of the original model and identified factors behind the earlier success. It then identified two approaches to implementation that could work at scale.[43] Even in fragile states, where system capabilities are limited, iterative approaches like this have been successful at restoring essential education services (box 11.7).

Policy makers can test policies before introducing them more widely. Whole-system reforms are difficult to evaluate because they lack an appropriate counterfactual, making it difficult to trace the impacts of policy change and adapt strategies to improve learning. Small pilots can overcome these difficulties, but it is hard to assess whether they will be effective without the attention and nurturing that can occur in a pilot. As a middle way, China and other countries have tested new policies in specific regions.[44] Policy makers first identify

---

Box 11.6 High-performing schools in the West Bank and Gaza offer some learning lessons

The United Nations Relief and Works Agency (UNRWA) provides over 300,000 refugees in the West Bank and Gaza with basic education services. In multiple rounds of international assessments, UNRWA schools outperformed public schools, delivering the equivalent of one year's additional learning despite the lower socioeconomic status of UNRWA students and lower per student spending.[a] Drivers of their better performance include:

- *Greater parental involvement* in school activities and a close partnership between schools, households, and refugee communities, which contributes to a shared sense of purpose and collaborative mechanisms for monitoring and support.
- *More effective teacher support systems.* Teachers are trained using standards that clearly articulate what students should know and be able to do in each grade.

Although preservice training is similar in UNRWA and public schools, UNRWA teachers complete a two-year training program in classroom instruction, resulting in teaching approaches that are better aligned with learning.

- *Assessment and evaluation.* UNRWA schools have more rigorous, more frequent student assessments and teacher evaluations than public schools.
- *Effective school leadership.* UNRWA invests in developing qualified principals who can support their teachers effectively.

Identifying lessons from high-performing schools is not always easy. Some factors such as school leadership that drive high performance may be idiosyncratic, making them hard to replicate. Drawing on large samples of schools can help identify more generalizable lessons.

Source: WDR 2018 team, based on Abdul-Hamid and others (2016).
a. This comparison is for UNRWA schools and public schools in Jordan.

Box 11.7 Burundi improved education services by iterating and adapting

After a protracted civil war and long peace process in Burundi, a new government and new constitution in 2005 led to a renewed emphasis on public services. Many schools had been destroyed, and management systems had collapsed. As the new government took office, primary net enrollment rates stood at just 56 percent, student-classroom ratios were 87:1, and 20 students shared a single mathematics textbook on average.

The government prioritized reducing the high student-textbook ratios and delays in delivery as part of a broader rapid-results initiative that had three stages:

- *Shaping.* In this stage, a reform team identified why there were not enough textbooks. To ensure practical solutions, the team comprised stakeholders from across the education system, including provincial education directors and parent-teacher associations.
- *Implementation.* Senior government officials gave the team authority to implement its new approach in a single province. As implementation progressed, the team regularly adjusted its action plan.
- *Planning for sustainability.* After reviewing the intervention's performance, senior government officials decided how to scale up the program to other provinces.

The initiative far exceeded its targets. Textbook availability increased, and average delivery times fell from over a year to 60 days. This success led to similar initiatives to tackle teacher payroll problems, as well as many other service delivery problems beyond education.

Source: WDR 2018 team, based on Campos, Randrianarivelo, and Winning (2015).

---

the main problems; then they agree on which solutions to subject to experimentation. They develop proposals for experiments, in part by analyzing solutions adopted in other countries to tackle similar issues, with different regions trying alternatives. Successful policies are then rolled out to other regions. Belgium and the Netherlands have adopted similar approaches.[45]

Giving stakeholders the authority and autonomy to adopt such approaches runs counter to how many education agencies operate. Closed systems limit the autonomy of system actors and judge performance based on compliance with formal rules over resource use, leaving little room for innovation. By contrast, more open systems that have a sharper focus on outcomes are more likely to see greater innovation across the education system (table 11.3).[46]

Good information systems and broad-based coalitions are also needed

A capacity to learn from the implementation of new innovations is vital. Information systems that provide rapid, regular, accurate feedback are crucial for more adaptive approaches to improving learning. Some countries are beginning to build these kinds of capabilities into their education agencies. Peru's MineduLAB in the Ministry of Education is a collaboration between government agencies and experienced researchers.[47] The lab introduces innovations directly

Table 11.3 Principles for encouraging innovation at scale and the roles that actors can play

Principles for encouraging innovation and agility in approaches to improving learning	Roles that different system actors can play
• Adopt a more iterative and adaptive approach to the design and implementation of policies. • Identify promising solutions from within the education system, as well as the global knowledge base. • Establish information systems that provide rapid feedback to support implementation. • Develop the capability of education agencies, an enabling environment, and autonomy to encourage innovation.	• *Government institutions:* Develop an enabling environment and incentives for innovation and a more iterative approach. • *Civil society and private sector providers:* Experiment with different approaches to improving learning.

Source: WDR 2018 team.

into government schools, and information from ministry systems (rather than individual data collection exercises) must be used by researchers to evaluate the new programs. Results must also be available within the same academic year. In MineduLAB's first year, innovations included providing more comparative information on school performance and introducing modules to encourage primary school students to adopt a growth mindset. The program is still new, but its approach is promising.

To be sustainable, these approaches need broad support. Though this iterative approach can help in developing more effective strategies, it comes with risks for actors in education systems. Politicians can incur significant costs if experiments fail or divert resources away from more traditional activities. Students can also suffer if new approaches disrupt their schooling without improving it. Yet some risk-taking is vital if education systems are to improve learning. Mobilizing stakeholder support and providing space for consultations from the outset can reduce the risks.

Education systems need to be agile to exploit critical moments

Politicians and education system managers also need to respond quickly when changes create opportunities to improve broad-based learning. This context changes infrequently, but when it does change it provides opportunities for significant changes in education policy. During the martial law period of the 1970s in the Philippines, government spending on education fell below 2 percent of the gross domestic product (GDP). In the 1980s, the People's Power Revolution restored democratic rule, ushering in a new government that was more responsive to demands for broader access to education. Trade liberalization increased the demand for skilled workers, further raising the incentives for better education. With these societal shifts, public investment in education increased by 2 percentage points of GDP between 1980 and 2000 (figure 11.3).

Critical junctures often arise from broader decentralization and reform efforts, as in the education reforms in Latin America during the 1990s.[48] Beyond shifting responsibility for education services to local governments and schools, decentralization can provide opportunities to better align important elements of education systems. After early decentralization reforms in Poland, the government introduced formula-based funding mechanisms to link school funding levels more closely to school needs. This

Figure 11.3 Trends in public education spending in the Philippines track changes in the broader political and economic context

Public education spending as percentage of GDP, and measures of democracy and trade openness, the Philippines (1960–2000)

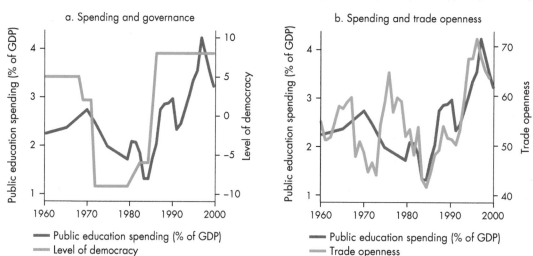

Source: Ansell (2006). Adapted with permission from Ben W. Ansell; further permission required for reuse. Data at http://bit.do/WDR2018-Fig_11-3.

Note: Level of democracy is measured by the polity score, which consists of an evaluation of the competitiveness and openness of elections, the nature of political participation in general, and the extent of checks on executive authority. A high positive score corresponds to strong democratic institutions; negative scores indicate more autocratic systems. Trade openness is measured by the inverted Hiscox Kastner score, which gauges the degree to which a country deviates from an optimal level of imports from a hypothetical protection-free environment. Higher scores indicate greater openness.

shift aligned funding with new realities, helping the system reduce inefficiencies.[49]

To innovate effectively—as indeed to build coalitions and use information for reform—education systems need strong, competent leadership. Research highlights three key attributes of effective leaders. First, they can clearly articulate problems and present clear visions for how to tackle them. Second, they mobilize human and financial resources around agreed-on goals and build coalitions to advocate for change and support implementation. Finally, effective leaders focus on identifying solutions that fit the institutional context.[50]

How can external actors support initiatives to improve learning?

Support the creation of objective, politically salient information

Global education initiatives can improve political incentives for action. The Millennium Development Goals (MDGs) were ssuccessful at mobilizing international and domestic actors on development challenges. Though the global impact of the MDGs—including the education goal—is still being debated, the legitimacy that progress could confer on weak or unstable governments was often a powerful incentive for change. Many countries introduced reforms to expand access to schooling in successful efforts to meet the MDGs. The Sustainable Development Goal (SDG) indicators, which will include a set of comparable learning measures, could play a similar role by motivating countries to shift their focus from schooling to learning.

By supporting improvements in learning assessment, external actors can help shine a light on low learning levels and their causes. For one thing, they can help developing countries participate in regional and global assessments, which are an important tool for opening up spaces for change and influencing policy debates.[51] They could also help ensure that test items are linked across countries and across time, which would allow results of different assessments to be more comparable. External actors can also help by supporting national assessment efforts, so that they can provide more politically salient information on learning. The READ program, a partnership among development partners, education practitioners, and low-income country governments, has helped countries strengthen their national assessments, while

also supporting their participation in international assessments.[52]

Beyond support to measure learning, external actors can also help build global knowledge on ways to diagnose system weaknesses and improve learning. This knowledge base has expanded rapidly, but more research is needed on how to adapt promising interventions to specific contexts. External actors can fund research and encourage collaboration among practitioners, researchers, and government institutions to build capacity and locally relevant knowledge on effective ways to improve learning.

Encourage flexibility and support reform coalitions

External actors can also encourage inclusive reforms through project development activities, policy discussions, and support to other system actors. Though there has been much progress on the aid effectiveness agenda first agreed on in the Paris Declaration in 2005, there is still room for improvement. A key aspect of this agenda is building inclusive reforms. But progress in this area has been slow. Across all sectors, only about half of countries were judged to have systems for meaningful dialogue with civil society organizations. Moreover, dialogue between the public and private sectors was judged to be difficult and rarely led to action.[53] Tackling these issues is vital for the emergence of the coalitions needed to design and implement effective policies.

In education, consultative groups and civil society organizations could promote more inclusive reforms. The Civil Society Education Fund (CSEF), launched in 2009, has supported national education coalitions in more than 40 developing countries, and the number of civil society organizations involved in education planning and policy has expanded rapidly.[54] For example, the fund has supported the Ghana National Education Campaign Coalition (GNECC) in lobbying for more participatory education planning, policy formulation, and monitoring. GNECC members have worked together to present new findings on education issues during annual education review meetings and to advocate for change.[55]

Link financing more closely to results that lead to learning

While the overall contribution of development assistance to country investments in education is relatively small, it is important in some low-income countries (figure 11.4). In 2015 international finance accounted for 14 percent of education spending in

Figure 11.4 Most funding for education comes from domestic sources, but international finance is important for low-income countries

Estimated sources of education spending, by income group (2015)

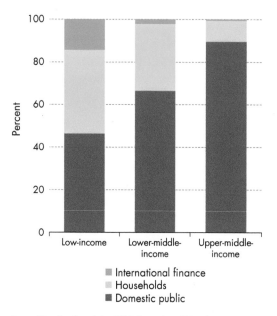

International finance
Households
Domestic public

Source: Education Commission (2016). Data at http://bit.do/WDR2018-Fig_11-4.

low-income countries. But support is much higher in some countries. In Mali, development assistance accounted for approximately 25 percent of public education spending between 2004 and 2010. Moreover, global estimates of the investments required to raise learning as part of the SDGs imply a need to increase development assistance, particularly to low-income countries.[56]

But external actors must provide financing in a way that aligns systems with learning. Projects aimed at narrow aspects of reform or on specific interventions, run the risk of exacerbating existing misalignments, if weaknesses in other parts of the system are not tackled at the same time. For example, projects that support professional development activities but are not aligned with career development incentives are likely to be less sustainable. External actors can support alignment by shifting the focus of systems toward learning, linking their financing to results rather than the provision of specific inputs or activities.

More development partners are using results-based financing in education. These approaches seek to align system components by linking financing to results. They shift the emphasis from inputs toward performance. Some financing is linked directly to student achievement. For example, a U.K. program that supports the education system in Ethiopia provides an agreed-on amount for net increases in the number of students who pass the examination at the end of lower secondary education. The multidonor-financed Big Results Now in Education program in Tanzania links financing to student learning and to intermediate outputs that support improvements in education quality. The ultimate impact of these approaches on system performance is still being evaluated, since they are new. But initial findings suggest they have the potential to tackle system-level constraints and improve system performance.[57]

* * *

There is nothing inevitable about poor learning outcomes, whatever a country's level of development. Some countries have used well-documented reforms to escape low-learning traps, successfully reorienting their systems toward learning. Others have achieved learning outcomes that far exceed what their development level would predict, indicating that they escaped the trap in the past. Though there is no single recipe for achieving broad-based learning, these cases identify three entry points for getting under way. First, deploy information and metrics to shine a light on the hidden exclusion of low learning. Second, build coalitions that can better align incentives toward learning, especially the learning of the most disadvantaged. Third, commit to innovation and agility, using feedback loops for continuous improvement. None of this is easy, but history shows that achieving education's promise will depend on taking up the challenge.

Notes

1. Cassen, McNally, and Vignoles (2015); Stannard and Huxford (2007); Tanner and others (2010).
2. Mullis and others (2016).
3. The numeracy strategy was introduced in 1999.
4. Evaluations of different aspects of the literacy and numeracy program are summarized in, for example, Machin and McNally (2008); McNally (2015); and Stannard and Huxford (2007).
5. Khemani (2015).
6. Banerjee and others (2011); Brender (2003).
7. Dias and Ferraz (2017); Toral (2016).
8. Andrabi, Das, and Khwaja (2015).
9. Barr, Packard, and Serra (2014).
10. Snilstveit and others (2015).
11. Carr-Hill and others (2015); Grandvoinnet, Aslam, and Raha (2015).
12. Banerjee and others (2010); World Bank (2017c).
13. Reinikka and Svensson (2011).
14. Filmer and Schady (2009).
15. Barrera-Osorio and Filmer (2016).
16. UNDP (2011).
17. UIS (2016).
18. Rath and others (2015).
19. Sutcliffe and Court (2005).
20. Di Tella and Franceschelli (2011).
21. Corrales (1999).
22. Bruns and Schneider (2016); Corrales (1999).
23. Bruns and Luque (2015).
24. Bruns and Luque (2015); World Bank (2017c).
25. Sabel and Jordan (2015); World Bank (2017b).
26. Jakubowski (2015); Jakubowski and others (2010).
27. Wojciuk (2017).
28. Beuchert and others (2016).
29. Chang and others (2013).
30. de Ree and others (2015).
31. Chang and others (2013).
32. Levy and others (2016).
33. Mansuri and Rao (2013).
34. Burde and Linden (2012).
35. Besley and Ghatak (2005); Finan, Olken, and Pande (2015).
36. Estrada (2015).
37. World Bank (2017c).
38. Andrews, Pritchett, and Woolcock (2017).
39. Besley and Persson (2009).
40. Andrews, Pritchett, and Woolcock (2017).
41. Andrews (2015).
42. Green (2016); Pascale, Sternin, and Sternin (2010).
43. Banerjee and others (2016).
44. Heilmann (2008).
45. Blanchenay (2016).
46. Andrews, Pritchett, and Woolcock (2013).
47. J-PAL and IPA Perú (2013).
48. Grindle (2004).
49. Alonso and Sánchez (2011).
50. Leftwich (2009).
51. Devarajan and Khemani (2016).
52. World Bank (2015).
53. OECD and UNDP (2016).
54. UNESCO (2015).
55. CSEF (2014). The CSEF is coordinated by the Global Campaign for Education (GCE), with funding from the Global Partnership for Education.
56. Education Commission (2016).
57. Sabarwal, Joshi, and Blackmon (2017).

References

Abdul-Hamid, Husein, Harry Anthony Patrinos, Joel Reyes, Jo Kelcey, and Andrea Diaz Varela. 2016. "Learning in the Face of Adversity: The UNRWA Education Program for Palestine Refugees." World Bank Study Series, World Bank, Washington, DC.

Alonso, Juan Diego, and Alonso Sánchez, eds. 2011. Reforming Education Finance in Transition Countries: Six Case Studies in Per Capita Financing Systems. World Bank Study Series, World Bank, Washington, DC.

Andrabi, Tahir, Jishnu Das, and Asim Ijaz Khwaja. 2015. "Report Cards: The Impact of Providing School and Child Test Scores on Educational Markets." Policy Research Working Paper 7226, World Bank, Washington, DC.

Andrews, Matt J. 2015. "Explaining Positive Deviance in Public Sector Reforms in Development." World Development 74: 197–208.

Andrews, Matt J., Lant Pritchett, and Michael Woolcock. 2013. "Escaping Capability Traps through Problem Driven Iterative Adaptation (PDIA)." World Development 51: 234–44.

———. 2017. Building State Capability: Evidence, Analysis, Action. New York: Oxford University Press.

Ansell, Ben W. 2006. "From the Ballot to the Blackboard: The Redistributive Political Economy of Education." PhD dissertation, Harvard University. http://users.polisci.umn .edu/~ansell/papers/Ben%20Ansell%20Dissertation.pdf.

Avalos, Beatrice, and Jenny Assael. 2006. "Moving from Resistance to Agreement: The Case of the Chilean Teacher Performance Evaluation." International Journal of Educational Research 45 (4): 254–66.

Banerjee, Abhijit Vinayak, Rukmini Banerji, James Berry, Esther Duflo, Harini Kannan, Shobhini Mukerji, Marc Shotland, and Michael Walton. 2016. "Mainstreaming an Effective Intervention: Evidence from Randomized Evaluations of 'Teaching at the Right Level' in India." CEPR Discussion Paper 11530, Centre for Economic Policy Research, London.

Banerjee, Abhijit Vinayak, Rukmini Banerji, Esther Duflo, Rachel Glennerster, and Stuti Khemani. 2010. "Pitfalls of Participatory Programs: Evidence from a Randomized Evaluation in Education in India." American Economic Journal: Economic Policy 2 (1): 1–30.

Banerjee, Abhijit Vinayak, Selvan Kumar, Rohini Pande, and Felix Su. 2011. "Do Informed Voters Make Better Choices? Experimental Evidence from Urban India." Working paper, Harvard University, Cambridge, MA.

Barr, Abigail, Truman Packard, and Danila Serra. 2014. "Participatory Accountability and Collective Action:

Experimental Evidence from Albania." *European Economic Review* 68: 250–69.

Barrera-Osorio, Felipe, and Deon Filmer. 2016. "Incentivizing Schooling for Learning: Evidence on the Impact of Alternative Targeting Approaches." *Journal of Human Resources* 51 (2): 461–99.

Besley, Timothy J., and Maitreesh Ghatak. 2005. "Competition and Incentives with Motivated Agents." *American Economic Review* 95 (3): 616–36.

Besley, Timothy J., and Torsten Persson. 2009. "The Origins of State Capacity: Property Rights, Taxation, and Politics." *American Economic Review* 99 (4): 1218–44.

Beuchert, Louise Voldby, Maria Knoth Humlum, Helena Skyt Nielsen, and Nina Smith. 2016. "The Short-Term Effects of School Consolidation on Student Achievement: Evidence of Disruption?" IZA Discussion Paper 10195, Institute for the Study of Labor, Bonn, Germany.

Blanchenay, Patrick. 2016. "Policy Experimentation in Complex Education Systems." In *Governing Education in a Complex World*, edited by Tracey Burns and Florian Köster, 161–86. Educational Research and Innovation Series. Paris: Centre for Educational Research and Innovation, Organisation for Economic Co-operation and Development.

Brender, Adi. 2003. "The Effect of Fiscal Performance on Local Government Election Results in Israel: 1989–1998." *Journal of Public Economics* 87 (9): 2187–2205.

Bruns, Barbara, David K. Evans, and Javier Luque. 2011. *Achieving World-Class Education in Brazil: The Next Agenda.* Report 65659. Directions in Development: Human Development Series. Washington, DC: World Bank.

Bruns, Barbara, and Javier Luque. 2015. *Great Teachers: How to Raise Student Learning in Latin America and the Caribbean.* With Soledad De Gregorio, David K. Evans, Marco Fernández, Martin Moreno, Jessica Rodriguez, Guillermo Toral, and Noah Yarrow. Latin American Development Forum Series. Washington, DC: World Bank.

Bruns, Barbara, and Ben Ross Schneider. 2016. "Managing the Politics of Quality Reforms in Education: Policy Lessons from Global Experience." Background Paper: The Learning Generation, International Commission on Financing Global Education Opportunity, New York.

Burde, Dana, and Leigh L. Linden. 2012. "The Effect of Village-Based Schools: Evidence from a Randomized Controlled Trial in Afghanistan." NBER Working Paper 18039, National Bureau of Economic Research, Cambridge, MA.

Campos, Jose Edgardo, Benjamina Randrianarivelo, and Kay Winning. 2015. "Escaping the 'Capability Trap': Turning 'Small' Development into 'Big' Development." *International Public Management Review* 16 (1): 99–131.

Carr-Hill, Roy, Caine Rolleston, Tejendra Pherali, Rebecca Schendel, Edwina Peart, and Emma Jones. 2015. *The Effects of School-Based Decision Making on Educational Outcomes in Low- and Middle-Income Contexts: A Systematic Review.* 3ie Grantee Final Review. London: International Initiative for Impact Evaluation.

Cassen, Robert, Sandra McNally, and Anna Vignoles. 2015. *Making a Difference in Education: What the Evidence Says.* Abingdon, U.K.: Routledge.

Chang, Mae Chu, Sheldon Shaeffer, Samer Al-Samarrai, Andrew B. Ragatz, Joppe de Ree, and Ritchie Stevenson. 2013. *Teacher Reform in Indonesia: The Role of Politics and Evidence in Policy Making.* Directions in Development: Human Development Series. Washington, DC: World Bank.

Chowdhury, A. Mushtaque Raza, Rasheda K. Choudhury, and Samir R. Nath. 1999. *Hope Not Complacency: State of Primary Education in Bangladesh 1999.* Dhaka, Bangladesh: Education Watch, Campaign for Popular Education; Dhaka, Bangladesh: University Press.

Contreras, Dante, and Tomás Rau. 2012. "Tournament Incentives for Teachers: Evidence from a Scaled-Up Intervention in Chile." *Economic Development and Cultural Change* 61 (1): 219–46.

Corrales, Javier. 1999. "The Politics of Education Reform: Bolstering the Supply and Demand, Overcoming Institutional Blocks." Report 22549, Education Reform and Management Series, World Bank, Washington, DC.

CSEF (Civil Society Education Fund). 2014. "Civil Society Advocacy: Good Practice Case Studies from Africa." Global Campaign for Education, Johannesburg.

Delannoy, Françoise. 2000. "Educational Reforms in Chile, 1980–1998: A Lesson in Pragmatism." Report 20806, Country Studies, Education Reform and Management Series, World Bank, Washington, DC.

de Ree, Joppe, Karthik Muralidharan, Menno Pradhan, and F. Halsey Rogers. 2015. "Double for Nothing? Experimental Evidence on the Impact of an Unconditional Teacher Salary Increase on Student Performance in Indonesia." NBER Working Paper 21806, National Bureau of Economic Research, Cambridge, MA.

Devarajan, Shantayanan, and Stuti Khemani. 2016. "If Politics Is the Problem, How Can External Actors Be Part of the Solution?" Policy Research Working Paper 7761, World Bank, Washington, DC.

Dias, Marina, and Claudio Ferraz. 2017. "Voting for Quality? The Impact of School Quality Information on Electoral Outcomes." Departamento de Economia, Pontifícia Universidade Católica do Rio de Janeiro, Rio de Janeiro.

Di Tella, Rafael, and Ignacio Franceschelli. 2011. "Government Advertising and Media Coverage of Corruption Scandals." *American Economic Journal: Applied Economics* 3 (4): 119–51.

Education Commission. 2016. *The Learning Generation: Investing in Education for a Changing World.* New York: International Commission on Financing Global Education Opportunity.

Estrada, Ricardo. 2015. "Rules Rather Than Discretion: Teacher Hiring and Rent Extraction." EUI Working Paper MWP 2015/14, Max Weber Program, European University Institute, San Domenico di Fiesole, Italy.

Ferraz, Claudio, and Barbara Bruns. 2012. "Paying Teachers to Perform: The Impact of Bonus Pay in Pernambuco, Brazil." Working paper, World Bank, Washington, DC.

Filmer, Deon, and Norbert R. Schady. 2009. "School Enrollment, Selection, and Test Scores." Policy Research Working Paper 4998, World Bank, Washington, DC.

Finan, Frederico S., Benjamin A. Olken, and Rohini Pande. 2015. "The Personnel Economics of the State." NBER

Working Paper 21825, National Bureau of Economic Research, Cambridge, MA.

Grandvoinnet, Helene, Ghazia Aslam, and Shomikho Raha. 2015. *Opening the Black Box: The Contextual Drivers of Social Accountability*. New Frontiers of Social Policy Series. Washington, DC: World Bank.

Green, Duncan. 2016. *How Change Happens*. Oxford, U.K.: Oxford University Press.

Grindle, Merilee Serrill. 2004. *Despite the Odds: The Contentious Politics of Education Reform*. Princeton, NJ: Princeton University Press.

Heilmann, Sebastian. 2008. "Policy Experimentation in China's Economic Rise." *Studies in Comparative International Development* 43 (1): 1–26.

Jakubowski, Maciej. 2015. "Opening Up Opportunities: Education Reforms in Poland." IBS Policy Paper 01/2015, Intelligent Business Solutions, Gliwice, Poland.

Jakubowski, Maciej, Harry Anthony Patrinos, Emilio Ernesto Porta, and Jerzy Wiśniewski. 2010. "The Impact of the 1999 Education Reform in Poland." Policy Research Working Paper 5263, World Bank, Washington, DC.

J-PAL (Abdul Latif Jameel Poverty Action Lab) and IPA Perú (Peru Country Office, Innovations for Poverty Action). 2013. "Implementación del Laboratorio de Innovación Costo-Efectiva de la Política Educativa: MineduLAB." J-PAL, Santo Domingo, Dominican Republic.

Khemani, Stuti. 2015. "Buying Votes versus Supplying Public Services: Political Incentives to Under-Invest in Pro-poor Policies." *Journal of Development Economics* 177: 84–93.

Leftwich, Adrian. 2009. "Bringing Agency Back In: Politics and Human Agency in Building Institutions and States, Synthesis and Overview Report." DLP Research Paper 6, Developmental Leadership Program, Birmingham, U.K.

Levy, Brian, Robert Cameron, Ursula Hoadley, and Vinothan Naidoo. 2016. "The Politics of Governance and Basic Education: A Tale of Two South African Provinces." Occasional Working Paper 2, Graduate School of Development Policy and Practice, University of Cape Town.

Machin, Stephen, and Sandra McNally. 2008. "The Literacy Hour." *Journal of Public Economics* 92 (5): 1441–62.

Mansuri, Ghazala, and Vijayendra Rao. 2013. *Localizing Development: Does Participation Work?* Policy Research Report Series. Washington, DC: World Bank.

McNally, Sandra. 2015. "Numeracy and Mathematics." In *Making a Difference in Education: What the Evidence Says*, edited by Robert Cassen, Sandra McNally, and A. Vignoles, 123–34. Abingdon, U.K.: Routledge.

Mizala, Alejandra, and Ben Ross Schneider. 2014. "Negotiating Education Reform: Teacher Evaluations and Incentives in Chile (1990–2010)." *Governance* 27 (1): 87–109.

Mullis, I. V. S., M. O. Martin, P. Foy, and M. Hooper. 2016. "TIMSS 2015 International Results in Mathematics." TIMSS and PIRLS International Study Center, Boston College, Chestnut Hill, MA. http://timssandpirls .bc.edu/timss2015/international-results/.

OECD (Organisation for Economic Co-operation and Development). 2016. *PISA 2015 Results: Excellence and Equity in Education*. Vol. 1. Paris: OECD.

OECD (Organisation for Economic Co-operation and Development) and UNDP (United Nations Development Programme). 2016. "Making Development Co-operation More Effective: 2016 Progress Report." Paris: OECD.

Pascale, Richard T., Jerry Sternin, and Monique Sternin. 2010. *The Power of Positive Deviance: How Unlikely Innovators Solve the World's Toughest Problems*. Boston: Harvard Business Press.

R4D (Results for Development Institute). 2015. "Bringing Learning to Light: The Role of Citizen-Led Assessments in Shifting the Education Agenda." R4D, Washington, DC.

Rath, Amitav, Pamela Branch, Dunstan Kishekya, Clement Kihinga, Terry Smutylo, and Kornelia Rassmann. 2015. *Evaluation Twaweza: Tanzania 2009–2014, Final Report*. With the assistance of Constance Lim, Yusra Uzair, and Maya Kovacevic. SIDA Decentralized Evaluation 2015. Stockholm: Department for Africa, Swedish International Development Cooperation Agency.

Reinikka, Ritva, and Jakob Svensson. 2011. "The Power of Information in Public Services: Evidence from Education in Uganda." *Journal of Public Economics* 95 (7): 956–66.

Rosser, Andrew J., and Anuradha Joshi. 2017. "Using Courts to Realize Education Rights and Create Opportunities to Improve Learning." Background paper, World Bank, Washington, DC.

Sabarwal, Shwetlena, Anuradha Joshi, and William Blackmon. 2017. "A Review of the World Bank's Results-Based Financing Mechanism Used for Tanzania's Big Results Now in Education Program: A Process Evaluation." World Bank, Washington, DC.

Sabel, Charles, and Luke Jordan. 2015. "Doing, Learning, Being: Some Lessons Learned from Malaysia's National Transformation Program." Competitive Industries and Innovation Program, World Bank, Washington, DC.

Snilstveit, Birte, Jennifer Stevenson, Daniel Phillips, Martina Vojtkova, Emma Gallagher, Tanja Schmidt, Hannah Jobse, et al. 2015. *Interventions for Improving Learning Outcomes and Access to Education in Low- and Middle-Income Countries*. 3ie Systematic Review 24, London: International Initiative for Impact Evaluation. http://www.3ie impact.org/media/filer_public/2016/07/12/sr24-education -review.pdf.

Stannard, John, and Laura Huxford. 2007. *The Literacy Game: The Story of the National Literacy Strategy*. New York: Routledge.

Sutcliffe, Sophie, and Julius Court. 2005. "Evidence-Based Policymaking: What Is It? How Does It Work? What Relevance for Developing Countries?" Research Reports and Studies Series, Overseas Development Institute, London.

Tanner, Emily, Ashley Brown, Naomi Day, Mehul Kotecha, Natalie Low, Gareth Morrell, Ola Turczuk, et al. 2010. *Evaluation of Every Child a Reader (ECaR)*. Research Report DFE-RR114. London: U.K. Department for Education.

Todd, Robin, and Ian Attfield. 2017. "Big Results Now! In Tanzanian Education: Has the Delivery Approach Delivered?" U.K. Department for International Development, London.

Toral, Guillermo. 2016. "When Are Local Governments and Bureaucrats Held Accountable for the Quality of Public Services? Evidence from Brazil's Education Sector."

MIT Political Science Research Paper 2016-11, Political Science Department, Massachusetts Institute of Technology, Cambridge, MA.

UIS (UNESCO Institute for Statistics). 2016. "Laying the Foundation to Measure Sustainable Development Goal 4." Sustainable Development Data Digest, UIS, Montreal.

UNDP (United Nations Development Programme). 2011. "Mexico: Scaling Up Progresa/Oportunidades, Conditional Cash Transfer Programme." UNDP, New York.

UNESCO (United Nations Educational, Scientific, and Cultural Organization). 2015. "Civil Society Education Fund 2013–2014/5." Biannual Progress and Supervision Report, January–June 2015, UNESCO, Paris.

Wojciuk, Anna. 2017. "Poland: A Notorious Case of Shock Therapy." Paper presented at Centro de Investigación y Docencia Económicas and Massachusetts Institute of Technology's conference, "Comparative Political Economy of Education Reforms," Mexico City, February 2–3.

World Bank. 2015. *Final READ Trust Fund Report 2008–2015.* Report 101527. Washington, DC: World Bank.

———. 2017a. "Case Study of Chile's Pay for Performance Reforms, 1995–2005." Background note, World Bank, Washington, DC.

———. 2017b. "Driving Performance from the Center: Malaysia's Experience with PEMANDU." Knowledge and Research, Malaysia Development Experience Series, Global Knowledge and Research Hub, World Bank, Washington, DC.

———. 2017c. *World Development Report 2017: Governance and the Law.* Washington, DC: World Bank.